Merchants and Manufacturers

Merchants

and Manufacturers

Studies in the Changing Structure of
Nineteenth-Century Marketing

GLENN PORTER AND HAROLD C. LIVESAY

ELEPHANT PAPERBACKS
Ivan R. Dee, Inc., Publisher, Chicago

First ELEPHANT PAPERBACK edition published 1989
by Ivan R. Dee, Inc., 1332 North Halsted Street, Chicago
60622. Manufactured in the United States of America.

Library of Congress Cataloging-in-Publication Data
Porter, Glenn.
    Merchants and manufacturers.
    Reprint. Originally published: Baltimore: Johns
Hopkins Press, 1971.
    Bibliography: p.
    Includes index.
    1. Marketing—Management—United
States—History—19th century. 2. United
States—Commerce—History—19th century. I. Livesay,
Harold C. II. Title.
[HF5415.1.P55   1989]   380.1'0973'09034   89-11972
ISBN 0-929587-10-3

This book is dedicated to two men
whose spirit all historians might contemplate with profit:
SUDDEN SAM McDOWELL,
the world's greatest drag bunter, and
EARL WEAVER,
who always has another pitcher ready.

Contents

Preface

The original impetus for this book developed while we were engaged in another project altogether: an attempt to construct an analysis of the appearance of concentration and vertical integration in American manufacturing. As the work progressed, we gradually became convinced that these phenomena had earlier antecedents in the history of American manufacturing than historians had indicated. We also felt that the explanation for the development of these patterns lay as much in the way problems of distribution had been solved as in the process by which mass production had been achieved.

In searching for material to test our hypotheses, we soon discovered that very little had been done in the way of historical investigations of the distribution of manufactured goods. The paucity of previous work, together with the adaptability of much of our accumulated research, made the idea of a study tracing major patterns of change in nineteenth-century American marketing—primarily in wholesaling—seem attractive and worthwhile.

What appears here is the culmination of three years of investigation. In both the research and the writing, we have benefited from the generous assistance of numerous individuals, of whom we can mention only a few here. Foremost among these is Professor Alfred D. Chandler, Jr., who was teacher and friend to both of us. Among the many others are Professors Louis Galambos, G. Heberton Evans, Jr., and Harold Williamson, all of whom read the manuscript in its entirety, and Professors James P. Baughman and Morton Rothstein, who read various sections.

Researching the topic and preparing the manuscript required extensive travel costs as well as additional expenses, and we wish to acknowledge the financial assistance of the following institutions: the Alfred P. Sloan Foundation, the Eleutherian Mills-Hagley Foundation, the Institute of Southern

History in conjunction with the Ford Foundation, the Division of Research at the Harvard University Graduate School of Business Administration, and the Horace H. Rackham School of Graduate Studies at the University of Michigan.

We also wish to express our gratitude to the editors of the *Business History Review*, the *Pennsylvania Magazine of History and Biography*, and *Pennsylvania History* for permission to use here portions of articles which have appeared in their journals.

Finally, while we realize that co-authors often accept (or disclaim) primary responsibility for specific chapters, we have concluded after hepatoscopy and meditation that we should not do so. We have served for so long as each other's critic, straight man, rewrite editor, and general dogsbody that our ideas and interpretations are very closely intertwined. This book is, in the broadest sense of the term, a joint venture.

Merchants and Manufacturers

CHAPTER I
Framework and Overview

During the nineteenth century, the American economy witnessed a process of fundamental change in the marketing of manufactured products. That process mirrored many vital elements in the transformation of the nation's economy from its mercantile, agrarian orientation in the period following the Revolution to its present status as the leading industrial economy in the twentieth century. Changes in distribution played at least as important a role in the story of our economic past as did changes in production, though the attention of historians has primarily been directed at developments in the latter area. This book attempts to redress part of the historical imbalance reflected in the many shelves groaning with the weight of volumes dealing with the means by which Americans have produced manufactured goods.

We have not tried to present a comprehensive history of the marketing of all commodities. The distribution of non-manufactured products, especially unprocessed agricultural products, has already been scrutinized by numerous historians, and many admirable studies have been completed.[1] Consequently we have excluded from our study the marketing of farm and mine products, except in some cases where such goods served as raw materials for manufacturers. Furthermore, although our research has involved an examination of the distribution networks employed in a multitude of nineteenth-century manufacturing industries, what appears here is a study of firms and industries that best illustrate prevailing distribution methods and best explain the causes and directions of change in the broad structural patterns of marketing.

By "distribution system" we mean the channels through which the manufacturer marketed his goods. Some consideration is also given to the means by which the manufacturer obtained his raw materials, since this also involved the

[1] A good recent example of such work is Harold D. Woodman's analysis of the marketing of raw cotton, *King Cotton and His Retainers*.

distribution of goods—some produced by manufacturers—but the primary focus is on marketing. We have made no attempt to trace the complete flow of the product through the entire marketing system to its ultimate consumer. Our vantage point is that of the manufacturer; once he had disposed of his goods, he was normally no longer concerned with their subsequent fate. As a consequence of this viewpoint, the book deals almost exclusively with wholesaling, for, insofar as the nineteenth-century producer marketed his goods to independent middlemen, he did so almost entirely to wholesalers, not retailers.

The marketing experience of manufacturing firms clearly indicates that the most important determinants of the marketing system employed by a firm were the nature of the product it manufactured and the nature of the market served by the enterprise. At the close of the eighteenth century, manufacturers shared broadly similar markets. In addition, almost all manufactured products of the time were "generic" goods, regarded by middlemen and by the market as susceptible to similar merchandising techniques.[2] As a result, a uniform distribution system prevailed throughout the entire economy. During the nineteenth century, however, shifts in the makeup of markets and of products in many industries led to fundamental changes in the way goods were distributed. This book describes and analyzes the changes and the reasons behind them, and it delineates and explains the survival of the older marketing order in those segments of the manufacturing sector which remained largely immune to change.[3]

DETERMINANTS OF THE STRUCTURE OF DISTRIBUTION

The analytical framework of this study holds that the structure of distribution in America at the beginning of the nineteenth century was in a state of equilibrium. All products, manufactured and otherwise, were distributed through a network of sedentary merchants, who were the dominant element in the economy. Moreover, this pattern was essentially the same as it had been for many centuries throughout the Western world. Although wars, conquests, political upheavals, and religious conflicts had repeatedly upset the social equilibrium, the nature of the market, the methods of production, and the means of transportation and communication had remained relatively static. Consequently the institutions of marketing had exhibited inertial tendencies. In the absence of forces necessitating change, little change had occurred.

[2] "Generic" goods are relatively simple, unspecific, general, or undifferentiated products. They are all marketed in similar ways through standard marketing channels, which handle a wide range of such goods. They create no special problems in the apparatus used to market them and they carry with them no particular merchandising difficulties. Almost all goods were generic at the beginning of the nineteenth century, but, as time passed, more and more products became more specific, more technologically complex, and more highly differentiated.

[3] The manufacturing sector of the economy includes firms which produced either finished or semifinished goods; it does not include firms engaged primarily in mining, transportation, agriculture, or finance.

As the nineteenth century progressed, however, several basic factors upset the equilibrium and brought widespread changes in the marketing patterns for many manufactured goods. Producers moved to replace merchants in the wholesale distribution of manufactured goods whenever one of two conditions evolved within an industry. First, they did so whenever it became possible for them to market their own products at a lower unit cost than could the mercantile network. Second, they did so whenever it became necessary as a result of shortcomings in the ability or willingness of independent wholesalers to merchandise goods effectively. If neither of these two conditions emerged over time, the producers in a particular industry tended to rely on the independent middlemen who had acted as the channels of distribution from the earliest colonial times.

Neither of the two causal conditions for structural change was widely operative in the American economy until the closing decades of the nineteenth century. Therefore the specialized wholesalers who evolved in the early national period constituted the dominant marketing mechanism for manufactured products until late in the century. It was not generally economically feasible for manufacturers to create and maintain a company wholesale force, because of the diffuse, unconcentrated nature of markets. The manufacturer of the early nineteenth century was a man of very limited horizons; he knew little of the markets outside his immediate area. He relied on his wholesaler to keep abreast of the changing needs of the many small consuming units to which his goods were transferred. Furthermore, the uncertain transportation and slow communications of the times inhibited efforts to establish direct contacts between a producer and his distant customers. By simply selling his goods to an urban wholesaler, the manufacturer avoided all the difficulties and expenses of marketing them to a diffuse, diverse mass of anonymous customers, the problems of arranging transportation for many small lots, and the uncertainties of collecting accounts from the scattered customers. The strength of this advantage lay at the heart of the merchants' long commercial reign. Only when the traditional, diffuse markets changed did the ability to handle his own wholesaling become a genuine possibility for the manufacturer.

The second condition which led manufacturers to bypass merchants, the existence of marketing problems which merchants could not or would not resolve, also did not emerge widely until the latter part of the century. Virtually all goods required neither special handling nor direct contact between producer and customer. The generic nature of products made the utilization of middlemen quite logical. The antebellum industries that constituted exceptions to this generalization were the very industries in which manufacturers were led to take the initiative in distribution.

In the three decades after 1870, changes in the nature of markets and of products brought about one or the other of the two necessary conditions for modifications in the structure of marketing. The first condition—the ability of manufacturers to wholesale more cheaply than merchants—arose in two ways. In many producers' goods industries the rise of the large corporation and the coming of oligopoly brought concentrated markets in which manufacturers sold to a relatively small number of customers who were no longer anonymous and whose orders were much larger than those of firms earlier in the century. In some consumers' goods industries the growth of urban markets produced concentrated markets wherein a firm could enjoy a sufficiently high sales volume in a city to warrant the creation of a permanent sales force there. In both cases the older, diffuse market of many small, scattered consuming units was replaced by a much denser market.

The second condition—the merchandising inadequacy of independent wholesalers—emerged in industries producing new goods that either were technologically complex, expensive items requiring close and often extended contact between manufacturer and consumer or required elaborate, innovative marketing apparatus. Technological advances in marketing facilities made expansion into the national market possible for many firms hitherto restricted to small, local sales. When these producers found existing wholesale channels unwilling or unable to avail themselves of new technology, they had to assume their own wholesaling. The appearance in the latter part of the century of many new products of considerable technological complexity also presented problems the old wholesalers could not solve—problems such as the need for demonstrations, extensive repair facilities, and the necessity for close consultation which resulted from the special needs of the customer. Such changes in the nature of products created marketing challenges undreamed of in the older era of generic, less complicated, less costly manufactured products. The established mercantile system often proved unable to make the needed adjustments and so watched the emergence of new industries in which the independent wholesaler was either entirely absent or considerably less important than he was in more traditional industries.

In those portions of the manufacturing sector where it neither became less costly for manufacturers to replace wholesalers nor became necessary for them to do so because of wholesalers' merchandising inadequacies, the old order endured. Throughout the industries where markets remained diffuse and products remained undifferentiated and inexpensive, the old structure of distribution survived. These industries generally were the least concentrated ones in the emerging twentieth-century economy and were populated by firms that were not examples of the large, modern corporation. They continued to rely on the independent middleman because neither the nature of markets nor that of products changed significantly in the nineteenth century.

This analytical construct, which rests on the assumption that economic institutions are inherently resistant to change so long as they can continue to function effectively, underlies our division of the history of nineteenth-century marketing into three distinct periods. The first was the age of the all-purpose merchant, which included the colonial experience and the early national period to 1815. Next came the age of the specialized wholesaler, which continued into the 1870s. Finally came the era of the manufacturer.

DISTRIBUTION IN THE AMERICAN ECONOMY:
THE AGE OF THE ALL-PURPOSE MERCHANT

During the first two centuries after the initial English settlements on the North American continent, urban merchants dominated the commerce of this extension of Europe, just as they had dominated European commerce since their supplanting of the petty capitalism of traveling merchants and peddlers in the late Middle Ages.[4] They were all-purpose, non-specialized merchants who dealt in a wide variety of goods ranging from lace to iron bars.[5] Usually they owned their own ships and engaged in commerce in coastwise and foreign trade, and often they acted as agents for British mercantile houses. They bought and sold items at wholesale and retail, and they acted as importers and exporters. They financed and insured the transport of goods with their own

[4] The best source on this topic is still the work of N. S. B. Gras; see especially his *Business and Capitalism*.

[5] Throughout this study a number of terms will be used to describe various marketing agents. The literature (both primary and secondary) of American economic history in the nineteenth century employs an array of terms for commercial middlemen—merchant, agent, factor, jobber, commission merchant, manufacturer's agent, wholesaler, forwarding merchant, and so forth. In the hope of making the distinctions between the kinds of wholesalers clearer, the terms used in this study are defined as follows:

(a) *Generalized merchant*—the all-purpose, non-specialized merchant of the colonial and early national periods. Synonyms include merchant capitalist, colonial merchant, and sedentary merchant.

(b) *Broker* or *factor*—a mercantile creature who is entirely a middleman. He never sells on his own account, but acts for others in his task of bringing buyer and seller together. He is more specialized than the colonial merchant, for he deals in a single line of goods, such as groceries, dry goods, drugs, iron, hardware, etc. Like the commission merchant described below, he takes a commission on his sales.

(c) *Commission merchant*—differs from the broker or factor in that he sells partly for his own account as well as for others. He, too, is a specialized man of business, and this differentiates him from the generalized or colonial merchant.

(d) *Jobber*—a wholesaler who buys and sells entirely on his own account, distributing his purchases either to other jobbers or to retailers.

(e) *Manufacturer's agent*—acts solely as a middleman, never selling on his own account. He differs from the broker or factor only in that he is even more highly specialized; he usually acts for a relatively small number of larger producers and sells to a smaller circle of customers than does the broker. If a particular firm authorizes him to be its sole representative in a specified geographic area, he is an exclusive manufacturer's agent; otherwise he is a non-exclusive manufacturer's agent. An exclusive manufacturer's agent acts for more than one producer, however; he is exclusive in the sense that he is a particular manufacturer's only sales agent in the area.

Other terms, including wholesaler, merchant, middleman, commercial agent, and mercantile agent, are general terms that cover any and all of the above types. The general sobriquets are used in the faint hope of relieving, slightly, the tedium of repeating the specific appelations.

capital or acted as factors for others. Often they loaned funds to capital-poor artisans and farmers who produced the goods in which the merchants traded.[6]

These great urban merchants were the key men in the early American economy. From their counting houses in the centers of urban business districts they coordinated the flow of goods through the arteries of commerce. They allocated the economy's capital, and they were competent in virtually every aspect of business. Merchants, farmers, and artisans in the back country looked to the urban merchant capitalists for leadership; they were the wealthiest, best-informed, and most powerful segment of early American society.

Producers in the rudimentary manufacturing sector relied entirely on the seaboard merchants for the distribution of all goods not sold in the manufacturing establishment's immediate surroundings. These goods involved no particular difficulties in marketing. The producer simply shipped his commodities to a nearby urban merchant and relied on him to dispose of them in the appropriate markets by means of the special knowledge and abilities that made him the high priest in charge of the mystic rites of trade. The goods then flowed to the diffuse, highly anonymous (as far as the manufacturer was concerned) markets of which contemporary commerce was composed.

The political upheavals that followed the end of the French and Indian War and led to the Revolutionary War and the subsequent initial years of the United States had virtually no effect on the position, role, or methods of the all-purpose merchants, who controlled the economic life of the colonial and early national era. Colonial historians, red in tooth and claw over the social and political meaning of the events of the last half of the eighteenth century, have paid much less attention to the economic role of the great sedentary merchants. To be sure, the Revolution, Confederation, and early national experiences created some problems and called forth adjustments in the short-run operations of merchants. The depressed conditions and the closing of much trade with Great Britain and her empire, for example, led American merchants to seek new commercial outlets such as the romantic, tantalizing Far East. Such temporary dislocations, however, did not alter the basic predominance of merchants in the economy, and they did not effect significant changes in the relations between merchants and manufacturers.

In the years following the desultory second conflict with Britain and the close of the Napoleonic Wars, however, the merchant capitalist witnessed a genuine change in his operations. The centuries-old tradition of omnicompe-

---

[6] Leading studies of the sedentary merchant include Bernard Bailyn, *The New England Merchants in the Seventeenth Century*; Stuart Bruchey, *Robert Oliver, Merchant of Baltimore, 1783–1819*; William T. Baxter, *The House of Hancock*; Byron Fairchild, *Messrs. William Pepperell*; Kenneth W. Porter, *The Jacksons and the Lees*; and James B. Hedges, *The Browns of Providence Plantations*. Also of interest is Bernard Bailyn, ed., *The Apologia of Robert Keayne*.

tence—of handling the entire range of economic activities, including importing and exporting, wholesaling and retailing, insuring and shipping virtually every item in which men traded—was eroded and eventually destroyed. The all-purpose merchant gave way to a new generation of businessmen who came to control the distribution of the products of the young nation.

THE DISTRIBUTION SYSTEM, 1815–1870:
THE AGE OF THE WHOLESALER

The new distribution network, like the old one, was in the hands of merchants. These businessmen, however, were largely jobbers or commission merchants rather than generalized merchants. The expansion of the economy in the first half of the nineteenth century led to a high-volume trade which compelled or allowed merchants to abandon their previous all-purpose orientation and to specialize. They became importers or exporters, wholesalers or retailers, and generally concentrated on a single line of goods such as hardware or dry goods.

As the frontier was pushed westward toward the Mississippi, natural increase and European immigration swelled the population. When the first federal census was taken in 1790, less than four million persons lived in the United States. By 1820 the population had more than doubled, and by 1860 it had grown almost eightfold from the original figure. This burgeoning increase called forth an expanding volume of trade.[7]

Another impetus of great importance was the British Industrial Revolution. That phenomenon created a large new market for American cotton, and the resulting changes in the American economy were profound. After the invention of new machines such as the spinning jenny, the water frame, and the mule, the explosive development of the British textile industry led to a corresponding rise in the export market for unmanufactured cotton. In the 1790s, for example, American exports of cotton averaged less than five million pounds annually. By the 1830s the cotton export level had risen to an annual average of more than 385 million pounds, and by the 1850s to more than a billion pounds.[8]

A whole new set of mercantile institutions was built to accommodate this expanded trade, including such innovations as the Black Ball Line's regularly scheduled packet service between New York and Liverpool and new forms of marine insurance and commercial banking. In order to facilitate the flow of goods and information to and from the interior of the United States, the seaboard merchants lent their support to the program of improved transportation through canals, turnpikes, and railroads. They also used some of their surplus

---

[7] U.S. Bureau of the Census, *Historical Statistics of the United States*, p. 8.
[8] *Ibid.*, p. 547.

capital generated from the new, higher-volume trade to invest in the nation's manufacturing sector.[9]

The specialized wholesalers, as this study makes clear, acted as the catalysts for economic growth by providing long-term and working capital to manufacturers interested in expansion. In many instances they took the lead in initiating manufacturing enterprises. Of even greater importance in an era of scarce capital, they extended credit to many businesses that could get no assistance from formal financial intermediaries such as commercial banks. The contributions of these specialized merchants to the process of economic growth in this country were absolutely essential, although heretofore their role has been little noted.

The ramifications of the nation's economic growth in the wake of the British Industrial Revolution were many and varied, but the important one for the purpose of this study was that the increased volume of trade led to specialization by merchants. The distribution of manufactured goods passed into the hands of a new breed of middlemen. Although their horizons were not so broad as those of the colonial merchants, the new middlemen were the most important men in the economy. They coordinated the flow of goods, allocated capital to farmers and manufacturers through the extension of credit, backed improvements in transportation, and served as primary economic integrators, at least through the Civil War years.[10]

The operations of specialized wholesalers are examined in the first half of this study. The distribution system in such lines as dry goods and drugs serves as an excellent example of the pattern that obtained throughout the consumers' goods industries. The marketing of textiles and the activities of a typical antebellum drug jobber illustrate the distribution network for such items as groceries, hardware, liquor, jewelry, notions, drugs, dry goods, and other staples of the early nineteenth-century consumer. In order to make clear the distribution system for producers' goods, the experience of the iron industry is explored. The chapters that delineate the marketing structure in these industries present a comprehensive portrait and analysis of the specialized wholesaler in the five decades after the War of 1812. They explain how he functioned, why

[9] The most impressive work analyzing the over-all impact of the cotton export trade on the American economy before the Civil War is Douglass C. North's *The Economic Growth of the United States, 1790–1860*. The best account of the changing patterns of trade and the new mercantile arrangements in the early decades of the nineteenth century is Robert G. Albion's *The Rise of New York Port*.

[10] An excellent brief treatment of the rise of the wholesaler in the first half of the nineteenth century can be found in Alfred D. Chandler, Jr., "The Role of Business in the United States," pp. 24–27; see also George R. Taylor, *The Transportation Revolution, 1815–1860*, chap. 1. Henrietta Larson observed in her *Guide to Business History*, p. 189, that "of the specialized wholesale merchants and commission dealers who grew to such importance in the nineteenth century very little is known." The work of the last twenty years has not done much to fill this substantial gap in our knowledge of our economic past.

he played a vital role in economic growth, and why the existing diffuse markets and generic products made him the logical distributor of the nation's manufactured goods.

The merchant gained much when he evolved from the all-purpose, omnicompetent businessman of colonial times into the much more highly specialized wholesaler of the first half of the nineteenth century. He knew his specialty much more thoroughly than the colonial merchant had known any particular service or product among the many in which he dealt. The increasing degree of division of labor in the mercantile realm after 1815 probably meant that commercial life was becoming more efficient, as each merchant grew to have a heightened command of all aspects of his specific line of business. By becoming more specialized, the merchant underwent a mutation that made him a better adapted economic organism, one capable of flourishing in the changed economic environment after 1815.

However, in making the transition from an all-purpose to a specialized man of business, the merchant also lost much. Because he handled all kinds of transactions pertaining to the distribution, finance, and transportation of a wide range of goods, the colonial merchant was insulated against unfavorable changes in the environment for any particular service or product. He operated on local, regional, national, and even international levels; his horizon was the wide world of commerce. Although he may not have been so efficient an economic component as his specialized successor, his omnicompetence assured him of a leading place somewhere in the economic system, despite virtually any alteration in the economic environment. The particularized merchant, for all his seeming invulnerability in the age of the wholesaler, was potentially far less secure in his dominance than had been his all-purpose predecessor. As long as the environment remained more or less the same, he had no problems; but, should the environment change significantly, he was potentially vulnerable as a result of his specialized state.

A detailed look at the one pre–Civil War industry in which conditions did shift markedly (with disastrous consequences for wholesalers)—the railroad supply industry—illustrates the possible dangerous results of specialization. In its initial phases, distribution in that business was similar to other producers' goods such as iron. As products grew more highly differentiated and technologically complex, and as the market grew more concentrated and less diffuse, producers and customers came to know one another, and the middlemen were swept aside; manufacturers and the railroads established direct contacts. In this respect, as in so many others, the experience of the railroads foreshadowed developments in many other industries.[11] Changes in the nature of markets and of products in the last part of the century brought about precisely the kind

[11] The theme of the railroads as prototypes for later corporations is developed in Alfred D. Chandler, Jr., ed., *The Railroads*.

of environmental changes to which the particularized wholesaler had been potentially vulnerable.

THE DECLINE OF THE MERCHANT AND THE
RISE OF THE MANUFACTURER

In the last half of the nineteenth century, the ancient and honorable dominion of the independent merchant over commerce came to a close. With the development of the modern manufacturing corporation in the last decades of the century, the role of independent middlemen in the distribution of manufactured goods greatly diminished. The rise of the factory and of mass production in the 1850s had tremendously increased the potential production rate of a single firm; the problem that remained for the manufacturers was how to solve the difficulties of mass distribution.

As producers in industry after industry learned to their grief in the decades following the Civil War, efficient production was not enough. Increased production seemed to bring only falling prices, as supply outran demand. The wholesale price index for all commodities in 1865 was 185; it declined fairly steadily thereafter to around eighty at the beginning of the 1890s.[12] Producers struggled mightily with the problem of adjusting output to meet the needs of the market, trying pools, gentlemen's agreements, trusts, and holding companies. During this search for economic order, some manufacturers began to create their own distribution networks and thus to eliminate or greatly reduce the role of the independent middlemen.

While not directly related to their role in the distribution process, one important reason for the decline of merchants was the atrophy of the manufacturers' financial dependence on them. During the 1860s, many manufacturers found that they were able to put their businesses on a cash basis as a result of the wartime boom and the infusion of greenbacks into the economy. This reduced their reliance on credit extended by wholesalers acting as their suppliers and distributors. Of even greater importance was the growing ability of producers to finance their operations out of retained earnings and the concomitant growth of financial intermediaries able and willing to lend funds to promising manufacturing enterprises. These developments hastened the decline of wholesalers in the economy, but their fate in the closing decades of the century was sealed by the increasing tendency of manufacturers in many industries to create their own distribution networks.

Changes in distribution came whenever a large firm faced either a concentrated market or serious problems in the marketing of its products. The independent middleman had always served to bring many buyers and sellers together, to connect and coordinate the diffuse markets of the older economy.

[12] The index was compiled by George F. Warren and Frank A. Pearson. See Bureau of the Census, *Historical Statistics*, p. 115.

Late in the nineteenth century, however, the structure of markets changed in many industries. The makers of producers' goods such as iron and steel and non-ferrous metals, like the makers of railroad supplies in antebellum days, found that the rise of the large firm and the coming of oligopoly had reduced the numbers and increased the size of buyers and sellers.[13] This resulted in a very different and much more concentrated market in which the network of independent merchants was no longer relevant. Manufacturers could now handle their own wholesaling more efficiently than could the middlemen, and they assumed the functions of the merchants by building their own marketing organizations. In many consumers' goods industries, manufacturers also faced a denser market because of the growth of America's cities, with their concentration of population and hence of customers. As more and more industries grew oligopolistic, manufacturers utilized the significantly improved transportation and communications systems to take over the wholesaling of their own goods in the expanding urban areas. In producers' and consumers' goods industries, manufacturers supplanted the mercantile agents primarily because of changed market conditions, not because of any serious inadequacies in the old distribution network's ability to market the goods effectively. Manufacturers in other industries, however, did encounter distribution problems that the middlemen could not solve.

The latter group of firms produced many of the new goods that appeared in the post–Civil War United States, some of which were quite technologically advanced. Processors of perishable items, such as ice, dressed beef, bananas, beer, and others, employed improved refrigeration techniques to forge marketing organizations that would tap the potential urban markets. Because the old mercantile agents were not in a position to distribute the perishables, producers built costly storage, transport, and marketing facilities, which brought economies of scale in distribution. Makers of complex products, such as industrial machinery, early electrical apparatus, harvesters, office machines, and other commodities, found that the necessity for close and continuing contact between manufacturer and consumer made the commission agents and brokers an unsuitable distribution channel. Accordingly they created their own marketing organizations to provide such services as technical consultation, instruction in the operation of products, replacement parts, and facilities for repairs. In the realm of perishable goods and those requiring intimate, extended contact between producer and customer, the inability of the established distribution

---

[13] Economists refer to a situation in which a few large firms constitute the market for particular production factors as "oligopsony." This term is singularly unwieldy and not entirely appropriate here, for it implies a set of controls and influences exercised by consuming firms over producers of inputs. We are concerned here with the effects of an increasingly dense market upon the distribution methods of producers, not with any theoretical purchasing advantages accruing to oligopolists. Therefore we prefer to designate the advent of a more concentrated market as the coming of oligopoly, not oligopsony.

channels to provide the facilities and services needed for the new products led manufacturers to bypass the independent middleman and to assume the whole-saling function.

Although erosion was common to the traditional distribution network of most American manufacturing, in some areas the middleman continued to act as the primary wholesale agent. In those industries in which the rise of the large firm and the coming of oligopoly were rare, and in which the structure of markets and the nature of products remained much the same as they had been throughout the nineteenth century, the independent middleman endured. Throughout the complex of industries in which a variety of simple, standard items was sold through many thousands of retailers—in the grocery, drug, hardware, jewelry, liquor, furniture, and dry goods businesses—the jobber continued to assemble and disperse goods through these diffuse markets. The highly unconcentrated structure of such markets made the jobber vital even in those industries dominated by a large firm such as the American Tobacco Company. In the areas in which the independent middleman survived as whole-saler, however, his old role as salesman atrophied because of the coming of national advertising and brand names. Advertising reduced the wholesaler's job to the rather mechanical satisfaction of consumer wants created by the manufacturer's direct appeal to the customer.

By the beginning of the twentieth century, the outlines of the new economic order had emerged. The concentration movement, the changing structure of markets, and the appearance of technologically advanced products that presented serious distribution and marketing problems all spelled the end of the merchant's dominance and the beginning of the manufacturer's pre-eminence. Only in those sectors of the manufacturing economy which retained many of the characteristics of the older, agrarian-based economy did the independent middleman retain his primary role as wholesaler. The long reign of the merchant had finally come to a close. In many industries the manufacturer of goods had also become their distributor. A new economy dominated by the modern, integrated manufacturing enterprise had arisen.

The changes in the distribution patterns of American manufacturing from 1815 to the opening years of this century reflected the broader pattern of the economy's shifting locus of power. The modern corporation emerged as the dominant institution in our economy and perhaps in our society. The twin engines of change in marketing—the concentration of production and population on the one hand, and the imperatives of advancing technology on the other—also proved to be the forces which shaped the broad outlines of change in all of American civilization. They have determined much of the context of economic, political, and social conflict in modern America.

CHAPTER II

The Merchant in Control: Marketing after 1815

In 1815 Americans faced the future with confidence. The federal Constitution promised political stability and continuity. The Treaty of Ghent and subsequent international agreements preserved the United States' independence, ended the threat of armed foreign intervention in American affairs, and brought to a close the long period of wartime blockades, embargoes, and restrictions which had disrupted and distorted international commerce. Freedom from these internal and external liabilities enabled Americans to concentrate on the tasks of geographic and commercial expansion. It was an imposing task, indeed. The land mass was large and partially unexplored; the population was small and scattered, with a limited capacity for manufacturing.

Enormous advantages offset these handicaps, however. The land proved to be fertile and rich in natural resources. The Indians who occupied it were scattered, disorganized, poorly armed, and easily subdued. The neighboring countries, while occasionally noisy and fractious, proved docile enough, thereby obviating the expense of defending the long national boundaries.

The people, although few in number compared to the size of the country, were relatively well educated, mechanically ingenious, and continued a long tradition of individual enterprise. "Capitalism," said Carl Degler, "came in the first ships."[1] It came primarily in the minds of a few ambitious men who hoped to transplant the English system of commercial agriculture to the soil of the New World, but circumstances soon made it the creed of the whole free

---

[1] Carl N. Degler, *Out of Our Past*, p. 1.

population. In America the sheer expanse of the country mitigated against oligarchical control; moreover, the offer of free land proved the only magnet capable of drawing the needed manpower across the Atlantic. Consequently land ownership, restricted to a fraction of the population in Europe, became a widespread phenomenon in America. As a result, Americans generally embraced the idea that each man had the right to apply his energy and talents to the development of his own property and to enjoy the results. In such an atmosphere, European social structures based on the tight control of scarce land soon decayed in New York, Maryland, and the Carolinas, and never got started elsewhere. Their absence served as a further inducement for frustrated Europeans to come to the New World seeking land and dignity of their own.[2]

But the American spirit of individual enterprise cannot simply be explained in terms of property ownership and social egalitarianism. Something must be said about the psychological impact of a land so vast, so unspoiled, so frighteningly beautiful on the minds of the men who beheld it for the first time. It was, in the words of Scott Fitzgerald,

a land that pandered in whispers to the last and greatest of all human dreams; for a transitory enchanted moment man must have held his breath in the presence of this continent . . . face to face for the last time in history with something commensurate to his capacity for wonder.[3]

In such a land anything seemed possible. In time the sense of wonder became mixed with a national spirit of chauvinistic optimism, for nothing so effectively converts dreams to doctrines as visible fulfillment; in America a man's labor often turned his yearning for plenitude into tangible prosperity.

By 1815 the once wondrous discovery that America could bring even the wildest schemes to fruition was a tradition nearly two hundred years old. Its effect on the populace was observed by Alexis de Tocqueville a few years later. Americans, he found, were eternally optimistic: "No natural boundary seems to be set to the efforts of man; and what is not yet done is only what he has not yet attempted to do." Entwined with this spirit was a willingness to accept innovation in everything: politics, religion, social theory, and business: "The idea of novelty is indissolubly connected with the idea of amelioration."[4]

Above all, Tocqueville's America was a land where "everyone finds facilities, unknown elsewhere, for making or increasing his fortune. . . . the spirit of gain is everywhere on the stretch, and the human . . . mind is there swayed by no impulse but the pursuit of wealth. . . . Not only are manufacturing and

---

[2] The impact of the new continent on old ideas has been the subject of some of the most stimulating speculation in American historical writing. See, for example, Sigmund Diamond, "Values as an Obstacle to Economic Growth"; Louis Hartz, *The Liberal Tradition in America*, esp. p. 1.

[3] F. Scott Fitzgerald, *The Great Gatsby*, p. 182.

[4] Alexis de Tocqueville, *Democracy in America*, 1: 510–11.

commercial classes to be found in the United States as they are in all other countries; but, what never occurred elsewhere, the whole community is simultaneously engaged in productive industry and commerce."[5]

The American spirit was not confined to industry and commerce, however, for, as Tocqueville found, "the Americans carry their business-like qualities into agriculture; and their trading passions are displayed in that, as in other pursuits."[6] Applied to agriculture, these "business-like qualities" were a boon to the growth of the American economy after 1815 because the southern section of the country proved admirably suited to produce the cotton for which English manufacturers had recently begun to clamor. The nation's "trading passions" were institutionalized in a highly sophisticated mercantile network that controlled the nation's commerce.

This mercantile network had been established almost as soon as the colonies were founded. Its original purpose (in keeping with the mercantilist theories of the time) had been to funnel the colonies' staple crops and raw materials to England, and to distribute British manufactured products in the colonies. It succeeded in doing both. Despite the vast difficulties of transportation and communication across the Atlantic, the system on the whole worked well for both sides. The colonists, of course, cried exploitation, and British merchants periodically complained of inadequate returns on their investments. But, whatever the validity of these arguments in any short-run crisis, such as that precipitated by the Stamp Act, there can be little doubt that the commercial ties established between Britain and North America worked to the advantage of both in the long run. Before the American Revolution, Britain received valuable materials for trade, such as tobacco, and established trading relationships that later helped supply the raw material for the looms of its Industrial Revolution. The colonists, on the other hand, had access to the capital, techniques, and products of the world's most advanced trading and manufacturing nation. Unlike their young and untried political counterparts, the American commercial institutions of 1815 were well established and thoroughly proven. Their viability was in large measure the result of their long association with, and backing from, British merchants.

At the center of the mercantile network was the all-purpose merchant. He was the key man in the American economy in 1815, as he always had been. He was the channel through which agricultural staples flowed to market, and he supplied manufactured goods and imported raw materials to city craftsmen

---

[5] *Ibid.*, 2: 41.

[6] *Ibid.*, p. 189. Visitors' observations on the relationship between American economic and social systems have continued to the present day, as witness this exchange between English satirists Alan Bennett and Peter Cook in the 1964 presentation of *Beyond the Fringe*.

COOK: There's no class system over here.

BENNETT: No class system? Well what's the incentive to get on?

COOK: Greed.

and country storekeepers. All of the important American merchants, such as the Hancocks of Boston, performed similar functions, and their methods of operation not only differed little from their colonial predecessors' but were essentially similar to the techniques of Western sedentary merchants since the late Middle Ages.[7] The all-purpose merchant lived and worked in port cities such as Boston, New York, Philadelphia, Baltimore, Charleston, and Savannah; he traded in markets all over the world. He bought and sold all kinds of goods at wholesale and retail, sometimes taking title to them, but frequently acting as an agent for others and receiving a commission for his services. He was often, though not always, the owner or part owner of the ships that carried his goods. Sometimes he joined with other merchants to insure a valuable cargo; often he shipped goods uninsured. Sometimes he bought goods as an individual, employing his own capital or credit alone. Frequently he pooled his resources with other merchants, and often he invested funds entrusted to him for that purpose by others less expert than he. A mastery of the maze of documents—notes, bills of lading, bills of exchange, letters of credit—by which foreign commerce was conducted was a necessity for the successful merchant.

Equally necessary was a knowledge of the credit standing of commercial correspondents (normally other all-purpose merchants). Business conducted in many places across vast distances had to be based upon faith in one's creditors, for the forceful collection of overdue bills was difficult if not impossible. The merchant's traditional solution to this problem was to restrict his dealings to a network of people known to be trustworthy. Often this group was bound together by ties of kinship or religion.[8] Some merchants, such as Robert Oliver of Baltimore, operated on the basis of credit supplied by a banking house, such as Baring Brothers of London, and such purely commercial arrangements became more prevalent in the late eighteenth century.[9] Successful merchants

[7] There is a wealth of material on colonial merchants. It shows a remarkable variety of personalities and an equally remarkable similarity in business methods. Among the best studies is Bernard Bailyn, *The New England Merchants in the Seventeenth Century*. Bailyn shows the utter dependence of colonial merchants on their colleagues in the mother country, and the importance of family ties in world-wide trade. Kenneth W. Porter, *The Jacksons and the Lees*, analyzes the operations of an important New England merchant group and includes a large number of annotated documents and letters typical of traditional mercantile operations. Also worthwhile is William T. Baxter, *The House of Hancock*. Stuart Bruchey, *Robert Oliver, Merchant of Baltimore, 1783–1819*, chronicles the work of an all-purpose merchant in the early national period. Bruchey, like many other scholars influenced by Frederic Lane and N. S. B. Gras, points out the similarity in the business methods of all general-purpose merchants since the late Middle Ages.

[8] These networks covered wide areas. American merchants often did business in India and China through family connected resident agents. See Porter, *The Jacksons and the Lees*, and Caroline F. Ware, *The Early New England Cotton Manufacture*, pp. 193–97.

[9] Stuart Bruchey, "Success and Failure Factors"; Ralph W. Hidy, "The Organization and Functions of Anglo-American Merchant Bankers, 1815–1860."

had access to flexible and reliable credit and to a network of responsible agents as the need arose.

The many histories of colonial merchants document the adaptability of such men to the needs of individual transactions. The merchant looked upon all of the techniques mentioned above as the tools of his trade, some suited to one particular exchange, some to another. The merchants' strength rested not so much on their mastery of the ancillary techniques of shipping, insurance, finance, and the like, as on their ability to use them in support of the fundamental trading function, buying and selling at a profit. The merchants exercised this function over a range of goods as varied as the commercial techniques they employed. The histories of individual firms, as well as merchants' advertisements in colonial and early national period newspapers, demonstrate the merchants' willingness to sell anything that offered a profit. Coffee, sugar, iron, cloth—all were grist for the merchants' mills.

There were two principal reasons for the unspecialized nature of American mercantile firms. First, they dealt with generic goods, a working knowledge of which was within reach of any intelligent man. Second, and most important, the volume of trade was low because supplies and markets were small and scattered; to do a volume business the merchant had to handle a variety of wares. Since virtually all generic goods of the time were marketed in the same way, he could easily diversify. Changes in technology might have forced specialization; changes in markets might have permitted it. Prior to 1815, however, only a few changes occurred in either, and the series of European wars retarded their effects until uninterrupted commerce was resumed.

After 1815 a series of events encouraged the rise of the specialized merchant, the man who replaced his all-purpose predecessor as the coordinator of the economy and who dominated the early industrialization of the United States through his control of the distribution of manufactured products.

THE RISE OF MERCANTILE SPECIALIZATION

The force which brought the specialized merchant to the forefront after 1815 was a dynamic increase in the volume of trade in generic goods. Since the kinds of goods traded and the markets in which they were sold remained basically the same, the services required to move goods to market also remained relatively unchanged. Increased volume, therefore, did not make the merchant's skills obsolete; rather, as the number of transactions rose, it encouraged a division of labor because the merchant found it increasingly difficult to exercise all his traditional functions in each transaction. Like any organism faced with changing conditions, the merchant had to adapt in order to survive, and that adaptation took the form of specialization in either commodity or function. Specialization enabled the merchant to operate efficiently by concentrating his efforts, but it weakened his position by tying him closely to a limited range of products and markets and by depriving him of the flexibility inherent in his previously diversified operations.

In the long run a number of factors contributed to the growth of American trade after 1815. These included population increase (from 8.5 million in 1815 to 31.5 million in 1860), geographic expansion (from 1.7 million square miles in 1815 to 3.0 million square miles in 1860), and the growth of domestic manufacturing. Together these powered a rapid expansion of domestic trade, as reflected in the Gross National Product, which rose from 1.6 billion in 1839 to 4.1 billion in 1860, and approximated the Gross National Product of Great Britain by 1840. The prime mover, however, in the rise of mercantile specialization was foreign trade, which grew from $166 million in 1815 to $762 million in 1860.[10] Much of this increase stemmed from the growing value of a single commodity, cotton. The importance of cotton resulted originally from a series of events which took place outside the United States and which occurred prior to 1815, the Industrial Revolution in Great Britain.

The Industrial Revolution created seemingly insatiable markets for American cotton by mechanizing the textile industry. This process was eventually completed in 1790, when steam power connected to Crompton's mule made possible the modern, integrated textile factory. Although most British producers were slow to integrate all operations in a single factory (the fully integrated mill was an American development), they quickly mechanized, thereby creating individual production units of great capacity.

Eli Whitney's cotton gin, invented in 1793, removed the last formidable obstacle to sustained, high-volume production in Britain. In America, in those areas where the climate and soil were well suited to cotton growing, planters quickly began to exploit the new market. Cotton, which had rarely been grown in North America before the Revolution, soon became the most important staple crop.[11]

The new staple soon flowed to Britain in large quantities; 93 million pounds were exported in 1810. The cotton trade, like all others, declined sharply during the periods of political vicissitude which ended in 1815 (11 million pounds were exported in 1808), but flourished immediately after hostilities ended. In subsequent years the volume of cotton exports rose from 83 million pounds in 1815 to 128 million pounds in 1820, 744 million pounds in 1840, and eventually exceeded one billion pounds annually in the late 1850s.[12]

---

[10] All figures are in constant dollars. Trade, population, and area statistics come from U.S. Bureau of the Census, *Historical Statistics of the United States*, pp. 538–39, 7, 8; GNP data from Robert E. Gallman, "Gross National Product in the United States, 1834–1909," pp. 7, 26.

[11] Robert G. Albion, *The Rise of New York Port*, p. 98; Norman S. Buck, *The Development of the Organization of the Anglo-American Trade*, pp. 33–36.

[12] All statistics in the paragraph are from Bureau of the Census, *Historical Statistics*, p. 547.

This unprecedented volume of trade in a single commodity changed the mercantile institutions through which it flowed. The process can best be seen through its effects on the commercial institutions of New York. Not only did the changes come first and have the most profound effects there, but the pattern of specialization caused by the cotton trade in New York subsequently developed in other locales as a result of large-scale domestic manufacturing. In addition, the flow of British textiles into New York led to the development of new types of mercantile middlemen, who retained control of the distribution of some commodities well into the twentieth century.

New York merchants entered the cotton trade almost as soon as it began, sending agents south to buy up bales for shipment overseas. Cotton was an attractive addition to the merchant's stock in trade, not only because British correspondents were anxious to buy it, but also because it presented a new way to pay for the manufactured goods that New Yorkers had long imported from Great Britain. In the early years of the cotton trade, many of the New York houses that engaged in it were all-purpose mercantile firms. As volume rose, they often dropped other lines to specialize in exporting raw cotton or importing textile manufactures. In later years specialized houses were established for the express purpose of participating in the cotton trade exclusively. Unlike all-purpose merchants, whose dealings had been primarily with London firms, the specialized cotton merchants did business largely through Liverpool, the port which dominated British cotton commerce.

Although shipment from southern ports to Liverpool via New York was obviously the long way around, New York merchants possessed powerful weapons with which to draw the trade into their hands. This arsenal consisted of geographic and institutional advantages. The harbor was sheltered and offered easy egress to southern coastal routes. Long Island Sound offered a sheltered passage to New England, and the Hudson and Mohawk valleys provided a highway into the hinterland. Because of these factors, New York merchants had a large, readily accesible exurban market.

To these natural advantages New Yorkers added their long mercantile experience, which produced not only a mastery of the intricacies of international trade but long-standing close ties with the British mercantile houses that imported cotton and exported manufactured goods to pay for it. New Yorkers also had the capital to make available to planters large credits against future crops. These elements combined to give them a strong advantage in the cotton trade from the outset; cotton might be shipped from any American port, but New York offered a market for British manufactures which no southern city could match.[18]

In order to exploit this market for manufactured goods, British manufacturing and mercantile firms sent agents to New York. Men such as Isaac Wright, Francis Thompson, and Benjamin Marshall sold British textiles in

[18] This discussion rests primarily on Albion, *New York Port.*

New York and purchased large quantities of raw cotton for shipment to British merchants and mills.[14] Like their native American competitors, they sent agents south to make purchases and to advance credit to planters. Thus New York's control of capital and its large hinterland markets combined to make it pre-eminent in the cotton export trade.

In 1815 British manufacturers disposed of their backed-up inventories by "dumping" them in the New York market. Enterprising New York merchants encouraged this trade by securing passage of a law which decreased taxes on auctions and guaranteed that goods would be sold to the highest bidder. As a result of these strategies the flow of trade through New York was heavy in both directions.

Under the impact of such large quantities the all-purpose merchants' cluster of competencies split apart into individual, specialized firms. Some of these firms concentrated on shipping and created transatlantic and coastal packet lines. Others handled marine insurance exclusively.[15] Even the fundamental mercantile function of buying and selling underwent specialization. Most of the major merchants dropped retailing to become wholesalers. In addition, some men concentrated on exporting or importing, and others limited their transactions to a particular line of goods. For example, Anson Phelps (who founded the firm of Phelps-Dodge) entered business as an all-purpose merchant in New York in 1812. He soon engaged in the cotton trade and, although he dealt in small quantities of general merchandise for many years, through the 1820s and 1830s he increasingly specialized in the export of cotton and the import of metals.[16] In his early years Phelps owned a number of ships which transported his goods, but gradually he disposed of them as regular shipping service became available. Phelps, like many of his contemporary colleagues, sent agents south to buy cotton, to advance credit to planters, and to sell manufactured products.

Phelps' gradual shift from all-purpose to specialized merchandising typified such transitions generally. "Specialized merchants" concentrated most of their efforts on the sale of certain commodities or the performance of certain functions; most of them, however, maintained a small general trade at wholesale and retail. Moreover, the changes did not come overnight, nor did they occur in all fields simultaneously. In general, the evidence indicates that the chronology and extent of specialization in specific commodities related directly to the volume of trade in those commodities. For example, some of the cotton factors who set up business in the South bought nothing but cotton, which was in great supply, but sold their planter customers a wide range of goods in small quantities. Thus they were specialized in one direction of trade and not

14 *Ibid.*, p. 40.
15 *Ibid.*, chaps. 3, 4, 6, and 13; Douglass C. North, *The Economic Growth of the United States, 1790 to 1860*, p. 60.
16 Robert G. Cleland, *A History of Phelps Dodge, 1834–1950*, chaps. 1 and 2.

in the other, whereas a trader like Anson Phelps, who bought and sold large volumes of single commodities, could specialize in both directions.[17]

The evolution of mercantile specialization thus indicates that Adam Smith's dictum that the extent of division of labor is a function of the size of the market held for marketing as well as for manufacturing institutions. Division of labor does not, of course, always result in specialized firms. Theoretically at least, mercantile houses could have continued to perform their traditional functions by altering the structure of their firms. Just as a single manufacturing plant often houses a number of specialized operations, a single mercantile house could have continued to operate as an all-purpose agency by adding specialists in various commodities as well as in shipping, insurance, wholesaling, and retailing. In practice this seldom occurred, however, because few merchants were willing to enlarge their firms. Most mercantile firms were established by an individual, or by a partnership of two or three men. Larger firms were rare. Subsequent additions to the firm generally resulted from the death or retirement of the original owners and were usually members of the family. For example, Anson Phelps took in his son-in-law William E. Dodge, and Nathan Trotter of Philadelphia added his sons. Occasionally a trusted employee was invited to join the partnership. Such changes assured continuity but rarely resulted in significant enlargement of the firm's membership.

The small size of the firm reflected the historical necessity for trustworthy associates. In a commercial world where communication and banking facilities were primitive, reliance on a few trusted individuals became a fundamental element of the merchant's creed. His reluctance to abandon it limited his options for change when the volume of trade rose. Because he was unwilling to expand the firm in order to continue his diversified operations, the merchant had little choice but to reduce the scope of his affairs. The result was specialization.

It is difficult to know just how merchants determined which functions to shed and which to retain, for there is a paucity of primary evidence. Presumably they specialized in those areas which they knew best. Nathan Trotter became a specialized metals dealer because he was an expert importer but knew little about domestic manufactures; imported copper and tin offered the best chance for success.[18] Some merchants were undoubtedly forced to specialize willy-nilly by the appearance of specialized competitors, whose large purchases enabled them to undercut the prices of their all-purpose colleagues.

Of course, continued specialization depended upon continued volume.[19] In a country where the population was as dispersed as it was in the United States

[17] See Louis E. Atherton, *The Southern Country Store, 1800–1860*, and Harold D. Woodman, *King Cotton and His Retainers*, for detailed treatments of the operations of cotton factors in the South.

[18] Elva Tooker, *Nathan Trotter*, p. 113.

[19] Theoretically, of course, specialization can also be supported by a low volume of large-unit-price, high-markup sales, but such trade was insignificant in this period.

in the early nineteenth century, this involved covering a wide geographic area, a circumstance which led merchants to be prime movers in the development of turnpikes, canals, and railroads. Urban merchants employed transportation facilities to widen their market coverage as soon as they were available.[20]

The increased volume of trade and the wide geographic area over which it spread combined to make it increasingly disadvantageous for the wholesale merchant to take title to all the goods he handled. After 1815 more and more merchants who concentrated on wholesaling operated either as brokers or as commission merchants because the quantity of goods would have required prohibitively large sums of capital for outright purchase and because merchants were unwilling to assume the financial risks involved in dealing with distant customers of unknown credit standing. Although the commission method had often been employed in colonial trade, it was perfected by New York merchants and became a widespread mercantile technique during the early years of the cotton trade.[21] It also played a vital role in the distribution of American manufactured goods in the nineteenth century.

THE EFFECT OF NEW ENGLAND TEXTILE MILLS ON MARKETING INSTITUTIONS

The textile industry that appeared in New England after 1790 was the first American manufacturing industry to influence domestic marketing institutions.[22] Before the development of the industry, American manufactures such as glass and iron either were sold directly to local customers or were marketed by all-purpose wholesalers and retailers. At the outset, textile producers endeavored to employ the same methods, but the development of integrated mills rendered the traditional channels unfeasible because they were unable to absorb the unprecedented volume of goods made possible by the new factories.

The first noteworthy American textile mill began operating in 1793 as a result of a partnership between the Providence merchants Moses Brown and Richard Almy (Brown's son-in-law) and the British technician Samuel Slater. The mill's capacity was small, several of the operations were carried out by hand, and the yarn it produced was sent elsewhere to be woven into cloth;

---

[20] The effect of transportation routes on a merchant's area of coverage is clearly demonstrated by the maps in Tooker, *Trotter*, p. 129.

[21] Buck, *Anglo-American Trade*, chaps. 1 and 4.

[22] In this study "manufacturing" refers to the production of finished or semi-finished goods through the use of tools and/or machinery, in buildings set up for the purpose, and conducted on a scale large enough for normal operations to require full-time employees. This excludes the work of individual artisans, as well as so called cottage industries and the like. The terms "manufacturer," "manufacturing entre-preneur," and "producer," designate men who owned and personally operated a manufacturing establishment as defined above. "Capitalist" refers to an individual who supplied capital to a manufacturing firm but normally took no active part in supervising production.

nevertheless, the mill embodied many of the essential characteristics of the large factory unit, which eventually dominated the American textile industry. All of the operations except weaving were carried out under one roof. Furthermore, unlike traditional production units in which the proprietor was also the production manager, the Almy and Brown firm separated ownership from production. Almy and Brown supplied the capital, Slater the mechanical expertise. In an arrangement that would prove typical of many American manufacturing enterprises in the years to come, Almy and Brown took little part in the actual production, leaving it to Slater. Like most American merchants, they had little knowledge of machine or craft techniques; they had previously failed in an attempt to run a mill themselves. What they did have was capital and a relentless drive to keep it profitably employed. Fortunately for the future of American enterprise, most merchants shared their countrymen's optimism about the nation's future and were willing to back it with their wealth.

The merchants' optimism and obsession with finding profitable employment for their idle capital led to the establishment of the Boston Manufacturing Company at Waltham, Massachusetts, in 1813. This was the first truly modern factory in the United States, for it integrated and mechanized production from raw material to finished product under a single management and within a single factory. Unlike Almy and Brown, who produced only yarn and thread, the Boston company used power looms to convert its spinning-machine products into cloth. The founder of the Boston Manufacturing Company, Francis Cabot Lowell, was familiar with mechanized British textile manufacturing, and he perceived that creation of such a mill in the United States would offer a solution to the lack of outlets for mercantile capital and the shortage of textile products caused by the war with Britain. In order to secure the capital necessary to create such a large enterprise, he enlisted the aid of his fellow Boston merchants Nathan Appleton and Patrick Tracy Jackson. Together they pooled $300,000, an unprecedented sum for an American manufacturing enterprise. They also secured the services of a British mechanic, Paul Moody, to assist in the perfection of power weaving.

A succession of such partnerships between merchant capital and technical expertise led to the construction of numerous mills on the "Waltham model," including the famous "Lowell Mills" built on the Merrimack River in the 1820s and 1830s. Largely as a result of these integrated mills the domestic production of textiles expanded swiftly. The number of spindles in U.S. cotton-spinning mills rose from 31,000 in 1810 to 250,000 in 1820, 2,284,631 in 1840, and 5,235,727 in 1860, a rate of growth almost double the rate of population increase in the same period.[23]

This burgeoning productive capacity soon led to distribution problems

[23] This discussion is based on Ware, *Early New England Cotton Manufacture*, chap. 2, and U.S. Census Office, *Eighth Census of the United States, 1860: Manufactures*, pp. ix–xx.

in a market where British imports presented fierce competition. Not only were large markets needed, but mill managers sought means of disposing of current production in order to keep factories from accumulating unwieldy surpluses. This was a difficult task in an economy in which demand fluctuated widely. Surpluses accumulated frequently before the Civil War, a fact which demonstrates that the cotton textile industry achieved mass production long before it solved the problems of mass distribution.[24]

The marketing problems encountered by these mills, the strategies adopted in attempts to solve them, and the institutional and financial arrangements that resulted established a pattern which was repeated many times over as other manufacturing industries expanded and were confronted by problems of mass distribution. The earliest spinning mills made small lots and sold directly to their consumers, principally weavers and storekeepers. Sometimes they accepted cotton, dyestuffs, and flour in payment. This crude method was obviously inadequate for the distribution of large volumes of goods, and rising production soon forced even early, relatively small-scale manufacturers (such as Almy and Brown) to seek other outlets. To induce retail storekeepers in New England to accept products for sale, the mills shipped on consignment; that is, the manufacturer retained title to the goods and the storekeeper did not pay until after they were sold. Although direct dealings with retailers was but a brief phase in the evolution of the textile distribution network, the consignment system remained a feature of the industry throughout most of the nineteenth century.

In order to expand their market coverage into the western regions, during the first decade of the nineteenth century New England mills turned to wholesale commission houses, which were appearing in coastal cities as a result of the importation of British textiles. These commission houses offered several advantages to manufacturers. They enabled producers to widen their markets while actually reducing the number of customers. They also made it possible to avoid the risk of dealing with a multitude of small, country merchants. Until 1817, New England mills dealt primarily through Philadelphia houses, such as Elijah Waring's, because Philadelphians had the best hinterland market for domestic textiles.[25] Institutional developments resulting from the distribution of British imports and reinforced by the expanded market created by the Erie Canal soon made New York the channel for the entire northwestern trade in domestic textiles. Moreover, buyers who secured imported textiles in New York were unwilling to go elsewhere to get domestic goods. Thus, after 1815, American goods passed increasingly through specialized New York

[24] In general the evolution of marketing techniques in the carpet industry followed the pattern set in cotton textiles. See John S. Ewing and Nancy P. Norton, *Broadlooms and Businessmen*; and Arthur H. Cole and Harold F. Williamson, *The American Carpet Manufacture*.

[25] New York had the largest total market, but imports took up much of it in the early years.

commission houses that had originally been created to handle imports. American mills also employed another import-spawned institution, the New York auction, to dispose of surplus inventories. Rhode Island manufacturers attempted to create a cloth cooperative through which to market their wares, but it failed in the late 1830s.

The institution that became the principal agency of distribution for large, integrated, cloth-producing mills was the "selling house," which evolved naturally from the specialized textile commission firm. Nathan Appleton, one of the principal stockholders of the Boston Manufacturing Company, took the first step in the creation of the "selling house" by making the commission firm of B. C. Ward and Company the sales agent for the entire Waltham output. (Appleton's choice of firms is easy to explain; he was one of the major financial backers of B. C. Ward.) Ward received a 1 per cent commission on sales, a low rate by previous standards, but an increasingly lucrative one as Waltham production rose. In 1828, stockholders of the Waltham, Merrimack, Hamilton, and Appleton companies (the last three were "Lowell Mills") formed J. W. Paige and Company, the first modern "textile selling house." Paige was agent for the entire output of the firms listed, and received a 1 per cent commission on most sales. In addition, the firm assumed all risks on credit sales (commission houses had passed such losses on to the manufacturers), financing this function by charging a guaranty fee of 2–4 per cent.[26]

Once developed, the selling house quickly became the dominant institution in the textile industry. Not only did it perform the indispensable sales function, but it soon played a crucial financial role. The New England textile mills involved an unprecedented investment of capital, and the prosperous New England merchants who founded them supplied the funds for initial construction and plowed back profits to start new mills and expand old ones. These investors, however, supplied funds primarily for buildings and equipment—the fixed capital required to start the industry. Once operations began, many of the mills quickly encountered a financial problem which was to dog most American manufacturers throughout the antebellum period—a chronic shortage of working capital.

This shortage arose because some fixed and variable costs—taxes, wages (at least in part), and transportation, for instance—often had to be paid in cash. These problems particularly affected integrated mills, which owned extensive taxable property and had large numbers of payroll employees. Cash, of course, was a scarce commodity in early nineteenth-century America, and manufacturers went to great lengths (as will be seen in later chapters) to minimize the need for it. Nevertheless, a certain irreducible minimum was always required, and the need increased as production rose. The problem was

[26] The emergence of the textile selling house is described in Ware, *Early New England Cotton Manufacture*, chap. 7. See also Evelyn Knowlton, *Pepperell's Progress*, chap. 5.

exacerbated by the fact that the time lag between production and final sale was often long when markets were diffuse and transportation and communication slow. The delay in realizing the proceeds of sales was extended by the fact that virtually all business was done on the basis of long-term credit. In order to continue production, textile makers had to find some agency that would advance funds on the basis of inventory on hand or accounts receivable, but no formal institutions existed to perform this service; banks and insurance companies would not lend on inventories. In prosperous times, banks would occasionally discount commercial paper, but they seldom did it without a merchant's endorsement.[27] Few banks would accept manufacturers' paper in times of credit stringency, no matter what sort of endorsement it carried. In these circumstances the manufacturers turned to the selling houses for working capital.[28]

The selling houses supplied the needed funds by making advances on goods received for sale. This, of course, was an industrial application of a traditional mercantile technique. Much of the commerce of the colonies had been funded by advances from British merchants against future shipments of tobacco, sugar, and other staples. Cotton factors financed planters in the same way. It is not surprising, therefore, that the merchants who dealt with early American manufacturers looked upon inventories as the same sort of security for cash advances. Some textile firms managed to avoid drawing on their agents, but the distributing firms' combination of mercantile expertise and control of working capital gave them a power over manufacturers which was nearly as great as that exercised by the cotton factor over his debtor-planters.

Mercantile expertise involved more than a knowledge of potential customers and their credit standing; the selling houses also engaged in a crude form of market forecasting. The agencies tried to estimate future tastes and markets, and then used these forecasts, together with current sales trends, to dictate to mill owners the kinds of goods they should produce and to fix the prices at which these should be sold.[29] Unfortunately their efforts at matching production to markets were often unsuccessful, and surpluses built up in good times as well as bad. Undoubtedly this failure was the result not only of the uncertainties of the market but also of the fact that commission houses, like most American business firms, were optimistic about business prospects and

---

[27] A more extensive discussion of the problems of borrowing on inventory and accounts receivable, and of operating in the pre–Civil War monetary system, appears in Chapters IV and V of this volume.

[28] Ware, *Early New England Cotton Manufacture*, chap. 7. Lance Davis has shown that selling houses usually supplied very short-term credit to textile mills, but often furnished long-term credit in times of capital scarcity; see his "The New England Textile Mills and the Capital Markets," pp. 6–7.

British manufacturers encountered similar shortages of working capital in the early stages of industrialization, and they too secured the needed funds from their distributors; see Sidney Pollard, "Fixed Capital in the Industrial Revolution in Britain."

[29] Hansjörg Siegenthaler, "What Price Style?"

often submitted overgenerous sales estimates. New England merchants founded most of the early selling houses, and so they naturally hoped to make Boston the center of the textile trade; but New York's advantages as a marketing center ineluctably attracted the Boston trade. One of the principal reasons for this trend was the fact that New York was the center of the network of textile jobbers, whose importance increased as markets expanded.

THE ROLE OF JOBBERS

The jobber, like the selling agent and specialized commission merchant, proved to be an extremely durable type of mercantile specialist in some lines. As a result of expanding trade flows through New York after 1815, he assumed a prominent role in the American distribution system. Jobbers appeared in the dry goods industry to fill a gap between increasingly specialized textile importers and commission merchants on the one hand, and the thousands of general-purpose retail stores that served as the consumer outlet for dry goods on the other. The retailers, who either came to New York periodically to purchase goods, or engaged agents to do so for them, found it a nuisance to go from merchant to merchant in order to secure the wide variety of goods they needed. In addition, the importers and selling houses were reluctant to break bales in order to sell the small quantities needed by retailers, and they often charged exorbitant fees for such services. Jobbers bought goods in large quantities and sold them in small assortments.

The jobbers' role became even more important with the advent of auctions as a means of disposing of imported and domestic goods, for out-of-town retailers obviously could not loiter in New York waiting for appropriate goods to go on the block, and auctioneers could not extend credit to country merchants. The jobber did both, and his performance of these services made him the most important link in the web of agencies which distributed textile products throughout America. In the words of one contemporary observer, the jobber "ruled the trade."[30]

The jobber achieved his position of dominance because his ability to connect the mills to their ultimate consumers was "essential to the orderly marketing of fabrics."[31] The jobber retained his position because the goods remained simple, the market remained diffuse, and because he adapted readily to the few changes which did occur in the industry. For example, when American mills began to produce wider varieties of textile products in the 1830s and 1840s, some jobbers specialized when volume permitted it. When geographic expansion made it difficult for customers in the hinterland to come to coastal cities

[30] Arthur H. Cole, *The American Wool Manufacture*, 1: 291.
[31] *Ibid.*

to do their buying, jobbers sent salesmen on the road and opened branch houses in inland cities. When the auction system declined as a means of textile distribution after 1830, jobbers bought increasingly from selling houses.

For the selling houses, jobbers were the most important and sometimes the only customers. Selling houses competed eagerly for the business of major jobbing houses and often had to agree to make no direct sales in order to secure a jobber's business. Despite the rapid expansion of settlement and population, jobbers in major eastern cities, particularly Boston and New York, were able to keep most of the industry's product flowing through their hands. For example, Pepperell's goods were marketed through the textile selling house of Francis Skinner and Company. In 1852 Francis Skinner sold Pepperell's output to 240 American firms. Of these, 130 were in New York, 51 in Boston. Together the two cities' jobbers absorbed 78 per cent of the total Pepperell production.[32]

In only one area did the jobbers' control of the marketing of textiles diminish—in sales to clothing manufacturers. In the decade 1850–60 the development of the sewing machine led to a rapid expansion of the ready-to-wear clothing industry. Clothing manufacturers viewed the jobber as an unnecessary middleman and repeatedly sought to purchase their supplies directly from the manufacturer. Jobbers reacted to this threat by refusing "to purchase of the commission houses which dealt directly with the clothier."[33] These tactics apparently succeeded for a time. Writing in 1873, one commentator said: "Clothing manufacturers in Boston, and not old men either, remember the time when they could not, on any terms, purchase their cloths directly of commission houses selling the goods of American mills."[34]

It is impossible to measure the precise share of the textile market represented by direct sales to clothiers in 1860. Clothing manufacture absorbed only 25 per cent of textile output in 1859, but by no means all of that was sold directly.[35] On the whole it seems likely that dry goods jobbers still distributed at least 80 per cent of all goods sold in the United States in 1860, and the figure may well have been higher. By collecting the individual small orders of dispersed customers and transmitting them to selling houses as large individual orders, by guaranteeing payment, and by maintaining contact with the expanding market area, the dry goods jobber performed an indispensable marketing function for the industry he served.

For similar reasons, antebellum jobbers became and remained the most important link in the distribution chain for such commodities as hardware (including simple hand tools), groceries, shoes, plumbing and building mate-

[32] *Ibid.*, pp. 291–96; Knowlton, *Pepperell's Progress*, pp. 82–85.
[33] Cole, *American Wool Manufacture*, 1: 294.
[34] *Ibid.*
[35] Estimated from data in Census Office, *Eighth Census.*

rials, and drugs.[36] Jobbers in all these fields operated similarly; thus, a detailed examination of one of them will illustrate the group as a whole.

TROTH AND COMPANY OF PHILADELPHIA:
A TYPICAL JOBBER IN OPERATION

The business records of the Philadelphia wholesale drug firm of Troth and Company disclose competitive problems, business methods, and economic significance typical of jobbers in the trades they served.[37] Drug jobbers, like most specialized urban merchants of the early nineteenth century, depended on extensive trade with the interior to provide a wide market area with a sufficient volume of trade to ensure success. This produced a fierce intercity rivalry for inland markets, and the competition forced urban merchants to make optimum use of developing transportation routes and to offer a variety of mercantile services to their hinterland customers.

Like all jobbers, the Troths had to maintain a large inventory of goods. They had to be prepared to ship goods in small lots on short notice because capital-poor wholesalers, retailers, and artisans in outlying towns and on the frontier kept inventories at a minimum, relying on urban jobbers to supply small lots as required. By extending credit to finance the establishment of storekeepers and artisans in inland towns, jobbers provided a vital link in westward expansion. The owners of general stores in small towns often simultaneously employed the services of several types of urban specialists, buying supplies on credit from dry goods jobbers, shoe jobbers, hardware jobbers, and others to maintain their motley stocks. As towns grew and specialized retail stores appeared, the owners remained dependent on jobbers as suppliers. Storekeepers made their purchases on periodic trips to the city or from drummers sent out by the wholesalers. Storekeepers also relied on their suppliers to act as bankers and urban agents for them, and merchants like the Troths had to give personal attention to these ancillary details in order to retain valuable accounts.

---

[36] Fred M. Jones, "Middlemen in the Domestic Trade of the United States, 1800–1860," chaps. 1–4. Jones details the network through which goods flowed from importing and manufacturing centers to outlying retailers, as does Louis E. Atherton in "The Pioneer Merchant in Mid-America," pp. 7–135, and in *Southern Country Store.* See also Arthur L. Throckmorton, "The Role of the Merchant on the Oregon Frontier."

[37] Arthur Cole noted long ago (*American Wool Manufacture,* 1: 291) the scarcity of information about jobbers. The Troth firm's papers are valuable because the correspondence contains detailed explanations of the way the firm did business. This is fairly unusual in any collection of antebellum business papers, and extremely rare in the papers of merchants, who were a close-mouthed lot. Aside from a few peculiarities associated with the drug business, the Troth firm's operations seem fairly typical of jobbers in general. For an extended discussion of the similarities between drug and hardware wholesalers, see William Becker, "The Wholesalers of Hardware and Drugs, 1870–1900."

Like most contemporary drug establishments,[38] Troth and Company dealt in a variety of goods, all of which were loosely termed "drugs."[39] Included under this general rubric were all medicinal items, paints, varnishes, and glass goods, but the wholesale trade in medicinal goods was the company's prime interest.[40] The Troths always acted as jobbers, buying goods outright from their suppliers.

Many of the suppliers of drugs were importers, for the majority of medicinal goods used in antebellum American were of foreign (especially British) origin. Quinine, ginger, arrowroot, opium, gum Arabic, and many other drugs were largely unobtainable from domestic sources and had to be secured abroad.[41] The Troths bought drugs from import houses such as H. H. Schieffelin and Company, Clark and McConnin, and Cummins and Reach (all of New York), from Baltimore's Smith and Atkinson and Brickhead and Pierce, and from local Philadelphia merchants such as Ziegler and Smith.[42]

In addition to purchases from importers and large wholesale houses in the port cities, Troth and Company obtained some of its goods from domestic manufacturers. These, however, were not drugs, but were usually raw materials for the paint and varnish business. The Brooklyn Lead Company and the Wetherills of Philadelphia, for example, supplied white and red lead for the production of pigments for paints.[43] Not until after the Civil War did the domestic manufacture of raw drugs reach significant proportions.

The Troths sold their goods primarily to two groups of customers. The

---

[38] The firm was founded in 1815 and remained in business until 1856. Like most mercantile firms of the time, Troth & Co. remained a family concern throughout its existence.

[39] A committee of the American Pharmaceutical Assoc. noted in 1868 that "the drug business is the most undefined of any. . . . It is said the term Drug applies especially *to all* commodities that are slow of sale, and for which there is little demand in the market." American Pharmaceutical Assoc., *Report of the Committee on the Drug Market*, p. 2. As used here, however, the term "drug" refers only to medicinal goods.

[40] The range of items sold by businesses such as Troth & Co. may be seen in the Eleutherian Mills Historical Library's collection of advertisements, price lists, circulars, and leaflets of various firms (mainly in Philadelphia) for drugs, patent medicines, etc., from 1840 to 1900 (hereafter cited as Drug Trade Collection).

[41] This made some drug prices very sensitive to aberrations in foreign trade. Samuel Troth wrote two Pittsburgh physicians that the price of quinine was abnormally high "owing to the great scarcity of the Quinine bark which scarcity is caused by the civil wars and unsettled state of affairs in the part of South America that the bark comes from." The cost of opium was similarly inflated whenever the crop in China was poor. Samuel Troth to Drs. R. and W. Young, May 3, 1844; Samuel Troth to Thomas Wainwright, November 10, 1845; and Samuel Troth to Dr. William W. Bancroft, June 29, 1844; Troth Papers.

[42] Correspondence from Troth & Co. to these and other wholesalers is in the Troth Papers.

[43] Letters from Samuel Troth to Samuel Newby (agent for Brooklyn Lead) are numerous in the Troth Papers. See also the entries of purchases from G. D. Wetherill & Co. in the Troth Ledger for the 1840s, *ibid*. The history of the Wetherill firm is ably recounted in Miriam Hussey, *From Merchants to "Colour Men."*

first group consisted of local drug retailers and physicians. Retail establishments such as Carter and Scattergood bought a wide variety of nostrums, spices, and drugs from the firm.[44] Local physicians often operated small drugstores in their offices, and they relied for their supplies on Philadelphia wholesalers such as the Troths.[45]

The second and larger portion of Troth and Company's many customers was composed of buyers in the interior of the United States.[46] Because so few drugs were produced in the inland areas, wholesalers, retailers, and physicians in the West and the South had to establish firm commercial ties with seaboard merchants who had ready access to the import trade.[47] In the West, Troth's customers included residents of central and western Pennsylvania, western Virginia, Tennessee, western Maryland, Ohio, and Missouri. In the South, customers in the Carolinas, Alabama, Mississippi, Georgia, and Louisiana had accounts with the Philadelphia firm.[48] Unlike the local purchasers, the reliability of these distant customers was often an unknown quantity; as a result, the Troths followed a careful credit policy toward inland orders.

In the interior and seacoast cities, the drug business, like most contemporary businesses, functioned on credit because of the scarcity of currency and the ubiquitous shortage of working capital. Importers and large wholesale houses normally sold on credit to other wholesalers and to retailers, who in turn sold on credit to physicians, pharmacists, and consumers. The usual credit in the drug trade in the 1840s and 1850s was six months, while a 5 per cent discount was offered for cash payments.[49]

In order to render business less risky and difficult for all, the Troths cooperated with other drug merchants in several ways. The merchants maintained a

[44] The Day Book of Carter & Scattergood, 1834–1835, contains many entries for goods bought from Troth & Co. This Day Book is in the Carter & Scattergood Papers.

[45] Troth also sold items used in the treatment of animals. Speaking of the merits of white as compared with yellow resin, Samuel Troth assured a buyer, "There is no doubt of its being as good for the hogs as the other article" (Troth to D. C. Miller, May 17, 1843, Troth Papers).

[46] In 1843 Samuel Troth estimated that he dealt with approximately 300 different customers. Troth to John Mitchell, April 17, 1843, ibid. The correspondence in the Troth collection indicates that a majority of those customers were outside the greater Philadelphia-Wilmington region.

[47] The pattern of southern and western druggists and doctors buying their supplies from wholesalers in northeastern cities was common. See, for example, W. H. Schieffelin & Co., 100 Years of Business Life 1794–1894, pp. 40–41, and McKesson & Robbins, The Road to Market, p. 21.

[48] Outgoing correspondence, Troth Papers.

[49] Several trade catalogs from the forties and fifties in the Drug Trade Collection at the Eleutherian Mills Library mention that goods were sold on the usual terms of six months; see, for example, the 1852 catalog of Bullock & Crenshaw. On trade catalogs in general, see George B. Griffenhagen and Lawrence B. Romaine, "Early U.S. Pharmaceutical Catalogues." If payment was not rendered by the end of the credit period, interest charges of 6 per cent per year were appended. "Nearly all of our trade," Samuel Troth informed a prospective customer, "charge after 6 months" (Troth to Dr. B. R. Owens, November 19, 1846, Troth Papers).

steady flow of information on the credit standing of wholesale houses and retail stores. In addition, they acted as fiscal agents for one another by paying local accounts for fellow merchants in other cities. Samuel Troth sent a check to a New York wholesale firm, for example, and instructed them thus: "In case you have drawn on me for the above amount, then please hand this check over to the Brooklyn White Lead Co. . . . to be placed to my credit on their books."[50] Sometimes a single check would be sent to the agent for the Brooklyn Lead Company, asking that part of the funds be credited to his account with that firm and that the remainder be divided between "Clark & McConnin and Isaac Lehman Commission Merchant and Broker of your city."[51] In the absence of specialized financial institutions to perform this function, such exchanges of services and information worked to the advantage of all and reduced the uncertainties of commerce.

Troth and Company also relied heavily on the cooperation of merchants in the interior, especially when a general grocery merchant or commission merchant sent an order from a retail druggist. These retailers were usually addressed as "doctor" by contemporaries, even though they were not physicians.[52] They were not so good a credit risk as physicians, and the Troths would not sell goods to drugstore operators without a favorable reference from a reliable merchant. Even when informed that a country retailer had a sound reputation, the Troth company never sold goods to the prospective customer without first requiring one-half of the amount in cash.

Merchants and physicians enjoyed a much stronger credit standing with the Troths than did the retail druggists. "We have for many years refused to open new accounts where the articles were wanted for Drug Stores, unless we had one half cash," Samuel Troth summarized his policy late in 1846, "while at the same time we have opened new accounts freely with merchants and Physicians."[53] Physicians in particular found quick cooperation and liberal credit if they could provide references. Credit terms were quite generous for physicians building a practice in the sparsely populated areas of the West. Indeed, such customers often were allowed a full year before their payments were due.[54]

The extension of credit to merchants, physicians, and retail druggists in the interior was an important contribution to the economic growth of the nation. Working capital constituted a large portion of the total capital needed by druggists and young physicians. For example, it was estimated in 1846 that as much working capital as fixed capital was necessary to open a retail drug business in the West. As Samuel Troth wrote, "We should suppose that $500

[50] Samuel Troth to Grinnell Minturn & Co., April 21, 1843, Troth Papers.
[51] Samuel Troth to Samuel Newby, May 20, 1843, *ibid.*
[52] David W. Ryder, *The First Hundred Years*, p. 1.
[53] Troth & Co. to Dr. David Petriken, December 18, 1846, Troth Papers.
[54] Samuel Troth to James M. Jetton, March 6, 1844, *ibid.*

for fixtures and such articles as could be procured cheaper in the west and $500 worth of medicine from the east would be sufficient to commence a very respectable store in St. Louis."[55] By extending a credit of one-half of the medicine, the Troth company made available to western entrepreneurs a portion of the northeastern capital. In addition, many physicians probably found the idea of establishing themselves in the interior a more palatable and practical proposition because of the available credit.

In addition to the extension of credit, Troth and Company provided a wide range of financial services to their customers (especially to physicians). The widespread mercantile connections of the Philadelphia house allowed it to accept bank notes and checks from inland cities without subjecting the customer's notes to the usual heavy Philadelphia discount rates for money or notes from the interior. "Thee mentions a preference paying in Nashville," Samuel Troth noted of a Tennessee customer. "If thee would prefer paying in six months from date of bill, thee may pay R. H. McEwen $50 which will be received in full."[56] Troth would sometimes even accept money from inland cities at face value, although he then gave no cash discount.[57]

Besides acting as banker for physicians, the Troths procured for frontier doctors many items obtainable only in the East. They bought copies of early pharmaceutical journals, general periodicals, and specialized texts on medicine and surgery, and packed them with physicians' drug orders. They made inquiries of manufacturers to secure information on the proper use of medical devices. "We could not find McCulloch on fevers—notwithstanding we enquired at most of our principal Book Stores," they told a South Carolina physician, "and the manufacturer of Chase's Supporters had not any printed directions, but thinks the article will sufficiently explain itself."[58] In addition to such errands, physicians often asked the Troths to arrange for the manufacture or purchase of items such as medical saddle bags, soda-water apparatus, artificial limbs, and imported French skeletons. The Troth partners performed all these tasks with diligence, thereby providing indispensable services to doctors in remote areas.

A similar diligence marked the Troth firm's performance of the primary function of packing and forwarding drugs. The wholesaler arranged for the transport of the goods to their ultimate destinations through specialized forwarding and commission agents in interior cities such as Pittsburgh and

[55] Samuel Troth to Eugene Massie, September 7, 1846, *ibid*. This figure may have been too high; a western druggist writing on the eve of the Civil War estimated that a retail drug operation could be started on as little as $500. James Bryan, *Bryan's Druggists' Manual*, pp. 202–3.

[56] Troth & Co. to Dr. B. R. Owens, April 8, 1843, Troth Papers. McEwen was a Tennessee merchant with whom Troth dealt.

[57] See, for example, Samuel Troth to Dr. John Heisley, May 10, 1843, *ibid*.

[58] Samuel Troth to Dr. F. W. Symmes, April 10, 1843, *ibid*.

Cincinnati.[59] In order to make the costs of their drugs competitive in areas served by houses in other seacoast cities, the Troths often paid the freight rates from Philadelphia to those cities. To a customer in upstate New York, for example, Troth and Company paid "all expenses on such of our goods as you may order, to New York [City], so as to place us on the same footing with you, as the New York druggists."[60]

Troth and Company usually employed water transport both to obtain and to distribute its merchandise, even when other means were available. Goods for the West usually went either around Florida to New Orleans and thence up the Mississippi, or else across the system of inland rivers and canals to distribution points such as Pittsburgh. The costs of water transportation were much lower than railroad rates. "I would prefer that the article should not be forwarded until the canal between your city and this opens," Samuel Troth cautioned a New York supplier, "as the Rail Road charges about four times as much as the tow boats and we are not in immediate want of the article."[61] Only when they were in "immediate want" of an item did the Troths' desire for speed overcome their desire for low-cost transport. They instructed a New York import house, for example, to "pack up the 40 lb. Blue Mass and send it over per railroad as soon as possible. The other articles we are in no hurry for."[62]

Thus, by performing the services of selling job lots from inventory, arranging for packing and shipping, assuming credit risks, and maintaining a flow of credit information on customers, the jobbers relieved domestic manufacturers (or their selling houses) and commission merchants importing foreign goods of a major burden.

CONCLUSION

The dynamic force of increased trade volume created a distribution chain in which each link specialized in some portion of the wide range of services traditionally offered by the all-purpose merchant. Through this chain flowed not only the domestic staples and imported goods which had initiated specialization, but the products of nascent American manufacturing industries as well.

In such industries as textiles, hardware, tools, groceries, plumbing and

[59] Samuel Troth to Poindexter & Rhey, April 5, 1843; and Troth to Isaac Thorn, May 22, 1843; *ibid.*

[60] Samuel Troth to Pritchard & Son, July 26, 1843, *ibid.* To a doctor in the Baltimore region Troth wrote, "To compete with the Baltimore Druggists I have paid the freight on thy goods to that place" (Samuel Troth to Dr. N. Marmion, August 30, 1843, *ibid.*).

[61] Samuel Troth to Isaac Lehman, March 6, 1843, *ibid.*

[62] Samuel Troth to Clark & McConnin, April 3, 1843, *ibid.* The Blue Mass was widely used as a cathartic. Like many remedies of the time, the cure was worse than the malady; repeated use of the Blue Pill (the ultimate form of the Blue Mass) caused systemic mercury poisoning. Paul Stecher, ed., *The Merck Index*, p. 662.

building materials, shoes, and drugs—that is, industries which manufactured retail generic goods in large quantities—specialized agencies such as selling houses and jobbers enabled manufacturers to reach their diffuse markets through a relatively small number of intermediaries. Jobber-dominated distribution networks appeared in all of these fields by the 1840s, and they retained their paramount position into the twentieth century. In addition to being retail generic goods, these products had in common the fact that they were produced (or imported) in large quantities, available from many sources, and relatively inexpensive per unit. Their final distribution came through small individual sales to a large number of customers spread over a wide area, usually through stores which handled a gallimaufry of goods.

It is worth noting that these industries are precisely those in which nineteenth-century horizontal mergers of many manufacturers into a few large firms usually failed; forward vertical integration rarely went beyond the wholesaling stage, and it did not reach that level until after World War I. Furthermore, manufacturers in these industries have rarely engaged in product diversification.[63] Such long-run stability in methods of production and distribution usually indicates little change in either production techniques or market characteristics, and this was precisely the case in the jobber-dominated industries. All of the products mentioned above continued throughout the nineteenth century to be generic goods produced by simple technology and sold in diffuse markets.[64] Because changes in technology and markets came slowly, the jobber-operated networks set up to distribute retail goods early in the nineteenth century remained adequate for many decades thereafter.[65]

Although most often associated with products of the new industrial economy, the jobber was in fact more representative of an earlier age. The services he performed and the techniques he employed to perform them were a legacy from his all-purpose predecessors, adapted through specialization to the rising volume of trade. Specialization itself resulted from conservatism, not innovation. The jobber, like other specialized merchants who appeared in the antebellum marketing system, simply dropped some of the all-purpose merchant's traditional activities in order to concentrate on others. Such flexibility, manifested in a willingness to match techniques to current market circumstances, had been a traditional hallmark of successful merchants through the centuries.

[63] Alfred D. Chandler, Jr., "The Structure of American Industry in the Twentieth Century"; P. Glenn Porter and Harold C. Livesay, "Oligopolists in American Manufacturing and Their Products, 1909–1963"; Harold C. Livesay and Patrick G. Porter, "Vertical Integration in American Manufacturing, 1899–1948."

[64] The major exception here is the meat packing industry, in which the application of a new technology, refrigeration, led to a concentrated, vertically integrated, and diversified industry. See Chandler's "Structure of American Industry," as well as Chapter X of this volume. It is also true that by the end of the nineteenth century drug jobbers and manufacturers had engaged in some vertical integration.

[65] The discussion of the role of jobbers in the marketing of retail goods after the Civil War is continued in detail in Chapter XIII of this volume.

By adapting to the shifting needs of trade, merchants had remained the dominant force in the Western economy since the late Middle Ages, and they remained so in pre–Civil War America. Retention of power was not without cost, however, for the merchant who specialized in the products of one industry over extended periods of time became tied to that industry, and his fortunes fluctuated with it. By sacrificing diversity for specialization, the merchant preserved his position of power at the cost of narrowing his horizons from the world and all its goods to specific markets for a single commodity.

The specialized merchant, then, adapted the techniques of the traditional mercantile economy to the new industrial environment. Specialization was economically logical, helped maintain an efficient distribution network, and cemented the merchants' role as coordinators, movers, and shakers of the American economy. By adapting themselves so thoroughly and effectively to their environment, however, specialized merchants made themselves vulnerable to future changes in it. In order to see the consequences of such changes before the Civil War, it is necessary to turn from retail goods to producers' goods industries. Most important of these—both in terms of the value of products and as illustrations of innovations in manufacturing and marketing—were the iron and machinery industries.

CHAPTER III

The Merchant
in Operation:
The Marketing of Iron

The years after 1815 saw the rapid development of the type of distribution networks through which most manufactured retail goods flowed for many decades thereafter. During the same period similar specialization appeared in the marketing of producers' goods—that is, goods sold to other manufacturers, or to transportation firms. In retail (consumers') goods, the selling agent and the jobber combined their mercantile expertise with their capital resources to dominate the industries they served. In producers' goods another type of specialized middleman—the commission merchant—applied the same levers to exercise control over manufacturers. In retail goods, expanding textile production forged the prototype network. In producers' goods, iron industries did so.

Iron, unlike textiles, was a very old industry in America—indeed, almost as old as the colonies themselves. Intrepid Europeans, bent on hacking and hewing civilization out of a primeval wilderness, required an array of iron tools and weapons to implement the job. British merchants not only were aware of the colonists' need; they counted on supplying it. In the counting houses of London it seemed a first-rate business to restrict the colonials to the production of pig iron, thereby protecting for British manufacturers the colonial market for British finished products.[1] In America this policy did not

---

[1] Whenever the term "finished products" appears in this study, it means those goods that required no further manufacturing processes (except assembly) before being put to their intended uses. In general, semifinished (or "intermediate") products were producers' goods, while finished products tended to be consumers' goods. This was not invariably the case, however. For example, yarn sold to frontier housewives was a semifinished product and a retail good; railroad rails were finished products and producers' goods.

seem so salutary: London was far away; the trees and the Indians were close by. The British passed laws to protect their market, while the colonists developed iron works to ensure their own supply.

Fortunately for the settlers, America had abundant supplies of iron ore, wood with which to smelt it, and craftsmen able to carry out the additional stages of manufacture culminating in finished products.[2] It is not known when American manufacture of iron began, but John Winthrop, Jr., set up the Saugus Iron Works near Lynn, Massachusetts, in 1645.[3] Although Saugus eventually failed, pig iron continued to be produced at a multitude of smelters throughout the colonies. It was converted to wrought iron by hammering in foundries. Pig and wrought iron eventually became major colonial exports, as well as important commodities in internal trade. Despite various unenforceable parliamentary acts prohibiting the manufacture of finished iron products, colonial craftsmen regularly produced pots, pans, anchors, chain, nails, axes, and the like.[4] Like the pig and bar iron sold within the colonies, some of these finished products were sold directly in local markets. Surplus production went to city merchants, who in turn disposed of the finished products in distant markets and sold bar and pig iron to blacksmiths, shipyards, and other fabricators.[5] Thus, like imported metalwares, both crude and finished colonial iron

[2] For the purpose of this study we have divided all iron-manufacturing processes into three categories. The first, *smelting*, involves the reduction of iron ore to pig iron. The second, *iron refining*, refers to those processes employed to convert pig iron into purer, more workable forms. These include hammering, puddling, and rolling, which produce wrought iron bars or rough slabs called "blooms." During the 1830s, puddling and rolling gradually began to replace hammering as the most important methods of iron refining. This change is discussed in Peter Temin, *Iron and Steel in Nineteenth Century America*, pp. 100–101. The third category, *iron processing*, comprises all other forms of iron manufacture except machinery making and includes all producers of finished products, whether they be producers' or consumers' goods.

This chapter is not, and does not attempt to be, a comprehensive history of the pre–Civil War American iron industry from either a technological or an institutional viewpoint. Such histories do not exist for the American iron and steel industries in any period. The material lies scattered in a myriad of primary and secondary sources. The best attempts to pull them together are Victor S. Clark, *History of Manufacturers in the United States*, and Temin, *Iron and Steel*.

[3] The detailed story of the Saugus Works is contained in Edward N. Hartley, *Iron Works on the Saugus*. Saugus is now a National Historic Site and is being restored by the National Park Service.

[4] Detailed statistics of colonial trade in iron can be found in U.S. Bureau of the Census, *Historical Statistics of the United States*, pp. 762–65; see also Keach Johnson, "The Baltimore Company Seeks English Markets."

[5] Sometimes the furnace had its own store in a nearby city to dispose of its wares. This practice declined, however, as specialization increased after the Revolution. Early American ironworks seem to have fascinated historians; the material in print is voluminous. The present discussion is drawn primarily from Arthur D. Pierce, *Iron in the Pines*, p. 132; Henry J. Noble, *History of the Cast Iron Pressure Pipe Industry in the United States of America*, pp. 17–18; James M. Ransom, *Vanishing Ironworks of the Ramapos*, *passim*; Lester J. Cappon, "Trend of the Southern Iron Industry Under the Plantation System," p. 370.

manufactures were regular items of trade for all-purpose American merchants and country storekeepers.

The early development of iron manufacture in the colonies, and the persistence with which it was pursued—despite frequent failures, and in the face of parliamentary prohibitions—demonstrates the interest in manufacturing which pervaded colonial America despite the essentially agricultural nature of its economy. An abundance of raw materials, the presence of skilled labor, the colonials' continual need for iron at home and for exportable goods to balance trade, and the demand for pig iron in England generated an incentive for the development of furnaces. Other factors, however, played an equally important part. Long before Alexander Hamilton, Americans sought manufacturing self-sufficiency as a means of reducing dependence on overseas suppliers, and the manufacturing enterprise enjoyed the support of some of the most prominent American families. Augustus Washington set up an iron furnace on the Potomac in 1732. He and his son George supplied capital to what later became Principio Furnace at the mouth of the Susquehanna in Maryland.[6]

Hamilton, Tench Coxe, Matthew Carey, and other apostles of autarky in the newly independent United States articulated ideas that had been common currency among their colonial predecessors. What these men advanced in theory, the shortages of manufactures during the two British wars and the troubled interim period advanced in substance. By 1815 the United States already contained many furnaces for smelting iron from ore, as well as forges, foundries, and blacksmith shops for converting pig iron into more useful forms.[7]

The need for raw materials and water power to run machinery largely determined the location of early American iron works. The ore lay scattered about the countryside, often far from urban markets. Smelting was done with charcoal made from timber, of which there was an abundant supply in the immediate vicinity of most iron mines. Because the quantity of raw materials put into the furnace was much greater than the quantity of iron that came out, and because transportation of bulky commodities was expensive and difficult,[8]

[6] Samuel E. Morison, *The Oxford History of the American People*, p. 143; Earl C. May, *From Principio to Wheeling*, chaps. 4–6.

[7] For evidence of the growth of interest in manufacturing see Samuel Rezneck, "The Rise and Early Development of Industrial Consciousness in the United States, 1760–1830." The part played by the federal government in creating a congenial environment for manufacturing is felicitously described in Stuart Bruchey, *The Roots of American Economic Growth, 1607–1861*, esp. chap. 5.

[8] Transportation costs were especially high if they involved wagonage. Precise comparisons between the costs of various forms of transportation are excruciatingly difficult to make for pre–Civil War America because the rates fluctuated so rapidly. It is clear, however, that a landlocked ironmaster had no chance to compete in a market served by colleagues with access to water transport. The best estimates of relative transportation costs are George R. Taylor's; an example is his *The Transportation Revolution, 1815–1860*, p. 442.

most iron smelting was done at the ore site.[9] The furnace owner commonly owned ore pits and timberlands as well, and was thus integrated backward to the raw materials. He was rarely, however, integrated forward into the refining and processing stages. Furnace owners shipped most of their pig iron to independent foundries, forges, and rolling mills for further manufacture.

Foundries made the casting for stoves, hardware, and simple machinery. Rolling mills turned out sheets for nails, plate iron for boilers, and the simple "merchant bars" used by tool makers and blacksmiths. All of these products were generic goods and remained so throughout the antebellum period. Foundries and smithies could be and were located almost anywhere, but ambitious entrepreneurs in this field had to locate near larger markets or on transportation routes. Rolling mills needed water power to operate the machinery (steam-powered rolling mills were not perfected until the mid 1840s and did not become common until mid-century), as well as transportation facilities. Although some refining establishments integrated backward by operating both furnaces and rolling mills or forges, the most common pattern in pre–Civil War America was a separation of these functions.[10]

There were several reasons why volume encouraged specialized, unintegrated manufacturing. First, the requirements for raw materials and water power were often mutually exclusive, thereby precluding the location of furnaces and rolling mills on the same site. Second, the management structure of the typical early nineteenth-century manufacturing firm (outside the textile industry) was similar to that of the mercantile firms already described. It was usually either a sole proprietorship or a limited partnership. Adequate supervision required continual attendance on the grounds, and the limited number of owners, together with slow transportation, discouraged single-firm ownership of several geographically separated plants.[11] Finally, increased production meant greater demands on limited capital, a significant barrier to integrated operations. A manufacturing entrepreneur usually had to choose between building new furnaces or constructing rolling mills. He could rarely afford to do both.

In the 1840s a few firms appeared which solved all these problems, thus clearing the way for integration of all three stages of manufacture within a

---

[9] An additional reason for locating the furnace near the charcoal ricks was the fact that charcoal, if hauled very far over rough surfaces, broke down into a grit unusable in furnaces; see David S. Landes, *The Unbound Prometheus*, p. 90.

[10] This pattern continued even after the shift was made from charcoal to anthracite coal as smelting fuel, a step that became common in eastern Pennsylvania in the 1840s.

[11] There were some exceptions to this generalization. Sometimes a single family owned more than one establishment, but these firms usually functioned as independent operations, not stages of a coordinated, integrated whole. See May, *Principio*, for a description of the multiple enterprises of the Whitaker family. Louis C. Hunter, "Financial Problems of the Early Pittsburgh Iron Manufacturers," lists a number of Pennsylvania ironmasters who controlled more than one firm concomitantly.

single firm. The integrated firm remained the exception, however, until after the Civil War; in 1860, unintegrated firms produced more than 75 per cent of U.S. pig iron.[12] The fact that most firms concentrated on a single stage of manufacture created a set of marketing and purchasing perplexities which opened the way for the commission merchant to dominate the industry.

THE MARKETING OF CRUDE IRON

The first stage of iron manufacturing was smelting. This consisted of converting the ore into pig iron. At some furnaces iron was further refined and shaped into rough slabs called blooms. Pig iron was used by bloomeries (refiners) and foundries (processors); blooms went to forges and rolling mills.[13] In either case the furnace owner faced serious problems of distribution and finance. In the first place he usually had a large capital investment in ore pits, timberlands, furnaces, and horses and wagons to move the materials about. The remote location of many iron furnaces forced the owners to build living quarters for their employees.[14] The total value of these assembled assets was often extremely large by the standards of the times. For example, according to the *McLane Report* published in 1832, there were 105 manufacturing firms in the United States with a capital investment of more than $100,000. Eighty-seven of these were textile mills; of the remainder, all but five were iron-smelting firms.[15]

Taxes and upkeep meant high fixed costs for proprietors. In addition, it was expensive to start up ("blow in") a furnace once it had been shut down. These costs, together with a natural desire to achieve steady returns on such sizable investments, constituted a strong incentive to operate as much of the time as possible. Sustained operation in turn made it imperative to find adequate markets and operating capital with which to meet cash expenses.

The problem of finding appropriate markets defied solution by the furnace

[12] Temin, *Iron and Steel*, p. 111. Henceforth the term "integrated iron firm" is used to describe only those producing units which combined more than one of the three stages of production: smelting, refining, and processing.

[13] In general, forges and rolling mills were refiners because they rarely made finished products. The most significant exceptions were those rolling mills which produced railroad rails.

[14] These self-sufficient communities were called "iron plantations." One may be seen in its entirety at Hopewell Village State Park in Berks County, Pa., where the Pennsylvania State Historical and Museum Commission has restored the buildings and works of the Hopewell Furnace, a nineteenth-century producer of pig iron and stoves. Temin estimates that a furnace owner needed at least 3,000 acres to have adequate supplies of fuel and ore (*Iron and Steel*, pp. 83–84).

[15] The remaining five included one firm in each of the following categories: nails and hoops, firearms, glass, salt, and hydraulic equipment. See U.S. Secretary of the Treasury, *Documents Relative to the Manufactures in the United States*. This survey is commonly referred to as *The McLane Report*. It covered only eleven states, but these contained the preponderance of extant manufacturing units.

owners themselves. Their production almost invariably exceeded local demands. In Berks County, Pennsylvania, for example, six operating furnaces produced approximately 3,000 tons of pig iron in 1819. The county's bloomeries and foundries used only half that much; therefore, even if Berks refineries monopolized the local market for pig iron (by no means a certainty), they still had a surplus of 1,500 tons to peddle somewhere else.[16] Conversely, no furnace could promise to make regular deliveries to specific processors, because iron smelting was a notoriously unpredictable affair plagued by troubles with furnaces, freeze-ups in ore pits, temporary shortages of labor, and the like.

These vagaries made large, direct ("on order") sales even to local consumers a chancy business at best, and they also tended to prevent furnace proprietors from roaming far afield in search of buyers. What was needed was an intermediate agency which could rationalize the flow of material by collecting large supplies from the sporadic output of many furnaces and matching them to the demands of a multitude of widely scattered foundries, bloomeries, and rolling mills. Only one man, the city merchant, was capable of performing this function, and iron smelters invariably turned to him.

Dealing in iron was nothing new for the mercantile community, of course; all-purpose colonial merchants had handled it regularly. In the years after 1815 the increased volume of trade in iron, facilitated by improving transportation and powered by continuing imports and rising domestic production on the supply side, together with increased population and the spread of manufacturing on the demand side, led to the development of merchants specializing in the iron trade.[17] Since the products themselves remained relatively simple and undifferentiated, specialization was the only adaptation necessary. It enabled merchants to retain control of the distribution of most iron products throughout the period.

These specialized iron dealers were usually commission merchants, who rarely took title to the goods. All over the United States, wherever iron was produced before the Civil War, a similar pattern emerged. Furnace owners sold what they could locally and shipped the balance to commission merchants (many of whom specialized in iron) in nearby cities for sale in the diffuse market. Pennsylvania producers (who accounted for the bulk of the national total) shipped to Baltimore, Pittsburgh, and Philadelphia; Kentucky and Ohio iron from the Hanging Rock District went to Cincinnati; Virginia iron was shipped to Richmond, Baltimore, New York, and Boston; South Carolina iron went to Charleston and Columbia; and Alabama iron was transported to

---

[16] Computed from data in U.S. Census Office, *Fourth Census of the United States, 1820.*

[17] The appropriate commercial directories show that there were specialized iron merchants in Boston, New York, Philadelphia, and Baltimore by the 1820s.

Montgomery and Mobile.[18] So long as iron smelting was conducted as a separate stage of manufacturing, success depended on the mercantile services of commission merchants, for success required volume. Volume in turn required large markets, and these the merchants opened to producers by organizing the trade effectively.[19]

Even the largest unintegrated iron-smelting firms relied heavily on the commission merchant until after the Civil War. The Coleman family of Lebanon County, Pennsylvania, owned the largest iron ore deposits in America (outside the Lake Superior region, which was not extensively exploited until late in the century), which they used to feed their Cornwall furnaces. The firm was not integrated; it produced almost nothing but pig iron, using charcoal and anthracite. It sold some of this directly to forges in Harrisburg and other nearby cities. Commission merchants sold the rest.[20] In the 1850s the firm utilized several iron brokers: Enoch Pratt in Baltimore, Henry G. Nichols in New York, and Cabeen and Company in Philadelphia.

As the decade advanced Cabeen became virtually the exclusive agent for Cornwall iron in all major markets, a position he retained throughout the 1860s.[21] For the producer he therefore operated as an exclusive manufacturer's agent. He sold Cornwall pig iron all over the East, and as far west as Pittsburgh, Wheeling, and Ironton, Ohio. These sales provided a clear majority of the Cornwall market. In 1866 (the first year for which complete records of pig iron orders are available) Cabeen's sales accounted for approximately 74 per cent of total production. Fragmentary evidence for earlier years indicates that the same ratio prevailed in the antebellum period.[22]

Hundreds of letters in several collections of manufacturers' papers disclose the nature of Cabeen's business methods and also indicate that they were typical for the industry.[23] Cabeen was extremely specialized, operated wholly on

[18] James B. McNair, *Simon Cameron's Adventure in Iron, 1837–1846*, p. 48; Hunter, "Early Pittsburgh Iron Manufacturers," p. 537; Vernon D. Keeler, "An Economic History of the Jackson County Iron Industry," p. 145; Wilbur Stout, "The Charcoal Iron Industry of the Hanging Rock Iron District," pp. 98–99; Cappon, "Trend of the Southern Iron Industry," p. 373; Kathleen Bruce, *Virginia Iron Manufacture in the Slave Era*, pp. 160, 190, 203–4; Ethel Armes, *The Story of Coal and Iron in Alabama*, pp. 30, 79; Ernest M. Lander, Jr., "The Iron Industry in Ante-Bellum South Carolina."

[19] Iron smelters also depended heavily on middlemen as sources of capital. This will be discussed in Chapter IV.

[20] Clark, *History of Manufactures*, 2: 197; Arthur C. Bining, *Pennsylvania Iron Manufacture in the Eighteenth Century*, p. 57; Frederick K. Miller, "The Rise of an Iron Community," pp. 141–42, 213.

[21] Incoming Correspondence for the 1850s and 1860s, Cornwall Furnace Papers.

[22] Computed from Pig Iron Order Book, Cornwall Anthracite and Donaghmore Furnaces, 1866–81, *ibid.*; see also Pig Iron Sales Book, R. W. & W. Coleman, 1858–78, and Incoming Correspondence for the 1860s, *ibid.*

[23] Manuscript collections containing extensive Cabeen correspondence include (in addition to the Cornwall Furnace Papers) the Lukens Steel Co. Papers, the Alan Wood Steel Co. Papers, and the Lobdell Car Wheel Co. Papers. The same collections also

commission, and dealt almost exclusively in pig iron and blooms, drawing supplies from New York, New Jersey, Pennsylvania, Delaware, and Maryland. He bought and sold almost entirely by mail. Because the supply of crude iron rarely matched current demands, prices fluctuated constantly. As the market rose and fell Cabeen fired off fusillades of letters to sellers and buyers, updating them on prices and offering "bargains" in the light of current market conditions. Because he dealt in such large volumes, he was often able to contract for future supplies at fixed prices, or at the lowest market price on the delivery date. Dealers in smaller volumes usually refused to guarantee future prices in such an unstable market.[24]

When a sale was arranged, Cabeen instructed the seller—the furnace owner—as to price, destination, means of shipment, quantity ordered, and date of delivery. The iron then went directly from furnace to buyer; Cabeen himself never saw it. The purchaser paid Cabeen, either in cash (most unusual), or by note. The broker deducted his commission (5 per cent for making the sale and guaranteeing payment) and disposed of the balance according to the refiner's instructions—discounting notes, making deposits, paying bills —thereby functioning as urban financial agent in the same way that drug, dry goods, and other jobbers did for their clients.

Specialization in function and commodity, coupled with a thorough familiarity with diffuse markets and credit standing, enabled Cabeen, Pratt, and their colleagues to perform an indispensable service to unintegrated iron firms by providing wide markets for producers and dependable supplies to consumers. The iron brokers prosecuted their business aggressively through constant contact with old customers and assiduous solicitation of new firms appearing in the industry.

THE DISTRIBUTION OF PROCESSED IRON

Unintegrated firms engaged in processing pig iron, wrought iron, and blooms faced a somewhat different set of market problems from those of iron smelters and refiners, depending on the nature of their products and the scale

---

contain much correspondence from the firm of Enoch Pratt & Bro. Virtually every manufacturer's collection cited in this study contains copious commission merchant correspondence. Among the most useful for developing a picture of the business relationships between producers and their agents are the exchanges between Gibbons & Huston and Kemble & Warner; the Lobdell Car Wheel Co. and Cabeen; and others to be cited subsequently.

[24] Detailed negotiations that culminated in a future contract at a fixed price can be seen in a series of letters between Richard Borden, treasurer of Fall River Iron Works, and Enoch Pratt, esp. in Borden to Pratt, August 23, 1853, Fall River Iron Works Papers. Pratt agreed to supply 2,400 tons of pig iron over twelve months at $32 per ton. Merchants met market prices by sending trusted customers blank invoices, telling them to fill in the lowest price offered by any competitor; see Cabeen to Gibbons & Huston, August 29, 1857, Lukens Papers.

of their operations. Small foundries, forges, and rolling mills required a miniscule capital investment compared with that of iron furnaces.[25] Small processing firms often operated quite successfully serving only a local market. As long as the proprietor was content to restrict the volume of production, he could buy his raw materials and sell his products without resorting to commercial intermediaries. Many firms did business exactly that way, remaining small through the proprietor's lack of ambition, or because of inadequate transportation facilities to larger markets.

Cheap transportation was an absolute precondition to servicing expanded markets, for, in an era of simple, inexpensive goods, transportation costs presented a barrier that protected local producers against outside competition. Before the Civil War cheap transportation almost always meant water transportation. Therefore, it is not surprising that iron-processing firms that expanded into distant markets were most often located on the seaboard, on rivers, or on a canal.

Whenever a manufacturing entrepreneur decided to expand beyond the local market, he became the object of eager solicitation by urban commission merchants who competed for his trade. Most manufacturers turned over their marketing problems to merchants in the city most accessible by water transport. In the early nineteenth century this usually meant that producers were firmly tied to the market of a single large city. As canals presented alternative routes, manufacturers acquired a wider choice of dealers and markets. The history of the New Cumberland Forge in Cumberland County, Pennsylvania, is a typical example of an unintegrated iron-processing firm that expanded beyond its local market by distributing its surplus production through urban commission merchants.

Jacob Haldeman, the proprietor of New Cumberland Forge, began operations in 1805 by setting up a forge and rolling mill at the confluence of Yellow Breeches Creek (which supplied water power) and the Susquehanna River.[26] He produced a variety of iron products typical of the times: barrel hoops, sledge runners, plow iron, horseshoe iron, nail and spike iron, scalloped iron, and large quantities of iron bars. Through 1815 he sold his products almost entirely in local markets to blacksmiths, gunsmiths, tool makers, and other artisans in towns such as Harrisburg, Hanover, York, Carlisle, Gettysburg, Elizabethtown, and Marietta. These sales were made directly, usually in cash, but often in exchange for produce.[27]

After the war Haldeman increased output and became by contemporary

[25] Integrated rolling mills, of course, required much larger capital investments; see Temin, *Iron and Steel*, chap. 5.

[26] The complex was built on a site that is now part of the borough of New Cumberland, Pa.

[27] Incoming Correspondence, 1805–21, Cornwall Papers; Orders for Iron, 1801–30, Jacob Haldeman Papers; Harold C. Livesay and Patrick G. Porter, "Iron on the Susquehanna."

standards a producer of considerable size.[28] He marketed his products through several outlets. His brother ran a general store in down-river Columbia, Pennsylvania, which marketed some iron.[29] In 1817 Haldeman began dealing with John Brooks, a Harrisburg commission merchant. Sales through Brooks provided about $4,000 average annual revenue in subsequent years, totaling more than $50,000 by 1830. Haldeman disposed of the balance of his iron through commission merchants in coastal cities.

Until the late 1820s, when the opening of the Chesapeake and Delaware Canal and the Union Canal linking the Susquehanna with the Schuylkill created short water routes to Philadelphia, Haldeman and his fellow businessmen in the Susquehanna River valley were tied firmly to Baltimore.[30] They floated their merchandise downstream to Port Deposit or Havre de Grace on rafts called "arks." There the arks were broken up for lumber, and all the goods were moved to Baltimore on a fleet of sloops which shuttled back and forth on the Chesapeake Bay.

Haldeman dealt with a number of Baltimore commission firms such as Hugh Boyle and Company, Ballard and Hall, Wilmer and Palmer, David Kizer and Company, Evan T. Ellicott, J. W. and E. Patterson, and Lambert Gittings.[31] These firms competed eagerly for Haldeman's trade by offering a variety of services.[32] They met the boats on arrival in Baltimore and, if a sale

[28] Although production data in the Haldeman Papers are incomplete, the firm appears to have had an annual capacity of about 650 tons. This was probably above average for similar Pennsylvania establishments in the 1820s, and about average in the 1830s. Size comparisons in this era can only be approximated, for the material on them is imprecise. See Bining, *Pennsylvania Iron Manufacture*, p. 85; Tench Coxe, *A Statement of the Arts and Manufactures of the United States of America for the Year 1810*, p. 50; and U.S. Census Office, *Fifth Census of the United States, 1840*.

[29] Christian Haldeman to Jacob Haldeman, February 23, 1829, Haldeman Papers.

[30] Taylor, *Transportation Revolution*, chap. 3, contains a comprehensive summary of canal construction in the era. Innumerable studies document the significance of waterways in tying urban merchants to hinterland markets and producers. For example, see Ralph D. Gray, "The Early History of the Chesapeake and Delaware Canal"; James W. Livingood, *The Philadelphia-Baltimore Trade Rivalry, 1780–1860*.

[31] See, for example, Hugh Boyle & Co. to Jacob Haldeman, June 28, 1817, and July 15, 1817; Ballard & Hall to Haldeman, June 5, 1818, February 22, 1819, April 21, 1819, and May 3, 1819; David Kizer & Co. to Haldeman, April 22, 1820; J. W. & E. Patterson to Haldeman, January 2, 1824; Evan T. Ellicott to Haldeman, December 31, 1823; and Lambert Gittings to Haldeman, February 14, 1829, and April 22, 1829; all in Haldeman Papers. Most of these were general commission merchants, but Joseph W. and Edward Patterson specialized in iron; see R. J. Matchett, *Matchett's Baltimore Directory for 1827* (Baltimore: By the author, 1827).

[32] Nothing deterred the competitors, not even death. When an agent died his competitors hastened to take over his accounts. "My object in visiting the towns of the Susquehanna is in part in pursuit of commission business," Edward Palmer wrote Jacob Haldeman, "supposing that since the death of our lamented friend Mr. Ballard that you have no agent in Baltimore" (Palmer to Haldeman, October 20, 1819, Haldeman Papers). See also George Winchester to Haldeman, October 14, 1819, and the circular from the late Ballard's partner, Andrew Hall, to Haldeman, December 31, 1819, *ibid*. A similar situation occurred upon the death of a partner in the Philadelphia commission firm of Haven & Smith, which sold flour and iron for Haldeman in the late twenties; see William F. Smith to Haldeman, November 17, 1829, *ibid*.

had not been previously arranged, they tried to sell the iron at the dock to buyers who congregated there daily. If no customer was immediately forthcoming, the brokers arranged for weighing, drayage, storage, and advertising.[33] They acted as financial agents by collecting and paying bills, discounting notes, making deposits, and so on.[34] They also purchased supplies, such as produce and millstones, and shipped them back to New Cumberland.[35]

Brokers kept Haldeman in touch with market conditions by writing him almost daily letters about market prospects and enclosing copies of *Baltimore Prices Current*. They advised him on the type of iron to produce and of upcoming large contracts for iron in various cities.[36] After 1830, Philadelphia commission merchants joined in the competition.[37]

The merchants thus provided Haldeman with the services necessary to reach a diffuse and expanding market, and he was absolutely dependent on them for sales outside his local area. This dependence (together with financial services to be discussed later) meant that merchants exercised considerable control over the way Haldeman operated his business, for merchants determined prices in relation to current markets, credit terms, and the kind of iron to be produced for sale in urban markets. The interaction between producers' capabilities and the commission merchants' marketing strategies determined trade practices throughout most of the iron industry before the Civil War. This is demonstrated not only by Haldeman's experiences but by the documents of other successful firms in the industry.

Among the most successful unintegrated firms in the antebellum iron industry were the rolling mills that produced boiler plate and sheet iron, and firms that manufactured nails and wire. Eastern Pennsylvania firms dominated the plate and sheet industry, accounting for 70 per cent of U.S. production in 1860.[38] The center of boiler-plate manufacture was the Schuylkill River valley, where a cluster of firms (known in the trade as the "Coatesville Mills") rode to prosperity on the increasing demand for steam engines as sources of sta-

---

[33] Ballard & Hall to Haldeman, April 23, 1819, and October 5, 1819; Wilmer & Palmer to Haldeman, April 28, 1825, and May 19, 1825; and Lambert Gittings to Haldeman, May 1, 1829, and October 10, 1830; *ibid.*

[34] Good examples are in Lambert Gittings to Haldeman, May 1, 1829, and September 12, 1829, *ibid.*

[35] James Keys to Haldeman, July 29, 1805; Isaac McPherson to Haldeman, September 22, 1825, and April 1, 1826; David Kizer to Haldeman, April 14, 1826; and Joseph M. Patterson to Haldeman, April 15, 1826; *ibid.*

[36] Ballard & Hall to Haldeman, May 3, 1819; Thomas Janvier to Haldeman, August 1, 1827; Lambert Gittings to Haldeman, February 14, 1829; and Christian Haldeman to Jacob Haldeman, February 23, 1829; *ibid.*

[37] See the correspondence in 1829 between Haldeman and Lambert Gittings of Baltimore, Hollingshead Platt of Philadelphia, and Haven & Smith of Philadelphia, esp. William F. Smith to Haldeman, November 17, 1829, *ibid.* The Philadelphia firms serving Haldeman are listed in Robert Desilver, *Desilver's Philadelphia Directory and Stranger's Guide* (Philadelphia: By the author, 1829).

[38] U.S. Census Office, *Eighth Census of the United States, 1860: Manufactures*, p. clxxii.

tionary and motive power. The business records of the firm of Gibbons and Huston of Coatesville, Pennsylvania, reveal the operating methods of boiler-plate manufacturers, not only because the firm was successful (it is now Lukens Steel, a major U.S. producer of plates), but because it corresponded continuously with its agents and competitors about conditions in the industry.[39]

Besides their markets, all of these mills had a great deal in common. They were unintegrated, employed water power, operated in an oligopolistic industry (few sellers, many buyers) and were well aware of it, and faced stiff competition from British imports. They bought their raw materials and sold their products almost entirely through commission merchants.

Gibbons and Huston bought some blooms directly from refiners, but they and other mills relied primarily on large-volume commission merchants such as Cabeen and Pratt. They sold boiler plate to specialized brokers such as Kemble and Warner of New York, Curtis Bouvé of Boston, and Charles B. Campbell of Philadelphia. The commission merchants also dealt in imported boiler plate and sold in two kinds of markets.

The most significant market, and the one which became increasingly important, consisted of a large number of steam engine and locomotive manufacturers such as Pusey and Jones of Wilmington, Delaware, and Baldwin of Philadelphia. The other market was even more diffuse; it consisted of the innumerable small boiler shops scattered throughout the country. Sales to engine manufacturers were usually by contract in large lots and, like pig iron, went directly from mill to factory without passing through the commission merchant's hands. The broker received the standard 5 per cent commission and guarantee fee on these sales.

Sales to boiler shops were usually in small lots, and the commission merchant had to keep an inventory of various sizes and thicknesses. Of course, these "job lot" sales involved storage, handling, and a disproportionate amount of bookkeeping. Brokers occasionally received a higher commission on such sales, but they habitually complained that "store sales" were unremunerative and demanded higher fees for handling them.[40]

Boiler-plate merchants, like the brokers who handled less sophisticated mill products, were in close touch with the market and demanded a high degree of autonomy in setting prices according to fluctuations in domestic demand and in competition from overseas producers. Their insistence on mercantile authority met with stiff resistance from Schuylkill millowners, whose position in the market made them a singularly independent lot.

---

[39] The Gibbons & Huston material is part of the Lukens Papers. We are indebted to Julian Skaggs, of the University of Delaware, who is currently writing a history of Lukens, for his generosity in sharing with us his familiarity with this large and valuable collection.

[40] Accounts of Sales by Agents, 1840–85; and Curtis Bouvé to Gibbons & Huston, July 9, 1857; Lukens Papers.

To some degree the millowners' independence was based on a paradox: boiler-plate manufacturers produced goods that were both scarcer in supply and higher in price than those of the iron smelters, but their capital investment was much smaller. It is difficult to say precisely how much smaller the investment was. Evaluating the fixed capital assets of pre–Civil War manufacturers is tricky business because of the variety and inconsistency of contemporary accounting methods; with no Bureau of Internal Revenue to answer to, and usually no stockholders to demand detailed accounts, firms employed whatever system satisfied the proprietors. Sometimes the cost of buildings and machinery can be discerned; often it remains unknown. Accounts such as "Real Estate" or "Machinery" may have indicated original cost, replacement costs, or simply what the proprietors thought they were worth to them. In addition, there was rarely any provision for depreciation in the modern sense. Occasionally there was a "Contingency" account, but it is often uncertain exactly what such an account implied. Many items that would be considered capital improvements today were often charged to an all-purpose "Repairs" account.

The railroads pioneered in developing guidelines to separate current expense from capital investment, but the most satisfactory way of doing so remained a subject of debate among railroad managers into the twentieth century.[41] It was scarcely an issue in iron manufacturing until the separation of ownership and management took place in integrated rail mills. One hopes that, when supplying information for government reports such as the census, millowners used original or replacement costs in calculating "Capital Invested," but it is by no means certain that they did. In the case of Gibbons and Huston, however, it can be seen that the investment was small. Modelbuilders at the Hagley Museum of Greenville, Delaware, have constructed a model of the mill from information found by Julian Skaggs in the Lukens Steel Company Papers. The entire plant consists of a small, one-room building (which the firm rented), a water wheel, sundry gears and shafts, two pairs of rollers, a set of shears, and furnaces for heating the iron. Whatever the actual value of this may have been, it was obviously very small compared to that of an "iron plantation."

Plate mills such as Gibbons and Huston, therefore, did not have the compulsion of high, fixed costs forcing them to run at almost any price. Short-run declines in the market were often met by putting the water wheel out of gear, sending the hands home, and waiting for better days. Long-run market declines were another matter, but, for much of the period before the Civil War, demand exceeded supply. Millowners and their brokers took advantage of the sellers' market and their oligopolistic situation to collude rather than to compete.

[41] See, for example, W. M. Acworth, "Railroad Accounting in America vs. England."

This collusion took many forms. For one thing, millowners consistently refused to compete for labor. Following a policy that apparently prevailed throughout the antebellum iron industry, owners of plate mills consulted each other constantly in order to maintain the same pay scale in all establishments.[42] They also pooled orders, dividing business among themselves. This process was facilitated by the fact that most millowners sold through the same commission merchants. Sometimes the merchant would send an entire order to one manufacturer, who would then parcel it out to cooperating firms. On other occasions the broker would divide the contract among his clients, informing each as to the amount of work given to the others. Above all, the Coatesville millowners conspired unceasingly to maintain prices at a level which would undersell foreign competitors yet yield an adequate profit. In order to make this policy work, the manufacturers expected their commission merchants to advise them of market conditions and to uphold agreed-upon prices by refusing to sell on any other terms.

This synergistic relationship worked well with respect to foreign competition. As William Kemble of the New York commission house of Kemble and Warner wrote in 1845:

I have uniformly pursued a policy which I considered in the best permanent interests of the mills, in endeavoring to regulate prices. . . . The first object of the manufacturing industry is obviously to set a limit to the prices, which shall obviate the necessity of importing foreign plate. With this in view, I opposed a heavy advance in price . . . & by keeping the price at a shade less than foreign plate could be imported, have succeeded in preventing any large importations.[43]

As long as demand exceeded supply, commission merchants were willing enough to permit millowners to determine prices. As Kemble described it, "While the manufacture of boiler iron in Pennsylvania fell short of the demand . . . prices were regulated by an understanding [among] the mill owners, & they reaped full advantages from adopting this course."[44] When a large contract was in the offing, the broker consulted his suppliers before submitting a bid. Kemble wrote Charles Huston in July, 1857, asking for a price on an order of from eighty to one hundred tons of boiler iron, the bid to be sub-

[42] Correspondence between Gibbons & Huston and Charles Bailey, C. E. Pennock, and others, Lukens Papers. See also letters to and from Fall River Iron Works, 1840–60, esp. Richard Borden to Crocker & Co., March 2, 1848, Fall River Iron Papers.

[43] William Kemble to Lukens and Gibbons, January 7, 1845, Lukens Papers. Such price-fixing was common practice among antebellum iron processors. For example, Abram Hewitt of Trenton Iron, and Henry Washburn of Washburn & Godard (Worcester, Mass.) conspired to control the price of wire in the 1850s. See Allan Nevins, *Abram S. Hewitt*, p. 109.

[44] Kemble to Lukens and Gibbons, January 7, 1845, Lukens Papers.

mitted by Huston after "consult[ing] our friends Pennock and Steele and Worth [other "Coatesville Mills"] on the subject."[45]

When demand declined, however, these harmonious relationships tended to break down. In a pattern which foreshadowed the collapse of trade associations and pools among manufacturers in the 1870s and 1880s, a drop in demand tempted some producers outside the Schuylkill River valley to the extent that, "although agreements were entered into establishing uniform prices, several of the parties, on various subterfuges . . . violated their agreements."[46] The reaction of the "Coatesville Mills" to this situation was to instruct their brokers to maintain prices, cut off credit, and quit handling imported plate altogether. If these tactics proved unsuccessful, the mills agreed to shut down, pending a rise in prices. Because all of these strategies were certain to drive business into the arms of competitors, the brokers resisted them and urged alternative policies.[47]

It was unrealistic, the plate merchants thought, to try to maintain prices during slumps. "In the present state of our country," wrote Kemble, "I do not believe it possible to maintain a uniform system of prices, by a certain number of proprietors combining to fix prices." Should the Schuylkill mills remain inflexible, "the result will be a cessation of large orders" because other manufacturers, who had interest payments to meet, would continue to sell at whatever the traffic would bear. Moreover, it was thought unnecessary to shut down. There was a better way.

The true policy of the proprietors of those mills who desire to pursue a uniform rate of prices [is to] authorize their agents to meet the market in all cases when underselling is attempted—the effect would be after a short time, that certain individuals, who have forced their iron into the market from time to time, would be compelled to resort to other measures & the business would be conducted on a more satisfactory footing.[48]

In the end the commission merchants' views prevailed, for beginning in the winter of 1857 a protracted slump hit the industry. Excess capacity meant enduring price competition, and an obstinate refusal to compete might have meant permanent shutdown and loss of livelihood. In an industry where products were alike, the market remained diffuse, and orders came to depend on competitive pricing, even the independent Schuylkill millowners had to yield. The "Coatesville Mills" continued to sell at a common price, but brokers, not manufacturers, determined what that price was to be. To unintegrated manu-

---

[45] Kemble & Warner to Charles Huston, July 8, 1857, *ibid.*
[46] Kemble to Lukens and Gibbons, January 7, 1845, *ibid.*
[47] Examples of the multitude of this kind of correspondence in the Lukens Papers are Kemble & Warner to Huston, November 25, 1857; December 14, 1857; and January 20, 1858; Charles Bailey to Huston, November 23, 1857; and Kemble & Warner to Huston and Penrose, November 18, 1852.
[48] Kemble & Warner to Lukens and Gibbons, January 17, 1845, *ibid.*

facturers the services of the commission merchant were essential, for, as William Kemble said, "The agent on the spot is the only person who can form a just estimate of the prices required for the district he supplies." Mill-owners had to agree that it was "absolutely necessary to give the agent sufficient discretionary power to enable him to conduct the business to best advantage."[49]

For similar reasons the specialized merchant occupied a critical position in other antebellum iron-processing fields. Whether they made producers' or consumers' goods, manufacturers turned to commission merchants for dependable supplies of refined iron. The wire-drawing firm of Washburn and Godard of Worcester, Massachusetts (predecessor to Washburn and Moen, later part of American Steel and Wire),[50] bought imported and domestic wire rods from the Boston commission houses of Samuel May and Charles Congdon. Agents such as Lamb and Hastings in Philadelphia, Stickney and Company in Baltimore, and A. R. Moen in New York distributed their products, selling wire for nails, musical instruments, and other manufacturing uses directly to factory owners. Fence wire and other types that required no further manufacture went through commission houses into the jobbing network that serviced the scattered retail market for hardware and other metalwares.[51]

The development of specialized hardware jobbers followed the same pattern as that already described for the dry goods industry. They originally appeared to fill the gap between the importing commission merchant and the consumer. An increased volume of trade supported specialization. As domestic manufacturing capacity increased, producers disposed of their surplus above local requirements by using commission merchants and jobbers to reach distant markets. Every city that was a regional distribution center had jobbing houses which serviced its hinterland.[52]

New York became the center of jobbing in the United States, not only for

---

[49] *Ibid.*

[50] Worcester was the center of wire manufacture in the United States (Census Office, *Eighth Census*, p. clxxiv). Washburn & Godard was the largest such firm in Worcester. John "Bet a Million" Gates put American Steel & Wire together. It became one of the components of U.S. Steel.

[51] Washburn & Godard Bill Book, Inventory and Record, 1833–48, American Steel & Wire Co. Papers. Commission merchants continued to sell most imported iron and steel products throughout the nineteenth century. For example, Thomas Prosser, a New York broker, was the U.S. agent for Krupp steel in the 1880s and 1890s (Prosser Letter File, James Reese & Co. Papers). Another New York commission house, Naylor & Co., supplied British and Norwegian steel to Samuel Colt in the 1850s, and British steel rails to American railroads in the 1880s and 1890s. This was long after the railroads had stopped using intermediaries in purchasing domestic rails. (See Steel Rail File, Chicago, Burlington & Quincy Railroad Papers.) The railroads' development of direct purchasing is discussed in Chapter V.

[52] The appearance of jobbers can be traced in city directories, and the number and variety of them serve as rough measures of a town's significance as a regional distribution center. This in turn was not simply a function of regional population but also that of the intraregional transportation facilities available.

dry goods, but for metal products as well, because of its importance as an entrepôt for foreign goods, its superior exurban markets, and its location close to the center of domestic manufacture. Most of the factories producing metal consumers' goods in pre–Civil War America were located in New England (many of them, such as Yale and Towne and Ames Tool, were clustered in the Connecticut River valley), and New York offered a convenient outlet for their production. As American manufactures multiplied in volume and variety, New York jobbers kept pace by increasing in numbers and specialization. Among the many manufacturers who benefited from the adaptability and expertise of New York jobbers was the Connecticut firearms manufacturer, Samuel Colt.

The jobbing network distributed Colt's rifles and pistols to the far-flung retail market for weapons which reached from border to border, from sea to frontier. The use of interchangeable parts and mass production techniques enabled Colt to make great numbers of cheap weapons. The government purchased most of his output, but surplus production went to New York wholesalers such as Cooper and Pond, who sold them far and wide.[53]

Other finished iron products also went into the jobbing network to reach consumers. These included nails, which were always an important commodity in the United States because of the new construction of homes, stores, and factories.[54] Fall River Iron Works in Fall River, Massachusetts, one of the largest American producers of nails before the Civil War, sold some of its products in its own store in Providence, Rhode Island. Expanded production, however, required wider distribution. After 1842 most of the firm's output went to the New York commission house of Borden and Lovell, which marketed it to New York hardware jobbers. Some nails went to southern customers through commission houses such as Dade Hurocthal and O. Mozangi of Mobile. Fall River Iron also depended on brokers for raw materials; it bought iron in large lots from Cabeen, Pratt, and Stickney.[55]

Like patterns prevailed in the manufacture and sale of simple castings. Many founders, of course, operated on a purely local scale. Those who sought wider markets, however, turned to brokers for raw materials, and they distributed finished products through the appropriate specialized mercantile channels. Stoves accounted for almost a third of the value of all cast iron products.[56] They were a consumers' good, and major stove manufacturers operated in the same way as Builders' Iron Foundry of Providence. Builders sold their stoves through specialized stove jobbers such as Robbins and Bibb of Balti-

[53] Correspondence, 1847–60, Samuel Colt Papers. Our colleague Russell Fries pointed out the relevance of Colt's purchasing and distribution methods to this study.
[54] Nails represented 10 per cent (by weight) of U.S. iron production in 1856; see J. P. Lesley, *The Iron Manufacturer's Guide*, p. 764.
[55] Iron Invoices; Invoice Books; and Annual Account of the New York Agency of the Fall River Iron Works; Fall River Iron Papers.
[56] Census Office, *Eighth Census*, p. clxxxvi.

more, Munsell, Thompson, and Munsell of New York, and Neman and Warwick of Philadelphia. Foundries making other consumers' goods, such as hardware, pipe, and simple tools, also relied on the jobber network for sales.[57]

On the other hand, the materials purchased by these processing firms were producers' goods, and as such were obtained from specialized commission merchants. Builders' Iron bought virtually all its inputs from specialized brokers. Iron came from Albert Root of New York and Cornell and Nightingale of Providence, sand from nearby commission merchants such as Henry C. Clark in Providence, and small lots of sash cords from John Roebling's plant in Trenton through the Philadelphia commission firm of Morris and Jones. E. S. Belknap and Sons of New York, wholesalers specializing in such goods as oils, paints, and varnishes, supplied stove putty.[58]

SUMMARY OF PREVAILING DISTRIBUTION PATTERNS IN THE ANTEBELLUM IRON INDUSTRY

Throughout most of the antebellum American iron industry, the unintegrated firm prevailed in smelting, refining, and processing. In all fields except smelting, volume producers turned to iron brokers for dependable supplies of raw materials. In all branches the majority of sales took place through specialized distributing agencies; commission merchants served as the sole intermediary for most producers' goods and as the first step toward the jobbing network for consumers' goods. In most industries, manufacturers and their agents evolved a symbiotic relationship suited to, and in large measure determined by, the nature of production methods and markets. So long as technology was simple, production unintegrated, products undifferentiated, and markets diffuse, the distribution of iron products required little knowledge of mechanics or metallurgy. It did demand men with an encyclopedic knowledge of buyers and sellers, men capable of arranging and financing transactions, to rationalize the flow of generic iron products from scattered refiners through dispersed processors into diffuse markets. The commission merchants' ability to perform these functions made them the key men in the iron-processing industry before the Civil War.

In the long run, ramifying technology, vertical integration, and concentrated markets deprived the broker of his paramount position. The process was a gradual one; it was not completed until the twentieth century. It began well before the Civil War, however, when a few firms espoused a strategy of production and sales which rendered middlemen irrelevant. These new firms were

[57] For example, see Pierce, *Iron in the Pines*, pp. 140–41, and Letter Books and Unbound Papers, C. G. and H. M. Plimpton Papers.

[58] Unbound Correspondence, 1851–60, and Bill Files, 1853–57, Builders' Iron Foundry Papers. Stove jobbers frequently sold at retail as well as wholesale; they also dictated style and price ranges to manufacturers.

the precursors—indeed, often the direct antecedents—of the modern, gigantic integrated iron and steel firms that dominate the industry today. The event which called forth these new firms was, of course, the coming of the railroads —one of the greatest causes of social and economic change in the nineteenth century.

INTEGRATED RAIL MILLS: A PRODROME
OF THE MIDDLEMAN'S DECLINE

American businessmen in many industries quickly realized that the railroads' needs for material offered a new and exciting market, and no group was more aware of the opportunity than American ironmasters. Almost as soon as construction plans were announced, iron firms began trying to sell to the new customer. Construction of the Baltimore and Ohio led the Mount Savage Iron Works (Maryland) to cast car wheels in 1828.[59] In 1829 Christian Haldeman wrote his brother Jacob that he was attempting to find out what sort of iron products the Philadelphia and Columbia would require so that he could sell it New Cumberland's products.[60]

Among the many types of iron that railroads needed, rails offered the most tempting market, for they were required in greater quantity than all others combined.[61] The rail market, however, proved a difficult one for unintegrated American producers to enter, for the vast quantities of iron demanded in railroad construction greatly exceeded their capacity and experience. In 1856, for example, the total tonnage of plates rolled by Gibbons and Huston, Benjamin Hatfield, Steele and Worth, and C. E. Pennock (four of the largest "Coatesville Mills") was less than 1 per cent of the tonnage of rails supplied to U.S. railroads. In the same year railroads laid 1,471 miles of new track. If the four mills had rolled rails instead of boiler iron, their total production would have sufficed for 54 miles (4 per cent) of new construction.[62]

The rail market was not only large, it was extremely competitive. After 1848, British manufacturers' capacity exceeded home demands, and they began to dump their surplus into the U.S. market at rock-bottom prices. Contract deadlines added to the problems of competing for rail business. The

[59] Lobdell Car Wheel Co., *Catalog and Price List, 1891* (Wilmington, Del.: Lobdell Car Wheel Co., 1891).

[60] Christian Haldeman to Jacob Haldeman, March 5, 1829, Haldeman Papers.

[61] Alfred D. Chandler, Jr., ed., *The Railroads*, p. 34.

[62] Tonnage for the "Coatesville Mills" was taken from Lesley, *Iron Manufacturer's Guide*, p. 233, the miles of track laid from tables in Chandler, *Railroads*, p. 14. The figure 54 miles was computed from Robert W. Fogel's estimate of the weight of rails per mile of track laid in 1856. We also used Fogel's figure for the total tonnage of rail consumption. Fogel's data are estimates at best, but they serve well enough for our purposes here. See Robert W. Fogel, *Railroads and American Economic Growth*, pp. 182, 194.

availability of large quantities of British rails permitted railroads to demand early and definite delivery dates. As railroad construction increased during the 1830s and 1840s, all of these conditions intensified. To compete successfully in this kind of market, a firm had to be able to minimize costs while maintaining a steady flow of high-volume production.

Contemporary American rolling mills encountered technical and structural handicaps that made it extremely difficult for them to meet all these conditions. Few American mills had the right kind of rolls; when these were obtained, water power often proved insufficient to roll rails; where hydraulic force was sufficient, it was subject to droughts and freezes that interrupted production.

The firms' unintegrated structures raised an additional barrier to sustained volume production. As noted before, they were dependent on commission merchants for supplies of raw material which often came from considerable distances. Since any form of transportation other than water was prohibitively expensive, the flow of pig iron stopped when winter prevented navigation. If production was not to stop as well, large inventories had to be assembled in advance—a costly step which millowners were loath to take. This method of raw-material procurement also added transportation and brokerage fees to the cost of the final product—a serious liability in such a competitive field.

In the event, the disadvantages of the unintegrated rolling mill proved impossible to overcome. Although some of them secured occasional rail orders, none ever succeeded in becoming a major producer on the strength of such business. Successful rail manufacture required integrated mass production, and few antebellum furnace or rolling mill proprietors had resources or imagination enough to adapt to the new conditions. A few rolling mills, such as Gibbons and Huston, and Alan Wood of Conshohocken, Pennsylvania, survived unintegrated by concentrating on the manufacture of a single specialized item like boiler plate or pattern sheet iron.[63]

A handful of talented manufacturers perceived the competitive advantages of integration and were flexible enough to adopt the new structure before the Civil War. Benjamin Jones of Jones and Laughlin integrated his bar mill by buying blast furnaces, and the Whitaker family of Principio Furnace, Maryland, gradually transferred their principal operations to an integrated nail, sheet, and rail mill in West Virginia.[64] (This facility is now one of the components of Wheeling-Pittsburgh Steel.) These few were the exceptions, however, for most unintegrated antebellum firms slipped into oblivion; they were forced out by competition or died with their proprietors. The integrated mills

[63] Both firms eventually had to integrate backward by adding blast furnaces in order to meet the competition of other integrated firms; however, this took place after the Civil War.

[64] The Whitakers also integrated the Principio works by adding a pipe foundry; see May, *Principio*, chaps. 13 ff.

played a part, nevertheless, in the subsequent development of the modern iron and steel complex; they were the training ground for the engineers and managers of the integrated rail mills, which were the real beginnings of that development.

Integrated rail mills in the United States began in the 1840s, when mercantile capitalists realized that traditional forms of production would not suffice in the new market. A new kind of mill was required, one which had ready access to large supplies of cheap raw material and could run day and night, turning out large quantities in a short time. To create such a facility, promoters had to overcome problems of capital, management, and technology. Capital requirements were met as they had been in building New England textile factories: prosperous Pennsylvania merchants like the Reeves family, George Trotter (Nathan Trotter's son), Edward Townsend, and Alfred Hunt formed joint stock companies. These men knew little or nothing about iron manufacture; therefore, they had to hire a superintendent to construct the works and operate it. In addition to a general manager, the size of the mill and the round-the-clock operations necessitated the employment of an elaborate supervisory staff of foremen for various departments and night superintendents. These men had learned their trade working in unintegrated iron firms; in the new mills they combined past experience with mechanical expediency to surmount technological problems.

The new mills used coal rather than charcoal for smelting after the process was perfected in the late 1830s by David Thomas, a Welchman imported to build the Lehigh Crane Iron Works at Catasauqua, Pennsylvania. Dispensing with charcoal removed one of the locational obstacles to integration. The other, and more important, obstacle—power to drive the mill machinery—was overcome by substituting steam for water power. This substitution in turn presented two major difficulties: first, an economical method of generating steam had to be devised; second, the steam engine had to be hooked up efficiently to the long trains of rolls required to shape rails.

The first of these problems—cheap steam—was solved by John Griffin while he was building an integrated mill for Moore and Hooven of Norristown, Pennsylvania, in 1846. Griffin heated the boilers by passing waste blast-furnace gasses through them, thereby obtaining plenty of steam at no additional cost. He perfected this method while building the Safe Harbor, Pennsylvania, Rolling Mill for David Reeves in 1847, and all eastern Pennsylvania rolling mills subsequently adopted it.[65]

The second problem involved in steam-powered mills—connecting the engine to the rolls—was a more persistent one, but it was eventually overcome

[65] Griffin was a West Chester County, N.Y., farm boy who learned the iron trade while working in an unintegrated, water-powered nail mill in Norristown, Pa. Prior to Griffin's innovation, it cost $3 per ton of iron produced to drive the mill with coal-fired boilers. See Howard Corning, ed., "A Letter from John Griffin, Ironmaster, 1878."

by John Fritz at Cambria Iron in 1857. Fritz began his career as an apprentice blacksmith and machinist in Parkesburg, Pennsylvania, and added to his skills by hanging around the Pennsylvania Railroad's Parkesburg locomotive shops. Then he became John Griffin's protegé at Norristown and Safe Harbor. These two men, backed by mercantile capitalists such as the Reeves and Trotters, left an enduring mark on the American iron and steel industry. Griffin left Safe Harbor to build the Buffalo Iron Works, now the Lackawanna Plant of Bethlehem Steel. He ended his career as general manager of Phoenix Iron, now Phoenix Steel. Fritz had an even more distinguished career. He became superintendent of Cambria Iron (later Cambria Steel) of Johnstown, Pennsylvania, in 1854 and turned a bankrupt concern into the largest U.S. rail producer. Cambria Steel eventually merged with Bethlehem Steel, a firm founded in 1860 with John Fritz as general superintendent and chief engineer.[66]

By overcoming the obstacles of inadequate capital, technology, and management, merchant entrepreneurs and their hired supervisors created a new and enduring institution in the American iron industry. In the last third of the nineteenth century, integrated firms, in control of their own raw materials and run by professional managers, dominated the industry. Even before the war, however, they demonstrated their ability to outproduce single-stage, owner-operated firms. The four largest American iron works in 1860—Trenton Iron, Phoenix Iron, Montour Iron, and Cambria—were all integrated rail mills. Nor can there be any doubt that the railroad was the principal agent of change. Not only were the largest producers integrated, but virtually all integrated mills owed their existence to the market for railroad iron. In 1854 there were eight integrated firms; seven of them were rail mills.[67] The new structure created enormous productive capacity. Compare, for example, the 1856 output of the four "Coatesville Mills"—3,900 tons—and that of the four rail mills—68,000 tons.[68]

It was this increased capacity of individual integrated producing units which made the influence of railroads on the American iron industry of such importance, despite the fact that the total production for railroad use represented only a minority of total iron output before the Civil War.[69] Industrial success depends (as Chairman Mao found with his backyard iron furnace experiment) not only on total productive capacity but on the flexibility of the

---

[66] *Ibid.* John Fritz, *Autobiography*, chap. 15, describes his perfection of the engine-driven rolling mill; the book also describes various ironworking processes such as puddling. See also R. D. Billinger, "Beginnings of Bethlehem Iron and Steel."

[67] Temin, *Iron and Steel*, pp. 109, 110, 117.

[68] Lesley, *Iron Manufacturer's Guide*, pp. 228, 233, 237.

[69] Just how much of a minority is a hotly debated question. According to Lesley (*ibid.*, p. 764), rails accounted for 17 per cent of U.S. tonnage in 1856. This is also the figure Fogel cites as the average annual consumption for *all* railroad purposes in the period 1840–60 (*Railroads and American Economic Growth*, p. 232). The precise figure is irrelevant here.

institutions involved.[70] Changing markets and technology, as in the case of the railroads, present manufacturers with new problems of production, purchasing, and distribution. The small, unintegrated firm, with its limited capital and human resources (often tied to the longevity of the owners or their heirs), found it difficult to adapt to these new conditions. They often had little incentive to change. It was easier to go out of business, as so many did, or to stay small like Gibbons and Huston.

The large, integrated firm, on the other hand, was a wholly new and different kind of business. It had both the ability and a positive incentive to adjust to changes in subsequent years. Its corporate form of organization not only supplied capital; it, together with the employment of professional managers, freed the firm from dependence on the life of any individual. Bureaucratic management, patterned after the railroads' and adopted to control complex, high-volume mill operations, led to an increased separation of ownership from management. Managers had to account to stockholders for income and expense. This led to strict accountability and lines of control from the general manager down to the foremen in the shop. These men filed periodic reports of costs and output. The general manager compiled these in an annual report to the stockholders which was similar in its exhaustive detail to the annual reports of the railroads.[71] The careful recording of expenditures and production ultimately provided integrated firms with unit-cost information not easily obtained by simple producing units.

The large firm could also broaden its technological base by hiring whatever experts were required. These engineers often succeeded merchant capitalists at a firm's head. The first president of Bethlehem Iron, for example, was a Philadelphia merchant, Alfred Hunt; all of his successors were college-trained engineers.[72] It was difficult for small firms to match their integrated competitors' expanding technology in the antebellum years. Men like Fritz and Griffin were few in number, and they commanded high salaries. Griffin, for example, declared that he never made less than $5,000 per year after 1856.[73] In these

[70] This point is important, for it illustrates the dangers inherent in using aggregate statistics as tools of growth analysis. Data showing total output for an entire industry, or even total production of sectors of that industry, often conceal the productive potency of individual units. This obscurity can lead to false estimations of the significance of various types of manufacturing firms to long-run economic growth. As David Landes has pointed out (*Unbound Prometheus*, pp. 512 ff.), it is indeed difficult "to balance macrostatistical calculations that attribute only a slight effect" to some development within the economic fabric "against what could easily be a myriad of individual examples" that demonstrate that the change had profound consequences. There is no easy way around this problem, but it can be minimized by disaggregating statistics as far as possible and by using quantitative data as the starting point rather than the ultimate goal of historical analysis.

[71] There is an excellent collection of these reports from John Griffin (General Manager) to David Reeves, President of Phoenix Iron, in the Phoenix Iron Co. Papers.

[72] Billinger, "Beginnings of Bethlehem Iron and Steel," *passim*.

[73] Corning, "Letter from John Griffin," p. 691.

circumstances the owner of an unintegrated mill often had no choice but to restrict his output to the line he knew best. He was therefore ill-equipped to meet a shift in demand or the appearance in the field of a diversifying, integrated firm. Large, integrated units proved able to do both.

When the principal market for iron and steel products shifted in the late nineteenth century from railroad material to urban construction components such as structural beams, strips for pipe ("skelp"), and wire products; and again in the twentieth century to sheets for automobiles and appliances, the new firms, unlike their unintegrated predecessors, shifted quickly and easily to meet the new demands.[74] They were able to do so because of their superior resources. The same resources encouraged innovation and diversification because, once assets were assembled, there was constant pressure from dividend-hungry stockholders and the obligation of fixed costs to keep them profitably employed. Managers felt these pressures acutely in periods of reduced demand. Contemplating a new mill idled by the depression of 1873, John Griffin wrote, "There are over $1,000,000 not only locked up and returning no interest, but it is subject to taxes . . . we hope in a year we shall have a use for it."[75]

In order to find "a use for it," integrated mills diversified their production into any promising market. For example, when British "dumping" drove the price of rails down in the late 1840s, Abram Hewitt diversified Trenton Iron by adding a wire mill. Trenton Iron, Phoenix, and Cambria also rolled structural iron beams before the Civil War, thereby demonstrating a versatility that would become the characteristic of giant firms later in the century. By 1872, Phoenix was producing not only rails and spikes but also bar, angle, and channel iron; beams, columns, and girders; iron roofs; and all the components for bridges.[76]

The versatility of integrated iron producers—derived from new institutional structures and initiated and developed before the Civil War to compete for the rail market—proved an invaluable asset in the drive toward industrial supremacy and concomitant urbanization. These firms supplied cheaply and in great quantities the widening range of products required for construction, machinery, and consumer durables. In the long run their contribution proved infinitely more important than that of the multitude of small-volume, single-stage bar mills, stove foundries, and the like, which accounted for the majority of antebellum production. Few in number though they were, the new mills such as Cambria and Bethlehem foreshadowed not only the dominant institu-

---

[74] Temin discusses changing patterns of iron and steel consumption in *Iron and Steel*, chap. 10.

[75] Corning, "Letter from John Griffin," p. 691.

[76] Annual Report to the President, 1872, Phoenix Papers; Nevins, *Hewitt*, pp. 104–5.

tions of production but also the decline of the middleman as the controlling force in the industry.[77]

The backward integration of rolling mills marked the beginning of the gradual removal of middlemen from the iron trade. The inability of brokers to supply enough pig iron for mass production year-round, together with the costs of their services, initially forced the mills to build their own furnaces at the same time that they built their high-volume rolling mills. Once integrated producers entered the field, competitors had to follow suit in self-defense. This process rendered the commission merchant redundant as a source of raw materials except when unusually high demand or mechanical breakdown forced a firm to seek outside supplies.

The broker's role as selling agent also began to diminish before the Civil War because the relatively small number of railroads and rail producers created a new situation in the American economy: a large, relatively concentrated market in which buyers and sellers could easily identify one another. Thus integration and a concentrating market combined to deprive the middleman of his mercantile relevance. Railroad purchases also pumped large sums of cash into integrated manufacturers' treasuries, thereby enabling them to avoid relying on middlemen to provide capital or to finance transactions. This was a key step toward autonomy, for mercantile agents used their supply of venture capital as a powerful weapon in the arsenal with which they controlled pre–Civil War manufacturing.

[77] By the end of the nineteenth century the U.S. iron and steel industry was dominated by a small number of giant firms. These firms made a diverse range of products, were integrated backward to control their raw materials, and were selling their products directly to consumers. See Chapter VIII for a discussion of the distribution of iron and steel products after the Civil War.

CHAPTER IV

The Merchant
as Catalyst:
Financing Economic
Growth

The years after 1815 presented ambitious American mechanics and artisans with steadily increasing opportunities. The rapid growth of population—it quadrupled between 1815 and 1860—created an ever larger market for manufactures. Much of this market remained accessible (as it had been in the colonial period) to ships that plied the coastal waters and the navigable rivers of the seaboard. As territorial expansion drew more and more people farther inland, proliferating transportation networks—turnpikes, canals, and then railroads—tied the new interior settlements to the nation's commerce.

Those men who possessed the mechanical knowledge necessary to operate a manufacturing facility had a choice: they could continue to produce for local customers, or they could create larger units, expand output, and try to take advantage of the emerging national market. As previously discussed, manufacturing entrepreneurs who chose expansion quickly encountered distribution problems that only the mercantile expertise of urban middlemen could solve. For most fledgling manufacturers, expansion also involved an excruciatingly difficult set of financial perplexities. First, there was the need for capital. Fixed (or long-term) capital was required for the purchase of land, buildings, and machinery, the fixed assets necessary for production. Successive moves toward expansion, or the need to replace obsolete plants and equipment, required repeated commitments of long-term capital.

An even more vexing difficulty was the need for short-term (working) capital with which to buy raw materials, pay wages, and meet other current operating costs such as taxes, advertising, transportation, loan interest, and the like.

Finally, doing business in distant markets with customers whose probity was unknown involved severe risks not encountered in selling locally. These included the dangers of extending credit to distant clients and of securing payment in funds or notes negotiable at or near par locally. Most manufacturers were as poorly equipped to resolve these dilemmas of capital and finance as they were to handle volume distribution in widespread markets.

LONG-TERM CAPITAL

Most early manufacturing firms were proprietorships or small partnerships. The owners were usually men of limited means. Assembling the fixed assets to commence or expand production often absorbed all the proprietors' resources. Additional fixed capital was extremely difficult to raise. Equity financing through the mass sale of securities did not begin in the United States until the introduction of the railroads, and it did not play a significant role in manufacturing finance before the Civil War.

The legal foundation for equity financing existed long before it found widespread employment in manufacturing. Prior to the Civil War many states had general incorporation laws embodying limited liability; however, for a variety of reasons, manufacturers seldom took advantage of them.[1] Among the reasons were lack of precedent, public skepticism toward such investments, lack of institutions to market shares, and entrepreneurial unwillingness to share ownership and control with "outsiders." Indeed, the correspondence and autobiographies of early American businessmen document the intensity with which the men identified themselves with their firms. Driven by pride, they labored continually to keep their affairs under their own control. This attitude often manifested itself in a reluctance to accept partners, and it certainly was not conducive to the adoption of financing methods that would have diluted ownership even further by selling shares in the business to the general public.

Financial institutions such as banks and insurance companies were of limited utility as sources of long-term capital. Banks would occasionally make long-term loans to manufacturers, but only on strong collateral. They did not make unsecured loans on business prospects, however glowing. In the first decade of the nineteenth century, for example, the Bank of New York supplied capital for the construction of a Paterson, New Jersey, textile mill, but the entire amount of the loan was secured by U.S. government bonds.[2]

---

[1] Thomas R. Navin and Marian V. Sears, "The Rise of a Market for Industrial Securities, 1887–1902."

[2] Joseph J. Klein, "The Development of Mercantile Instruments of Credit in the United States," p. 437.

A mortgage on real estate was another acceptable form of security. In the 1820s and 1830s, Washburn and Godard obtained long-term capital from a Worcester savings bank. The bank in turn held a mortgage on the firm's machine shop and on the millowners' real estate.[3] In 1856 the Baltimore iron-master S. S. Keyser obtained funds to build a warehouse by mortgaging his family's property to a local bank.[4] Such conservative lending policies seem to have been typical of most sound eastern banks throughout the period. In 1856, for example, the Savings Bank of Baltimore had $190,000 outstanding in long-term industrial loans, all of which was secured by real estate, bank stock, or U.S. government bonds.[5]

Insurance companies, like savings banks, were in the business of pooling individuals' savings and investing them at a profit. Insurance firms were, however, even less inclined than banks to make manufacturing loans. Refusing a loan request submitted by the Shawmut Fibre Company of Shawmut, Massachusetts, an officer of the Union Mutual Life Insurance Company commented that his firm had stopped making such loans "long ago." He added, "It is the custom of our company, which has become practically a law with us, that we do not loan on manufacturing establishments."[6]

Massachusetts Hospital Life Insurance Company, which opened for business in 1818, invested heavily in the stock of New England textile mills and made large loans to individual stockholders in textile firms, but it made few other investments in manufacturing. Massachusetts Life's participation in textile financing is doubtless explained by the fact that its list of stockholders consisted of names such as Lawrence, Lowell, Jackson, Cabot, Appleton, and other prominant New England merchants.[7] These were, of course, the same families that owned controlling interest in the textile mills, and the merchants were, in effect, lending to themselves by siphoning funds from one family enterprise into another. This pattern of a merchant-controlled financial institution underwriting its stockholders' industrial investments while refusing loans to other manufacturing proprietors and partners was commonplace in the period. It was one of the principal ways in which merchants were able to control antebellum manufacturing developments.

Modern industrial firms secure long-term capital for expansion or modernization by tapping the savings of the general public. They do so through mass sales of securities, or through loans from financial institutions such as

[3] Washburn & Godard Bill Book, Inventory and Record, 1822–48, American Steel & Wire Papers.

[4] Credit Report on S. S. Keyser & Co., Baltimore, Md., Dun & Bradstreet Collection, 8: 12, 397. Many similar examples could be listed.

[5] Peter L. Payne and Lance E. Davis, *The Savings Bank of Baltimore*.

[6] Josiah Drummond to Alexander H. Rice, October 21, 1889, Shawmut Fibre Co. Papers.

[7] Gerald T. White, *A History of the Massachusetts Hospital Life Insurance Company*, pp. 41–55, 85–104.

banks and insurance companies. Since neither of these methods was open to pre–Civil War entrepreneurs, growth depended upon personal resources and retained earnings (both of which were usually inadequate), or upon financial assistance from wealthy merchants. In such circumstances it is not surprising that many of the most successful firms were either those founded by the merchants themselves or those in which the entrepreneur was able to secure funds for fixed capital assets through an alliance with members of the mercantile community.

The outstanding examples of the first case were the Waltham and Lowell textile mills and such integrated rail mills as Cambria and Bethlehem—the largest manufacturing enterprises of their times. All of these firms were originally created through merchants' initiative. The merchants raised fixed capital by forming a corporation and selling stock privately to limited numbers of their colleagues.[8] Because many of these firms prospered, and because many of their histories have been written, this method of finance is the best known, but it was in fact the least often used.[9]

The second case, in which an established manufacturer financed expansion through an alliance with wealthy merchants, occurred far more often. Sometimes these alliances took the form of a closely held stock corporation; often they were a formal or informal partnership. Whitaker Iron (the forerunner of Wheeling Steel) illustrates the corporate method. In the 1840s George and Joseph Whitaker, the Maryland ironmasters who controlled Principio Furnace, financed their firm's growth by securing capital from the Baltimore merchants Thomas Garrett and William Chandler. The new firm issued 4,000 shares of stock, of which the Whitakers owned 2,400, the merchants 1,600.[10]

Often a firm sought to acquire investment capital by inveigling the merchants who distributed its products into buying shares in the firm, or into becoming partners. The Mount Hope Iron Company (Massachusetts), for example, tried to increase its capitalization in 1858 by selling shares to several iron commission merchants in Boston.[11] The most dramatically successful example of the partnership method was Jones and Laughlin of Pittsburgh, a firm built through the union of manufacturing entrepreneurs and merchant capital.[12]

---

[8] A firm in which all the stock is closely held by a few individuals is called a "close corporation."

[9] Victor S. Clark commented: "Commerce supplied capital to manufacturing in two ways: by direct investment and by credits to industrial companies. The latter way, although less conspicuous, was probably the more important of the two" (*History of Manufactures in the United States*, 1: 368).

[10] Minutes of Stockholders Meeting, 1842, 1843, 1844; Statement of Stock, Principio Furnace, 1841; both in Principio Furnace Papers.

[11] Minutes of Directors' Meeting, October 4, 1958, Mount Hope Iron Co. Papers. This method was more often used to obtain working capital.

[12] Jones & Laughlin is particularly interesting to study because it is the only one of the modern "Big Steel" firms which grew entirely through internal expansion. It absorbed no other producing firms until 1943.

The firm began in 1853 as a partnership between Benjamin Lauth, Francis Lauth, Benjamin Jones, and Samuel Kier. The Lauths were immigrant German metalworkers who had built a rolling mill on the south side of the Monongahela River in 1850. Although the Lauths were mechanically ingenious (they perfected a cold-rolling process that produced a very hard iron with a smooth, shiny exterior surface),[13] they quickly encountered the financial difficulties that were the bane of all western Pennsylvania ironmasters' existence before the Civil War.[14] By 1853 they were floundering, and they began to seek added capital in the Pittsburgh mercantile community. This search eventuated in the alliance with Jones and Kier, who contributed $10,000 cash to the business, paid the Lauths $2,700 for their previous efforts, and became equal partners in the business.[15]

Jones and Kier were specialized freight commission brokers who had operated the "Mechanics' Line of Packets" between Philadelphia and Pittsburgh over the Main Line Canal and Portage Railroad. When the Pennsylvania Railroad reached Pittsburgh in 1852, Jones and Kier shrewdly perceived that the heyday of the freight commission broker had passed; they sold out, opened an iron commission business, and became partners with the Lauths.[16]

Under the terms of the partnership, Jones and both Lauths received salaries of $1,500. The partners agreed to draw no other funds from the business; all profits were to be added to the firm's capital. The Lauths ran the rolling mill; Jones had charge of "warehouses, books, accounts and finances."[17] Jones soon proved a singularly nimble financial manager. He saved the business, for,

[13] Thomas E. Lloyd, "History of Jones and Laughlin Steel Corporation," mimeographed copy dated 1938, Old History Papers, Jones & Laughlin Steel Corp. Papers.

[14] Capital shortages in Pittsburgh are elaborated in Louis C. Hunter, "Financial Problems of the Early Pittsburgh Iron Manufacturers," *passim*. See also Willis L. King, "Speech Delivered Before Aliquippa Engineers Institute on the History of Jones and Laughlin Steel Corporation," mimeographed copy in Jones & Laughlin Papers. King was Benjamin Jones's nephew.

[15] Agreement between Benjamin Lauth and Francis Lauth with S. M. Kier and B. F. Jones, December 3, 1853, Jones & Laughlin Papers.

[16] Kier was never an active partner in the rolling mill. In 1856 he made a spectacular error in judgment by trading his one-quarter interest in the firm in exchange for Jones's share of their commission business. Kier was a fabulous, multifaceted character. In addition to his freight, iron, and commission businesses, he also owned a fire-brick and pottery factory. In a more exotic vein, he drew off the crude oil that seeped into his father's salt wells near Tarentum, Pa., and bottled it as a panacea called "Kier's Rock Oil." He developed a following for this wondrous concoction by sending a "medicine road show" around the country in the 1840s. When a steady demand arose, he sold through regular drug channels. In the 1850s he developed a method of distilling crude oil for use as an illuminant, as well as a patent lamp in which to burn it. See Release: Benjamin F. Jones from All Liability to Co-Partners in Firms of Grover, Kier & Co. and Jones, Kier & Co., and Samuel M. Kier from All Liability to Co-Partners in Jones, Lauth & Co., January 17, 1856, *ibid.*; Allen Johnson et al., eds., *Dictionary of American Biography*, 5: 371–72.

[17] Article of Partnership between Benjamin Lauth and Francis Lauth with S. M. Kier and B. F. Jones, December 3, 1853, Jones & Laughlin Papers.

despite the fresh injection of cash and the agreement to plow profits back into the business, the new firm almost immediately needed additional long-term and working capital. Jones was able to arrange for both; moreover, he did so on extremely favorable terms in a region where dozens of manufacturers competed for the limited quantity of capital available. The "angel" was a Pittsburgh commission merchant, James Laughlin.

Laughlin was an Irish immigrant who had made his fortune as a pork packer and a seller of provisions to settlers passing through Pittsburgh on their way west. In the 1850s he operated commission houses dealing in iron and groceries in Pittsburgh and in Evansville, Indiana. Laughlin sold iron from the Jones and Lauth works, and he apparently had great faith in the future of the firm, for he soon became its financial backer. By March, 1855, he had already contributed $8,200 cash to the firm's capital. In that year he contributed $40,000 more and became a partner in the business.[18] As a partner Laughlin was a manufacturing entrepreneur's dream. He took no part in the active management of the business,[19] but he backed the firm with his entire financial resources through the crucial first decade of its existence. He contributed his personal wealth to the firm's long-term capital and used his personal credit standing to arrange for adequate working capital.

Whether Jones and Laughlin could have survived without Laughlin's all-out support is debatable. It was the only pre–Civil War iron firm, other than integrated rail mills, that survived to become one of the giant twentieth-century steel producers; and it was one of the few unintegrated antebellum iron firms that succeeded in adopting the integrated, high-volume structure. As described in the previous chapter, the integrated mill required large sums of capital. The rail mills obtained theirs from the pooled resources of several merchants. In the 1850s, Jones and Laughlin transformed the Lauths' small, single-stage bar mill into a large, integrated unit. By 1857 the firm had its own blast furnaces to furnish pig iron, thirty-one puddling and heating furnaces to refine the iron and prepare it for rolling, five trains of steam-driven rolls to produce bar iron and shafting, and twenty-five nail-making machines.[20] As a result of expansion and integration, capital invested rose from $20,000 in 1853 to $176,000 in 1861. The increase came entirely from profits and

[18] Agreement between James Laughlin and Jones, Lauth & Co., March 8, 1855; Limited Patrnership: Benjamin F. Jones, Benjamin Lauth, and James Laughlin (James Laughlin Special Partner), Term Five Years from August 1, 1856, *ibid*. Francis Lauth had already dropped out of the business. His brother sold out in 1864 for $10,000, went back to Germany, and made a fortune in iron and steel there.

[19] His sons did, however; two of them became partners in 1861. Others joined in 1870. With one or two exceptions, a member of the Jones and Laughlin families has headed the firm since its inception.

[20] Lloyd, "History of Jones and Laughlin"; J. P. Lesley, *The Iron Manufacturer's Guide*, pp. 247–48. The mill's capacity rose from 15 tons per day in 1853 to 100 tons in 1869; see King, "Speech before the Aliquippa Engineers," Jones & Laughlin Papers.

James Laughlin's cash contributions. Retained earnings alone fell far short of supplying the total additions to capital, as Table I indicates.

TABLE I. CAPITAL INVESTED IN JONES & LAUGHLIN STEEL CORP., 1853–1861

Year	Total Capital ($)	Capital Added ($)	Capital Added from Profits ($)	Capital Added by Cash from Laughlin ($)
1853	20,000	—	—	—
1853–1856	127,000	107,000	55,000	52,000
1856–1861	176,000	49,000	30,000	19,000
Total	323,000	156,000	85,000	71,000

Source: Computed from data in various articles of partnership cited previously, the partnership agreement of 1861, and a table of earnings and dividends in H. S. Geneen, Comptroller of Jones & Laughlin, to W. R. Compton, Assistant Chairman of the Board, December 2, 1952, all Jones & Laughlin Steel Corp. Papers.
Note: After 1861 the firm continued its policy of financing expansion with retained earnings. From 1861 to 1908, the firm's profits totaled $70,000,000. Eighty per cent of this was plowed back into the business.

As great as Laughlin's contributions to the firm's long-term capital were, they were probably less important to its ultimate success than his ability to secure adequate working capital. He was able to do so because his endorsements enabled Jones and Laughlin to discount its own and its customers' short-term notes for cash to meet operating expenses. Working capital not only was far more difficult for most manufacturers to come by, but the annual requirements for it greatly exceeded the average annual additions to fixed assets. In 1860, for example, when Jones and Laughlin's fixed assets totaled about $176,000, it had short-term obligations of $200,000 to the Pittsburgh Trust Company.[21]

The firm was able to secure such extensive credit only because its paper carried the endorsement of Laughlin, a merchant and a stockholder in several Pittsburgh banks.[22] Jones could never have secured such advances on the strength of his own (or his firm's) credit alone. Virtually all antebellum manufacturers faced similar requirements for short-term capital relative to total investments; very few had a James Laughlin to obtain it for them. Their ability to secure such funds often determined their success or failure, and the

[21] Acknowledgment of Obligation of James Laughlin and Benjamin F. Jones to the Pittsburgh Trust Co. to the Extent of $200,000, March 16, 1860, Jones & Laughlin Papers. Laughlin was president of Pittsburgh Trust when he first became interested in the rolling mill.

[22] In order to get the bank of Pittsburgh to discount the firm's notes and bills, Laughlin (in his role as endorser) submitted a statement of his personal wealth. In addition to a 13/32 interest in the iron works, he had $50,000 in real estate, $75,000 cash capital in his commission houses, and $25,000 in bank stock. See James Laughlin to President and Cashier, Bank of Pittsburgh, August 26, 1857, *ibid*.

way in which the funds were obtained often determined the conduct of the business.

PROBLEMS OF WORKING CAPITAL

Working capital presented particularly perplexing problems to early manufacturers because of the large quantity required and the paucity of agencies, formal or informal, prepared to supply it. The quantity required was primarily a result of high operating costs and of the credit, banking, and monetary systems that prevailed in the United States prior to the Civil War.

The Jones and Laughlin case cited above, in which short-term obligations incurred in meeting operating costs roughly equaled the fixed assets accumulated through the entire life of the business, was not at all unusual among pre–Civil War American manufacturing firms. For example, E. I. du Pont de Nemours, the Wilmington, Delaware, powder firm founded in 1802, had capital assets of $500,000 in 1860. Its operating expenses during the same year were $440,000. In smaller firms the ratio of current expenses to capital assets was often much higher. John Roebling's wire rope factory at Trenton, New Jersey, had fixed assets of $20,000 in 1850; labor and material costs totaled $42,000.[23]

The bulk of current operating expenses consisted of the cost of raw materials and wages. Both of these were "variable costs," which rose and fell with the level of production. When an entrepreneur decided to expand production, he almost immediately encountered increased payroll expenses. Raw-material costs also rose, but these could often be deferred to some extent by purchasing on credit. Suppliers, however, had payrolls of their own to meet, and they persistently pressed for punctual payment. Transportation costs (another variable) also had to be paid in cash or on short-term credit (usually within thirty days or less). All of these factors combined to present manufacturing entrepreneurs with a critical shortage of operating capital with which to meet production expenses.

Income, on the other hand, came from sales almost invariably made on long-term credit.[24] The average term of credit in most manufacturing lines was six months, but this often fluctuated. In competitive markets, manufacturers often had to offer more generous terms. The prevalence of extended

---

[23] U.S. Census Office, *Eighth Census of the United States, 1860: Manufactures*, pp. 53, 55, *et passim*; D. B. Steinman, *Builders of the Bridge*, p. 147.

[24] Cash payment was extremely rare, despite the considerable savings it offered through the avoidance of discount costs. Manufacturers and merchants usually offered price reductions of up to 10 per cent for payment in cash. Despite these inducements, the only antebellum firm (among the dozens whose papers we have seen) that habitually paid cash, in good times and bad, was the Conshohocken, Pa., rolling mill of James and John Wood. Not only did the Woods pay cash for supplies, but they invariably held their customers' notes until maturity, a remarkable feat at the time. See the Correspondence and Account Books in the Alan Wood Steel Co. Papers.

credit terms was a function not so much of the money supply as of the pre-
dominantly agricultural nature of the economy. The best available estimates
indicate that manufacturing contributed about one-quarter of the total value
added in all American industries in 1839. By 1850, manufacturing's share had
risen to about one-third.[25] In such an economy, manufacturing credit terms
were necessarily tied to agricultural credit terms. The latter, of course, were a
function of the harvest cycle. In either case there was considerable delay
before suppliers received payment in full.

Customers paid for their purchases by sending a note—in effect, a post-
dated check payable at the expiration of the credit period. The manufacturer
needed immediate cash to meet expenses. If the note came from a local resident of good credit standing, it could sometimes be cashed at a local bank for
a fee (discount), which varied according to the prevailing demand for money.
The discount, of course, reduced the profit on sales and added to the cost of
doing business.[26] To avoid this cost, manufacturers sometimes accepted payment in produce, which they foisted off on employees as partial payment of
wages.[27]

These methods broke down as production increased and markets expanded
geographically. Banks refused to accept out-of-town notes, or would accept
them only at prohibitive discounts.[28] Even if the manufacturer could afford to
hold the note until its payment date, and even if the note did not prove worthless, his troubles were not over, for checks drawn on distant banks, or notes
issued by them, also were subject to discount. Manufacturers therefore tried to
insist on payment in local funds, or in paper that traded at face value
locally.[29] All the while, of course, their suppliers were making similar demands on them. Factory owners generally were ill-equipped to deal with these
perplexities; they had neither the time nor the experience. What they needed
were financial intermediaries capable of supplying reliable credit information,
rationalizing payments in order to minimize discount costs, and furnishing
operating cash either by discounting notes, making advances on accounts
receivable, or lending on inventories.

[25] U.S. Bureau of the Census, *Historical Statistics of the United States*, p. 139. An
explanation of the term "value added" appears on p. 133 in the same volume.
[26] Discount and interest costs often absorbed as much as 20–25 per cent of gross
revenues in the period 1830–60. Presumably the most successful entrepreneurs took
this into account when setting prices.
[27] This questionable practice was later outlawed by some states, but was institutionalized in company stores in others. Payment in produce continued in small firms
for many decades; however, it had pretty well disappeared by 1840 in the firms with
which we are concerned here.
[28] This was particularly true after the demise of the Second Bank of the United
States rendered the transfer of funds difficult and diminished the reliability of state
bank notes.
[29] See George R. Taylor, *The Transportation Revolution, 1815–1860*, pp. 312–23
and chap. 15, for a lucid description of monetary and banking practices, their hazards
and abuses.

In the modern economy a complex network of formal institutions performs all these functions. National and local credit agencies abound. Banks discount reliable manufacturers' notes and lend on receivables. Two types of companies specialize in industrial finance: commercial credit companies discount notes and lend on receivables; factoring companies buy accounts receivable outright and lend on inventories.[30] Before the Civil War no such salubrious conditions obtained. Credit-rating agencies existed, but they primarily served mercantile clients. Banks grew progressively more reluctant to discount notes bearing a manufacturer's endorsement; they rarely (if ever) lent on receivables. Commercial credit and factoring companies were twentieth-century developments; it is thought that the first of each type appeared in 1903 and 1925 respectively.[31]

The late development of formal fiduciary institutions geared to manufacturers' needs, together with the enduring reluctance of banks to provide working capital or to finance transactions, was, like the prevalence of long-term credit, largely attributable to the pre-eminence of the agricultural sector of the economy. Not until the 1880s did the total annual value of manufacturing production exceed the total value of agricultural output.[32] Credit institutions (particularly commercial banks) were therefore oriented toward financing the movement of crops to market at home and abroad. They tended to remain so for two reasons.

The first reason was a philosophical conservatism which deeply influenced banking policies. Early nineteenth-century banks were not in business to take "risks" in the sense that we understand the term today. Savings banks were in business to accept deposits, pool them, and use the resulting fund of capital to invest in mortgages or government bonds. The value of the property or the credit of the U.S. government eliminated the element of risk.

Most commercial banks had been founded by merchants to service the needs of the agricultural and commercial economy. They facilitated commerce at home and abroad by discounting notes and serving as clearing houses for bills of exchange. These transactions were not considered hazardous, because the value of the goods for which notes and bills were issued, together with the personal assets of the merchants involved in the transaction, protected the bank against losses. Because banks were not accustomed to extending these services to manufacturers, and because most early producers were men of limited means, bankers tended to regard manufacturing finance as unknown and risky, and therefore beyond the scope of sound banking practice. It took decades of manufacturing growth to alter this conservative philosophy.

---

[30] Terris Moore, "Unsecured Bank Loans as Permanent Working Capital for Industry," pp. 116–17; William T. Rhame, "Competitive Advantages and Disadvantages of Agencies Making Short and Medium Term Loans to Industry," pp. 5–42.

[31] Moore, "Bank Loans as Working Capital," pp. 116–17; Joseph E. Hedges, *Commercial Banking and the Stock Market Before 1863*, p. 86.

[32] Bureau of the Census, *Historical Statistics*, pp. 139–40.

The second reason for the delayed entry of formal institutions into manufacturing finance was the fact that early manufacturers, finding no formal agencies willing or able to assume the financial risks of expanding production and markets, turned to merchants for help. Merchants supplied the needed capital and expertise, and in the process became so deeply entrenched in the manufacturing sector that they were extremely difficult to supplant.

MERCHANTS AS FINANCIAL AGENTS AND SUPPLIERS OF SHORT-TERM CAPITAL

Merchants handled most of the financial transactions of the expanding national market as they managed the growing flow of goods throughout the economy. They were able to do so because, in contradistinction to manufacturers, they were appropriately equipped in resources, temperament, and training.

Throughout the pre–Civil War period, merchants controlled most of the available capital in the United States. Many merchants had large sums of personal cash available[33] and had access to additional funds through credit at home and abroad. Unlike manufacturers, who could obtain bank loans only on tangible collateral, prosperous merchants could borrow extensively from commercial and savings banks, often on their signature alone. This seeming paradox is explained by the prevailing banking philosophy and by the fact that merchants usually *were* the banks. An analysis of the directors and officers of the banks of New York, Philadelphia, and Baltimore in 1840, 1850, and 1860 reveals that more than two-thirds of the officials were or had been merchants. The same was true of virtually all the private bankers in those cities.[34] Middlemen therefore had ready access both to accumulated mercantile profits and to the savings deposits of the populace.

Merchants not only had resources, they were temperamentally inclined to use them to finance commerce. They were professional risk takers. Men who did not hesitate to send ships from the East Coast of the United States around the world, on voyages that lasted for years, were not as likely to be defeated by the financial intricacies of a transaction between Baltimore and Pittsburgh as was a manufacturer accustomed to dealing locally. In addition, as many historians have noted, successful merchants seem perpetually driven to find profitable employment for surplus funds.

In previous centuries this drive led merchants such as the Fuggers and

[33] A forceful demonstration of the profitability of mercantile trade is the fact that Baltimore merchant Robert Oliver made a net profit of $775,000 in 1806–7 in his trade with Vera Cruz alone; see Stuart Bruchey, *Robert Oliver, Merchant of Baltimore, 1783–1819*, chap. 6.

[34] Based on data taken from appropriate city and commercial directories. Among the many biographies of merchants who turned bankers are Richard H. Hart, *Enoch Pratt*, and John B. McMaster, *The Life and Times of Stephen Girard*.

Rothschilds into banking. Others poured their profits back into trade, buying and selling more goods, and building more ships to haul them in. Of necessity, expanded trade required larger markets, and this dynamic led Nicolo Polo and his successors to travel about the world themselves and to finance explorations in search of trading routes and markets in the Indies.

Many American merchants followed these traditional paths in the early nineteenth century. Stephen Girard of Philadelphia became an enormously wealthy private banker. Merchant families such as the Jacksons and Lees of Boston built world-wide trading networks with branch houses in India and China. The need for greater market coverage made merchants the driving force behind such early internal improvements as the Erie and Chesapeake and Delaware canals.

Many merchants, however, found an outlet for their surplus capital in manufacturing finance. Some, like Francis Cabot Lowell, did so at first because the Napoleonic Wars and the War of 1812 made reinvestment in foreign trade impractical. Lowell had been to England, and he realized that potential profits lay in textile manufacturing. Once he and his associates demonstrated the profitability of textile enterprises, other merchants were quick to make similar investments.

Some of these traders turned to manufacturing investment because of the changing American market. Population growth presented greater trading opportunities at home, and the advance of mechanization widened the market for manufactures. In selecting their investments, merchants used their knowledge of expanding domestic markets and usually financed those manufacturing fields for which their own trading regions were particularly suited in terms of natural resources, skilled labor, and transportation facilities. For example, the Pennsylvania merchants who underwrote the state's iron industry included the Trotter family, which dealt in tin and copper, but invested heavily in the Lehigh Crane Iron Works; Richard Wood, Charles Wood, and Edward Townsend, Philadelphia dry goods merchants who took over the bankrupt Cambria Iron Works and hired John Fritz to resuscitate it; and, of course, the pork packer turned iron dealer, James Laughlin.

Many specialized merchants invested in firms that produced the particular types of goods they sold. In effect, this was a loose form of backward integration which assured continuing supplies in expanding markets and decreased the merchants' dependence on overseas producers. Anson Phelps supplemented his supply of copper and brass wares by supporting factories in the Connecticut River valley. David Reeves used his profits from importing British rails to start the first integrated American rail mill, Phoenix Iron. Specialized merchants also supplied working capital and became financial agents for their clients.

In so doing they brought their experience and skill to bear on the assortment of capital, credit, banking, and monetary woes which beset ambitious manufacturers. Problems that defied solution by manufacturing entrepreneurs were often resolved by merchants through the application of traditional techniques. Traders since the Middle Ages had had to assemble capital, evaluate investment risks, maintain a flow of credit information, function as investment and commercial bankers, and master the art of doing business over long distances with a polyglot assortment of currencies and commercial paper. In short, merchants routinely performed all the functions later institutionalized in formal agencies such as banks, credit bureaus, and factoring companies. Their financial versatility, developed through the centuries in a preindustrial economy, proved readily adaptable to manufacturing. Entrepreneurs who sought outlying markets were pioneers in American manufacturing, but the commission merchants and jobbers who distributed their products functioned as they and their predecessors always had in arranging and financing transactions.

In the process, commission merchants and jobbers naturally kept current records on the credit standing of clients, and, as previously shown, brokers such as Cabeen and Kemble, and jobbers such as the Troths, relieved manufacturers of credit risks by guaranteeing payment. They also brought some measure of order to the chaos of notes and currency. Through widespread connections in the trading and banking community they were able to absorb and dispose of commercial paper at much less loss than manufacturers. Commission merchants customarily rendered payment in their own notes, which discounted more readily. This accelerated the cash flow and decreased the pressure for working capital. They also furnished short-term funds in other ways. Some, like Laughlin, endorsed notes so that banks would accept them. Unlike Laughlin, most brokers were not partners in the business and therefore charged a fee for the service.

Other merchants acted as note brokers, using their own funds to discount manufacturers' paper. The risks in such dealings were high, but so were the returns. Merchants' discount rates often were not subject to usury laws, or the laws were evaded. In a period when 6 per cent or less was the normal bank interest rate to preferred borrowers, note brokers often charged as much as 30 per cent and rarely less than 12 per cent.[35] In such circumstances it is not surprising to find that many merchants borrowed heavily from banks to underwrite their discounting activities. For example, the Baltimore iron brokers John Gittings and E. J. Stickney borrowed hundreds of thousands of dollars from the Savings Bank of Baltimore in the period 1845–66. During that time they made loans and discounted notes for several iron manufacturers, includ-

---

[35] Don M. Dailey, "The Early Development of the Note Brokerage Business in Chicago"; Lance E. Davis, "The New England Textile Mills and the Capital Markets"; Elva Tooker, "A Merchant Turns to Money-Lending in Philadelphia"; and Klein, "Mercantile Instruments of Credit," p. 603.

ing Gibbons and Huston, and for the Locust Point Furnace (Maryland).[36] Some measure of the profitability of such operations when prudently managed can be seen in the career of the Philadelphia metal dealer Nathan Trotter. Trotter habitually put his surplus funds into discounting. Between 1833 and 1852 he cleared almost half a million dollars from such deals.[37]

With such widespread demand for discounting, and such great profits to be made, many merchants quit dealing in merchandise altogether and became specialized note brokers. Their services were expensive, but, because they were available nowhere else, note brokers proved indispensable to many manufacturers. As the volume of trade increased, so did specialization. Note brokerage as a speculation by commission merchants with surplus funds was commonplace by 1830. Specialized note brokers appeared by 1840. By 1850 some of them had become further specialized and handled only one kind of paper— for example, iron or dry goods.[38] Thus, volume brought disintegration of the merchants' cluster of financial competencies, just at it had transformed the manifold mercantile functions of the all-purpose merchant into specialized fields such as dry goods jobbing. In time the process of disintegration produced specialists in every sphere of financial responsibility, and these were the precursors of the formal institutions that appeared after the Civil War.

Commission merchants also supplied working capital by making advances on sales. Brokers paid producers some portion of the total value of the goods as soon as they had been shipped. Baltimore commission merchants Ballard and Hall wrote Jacob Haldeman after receipt of a shipment of iron, "You are at liberty to value on us payable in 90 days and your draft will meet due honor." The commission house declared itself "always willing to make advances to any desired extent on goods in hand . . . if you continue your shipments of iron."[39]

The merchants, it is important to note, did not make these payments and advances in cash. As in the case of Ballard and Hall, wholesalers issued notes payable at some later date, usually from three to six months after issuance. They did so by authorizing manufacturers to "draw" on them. The manufacturer then filled out a promissory note showing the amount and the date of maturity. He sent the note to the merchant, who signed ("accepted") and

---

[36] Payne and Davis, *Savings Bank of Baltimore*; Credit Report of Locust Point Furnace, Baltimore, Md., Dun & Bradstreet Collection, 8: 348. On occasion Baltimore banks were reportedly unable to discount any kind of paper because the entire supply of loanable funds was in the hands of merchants and note brokers; see Klein, "Mercantile Instruments of Credit," p. 603.

[37] Elva Tooker, *Nathan Trotter*, p. 182. Not all the paper Trotter handled was manufacturers'. He also dealt in bills of exchange and the like.

[38] Klein, "Mercantile Instruments of Credit," pp. 533–35.

[39] Ballard & Hall to Jacob Haldeman, May 18, 1819, and February 24, 1820; Andrew Hall to Haldeman, December 31, 1819; and David Wizer to Haldeman, March 24, 1820; Jacob Haldeman Papers. Frequently such advances were subject to interest charges.

returned it. The manufacturer then discounted the note for cash, or used the note itself to pay current bills. The notes of many prominent, wealthy merchants, such as Enoch Pratt, circulated at near face value, and they formed an important addition to the money supply in an era of chronic shortages of currency.

From the manufacturer's point of view, the advantages of receiving advances were negated to some extent by the fact that sales revenue was reduced by the amount of the discount cost; nevertheless, the practice was universal before the Civil War and was not restricted to proprietorships like Haldeman's. Equity-financed firms used it as well. Advances from selling houses supplied crucial working capital to textile mills, and Whitaker Iron often kept its Wheeling mill running on advances from Pratt.[40] Sometimes a firm's success or failure depended upon its ability to make arrangements with a wholesaler for guaranteed advances. To obtain such guarantees, a producer often had to agree to consign his output to a single merchant, thus sacrificing a large measure of control over his business.

Agreements on guaranteed advances and marketing rights were often formalized by a contract between a manufacturing firm and a commission house. Typical of such agreements was one between Robeson, Brooke Company, blast furnace operators of Berks County, Pennsylvania, and the Philadelphia iron brokerage house Whitaker and Coudon. The brokers bound themselves to "undertake the sale of your iron for two years ... charging you 5% commission and guarantee on the entire product of said furnace [plus] the usual charges for weighing, wharfage &c., and will advance you either in cash or our paper—monthly, the amount of sales, fast as made less charges and interest." Whitaker and Coudon thus assumed the role of exclusive manufacturer's agent for Robeson, Brooke, as did Cabeen for Cornwall Furnace. In return for exclusive sales rights, the brokers promised to supply working capital. "We will agree to loan you our paper to the amount of Thirty thousand dollars for which we will charge you two & one half per cent."[41]

Several important stipulations were involved. First, the furnace had to supply 5,000 tons of pig iron annually. If it failed to do so, the interest on the loan jumped to 5 per cent. Second, the brokers reserved the right to discount their own paper (thereby adding brokerage fees to the interest charges), and the furnace could cash it elsewhere only with permission. Third, if the loan was not repaid within a year, "We will charge you over and above the commission the street rate or charge for the money."[42]

Whitaker and Coudon's loan was, in effect, an advance against future pro-

[40] Davis, "New England Textile Mills," pp. 6–7; Nelson Whitaker to George P. Whitaker, November 17, 1868, Whitaker Iron Papers; Klein, "Mercantile Instruments of Credit," pp. 526–28.

[41] Whitaker & Coudon to Robeson, Brooke Co., March 8, 1858, Whitaker Iron Papers.

[42] Ibid.

duction. As such, it represented another classic mercantile technique developed for the preindustrial economy in the form of advances against crops, a technique practiced throughout the nineteenth century by cotton and grain factors.[43] Sometimes such bargains paid off. Gibbons and Huston weathered the slump of 1857 with the help of advances from Curtis Bouvé, a Boston commission house, and went on to renewed prosperity. Samuel Colt's suppliers, including Naylor and Company of New York, financed him until his first government contract in the 1840s assured him of success. On other occasions the gamble proved unwise. The Columbia, South Carolina, commission firm of Polock, Solomon, and Company lost $9,000 when an iron furnace went bankrupt.[44]

Middlemen also engaged in barter transactions with manufacturers, thereby reducing the need for cash operating capital. John Wood, the Conshohocken, Pennsylvania, rolling mill operator, shipped sheet iron to Anson Phelps in return for copper and brass. Fall River Iron regularly paid Enoch Pratt and E. J. Stickney for pig iron by shipping them nails.[45] Such transactions were often advantageous for both parties, for the manufacturer disposed of his products and secured raw materials without adding to his debts or undergoing discount costs. Brokers, of course, profited on the sale of both raw materials and finished products.

Through the application of their financial expertise concomitantly with their role as distributors and suppliers, merchants made it possible for American manufacturers to function in expanding markets. Their control of finances often allowed them to dictate policy to manufacturers. Some merchants became partners in, or owners of, producing firms as a result of their advances. In this way Joseph Anderson became president of Tredegar Iron in Richmond, Virginia. The New York commission merchant Augustus Moen joined the wiremaking firm of Washburn and Godard.[46] Similar examples abound in the histories of antebellum manufacturing firms.

[43] This mercantile technique was traditionally employed in agriculture, but it was used for centuries in other industries as well. In the seventeenth century, British wool merchants made advances to weavers, and London coal merchants financed the operations of mining entrepreneurs in order to assure future supplies of coal. See William Hillyer, "Four Centuries of Factoring"; and John U. Nef, "Dominance of the Trader in the English Coal Industry in the Seventeenth Century." As later happened in U.S. manufacturing, the London coal merchants' advances of short-term capital often led to their ownership of the producing property.

[44] Curtis Bouvé to Charles Huston, October 8 and December 11, 1857, and January 15, 1858, Lukens Steel Co. Papers; Correspondence, 1847–50, Samuel Colt Papers; Ernest M. Lander, Jr., "The Iron Industry in Ante-Bellum South Carolina," p. 348.

[45] Correspondence, 1840–50, Alan Wood Papers; Correspondence, Iron Invoices, and Richard Borden to E. J. Stickney Co., February 18, 1848, Fall River Iron Works Papers.

[46] Kathleen Bruce, *Virginia Iron Manufacture in the Slave Era*, chap. 4. The Washburn & Moen Papers are part of the American Steel & Wire Papers.

CONCLUSION

Thus, most early American manufacturing firms existed as partnerships (formal or informal) between technically knowledgeable factory owners or managers and mercantile capitalists. Sometimes (as in the case of rail and textile mills) these alliances developed when merchants, perceiving a new market and seeking a profitable outlet for unused resources, pooled their funds to construct a factory, engage a supervisory staff, and commence production. On other occasions (as in the case of Jones and Laughlin) established manufacturers took in merchant partners in order to secure capital. Jobbers and commission merchants became involved as a logical consequence of their roles as distributors and suppliers.

Whatever the particular circumstances, the ultimate effect of these relationships was to open a channel through which capital poured from the mercantile sector of the economy into the manufacturing sector.

Merchants were the agents of transfer, a role which resulted naturally from their position at the nexus of American commerce. The growth of American markets for manufactures in the early nineteenth century presented an incentive and a compulsion for mercantile participation in manufacturing finance. The incentive was the profit potential of trade in domestic products; the compulsion derived from the need to control large and dependable supplies in order to maintain control of trade flows. Some merchants found their role as capitalists and financial manipulators so profitable that they dropped marketing to specialize in finance. These private bankers and note brokers were the forerunners of formal agencies specializing in commercial credit which appeared in a subsequent era.

By bringing their capital resources and financial expertise into the manufacturing sector, merchants played an indispensable part in American industrialization. All but a handful of antebellum American manufacturers who produced for outlying markets and operated successfully for at least a generation received some form of financial assistance from merchants. Nowhere was this more true than in the group of industries which sprang up as a result of the coming of the railroads.

CHAPTER V

Marketing in a Changing Environment: The Railway Supply Industry, 1830–1842

Between 1830 and 1860 the American railroad network grew from thirty to thirty thousand miles. This growth created a large market for rails, cars, locomotives, wheels, and miscellaneous fixtures and fittings. American producers competed eagerly to supply this new demand, and in the process they created a new industry. In the 1830s the railroad supply industry was made up of a multitude of small, local producers, such as blacksmiths, machinists, and carriage builders, who began to produce railroad equipment as a sideline. By 1860 the industry had become highly concentrated; that is, most production was in the hands of a small number of specialized firms. This transformation took place in three distinct periods, each of which was characterized by changing methods of production and distribution resulting from the nature of the market and the interlocking problems of finance and technology which confronted producers.

In the first period, 1830–42, markets were small and localized, and technology was simple. Producers entered and left the field with relative ease. Products were sold unsystematically to railroad officers, or through all-purpose and metal commission merchants. The Panic of 1837, and the recession that followed, eliminated all but the handful of firms that were well-financed and efficient producers.

In the second period, 1842–57, the market grew rapidly, and the railway supply industry enjoyed a period of expansion and prosperity. It exhibited characteristics typical of other contemporary producers' competing for distant markets: an increase in output resulting in specialized production; and the appearance of specialized commission merchants, who supplied raw materials and fixed and working capital, and who arranged and financed transactions. By the late 1840s a network of these specialized merchants controlled much of the distribution of railway equipment, just as they controlled boiler iron and other producers' goods.

Concurrently, the industry developed a method of distribution which was a forerunner of sales techniques that became prevalent in most producers' goods industries in the late nineteenth century. This new pattern, in which manufacturers dealt directly with their customers and many middlemen were eliminated, appeared in the late 1840s and 1850s as a result of three conditions that were peculiar to the market for railroad equipment.

First, the railroads offered the only truly concentrated market for manufactured products in the antebellum economy.[1] Never before had so few customers demanded so much material. In 1855, for example, 36 railroads 150 miles or more in length were in operation or under construction. These provided the bulk of the domestic market for railroad equipment. To supply this market there were in the United States 15 rail mills, about 40 locomotive builders, and 15 wheel foundries. These numbers were small compared to the number of producers in other antebellum industries. In 1856, for example, there were 560 iron furnaces, 389 forges, 210 rolling mills, and approximately 1,100 foundries.[2] The relatively small number of producers and consumers in the railroad supply industry enabled buyers and sellers to identify each other without the assistance of mercantile intermediaries.

Second, the railroads pioneered in the development of sophisticated management structures.[3] As they created bureaucratic methods of control, they systematized purchasing, assigning it to a particular officer or department. The railroad bureaucracy therefore institutionalized the middleman's mercantile functions within a larger business enterprise. The railroads also developed detailed technical specifications for the materials they purchased;

[1] Concentrated markets are of two kinds. The first, represented by the railroads, is one in which a small number of consumers demand a large volume of material. The second is a market in which a large number of consumers are concentrated in a small geographic area. The latter type is a function of urbanization, and became an increasingly significant factor in the American economy in the last two decades of the nineteenth century.

[2] Alfred D. Chandler, Jr., ed., *The Railroads*, p. 16; J. P. Lesley, *The Iron Manufacturer's Guide*, pp. 747, 757; and John H. White, Jr., *American Locomotives*, p. 13. The number of foundries is an average based on data for 1850 and 1860; see U.S. Census Office, *Eighth Census of the United States, 1860: Manufactures*, p. clxxxvi.

[3] The best discussions of the railroads' development of bureaucratic management are found in Chandler, *Railroads*, and Thomas C. Cochran, *Railroad Leaders, 1845–1890*.

by tailoring their equipment to fit individual operating conditions, they created the first important market for specific, non-generic goods. Thus, more and more negotiations between railroad purchasing agents and equipment manufacturers were carried on in a complex technical language that few commission merchants could speak.

Third, railroads were also pioneers in methods of finance. Most of them raised capital through the mass sale of securities, so they had funds available for initial equipment purchases. Many of them were extremely profitable as well; therefore, they often had no need of middlemen to underwrite their subsequent purchasing operations. In response to this new kind of market in which the railroads' purchasing methods either institutionalized or made redundant the independent dealers' mercantile and financial expertise, the supply industry developed, by the late 1850s, modern strategies of direct sales. Among these were the employment of traveling salesmen, who used passenger trains to reach many customers quickly, and extensive use of the telegraph to communicate with customers, salesmen, and shipping agents.

For several reasons, these new, direct sales methods did not completely replace the indirect channels of distribution. Not all railroads were well financed or prosperous. Not all adopted the new methods of management before the Civil War, and those which did, did not do so simultaneously. Many firms, such as wheel foundries or boiler works, produced components that were sold not only to railroads but also to other suppliers such as car and locomotive builders. Finally, many manufacturers produced some material for customers in other industries. For all these reasons, most firms utilized new and old distribution methods simultaneously. It is this coexistence of traditional and modern patterns which makes the railway supply industry a uniquely valuable source for the study of antebellum manufacturing distribution.

The third period of change in the industry occurred between 1857 and 1861. By 1857 the long era of prosperity had drawn a number of firms into the field. The Panic of 1857 and the severe recession that followed brought on an era of ruthless competition which swiftly eliminated marginal firms. The diminished market supported only the few strong firms that managed to survive until the Civil War boom brought renewed prosperity. This period of attrition completed the transformation of the railroad supply industry from a large, diffuse group of unspecialized local producers typical of the agrarian economy into a concentrated cluster of specialized, high-volume producers which served national (and sometimes international) markets dominated by a small number of large consumers. Thus, not only the railroads, but their suppliers as well, pioneered in developing institutions and methods that became hallmarks of the modern, industrial economy.

THE BEGINNINGS, 1830–1842

The railroads excited the imagination of Americans as had no other development in transportation in American history. Unlike the British railways, which often encountered hostility rooted in social, political, and economic traditions,[4] American railroads enjoyed the support of almost all elements of society.[5] The general public not only welcomed them as an advance in transportation but saw them as evidence of America's growth, prosperity, and ability to match European achievements. The merchants of seaport cities such as Boston, New York, Philadelphia, Baltimore, and Charleston, who were the prime movers in establishing the first American railroads, looked upon them as a means of tying hinterland producers and consumers to coastal cities. American artisans saw the railroads as another market for their products. Moreover, they could supply this market by combining existing techniques of production, for the only thing new about early railroads was the combination of roadbed, cars, and locomotives. There was nothing novel about the components themselves.

The roadbed, or track, of wooden rails faced with thin strips of bar iron, and the flanged iron wheels that ran on it, had been developed in Britain by 1753 as a means of carrying coal from pithead to dockside.[6] Freight cars were wooden wagon bodies mounted on iron wheels. Early railroad passenger coaches were stagecoach bodies on similar wheels. Even the steam locomotive, the quintessential component of successful railway transport, was a new adaptation of pre-existing ideas. The steam engine had been successfully applied to water transport long before. Fulton and Livingston ran the *Clermont* on the Hudson in 1807, and sent their steamboat the *New Orleans* on a successful round trip between New Orleans and Pittsburgh in 1817, thirteen years before steam-powered train service appeared in the United States.

[4] For accounts of opposition to railways in Britain, see W. T. Jackman, *The Development of Transportation in Modern Britain*, chap. 7. Railroads have generated an enormous volume of historical writing in Britain and America. George Ottley's *Bibliography of British Railway History* contains 683 pages and excludes articles. In general, British historians have been more concerned with the social effects of railways. John R. Hellet, *The Impact of Railways on Victorian Cities*, is a typical example of recent vintage. American historians, on the other hand, have concerned themselves with economic effects. Institutional studies such as Chandler's *Railroads* and Cochran's *Railroad Leaders* preceded Robert W. Fogel's *Railroads and American Economic Growth*, which in turn set off a burst of frenzied econometric activity by critics and imitators. The best of these is Albert Fishlow, *American Railroads and the Transformation of the Ante-Bellum Economy*. Extensive studies of the economic effects of railways in Britain are now under way. Some of the preliminary findings are discussed in B. R. Mitchell, "Coming of the Railways and British Economic Growth," and Derek Aldcroft, "The Efficiency and Enterprise of British Railways, 1870–1914."

[5] George R. Taylor, *The Transportation Revolution, 1815–1860*, chap. 5.

[6] Jackman, *Transportation in Modern Britain*, pp. 473–74.

By 1830 steamboats were common on eastern and western rivers and in sheltered coastal waters.[7]

Inventors on both sides of the Atlantic had also explored the possibility of steam-powered land carriages long before the advent of railroads. Philadelphia inventor Oliver Evans (one of the most visionary geniuses of his or any other time) secured a Maryland patent for a steam-powered wagon in 1787. In 1816 he tried unsuccessfully to interest Congress in supporting the application of steam power to railways or road vehicles. Evans died in 1819, his hopes frustrated, but still convinced of the efficacy of steam-driven land conveyances. It took developments in Britain to convince his skeptical countrymen.[8]

The British inventor Richard Trevithick built a steam carriage which ran on London streets in 1803. The difficulty of running on rough pavements caused him to turn his attention to the development of a railway locomotive,[9] and in 1804 he put one to work on a tram road near Methyr Tydvil in Wales.[10] Similar experiments culminated in the birth of the first modern railroad on September 27, 1825, when the Stockton and Darlington opened for business.[11] The chief engineer of the Stockton and Darlington, George Stephenson, succeeded in putting together the railroad's components in a form that proved both mechanically practicable and economically viable.

Americans were quick to imitate Britain's success. Baltimore merchants chartered the Baltimore and Ohio in 1828, and it began service in 1830. A year later the South Carolina Railroad, designed to connect Charleston with the Savannah River, began operations. In 1830–31, Bostonians, frightened by the rising commercial dominance of New York and desirous of connecting textile mills directly with their port, chartered three railroads: one north to Lowell, one west to Worcester, one south to Providence. All three were functioning by 1835. These early American railroads bought some of their

---

[7] Taylor, *Transportation Revolution*, chap. 4.

[8] Eugene Ferguson, ed., *Early Engineering Reminiscences [1815–40] of George Escol Sellers*, p. 37; Taylor, *Transportation Revolution*, p. 76.

[9] Other inventors, however, carried on the experiment. In the 1820s a number of them rambled about the British countryside, rolling up hill and down dale trailing clouds of steam and curious bystanders. In 1829, Goldsworthy Gurney made a two-hundred-mile round trip in his steam carriage at an average speed of twelve miles an hour. By 1827 several steam-powered carriage lines were in operation in Britain. Their decline came not as a result of mechanical impracticability but because the landowners who controlled Parliament, fearing that steam carriages would destroy the roads and the tranquility of their estates, as well as frighten their horses, soon taxed them out of existence. See Jackman, *Transportation in Modern Britain*, pp. 328–35; C. Hamilton Ellis, *British Railway History*, 2: 45–48.

[10] Jackman, *Transportation in Modern Britain*, pp. 329–30.

[11] The terms "railroad" and "railway" are used here as defined by Michael Robbins, "The modern railway [is] a combination of four main features, namely: (a) specialized track; (b) accommodation of public traffic; (c) conveyance of passengers; and (d) mechanical traction" (*The Railway Age*, p. 3).

equipment (particularly locomotives) in Britain, but local craftsmen supplied much of it.

Sawmills produced cross-ties and lumber for freight and passenger cars; carriage makers built coaches; rolling mills produced strap iron and T rails; steam engine builders and machinists made locomotives; foundries cast wheels and other metal parts for rolling stock. For the majority of these firms, participation in the new market was only a brief excursion—for some, a profitable sideline dropped when local railroad construction ended; for most, an abortive venture that culminated in failure or bankruptcy. A few, however, survived to grow with the industry that supported them, and these survivors exhibited two common characteristics. First, they were versatile enough to manufacture a variety of products until the 1840s, when railroad demand became large enough to permit specialization. Second, they were able to adapt to a market which changed from a small, local, technologically simple one to a far-flung network of specialized, high-volume buyers who demanded adherence to increasingly complex technical specifications. In addition, American producers had to meet competition from British manufacturers. In such trying circumstances it is scarcely surprising that most competitors dropped out, or that those who survived the early years often remained dominant in the industry throughout the nineteenth century. Among the durable survivors were the Norris Locomotive Works and the Baldwin Locomotive Works, both of Philadelphia; the Rogers Locomotive and Machine Works of Paterson, New Jersey; and two Wilmington, Delaware, firms, Harlan and Hollingsworth (car builders) and the Lobdell Car Wheel Company.[12]

The Lobdell firm, founded in 1830, was one of the earliest competitors in the field. It began business as a small foundry producing castings of all kinds, but rose to be the world's largest manufacturer of railroad wheels by 1860. It had an annual capacity of 30,000 wheels, a capital investment of $200,000, and a gross income of $562,000. During its period of growth, the firm encountered all the obstacles inherent in its markets and surmounted them with a variety of production and sales strategies. The firm's records not only disclose these obstacles and strategies in detail but also demonstrate that they were typical of other successful producers in the field.[13]

The Lobdell Car Wheel Company began as a partnership between Jonathon Bonney and Charles Bush. This partnership, like so many other early American manufacturing ventures, was a union of technical skill and mer-

[12] This discussion of the railroad equipment industries centers on manufacturers of locomotives, cars, and wheels because they, together with the iron producers discussed earlier, supplied the bulk of equipment purchased by antebellum railroads.

[13] The Lobdell records provide a clear picture of conditions in the antebellum railroad supply industry because they contain correspondence with every major firm in the field. We have also used other germane manuscript collections, trade journals, and the handful of useful secondary sources. All of these confirm in detail the conclusions derived from the Lobdell material.

cantile capital. Jonathon Bonney was a founder and iron worker who learned his trade at the Mount Savage Iron Works near Frostburg, Maryland. He cast some experimental wheels for the Baltimore and Ohio Railroad in 1828 and was thus one of the first American craftsmen to become involved in the manufacture of railroad equipment.[14] In 1830 he moved to Wilmington and formed a partnership with Charles Bush.

Bonney chose his partner wisely, for Bush was a member of one of Wilmington's oldest and wealthiest mercantile families. His father owned a shipping line which operated a daily packet service between Wilmington and Philadelphia. He supplied the original capital for the partnership of Bonney and Bush,[15] and the Bush family's wealth played a crucial role in the subsequent development of the business.

All of the other railway manufacturers listed above either began with mercantile capital or subsequently obtained a transfusion of it in order to survive. In the former category were Rogers, Ketchum, and Grosvenor, the predecessor firm of Rogers Locomotive, and Betts, Pusey, and Harlan, the antecedent of Harlan and Hollingsworth. Rogers, Ketchum, and Grosvenor, which produced its first locomotive in 1837, combined the skills of the machinist Thomas Rogers with the wealth of the New York merchant-banker Morris Ketchum.[16] Samuel Pusey, a journeyman-machinist, and Samuel Harlan, a cabinetmaker, built their first cars in 1836. They benefited from the financial resources of the third partner, Mahlon Betts. Betts was a member of a wealthy Quaker family active in banking and insurance. Although he himself had been trained as a machinist, Betts devoted the greater part of his energies to a career as a capitalist. He was a director of the Bank of Wilmington and Brandywine and the Savings Bank of Wilmington, as well as of three railroads: the Wilmington and Susquehanna, the Delaware and Maryland, and the Philadelphia, Wilmington, and Baltimore.[17]

Norris and Baldwin belong to the category of firms rescued by the timely

---

[14] Lobdell Car Wheel Co., *Catalog and Price List, 1891* (Wilmington, Del.: Lobdell Car Wheel Co., 1891), p. 4. The Mount Savage Iron Works pioneered in making railroad equipment. It rolled rails in the 1830s, and T rails by 1844. It was also one of the first American furnaces to use ccal for fuel. See Peter Temin, *Iron and Steel in Nineteenth Century America*, p. 48; and Edward Hungerford, *The Story of the Baltimore and Ohio Railroad*, p. 72.

[15] *Historical and Biographical Encyclopedia of Delaware*, p. 385; *Biographical and Genealogical History of Delaware*, 2: 1151.

[16] Allen Johnson et al., eds., *Dictionary of American Biography*, 8: 112–13 (hereafter cited as *DAB*). Ketchum was an invaluable partner. Not only did his wealth spare the firm the financial vicissitudes that beset its chief competitors, Baldwin and Norris, but, in addition, Ketchum became a director of the Illinois Central Railroad in the 1850s and channeled the road's locomotive orders to Rogers (White, *American Locomotives*, p. 24).

[17] *Semi-Centennial Memoir of the Harlan and Hollingsworth Company*, pp. 125–39, 174–75; *Annual Report of the Philadelphia, Wilmington, and Baltimore Railroad*, 1840–66; *Wilmington City Directory*, 1845, p. 81; *Delaware Gazette*, December 9, 1834; Jack C. Potter, "The Philadelphia, Wilmington, and Baltimore Railroad, 1831–1840," pp. 73–171.

infusion of outside capital. William Norris began business in 1832 as the American Steam Carriage Company. By 1842 he was bankrupt and had to be rescued by his brother Richard, who came armed with a fortune made in the family's dry goods business.[18] Matthias Baldwin, a jeweler and instrument maker turned machinery builder, constructed his first locomotive in 1832. He avoided bankruptcy in 1837 because mercantile creditors such as Anson Phelps of New York and Hendricks and Brother of Philadelphia extended his notes for as much as six years. He also secured capital from a succession of partners, including the New Jersey industrialist and capitalist Stephen Vail (1839) and Asa Whitney of Philadelphia (1842).[19]

All of these firms enjoyed advantageous locations which provided access to skilled labor, commercial agencies, and transportation facilities. Paterson, the home of Rogers, Ketchum, and Grosvenor, was founded in 1791 by the Society for Useful Manufactures, which built a textile mill there to take advantage of the seventy-foot fall in the Passaic River. The town remained a center of textile and metal manufacture thereafter, creating a pool of skilled machinists trained in local factories. Paterson was close to New York mercantile centers. The Morris Canal connected it to Newark and New York Harbor in 1831; the Paterson and Hudson Railway (later part of the Erie) opened to Jersey City in 1832. Philadelphia, where the Norris and Baldwin works were located, offered the labor and commercial resources of one of the nation's oldest and largest cities, as well as transportation via the Delaware River and the network of canals that radiated from the Delaware River valley. Wilmington, however, offered the ideal combination of these assets. It eventually became the center of railroad car and car wheel manufacture in the United States, a development that began in 1830 with the foundry of Bonney and Bush.[20]

In 1830, Wilmington was a prosperous town of 8,000 inhabitants. The

[18] DAB, 7: 555–56.
[19] DAB, 1: 541–42. Malcolm C. Clark, "The Birth of an Enterprise," details Baldwin's financial struggles in his early years. Judge Stephen Vail was the owner of the Speedwell Iron Works in Morristown, N.J., the firm that supplied Baldwin with cranks and axles for his locomotives. The judge took no active part in the locomotive works; he turned his interest over to his sons George and Alfred. Alfred Vail is better known to history as the operator who received Samuel Morse's first message, "What hath God wrought!" in Baltimore on May 24, 1844. He had become Morse's partner in 1837, and he designed most of the telegraphic apparatus used in the first transmission. Alfred apparently was a man of acute perceptions, but little faith. He spotted the potential of Morse and Baldwin, but dropped out of both partnerships too soon and died broke. See DAB, 10: 136–37.

Asa Whitney had been superintendent of the Mohawk & Hudson Railroad and a New York State Canal commissioner before joining Baldwin's firm. A member of an old Massachusetts mercantile family, he was a careful business man who brought order to Baldwin's chaotic business methods (DAB, 10: 156–57). He left Baldwin in 1846 and opened a car wheel foundry which became Lobdell's chief competitor. He became president of the Philadelphia & Reading Railroad in 1860.

[20] Richard Edwards, ed., Industries of Delaware, p. 62.

proximity of the fall line of northern Delaware streams to the tidewater provided a combination of water power and shipping facilities which had made the Wilmington area the most important flour-milling center in the country by 1815. In 1830 the Brandywine flour mills, although no longer the country's largest, were still a major source of income. The du Pont powder mills, the paper mills of Joshua Gilpin, and the textile mills of the Bancroft family added to the economic vitality of the community.[21]

The development of the milling industry induced the establishment of foundries and machine shops. These in turn produced the castings and machinery required by the mills, and trained craftsmen in the skills necessary to manufacturing. In addition to mills and shops, Wilmington had other essential elements of commerce. It was located at the confluence of three navigable waterways: the Delaware River and the Brandywine and Christina creeks. It had wharves and warehouses serviced by regular shipping lines. Also, Wilmington lay astride the land route connecting Boston, New York, Philadelphia, and Baltimore with the South, and it maintained regular stage service, despite the atrocious condition of the roads.[22] Local banks had been in business since 1795. In 1810 the Farmers Bank established a company which insured the buildings and cargoes of local industries.

Blessed with these advantages, Wilmington businessmen viewed the future with an optimism which was reflected in the state legislature's sympathetic attitude toward commercial enterprise. Although there was no general incorporation law, by 1807 Delaware had recognized the principle of limited liability, and the state government granted corporate charters readily.[23] Legislators and businessmen shared an interest in the development of transportation networks. Before 1830 they had cooperated in supporting the construction of turnpikes that radiated from Wilmington, and of the Chesapeake and Delaware Canal, which permitted a shortened water route from Philadelphia to Wilmington and Baltimore. By 1830 the limitations of roads and canals had attracted the attention of Delaware businessmen to the railroads being promoted by the merchants of Boston, Philadelphia, Charleston, and Baltimore.[24] Support was growing for projected railroads to Philadelphia and Baltimore, and it was stimulated by articles in the *Delaware Gazette*, which

[21] Arthur E. Warner, *A Historic Sketch of Economic Developments in Wilmington, Delaware, and Environs*, p. 12; Henry S. Canby, *The Brandywine*, gives a literate, detailed description of the early years of Wilmington industries.

[22] Henry C. Conrad, *History of the State of Delaware*, 1: 342; Dudley C. Lunt, "The Farmers Bank."

[23] William B. Whitman, "Business and Government in Nineteenth Century Delaware," pp. 8, 53, 67.

[24] Ralph D. Gray, "The Early History of the Chesapeake and Delaware Canal," p. 76; *idem*, "Transportation and Brandywine Industries." Betts became a member of the Board of Directors of the Wilmington & Susquehanna in 1835. See *Delaware Gazette*, March 13, 1935; and Potter, "The Philadelphia, Wilmington, and Baltimore," pp. 71–72, 154.

printed glowing reports of railroad prospects. Wilmingtonians apparently were convinced. When 3,000 shares of Wilmington and Susquehanna stock went on sale on March 12, 1835, they were sold in twenty minutes. Among the lucky buyers were Jonathon Bonney and Mahlon Betts, who had been a member of the original committee formed to investigate the feasibility of construction.

Bonney and Bush thus began operation in an area supplied with many of the essential factors of production: plentiful land, pools of capital and skilled labor, advanced banking and insurance facilities, adequate transportation, and nearby raw materials. The principal limitation on manufacturing was the nature of the market. Unlike the flour and paper mills, which shipped their products to all the major ports of the United States and Europe, the foundries and machine shops of Wilmington were largely confined to the production of castings and machinery for local mills and farms. For ambitious producers there were two possible ways of increasing sales. They could develop new products for new markets, or they could widen their coverage of the market for existing products. Bonney and Bush did both. They developed a cast iron car wheel in order to obtain entry into the new railroad equipment field, and they tried to sell castings outside the Wilmington market.

In the 1830s few merchants specialized in railroad equipment, and the railroads themselves had no systematic purchasing policies. Therefore Bonney and Bush adopted tactics appropriate to the market and typical of other railroad equipment producers of the time. Both partners made sales trips up and down the coast to talk to car and locomotive builders, railroad officials, promoters, and contractors. They also arranged for hardware and iron brokers, such as A. and G. Ralston of Philadelphia, to sell their wheels on commission. To keep up with construction plans, Bonney and Bush subscribed to *American Railroad Journal*. When a new road was announced, the firm contacted the railroad's officers in person or by mail. Although the firm sold its wheels to many of the first railroads, including the Philadelphia and Columbia, New Castle and Frenchtown, and Wilmington and Susquehanna, the volume of business in the 1830s was insufficient to support specialization.[25]

Other railway suppliers also found specialization impractical in the 1830s. Norris tried to concentrate on locomotives and went bankrupt in 1842. Baldwin built 159 locomotives from 1832 to 1840, but the firm kept going only through credit extensions and by building stationary steam engines and other

[25] Inventory, Bush & Lobdell Old Firm, July 31, 1859, showed that the firm possessed bound volumes of the *American Railroad Journal*, 1832–58. The firm's correspondence reveals the travels of its partners and the names of its customers. See, for example, Bonney to Charles Bush, July 25, 1836; Charles Bush to Bonney, July 18, 1836; Ralston & Co. to Bonney & Bush, February 7, 1837; and the firm's lengthy correspondence with Miller & Alexander of Philadelphia and Jeffrey Smedley of Columbia, Pa.; Lobdell Car Wheel Co. Papers.

machinery. Rogers, Ketchum, and Grosvenor was originally founded in 1832 to manufacture textile machinery, and it continued to do so until the 1850s. It entered the railway supply business gradually in the 1830s, first making car wheels and other castings, then building locomotives.[26]

Like Norris, Betts, Pusey, and Harlan entered business intending to concentrate on railroad equipment exclusively. Betts, who was a prime mover in the Wilmington and Susquehanna, rightly anticipated a contract to build the road's cars. The partners planned meticulously. They traveled to Lowell, Massachusetts, in 1835 to inspect the car works there, but found it to be a made-over carriage factory and decided to build from scratch. Their new factory, which began production in 1836, was a two-story building. The car body was built on the upper floor and then was dropped through a hole onto the undercarriage, which was assembled on the ground floor. Despite these innovations, as well as considerable success in selling its cars (176 sold by 1839), the firm found railroad business alone inadequate to support it and turned to general machine building and repairs and iron ship building. The latter was a success. In 1844 the firm launched the first iron, propeller-driven sea-going steamship built in the United States. Between 1845 and 1857, Harlan and Hollingsworth built more tonnage of iron ships than all other American shipyards combined, and it continued to be a major shipbuilder and railway car manufacturer throughout the rest of the century.[27]

In order to supplement the market for car wheels, Bonney and Bush concentrated their efforts on expanding sales of castings. The principal obstacle was the diffuse market, for castings were made by innumerable foundries throughout the country, and the market in any given locale was relatively small. In milling and manufacturing centers like Wilmington, Philadelphia, and the New England river valleys, local iron processors supplied local needs. Outsiders like Bonney and Bush found these local producers difficult to supplant. Their proximity to consumers gave them a great advantage because transportation charges on small lots added appreciably to costs. This was particularly true if shipment involved overland cartage. Since most of the castings sold in the 1830s were generic goods such as simple parts for mills, or crude farm implements like rakes or straw cutters, it was difficult to capture distant markets through technological superiority. In the northern states,

---

[26] White, *American Locomotives*, pp. 20, 23, 24, 457; Clark, "Birth of an Enterprise," *passim*; *DAB*, 1: 541–42, 7: 555–56, and 8: 112–13.

[27] *Memoir of Harlan and Hollingsworth*, pp. 174–75, 181, 186–91, 206–8, 215; George A. Richardson, "History and Development of Passenger Car Building"; David B. Tyler, *The American Clyde*, pp. 1–25. Until railroad work and shipbuilding picked up, Harlan & Hollingsworth sought any kind of machine work. Submitting a bid on a boiler in 1838, they wrote, "One thing is certain that we will do any kind of work that we have tools and workmen to do, as cheap as it can be had in Philadelphia or anywhere in the vicinity" (Betts, Pusey & Harlan to E. I. du Pont de Nemours Co., May 11, 1838, Betts, Pusey & Harlan Papers).

where competitors were numerous, Bonney and Bush never succeeded in making large sales of castings except in the Wilmington area. In the southern states, where competitors were fewer, the partners devised sales and distribution methods that secured customers throughout the region.

Bush made frequent trips to the South in the 1830s to arrange for agents to sell castings and machinery. Cast farm tools such as rakes, straw cutters, plowshares, and the like, were, in effect, consumers' goods (that is, they were sold to a very large number of customers), and they were sold like other generic consumers' goods at the time. Southern commission merchants, such as Lamden and Bennett in Natchez, and Murphy and Brach in Mobile, accepted the goods on consignment, remitting payment when and if the goods were sold. From the commission houses the implements went to jobbers, and thence into the network of retail country stores which distributed them throughout the rural South. Bonney and Bush's castings thus followed the same route (often through the same commission houses) to southern consumers as did nails from Fall River Iron and wire from Washburn and Godard.

Bush also arranged for southern commission merchants to inform their customers that Bonney and Bush stood ready to build, on order, mill machinery ranging from replacement parts to complete steam-powered units.[28] When orders for mill installations were received, the firm manufactured the castings, but it generally subcontracted the machine work and engine building to shops such as Cartwright's in Philadelphia. If the unit was a complex one, Bush and a mechanic would accompany it south, supervise its assembly, and make sure it operated properly.[29]

In addition to agents in major cities, the firm was represented in the South in the 1830s and 1840s by Peter McIntyre of Claiborne, Alabama. McIntyre was a non-exclusive manufacturer's agent. He worked strictly on commission and traveled through the South for various northern factories. He made sales, supervised installations, and collected payments from customers. He also followed up inquiries received in Wilmington in response to advertisements run in the *United States Gazette*.[30]

The combination of advertising returns, dealers in major southern cities, and the travels of McIntyre and Bush enabled Bonney and Bush to operate successfully in the southern market. By shipping castings in large quantities and machinery in large units, the transportation cost per unit was kept low. Shipments were made by water as far as possible—either directly from Wil-

---

[28] Bonney & Bush to Lamden & Bennett, and Bonney & Bush to Murphy & Brach, 1830–40, Lobdell Car Wheel Papers.

[29] Bonney & Bush to Murphy & Brach, June 23, 1838, *ibid*.

[30] McIntyre's letters are scattered throughout the Lobdell records. For McIntyre's relationship to the firm, see George Abbott to Bonney & Bush, February 18, 1840, *ibid*.

mington or via transshipment at Philadelphia to ports such as Mobile, Charleston, and New Orleans.[31] Throughout the 1840s, and particularly prior to the Panic of 1837, sales of castings and machinery provided a majority of the firm's revenue. They accounted for all but a small fraction of sales in 1830, and still supplied two-thirds of the firm's income as late as 1840.[32]

Despite the partners' success in southern sales, conducting business over such distances involved many difficulties. Shipment by sailing vessel was slow and unreliable. Goods sometimes waited weeks for a ship going to the right port. In winter the Delaware River often froze, making shipment impossible. Once the goods were picked up, they were subject to further delays and damage by the weather. Sales of farm equipment were slow, and payment for the goods was slower yet.[33] Additional problems resulted from customers' dissatisfaction with mill installations. Steam-driven mills of the period were huge, clumsy, cantankerous machines.[34] They exhibited an annoying tendency to expire as soon as the mechanic had disappeared on the northbound boat. Breakdowns were difficult to repair in the South because mechanics were scarce and spare parts often took months in transit. The brunt of customers' anger fell upon the firm's dealers and the unhappy McIntyre. After one particularly vexatious series of breakdowns, he wrote that the machine was "a most raskely piece of work." He did not have "to sell such junk," he added, for he "could get good machines in Paterson or Providence."[35]

Problems of transportation and mechanical failures were irritating; these difficulties were further compounded by the demise of the Second Bank of the United States and the panic which followed. The collapse of the Bank was viewed with regret by Bonney and Bush, who, like most of their fellow

[31] Many northern manufacturers used similar methods to sell throughout the South. They succeeded so well in supplying southern requirements that the South developed few iron-processing facilities before the Civil War. In 1860, 17.5 million dollars' worth of "labor-saving machinery" was manufactured in the United States, but only a little more than a million dollars' worth of it originated in the South. See Census Office, *Eighth Census: Manufactures*, p. ccvii.

According to Robert C. Black, southern railroads depended almost entirely on northern foundries for basic castings throughout the antebellum period (*Railroads of the Confederacy*, p. 24). In 1859 there were 210 rolling mills in the United States; of these, 21 were in the South (Lesley, *Iron Manufacturer's Guide*, p. 747).

Shipping patterns and raw-material sources were reconstructed from insurance receipts, bills of lading, shipping receipts, railroad freight bills, and material invoices in the Lobdell Car Wheel Papers.

[32] This conclusion rests on an analysis of orders received and bills of lading for outbound shipments found in the Lobdell Car Wheel Papers.

[33] George Farcis to Bonney & Bush, October 23, 1840; and Lamden & Bennett to Bonney & Bush, July 12, 1841; *ibid.*

[34] The firm offered one customer a three-horse-power steam engine for $500. The boiler was four feet wide and twenty feet long. Bonney & Bush to Jesper Cardin, December 20, 1838, *ibid.*

[35] McIntyre to Bonney & Bush, March 16, 1840, *ibid.*

Wilmington businessmen, were staunch Whigs.[36] Their fears that evil consequences would follow were quickly confirmed. The transfer of funds from
southern customers, which hitherto had been made at little cost under the
Second Bank's system, became an expensive, makeshift affair. Collections
were made by McIntyre and other agents in drafts on local southern banks.[37]
After the removal of the stabilizing influence of the Second Bank, these
drafts and notes were often unsalable in Wilmington and had to be discounted through a Philadelphia note broker, George Abbott. Sometimes they
could not be disposed of at all; often the discount rate was so high as to
eliminate any profit from the sale. On at least one occasion, Bush, on Abbott's advice, instructed his New Orleans agent to purchase cotton with
Bonney and Bush funds. The cotton was shipped to Philadelphia and sold
by Abbott.[38]

Such financial difficulties added to the disadvantages of southern trade
and contributed to the gradual withdrawal of Bonney and Bush from the
machinery business as the market for car wheels grew. Trade with the South
nevertheless played a decisive role in the firm's early years. It financed an
expansion of facilities, established contacts with suppliers, customers, and
shipping agents which were valuable in the subsequent development of railroad business, and provided the funds for developing a satisfactory iron car
wheel.

Bonney had cast his first wheels for the Baltimore and Ohio in 1828.
Shortly after he moved to Wilmington, he contracted to build cars for the
New Castle and Frenchtown Railroad, which was under construction nearby.
The work ended in catastrophe; the wheels broke, derailing the train and
tearing up the track. The railroad bought the balance of its cars from
Richard Imlay in Baltimore. These cars were equipped with wheels made by
Ross Winans.[39] Despite the failure of his first efforts, Bonney realized the

[36] George Bush to Charles Bush, January 22, 1836; and John Pedrick to Charles
Bush, November 25, 1840; *ibid.* Matthias Baldwin shared these political sentiments.
He exhorted Judge Vail, "Stand for Harrison, if you don't you will be left all alone"
(Clark, "Birth of an Enterprise," p. 439).

[37] Seamans & Shackleford to Bonney & Bush, April 13, 1838; Bonney & Bush to
McIntyre, August 13, 1838; and George Abbott to Bush & Lobdell, February 18, 1840;
Lobdell Car Wheel Papers.

[38] Abbott to Bonney & Bush, March 7, 1838; and Seamans & Shackleford to Bonney & Bush, April 13, 1838; *ibid.* Similar problems beset Baldwin. After 1837 he
demanded payment in Philadelphia funds or in paper that traded at par in the East.
He often refused to make delivery until such payment was guaranteed. See Letterbooks, Baldwin Locomotive Works Papers; and Clark, "Birth of an Enterprise,"
pp. 431–32, 436–37.

[39] William D. Lewis Manuscript Diary, entry for July 27, 1831; and William F.
Holmes, "The New Castle and Frenchtown Turnpike and Railroad Company," pp. 101,
125. Ross Winans was a New Jersey horsebreeder turned designer-manufacturer. He
made a fortune building locomotives and cars for the Baltimore & Ohio, much of
which he later dissipated in support of low-rental housing, ecumenism, and the Confederate States of America. See *DAB*, 7: 555–56.

potential growth of railroads[40] and determined to develop a wheel that would hold up under increasingly heavy railroad equipment.[41] By the time the firm decided to withdraw from the southern market for machinery, Bonney had solved the technological problems of casting durable wheels. A patent for his method was secured in March, 1838,[42] and thereafter the firm increasingly specialized in the manufacture and sale of wheels.

Bonney was aided in his development of a wheel cast in one piece by his young, orphaned nephew, George Lobdell, who had come to Wilmington in 1832 as an apprentice to his uncle. Lobdell must have been a singularly attentive student, for at the age of eighteen he was competent to take charge of the shop during his uncle's absences.[43] In 1838 Bonney died (of diarrhea brought on by worry over non-payment by southern customers, if Bush is to be believed[44]), and Lobdell, at the age of twenty-one, purchased his uncle's interest in the business with funds borrowed from the Bush family.[45] The name of the firm was changed to Bush and Lobdell, but henceforth Lobdell dominated its affairs.

THE IMPACT OF RECESSION, 1837–1842

The recession of 1837–42 brought on the credit stringencies previously mentioned and was, as well, a period of severely reduced demand for manufactured products. Railroad construction and expansion declined, and mill and factory owners postponed the replacement of old machinery or the installation of new. Firms supplying equipment to railroads were perhaps more fortunate than most, for, although their general machinery business declined, continuing railroad maintenance provided some sales. In addition, railroad construction revived before the rest of the economy. In order to survive the

---

[40] Bonney served on the committee appointed in 1834 to secure financial support for the proposed Wilmington & Susquehanna. *Delaware Gazette*, December 19, 1834.

[41] The first railroad coaches were stagecoach bodies on flanged wheels. The wheels themselves resembled carriage wheels. They had wooden spokes and metal rims and flanges. This arrangement soon proved unsatisfactory because it would not support the weight of the car and passengers. Even the earliest coaches were larger than stagecoaches. For example, the carriages Imlay built for the New Castle & Frenchtown in 1832 carried fifty passengers inside and out. By the late 1830s, progressive American railroads had begun to employ the prototypes of the eight-wheel, center-aisle coaches that are still in use. Heavier coaches required stronger wheels; therefore, all-metal wheels soon replaced the part-wood variety. See John M. Clayton, "Railroad Building in Delaware," p. 6; and August Mencken, *The Railroad Passenger Car*, chap. 1. The Baltimore & Ohio transportation museum in Baltimore contains a variety of cars, locomotives, wheels, and other equipment which graphically illustrate the growing complexity of railroad technology before the Civil War.

[42] Association of Manufacturers of Chilled Car Wheels, *Historical Sketch of the Lobdell Car Wheel Company*, p. 1.

[43] *Ibid.*

[44] Charles Bush to McIntyre, August 13, 1838, Lobdell Car Wheel Papers.

[45] Notes, William Bush for George G. Lobdell, 1838, *ibid.*

period of stringency, railroad equipment firms had to find capital with which to tide themselves over. In a later period, such firms received assistance from specialized commission merchants who sold their products. Before 1837, however, few such alliances had been formed between producers and distributors. The strategies that George Lobdell employed to survive the recession are illustrative of those adopted by other firms in the industry.

Lobdell's first problem was keeping the firm afloat during the difficulties caused by the depression's effect on southern business. In addition, there was a general collapse of local commerce as mills shut down and repairs and improvements were postponed.[46] Sales to railroads continued, but most railroads paid their bills with sixty- or ninety-day notes, which became impossible to discount at reasonable rates. Payments to suppliers could be deferred until the railroad notes matured and were collected, but continued operation required a steady flow of cash to meet payrolls, which ran as high as $1,000 a month in 1838.[47]

A majority of the firm's correspondence for 1837–39 concerned financial problems and their solutions.[48] The firm survived by floating a $2,000 loan from the Bush family, by obtaining a $4,500 government contract to build an iron fence around Frankford Arsenal in Philadelphia, by laying off half its employees, and by getting credit extensions from its suppliers.[49] It also obtained a contract to do all wheel and axle work for the newly formed Philadelphia, Wilmington, and Baltimore Railroad.[50] The new road paid its bills monthly and in cash. This steady income helped Bush and Lobdell recover well before the general return to prosperity which came in the Northeast in 1843. By early 1840 the firm was able to take up many of the notes that it had previously renewed. In March the loan from the Bush family was repaid, and the firm's first severe financial crisis ended.

CONCLUSION

For Lobdell, Baldwin, Norris, Rogers, Harlan and Hollingsworth, and other railway suppliers who managed to survive the depression years, the

46 John P. Crozier to Bonney & Bush, July 8, 1837; and J. Johnston to Bush & Lobdell, June 16, 1838; *ibid.*

47 Bush & Lobdell to McIntyre, March 9, 1838, *ibid.*

48 The same pattern appeared in the Baldwin correspondence; see Clark, "Birth of an Enterprise," p. 439.

49 Frankford Arsenal to Bonney & Bush, 1837–38; Promissory Note from Bush & Lobdell to David Bush, dated October 10, 1837, paid March 1, 1840; Bush & Lobdell to McIntyre, March 9, 1838; *ibid.*

50 The Philadelphia, Wilmington & Baltimore was a staunch proponent of the policy, much debated among early railroad leaders, of turning maintenance work over to outside contractors. The road did so regularly before the Civil War. See Cochran, *Railroad Leaders*, pp. 83, 115–16; and *Annual Report of the Philadelphia, Wilmington, and Baltimore Railroad*, 1840–66.

period 1830–42 was a crucial one. During those years the level of demand was too low to permit specialization, and the manufacture of railroad equipment was, in effect, a branch of the general machinery industry. Railroad demand was, however, sufficient to permit producers to perfect products good enough to compete with imports from Britain. Suppliers also began to develop sales techniques that were perfected in the years after the depression. Only a few survived the years of reduced demand, and they became the nucleus of the highly specialized, concentrated industry that developed between 1842 and 1860.

CHAPTER VI

The Future Foreshadowed: The Railway Supply Industry, 1842–1860

The years of financial stringency following the Panic of 1837 eliminated many railway supply firms. The producers that survived entered a period of relative prosperity unbroken after 1842 until the recession of 1857. In the 1840s 21,000 more miles of rails were added.[1] The combination of new construction, expansion of existing facilities, and the need for replacement parts and equipment created a high-volume market. As a result of this market, the 1840s and 1850s brought specialization to the railway supply industry. Manufacturers dropped or curtailed other lines to concentrate on railway materials, railroads developed systematic purchasing methods, and the number of specialized commission merchants multiplied.

During this period the quantities of materials required by the largest railroads became great enough to present American manufacturers with their first concentrated market. As a result of this market and the systematic purchasing techniques adopted by some railroads, direct marketing became a significant method of distribution for the first time. These new methods coexisted with indirect distribution channels controlled by the specialized commission merchants who handled those goods not sold directly. Successful manufacturers employed both direct and indirect channels to dispose of their expanding production.

[1] Alfred D. Chandler, Jr., ed., *The Railroads*, p. 13.

96

The Rise of Specialization, 1842–1857

Matthias Baldwin, who built only 159 locomotives between 1832 and 1840, built 850 in the next twenty years, concentrating almost exclusively on their development and manufacture. Thomas Rogers curtailed his manufacture of textile machinery and built 950 locomotives between 1840 and 1860. Richard Norris and his son succeeded where William Norris had failed, producing 900 units from 1842 through 1860.[2] Harlan and Hollingsworth, while continuing their shipyard, built a new plant in 1841 especially designed for the manufacture of railroad cars.[3] After 1840, Bush and Lobdell's production of castings and machinery steadily declined as the firm concentrated on car wheels and expanded its capacity from 40 wheels per day in 1840 to 200 per day in 1860.

In converting his firm to specialized, high-volume production, George Lobdell had to discharge complex responsibilities, for Charles Bush, despite some training as a machinist, "was not a practical man."[4] As practical head of the firm, Lobdell purchased materials, supervised production, set wage rates, hired and fired employees, developed work rules for the shop, arranged for loans and credit, calculated costs, and decided prices. He handled all technical correspondence and research,[5] developed the methods by which the wheels were advertised and sold in a changing market, and selected and purchased all raw materials.[6] The most important raw material was iron, and the firm's location at the center of the pre-Civil War iron industry made it possible to purchase from an assortment of furnaces,[7] playing one off against the other to obtain the lowest prices.

[2] John H. White, Jr., *American Locomotives*, p. 20.

[3] George A. Richardson, "History and Development of Railway Passenger Car Building," p. 1136; *Semi-Centennial Memoir of the Harlan and Hollingsworth Company*, pp. 176–81.

[4] Association of Manufacturers of Chilled Car Wheels, *Historical Sketch of the Lobdell Car Wheel Company*, p. 1.

[5] Lobdell personally supervised the mixture of pig irons that went into the furnaces, prescribed the casting techniques, and inspected the finished product. His practice, he declared, was always "to break up any wheel about which there is the least doubt; to break up hundreds rather than run the risk of sending one bad wheel away" (quoted in *ibid.*, p. 3).

[6] At this time metallurgy was an inexact science. The master founder had to depend on his personal knowledge of irons to make selections. By 1840 Lobdell had concluded that charcoal iron from cold-blast furnaces made the least frangible wheels. The firm used this type of iron well into the twentieth century. Charcoal iron was in general use in car wheels as late as the 1880s.

In cold-blast furnaces the air flowed through the mixture of ore and charcoal without preheating. Cold-blast iron cost more than hot-blast because it required more fuel in smelting.

[7] J. P. Lesley, *The Iron Manufacturer's Guide*, p. 751.

In the 1830s iron was usually purchased in small lots (thirty tons or less) directly from furnaces on the Susquehanna River and was shipped to Wilmington the cheapest way. In the 1830s and 1840s this meant it came by ship via the Chesapeake and Delaware Canal to the Lobdell wharf on Christina Creek, even though rail transportation was available after 1838. By the mid-1850s rail shipment had become cheaper from furnaces like the Whitaker Iron Works at Principio because these firms were on the rail line rather than on a waterway. Such cases remained the exception, however, until the Civil War.

Although the methods by which iron moved from furnace to foundry changed little in the period 1830–60, the manner in which it was bought changed radically. After 1840, Lobdell bought increasingly from iron commission merchants in Philadelphia and Baltimore. Among his most important suppliers were the familiar brokers Cabeen, Pratt, Stickney, and Gittings. By 1860 these brokers were furnishing the entire supply. There were two basic reasons for the shift. First, the expansion of productive capacity from forty wheels per day in 1840 to five times as many in 1860 resulted in a corresponding increase in the quantity of pig iron required. Consumption of pig iron sometimes reached forty tons per day in the 1850s. No single charcoal furnace could undertake to furnish such quantities, but the commission merchants, who gathered the output of furnaces in five states, could be counted on to provide steady supplies.

The other reason Lobdell turned to brokers for iron supplies was financial. He needed long-term credit, and the furnace owners, who had cash payroll problems of their own, could seldom extend adequate terms. The iron commission merchants provided the necessary credit, allowing Lobdell six months to pay, and often extended the time period if asked. This method of purchasing facilitated production increases, but it also increased interest costs and thus reduced Lobdell's ability to bargain effectively with his suppliers.

Specializing in a single basic product permitted Lobdell to carry on numerous experiments. From this research there emerged a wide variety of wheels which embodied a series of technical improvements. The firm created an extensive line of railroad wheels that met the requirements of rapidly multiplying types of rolling stock. Lobdell also produced a complete line of wheels for the horse cars that began to appear in eastern cities in the 1840s, as well as wheels for mine, quarry, and factory cars. His methods reflected a determination always to offer equipment as good as any competitor's. He patented improved versions of the original double-plate wheel of 1838.[8] When competitors like Asa Whitney of Philadelphia developed products Lobdell considered equal to his own, he traded patents with them. When

8 Lobdell Car Wheel Co., *Catalog and Price List, 1891* (Wilmington, Del.: Lobdell Car Wheel Co., 1891), pp. 3–12.

other foundries developed hammered and rolled axles that were better than his, he stopped making axles and bought theirs.[9]

These strategies of specialization and development enabled Lobdell to keep pace with the rapidly changing technology of the railway supply industry. All manufacturers who serviced this market had to do the same in order to remain competitive. The railroads' demands for more powerful locomotives, larger and more comfortable cars, and more durable rails—all manufactured to increasingly rigid specifications—gradually shifted most railroad equipment from the category of generic goods to that of specific goods. Producing firms had to adjust to this development, and those which did so most successfully maintained leadership in their fields. Baldwin, Norris, and Rogers developed a series of faster, more efficient locomotives; Harlan and Hollingsworth maintained the innovative spirit that had characterized their entry into the field by producing freight and passenger cars to fit the manifold requirements of their customers.

In addition to this continuing product development, manufacturers had to adjust their sales and promotion methods to the new technological competition that accompanied the appearance of a market for specific goods. Lobdell, for example, promised to supply wheels that would outwear his competitors', and to deliver them at prices as low as, or lower than, any competitive wheel of similar quality.[10] Although he guaranteed his wheels for various lengths of time (using this as a bargaining point in negotiations), it was his general policy to replace any wheel that broke, regardless of its age, provided the broken wheel was returned.[11]

Sure of his wheels' strength, Lobdell agreed to submit them to comparative tests against his competitors'. Under the aegis of the general superintendent of the Boston and Worcester Railroad, a grand smash-off was held in March, 1843, at the road's Boston yard. Before several New England railroad executives, and two of Lobdell's principal competitors, Lyman Kinsley of Boston and Ross Winans of Baltimore, the wheels were tested by dropping a car axle on them from various heights. All wheels but Lobdell's broke. Word of the test spread quickly—with gratifying effects on sales.[12]

[9] Such patent trades between manufacturers were common before the Civil War. They enabled producers to offer a wider line of products. Patent holders received a royalty on each unit sold. See the letters between Lobdell and Asa Whitney, Lyman Kinsley, Ebenezer Lester, L. B. Tyng, and Trego and Co., 1840–65, in Lobdell Car Wheel Co. Papers.

[10] Charles Hewitt of Trenton Iron Works invented a wheel similar to Lobdell's in 1855, but Trenton Iron could not produce it at a competitive price; see Allan Nevins, *Abram S. Hewitt*, p. 119.

[11] Bush & Lobdell to Erie Railroad, August 28, 1840; Bush & Lobdell to Philadelphia, Wilmington & Baltimore Railroad, February 8, 1842; and Bush & Lobdell to Murphy & Allison, September 11, 1860; Lobdell Car Wheel Papers. Lobdell recorded the types of iron that went into various lots of wheels; examining broken wheels was an integral part of his research and development methods.

[12] Bush & Lobdell, *Catalog, 1851*, pp. 6–7; T. Lapham to Bush & Lobdell, February 19, 1843, Lobdell Car Wheel Papers.

A catalog issued in 1851 summarized the results of the Worcester trial and included testimonials from satisfied customers. Norris declared Lobdell's "the very best wheels which are manufactured" and added that his European customers thought the wheels superior to any made in Britain or on the Continent. Comments from other railroad officials included such remarks as "safer and more durable than any other wheel," and "I have never known one to break."[13] Lobdell's products received further signficant endorsement in the 1850s. When Henry Varnum Poor revived the technical columns of the *American Railroad Journal* in the early fifties, one article praised the economy and durability of Lobdell products. Subsequent articles reported that some Lobdell wheels had run for more than fifteen years without a failure. Similar comments appeared in the *Railroad Record* and other trade journals.[14] The products' reputation remained an essential ingredient of the firm's merchandising methods, although the methods themselves changed as more sophisticated purchasing systems evolved. In the 1840s and 1850s wheels continued to be sold to railroads and to car and locomotive builders. Each case involved direct and indirect sales methods.

Railroad sales fell into two categories. The first category was sales made to railroads under construction. In the 1830s such roads often bought directly from suppliers, a satisfactory method when the total quantities required were small. In subsequent decades, however, new railroads increasingly bought through specialized commission merchants. They did so for mercantile and financial reasons. Several factors made the commission merchants' mercantile services valuable. First, they were the principal source for British railway equipment. Second, as railroads expanded into areas where no local manufacturers capable of supplying equipment existed, commission merchants were able to arrange for the necessary supplies. Third, as railroads expanded they often required quantities of material which exceeded the capacity of individual manufacturers. Railroad commission merchants, like the specialized iron brokers, pooled the outputs of many producers to assure adequate supplies. Fourth, railroads required such large quantities of such a wide variety of materials that attempts at direct purchasing involved promoters and contractors in time-consuming negotiations with a large number of prospective suppliers. Turning this burden over to a single broker enabled officers and contractors of new roads to concentrate on raising capital, buying land, and building the railroads.

---

[13] Bush & Lobdell, *Catalog, 1851*, pp. 9–14. Norris sold locomotives in England in the 1840s; see William Norris to Bush & Lobdell, January 14, 1840, Lobdell Car Wheel Papers.

[14] Alfred D. Chandler, Jr., *Henry Varnum Poor*, pp. 42–43. The technical editor from 1851 to 1854 was Zerah Colburn, author of many technical treatises on railroad equipment. See White, *American Locomotives*, p. 451; *American Railroad Journal* 26 (1853):566–67, 620; *ibid.* 32 (1859):842; and *Railroad Record* 9 (1861):79.

Commission merchants also performed valuable financial functions for the new railroads and their suppliers. Before the Panic of 1837, many new railroads were well financed and were able to pay cash for their equipment. During and after the recession, funds were tighter, and railroads often sought long credit terms. Commission merchants, for the reasons discussed in the previous chapter, were better able to offer the necessary credit than were manufacturers. Railroads also wanted to make partial payment with their stock and bonds. Producers were extremely reluctant to accept securities. For one thing, many of them had sustained losses in the early years of railroad construction. For instance, Harlan and Hollingsworth accepted stock in the Annapolis and Elk Ridge Railroad in partial payment for some cars delivered in 1838. The railroad soon collapsed, and the car builders received only "some curious and antiquated specimens of the wagoner's art" in payment.[15] Bad news like this traveled fast among railroad suppliers, most of whom knew each other personally and corresponded regularly.

The principal objection manufacturers had to accepting stock or bonds in payment was, of course, the fact that they were not cash, and could be converted only at a discount. Altogether, such securities represented a heavy risk, and, as often as possible, manufacturers resisted the pressure to accept them. When forced to take them, as all manufacturers eventually were, they tried to minimize the risk by insisting on overpayment—for example, $1.50 in stock or bonds for each $1.00 in material delivered.

Commission merchants were better equipped to accept large quantities of railroad securities. They had superior knowledge of the roads' finances because of their access to a constant flow of credit information. They were, therefore, better able to judge which securities were sound and which were not. They were also often willing to invest their surplus capital in railroad shares and did so by taking securities in payment for material, using their cash or credit to pay suppliers. Through this process many commission merchants became important railroad stockholders. The combination of mercantile and financial leverage made specialized commission merchants a major factor in the distribution of railway equipment from the 1830s until the 1870s.

Commission firms that appeared in the first decade of American railroad construction, such as T. and E. George and A. and G. Ralston of Philadelphia, handled British rails and equipment exclusively. Ralston advertised that it kept on hand a supply of rails, boiler iron, car and locomotive wheels, and stood ready to import "at the shortest notice . . . every description of railroad iron [rails] and locomotive engines . . . under the direction of one of our partners who resides in England for this purpose." The firm also retained the services of "Mr. Solomon W. Roberts, a highly respectable American engi-

[15] *Memoir of Harlan and Hollingsworth*, p. 176.

neer, [who] resides in England for the purpose of inspecting all Locomotives, Machinery, Railway Iron, &c. ordered by us."[16]

In the 1840s, geographic expansion of the railway network, increasing
demands for material, and the rise of domestic producers induced a proliferation of specialized brokers who handled both domestic and imported
products. Ralston added Pennsylvania boiler iron and rails to its stock in
trade. Reeves, Buck, and Company of Philadelphia was agent for the Reeves-
controlled Phoenix rail mill. Cooper and Hewitt of New York sold the
products of its firm, Trenton Iron. Both these agencies also handled the output of other American and British firms. Other brokers, such as Manning
and Lee of Baltimore, Williams and Page, Thomas Lapham, and George
Gardner of Boston, and A. Wyatt and D. and H. Riker of Charleston, operated independently, pooling the outputs of various manufacturers in order
to fill volume orders.[17]

During the 1840s and 1850s these commission merchants also rationalized
purchasing for new railroads by making it possible for them to deal with one
supplier rather than become embrangled with a number of manufacturers.
When a new railroad compiled a list of the materials it required, it called
for competitive bids on the whole lot. Since the contract called for an assortment of rails, cars, locomotives, and miscellaneous equipment, and usually
required the supplier to take part-payment in securities, no one manufacturer
was in a position to bid on it. The contract went to the commission merchant
who agreed to supply all the needed material at the lowest price. He then
went into the market and assembled the order from various manufacturers
who bid against one another to obtain a share of it.

When the contract was completed, the broker collected from the railroad
and pocketed the difference in price. He received a commission from the
road on the total value of the contract, and sometimes from manufacturers as
well. In addition to commissions and profits, middlemen could gain in other
ways. If they advanced working capital to manufacturers, they charged interest on the loan and deducted it before making payment. They also had a
chance to profit from railroad securities through bond interest, stock dividends, and appreciated values if the shares rose in the market. The risks, of
course, were equally great, but an astute merchant could parlay his capital,
expertise, and the advantages of his position into wealth and power in the
industry.

One of the most successful railroad commission merchants was Morris
Ketchum Jesup of New York, and his career is illustrative of such merchants
generally. Jesup, who was born in 1832, was named after his godfather

[16] See A. and G. Ralston advertising circulars in Miscellaneous Papers of Philadelphia Merchants, 1774–1890.
[17] See advertisements by commission merchants in *American Railroad Journal*,
1835–1860.

Morris Ketchum, the New York banker who was a partner in the Rogers Locomotive Works. Ketchum apparently took his duties as godfather seriously, for he played a significant role in Jesup's career. In 1842, Jesup went to work in the Rogers Locomotive's New York office. In subsequent years he learned both the mercantile and financial sides of the railway supply business. In 1852 he opened a railway commission house in partnership with Charles Clark, a clerk in Ketchum's bank. The firm's capital came from a $2,000 bank credit arranged by Joseph Grosvenor, Ketchum's banking partner.[18]

The railroad commission house of Clark and Jesup was an almost instantaneous success. One of its first contracts was with the Illinois Central Railroad (Ketchum was a director of the road). The contract specified that Clark and Jesup was to "receive all orders sent to the Eastern Market [in effect this meant all orders] . . . purchase for the account of your road and see goods are shipped and insured. We get two and one half percent commission." The firm also got an additional commission of fifteen cents per ton on all rails purchased, regardless of price.[19]

Jesup dealt in imported as well as domestic equipment, and Clark's place in the firm was taken in 1859 by John S. Kennedy, an agent for British boiler-tube manufacturers. In order to cover a wider area more effectively, Kennedy opened an office in Chicago (later headed by John Crerar). Jesup developed close ties with all the leading railroad equipment producers in the United States, which enabled him to fill large orders promptly. His sales abilities opened large and distant markets for producers. For example, he sold 5,000 wheels to the Illinois Central Railroad alone in 1855–56. He also performed financial services by making cash advances on orders and by absorbing railroad securities. In the process, he and his partners became stock or bond holders in many U.S. railroads, including the Chicago and Alton, the Toledo, Peoria, and Western, the Cleveland and Marietta, and a number of others.[20]

All three partners, Jesup, Kennedy, and Crerar, subsequently had careers which demonstrated the potential power inherent in railroad commission work. After the Civil War, they stopped dealing in merchandise and became investment bankers specializing in railroad securities. Jesup became a director of the Southern Railroad Securities Company, which controlled the Southern, the Atlantic Coast Line, and others. Congress appointed J. S. Kennedy one of the directors of the Union Pacific. He was also a director of the Chicago, Burlington, and Quincy; the Pittsburgh, Fort Wayne, and Chicago; and the New York, Chicago, and Saint Louis. He joined the syndicate that built the Canadian Pacific, and he was James J. Hill's closest associate and a cofounder

[18] William A. Brown, *Morris Ketchum Jesup*, pp. 8–34.
[19] Clark & Jesup to W. K. Ackerman, May 17, 1856, in Contracts, 1851–82, Illinois Central Railroad Papers.
[20] Contracts, 1851–82, *ibid.*; Brown, *Jesup*, pp. 34–37.

of Northern Securities. John Crerar, one of George Pullman's principal backers, was an incorporator and a director of the Pullman Company, as well as a director of Illinois Trust and Savings Bank.

The long-run success of Jesup and his partners resulted from their ability to shift, through specialization of their financial functions, from commission work to investment banking in the post–Civil War period. The foundation for their later careers was laid long before, however, when the Jesup firm managed to secure many large contracts to supply equipment to railroads under construction. It was in this first category of sales to railroads that commission merchants played their most prominent role.

The second category of sales to railroads was equipment sold to operating railroads, which bought new equipment to replace old, or to expand track mileage and add to the stock of cars and engines. Inefficiently managed or unprosperous railroads often had to make such purchases through commission merchants in order to obtain the necessary credit terms.

In the 1840s and 1850s, however, prosperous and progressively managed railroads began to purchase an increasing amount of material directly from manufacturers. They did so for two principal reasons. First, progressive railroads were becoming more cost conscious; innovators like Daniel McCallum of the Erie, and Albert Fink of the Louisville and Nashville, pioneered in developing accounting procedures and management structures designed to analyze and minimize costs.[21] One obvious cost to be eliminated was the middleman's fees. Second, railroad technology ramified very quickly, and mechanical officers often had to consult with manufacturers and designers in order to obtain the kind of equipment they required for their roads.

Successful railroads were able to eliminate the commission merchant because they found ways to dispense with his mercantile and financial services. The total number of prosperous railroads and large-volume equipment producers was small enough for both parties readily to locate each other. By the 1850s American producers were able to supply most domestic requirements (except for rails), so railroads had no further need to deal with importing merchants. The problem of conducting negotiations with many manufacturers was surmounted by assigning purchasing duties to members of the railroad's staff. In the 1840s the officers of mechanical departments dealt with their respective suppliers: superintendents of track bought rails; motive-power superintendents purchased locomotives; master mechanics ordered cars and wheels.[22]

---

[21] Thomas C. Cochran, *Railroad Leaders, 1845–1890*, p. 407; Chandler, *Railroads*, pt. 3.

[22] Direct negotiations between manufacturers and railroads in the 1840s and 1850s make up much of the material in the following collections: Lobdell Car Wheel Papers; Steel File, Steel Rail File, Steel Papers, and Contracts, 1850–76, Chicago, Burlington, and Quincy Railroad Papers; Contracts, 1851–82, Illinois Central Papers; and Baldwin Locomotive Works Papers. See also W. H. Wilson to Phoenix Iron, and

In the 1850s this system was further modified by having mechanical officers draw up standard technical specifications for the equipment that their departments ordered and maintained. These specifications were assembled into a manual for purchasing agents, who were assigned the full-time job of obtaining equipment and parts. By relieving department heads of the job of negotiating with manufacturers, and by providing a steady flow of material bought at the lowest possible price, purchasing agents absorbed the commission merchants' mercantile function into the bureaucratic management structure of the railroads.[23]

Progressive railroads also dispensed with the financial services of middlemen. They paid cash on delivery, settled their accounts monthly, or gave their own notes in payment. Since the notes of solvent railroads discounted readily after 1842, manufacturers would almost always accept them. The total number of American railroads that developed direct buying through purchasing agents before the Civil War was relatively small, but these included many of the largest, such as the Pennsylvania, the Louisville and Nashville, the Erie, and the Baltimore and Ohio. The orders from these roads constituted a significant proportion of the total market. For example, Bush and Lobdell sold thousands of wheels to the purchasing agents of the Erie and the Baltimore and Ohio in the 1850s.

Sales of wheels to car and locomotive builders, like sales to railroads, depended on a combination of indirect and direct sales methods. Wheels were usually sold through commission merchants, as were most other producers' goods of the time.[24] The principal reason for this reliance on intermediaries was financial. Manufacturers did not have the capital resources of the prosperous railroads; therefore, usually either the wheelmaker, the rolling-stock manufacturer, or both, needed financial assistance in order to complete the transaction. Many apparently direct sales to manufacturers actually were the result of a commission merchant's intercession. Purchasers of cars and locomotives reserved the right to specify the brand of wheels used. As a result Lobdell sold many wheels to Baldwin in the 1850s because Lobdell agreed to pay Morris Jesup a commission on any wheels sold directly to a manufacturer through Jesup's efforts. Jesup sold many locomotives for

---

George A. Kettel to Phoenix Iron, both dated April 6, 1861, Phoenix Iron Co. Papers; numerous entries in Letterbooks, Stone & Harris Papers; and Abbott & Cartwright to Enoch Laws, General Superintendent, Pennsylvania Railroad, October 7, 1861, Andrew Carnegie Papers, 1: 127.

[23] These worthies were sometimes dishonest; occasionally "arrangements" could be made with them to give preference to one firm's products regardless of price. Most of them, however, appear to have functioned as they were supposed to, driving hard bargains and demanding the lowest prices and quick deliveries. See Colby to Bush & Lobdell, December 2, 1860, Lobdell Car Wheel Papers.

[24] Gibbons & Huston, for example, sold boiler iron to Baldwin, Norris, and Rogers through commission merchants. Railroad boiler shops usually bought directly. See O. N. Lull to Charles Huston, August 19, 1857, Lukens Steel Co. Papers.

Baldwin, and reminded him to "remember our friend [Lobdell] when ordering wheels."[25] Lobdell also made many sales to Rogers Locomotive Works after Jesup became vice-president of that firm in 1856.[26]

Successful operation in the railroad supply market in the 1840s and 1850s thus required close contacts with railroad purchasing agents, rolling-stock manufacturers, and specialized commission merchants. At first, Bush and Lobdell accomplished this by making periodic sales trips around the country. As the number of prospective customers multiplied, however, it became impossible for the partners to make all calls personally. The ubiquitous Peter McIntyre was often detailed to call on southern clients. After 1840 the firm continuously employed one, and often two or three, full-time salesmen to call on the users of its products and the railroad commission merchants.[27]

Developments in the 1850s brought further modifications in sales techniques. Expanding production forced Lobdell to spend more time in the shop, and he gradually limited his sales calls to the firm's most important customers (for instance, Jesup). The firm ordered its salesmen to use passenger trains whenever possible to widen their territories and used the telegraph extensively to give salesmen instructions, bargain over prices, and arrange for shipments. It also advertised in *Railroad Record, American Railroad Journal, Hillyer's American Railroad Magazine, The American Railway Times, Railway Directory,* and *U.S. Advertising Atlas*.[28] So successful was this assortment of sales methods that a list of the firm's customers would serve as a tolerably complete index to antebellum railroads, commission merchants, and rolling-stock producers. The combination of specialized manufacture, a quality product that met technical requirements, and aggressive merchandising techniques brought an increasing volume of business to Bush and Lobdell and necessitated an augmentation of capacity.

The original foundry built in 1830 could cast 10 wheels per day. By 1844 the firm had outgrown the original building, and it built a new foundry capable of casting 150 wheels daily. By 1860 this output had risen to 200 wheels and 30 locomotive tires,[29] and the sale of wheels in lots of thousands

---

[25] Jesup to Baldwin, May 18, 1859, Baldwin Papers.

[26] When Thomas Rogers died in 1856, the firm was reorganized as a close corporation. J. S. Rogers, the founder's son, became president. Jesup's participation in the company assured the perpetuation of its enviable record of support by mercantile capital.

[27] Bush & Lobdell to McIntyre, 1840–45, Lobdell Car Wheel Papers. There are many letters to and from salesmen in this collection. Some of them received straight salaries; others received salaries plus a commission. In 1860 G. W. Colby got $40 a month plus $.50 per wheel; A. B. Day received a salary of $1,500 per year.

[28] This list of magazines was compiled from advertisements found in journals in the Bureau of Railway Economics Library, Washington, D.C., and from receipts for advertising bills found in Lobdell Car Wheel Papers.

[29] Lobdell Car Wheel Co., *Catalog, 1891*, pp. 11–12. In 1867 the firm's capacity rose to 250 wheels per day.

to the Erie and the Baltimore and Ohio often taxed even this capacity. In addition, the nature of competition changed as products became standardized in price and quality. Orders often went to the firm which could deliver the widest range of products in the shortest time. These demands necessitated inventories that were large for the times. An 1859 accounting showed that Bush and Lobdell had on hand 2,000 tons of pig and scrap iron valued at $75,000, and 3,700 wheels worth $54,000. In 1860 the firm used 10,000 tons of pig iron (approximately 1¼ per cent of the total national output) and sold 30,000 wheels (22 per cent of total U.S. production) valued at $518,000 and 300 tons of other castings worth $44,000.[30]

Like most manufacturing entrepreneurs with expanding production and sales, Lobdell grappled perpetually with the need for long-term and working capital, as well as with the vexing problems of credit and payments. Because the period 1841–57 was a prosperous one, successful railway equipment makers generated sufficient retained earnings to pay for new plant and equipment in the long run. In the short run, however, most firms faced crippling shortages of working capital, for the high ratio of short- to long-term capital requirements generally characteristic of antebellum manufacturing prevailed throughout the railway supply industry as well, as seen in Table II.

TABLE II. RATIO OF SHORT- TO LONG-TERM CAPITAL REQUIREMENTS IN THE RAILWAY SUPPLY INDUSTRY, 1860

| Firm | Fixed Capital Assets | Operating Costs | | Value of Products |
		Wages	Material	
Harlan & Hollingsworth[a]	$ 50,000	$ 36,000	$ 54,000	$102,000
Lobdell	200,000	76,000	363,000	562,000
Rogers	350,000	225,000	382,000	765,000
Baldwin	350,000	251,000	376,000	750,000
Norris	290,000	214,000	320,000	670,000

Sources: John H. White, Jr., American Locomotives, p. 20; Semi-Centennial Memoir of the Harlan and Hollingsworth Company, pp. 535–38; Baldwin Ledgers, Baldwin Locomotive Works Papers; U.S. Census Office, Eighth Census of the United States, 1860: Manufactures, pp. clxxxviii, clxxxix, 53, 333, 343.
   [a] Figures are for car shops only; they do not include the shipbuilding division.

Expenditures for labor, transportation, and raw materials spiraled as production increased. The total payroll rose from an average $1,000 per

[30] Inventory, Bush & Lobdell Old Firm, July 31, 1859, Lobdell Car Wheel Papers; U.S. Census Office, Eighth Census of the United States, 1860: Manufactures, p. 24; Peter Temin, Iron and Steel in Nineteenth Century America, p. 266.

month in 1838 to $4,000 in 1856 and $6,000 in 1860.[31] Transportation costs rose proportionately.

Cash to meet these operating expenses came from three sources. The first was C.O.D. payments and monthly account settlements from prosperous railroads such as the Philadelphia, Wilmington, and Baltimore. The second source was long-term notes from railroads such as the Mississippi Central, and commission merchants such as Wyatt in Charleston. After 1842 and until the Panic of 1857, Lobdell could often discount good quality notes at Wilmington or New York banks with Bush's or Jesup's endorsement. If the customer's credit standing was questionable, it was necessary to turn to note brokers or commission merchants. Enoch Pratt, John Gittings, and Robert Cabeen were among those who accepted notes for Lobdell and other equipment makers. All such transactions were, of course, subject to heavy discount fees.

The third source of cash was advances on wheels ordered but not yet delivered. This was particularly important to Lobdell because, unlike locomotive and car builders, who often received partial payment from railroads when the work was 50 per cent complete, he was usually entitled to payment only on delivery. Commission merchants supplied the needed advances. In the 1850s Lobdell increasingly relied on Morris Jesup for such help, as did Baldwin and Harlan and Hollingsworth.[32]

As production advanced, Lobdell and his colleagues often found themselves running expanding, profitable businesses and accumulating larger debts in the process. Advances from Jesup and other railroad merchants, and credit extensions from iron commission merchants Pratt, Stickney, Cabeen, and Gittings, were, in effect, converted into long-term loans through the process of repeated renewal. This enabled producers to use cash income to meet operating expenses, to build inventories, and to expand factories.

The death of Charles Bush in a carriage accident in 1855 added to Lobdell's burden of debt. In order to retain control of his business, Lobdell assumed a debt of $100,000 to Bush's heirs, a debt secured by a series of ten long-term notes bearing 6 per cent interest. The settlement saddled Lobdell with an annual fixed cost, for it obligated the firm to make regular payments regardless of the level of business.[33]

[31] Bonney & Bush to McIntyre, March 9, 1838; and Account, New Firm with Old Firm, or G. G. Lobdell with Bush & Lobdell; Lobdell Papers; Census Office, *Eighth Census: Manufactures*, pp. 23–24.

[32] See Letterbooks, Baldwin Papers; and correspondence between Lobdell and Harlan & Hollingsworth, Lobdell Car Wheel Papers. It seems likely that Jesup rendered similar aid to Rogers Locomotive, since he was vice-president of the firm.

[33] The settlement also injected a forceful new personality into the business in the person of Henry S. McComb, Charles Bush's son-in-law and the designated trustee for Bush's heirs. McComb, a self-made man who had risen from apprentice currier to millionaire leather manufacturer. He assumed $50,000 of Lobdell's debt to Bush's heirs and became the firm's chief salesman. See An Agreement between H. S. McComb, William Bush, and George G. Lobdell, June 19, 1856, Lobdell Car Wheel Papers; and J. Thomas Scharf, *History of Delaware*, 2: 755–56.

Faced with steadily increasing costs, Lobdell tried to economize wherever possible. Like many of his contemporaries, he used the barter system to avoid the costs of commercial paper. Lobdell was always willing to trade wheels for scrap or pig iron, pig iron for coal, and coal for sand. All such transactions were calculated at current market prices. Lobdell took scrap wheels in payment for new ones and either used the scrap himself or traded it for other materials. Throughout the late fifties he sold new wheels to the Erie and took partial payment in scrap at $20 per ton. He traded the scrap to Trego and Company in Baltimore for car axles, receiving credit on his account at the rate of $21 per ton. The $1 differential covered the freight on the scrap, which often went directly from the Erie at Piermont, New York, to Trego in Baltimore.[34]

In addition to practicing economies in purchasing and finance, Lobdell always tried to keep transportation costs to a minimum. Finished products were shipped the same way as raw materials, by water. Railroads were used only when the need for haste overrode economic considerations, or in the rare instances when rail transport was cheaper. Wheels for the South went the same way that machinery had gone earlier—directly from the Lobdell pier on Christina Creek, or to Philadelphia on the Bush packet for transshipment. Wheels for northeastern points traveled by ship as far as possible. Goods for the West went to New York for forwarding via the Erie Canal.

In the 1850s the expanding volume of shipments and the growing reluctance of sailing masters to call at the Wilmington pier induced Lobdell to purchase two schooners, the *Maria Fleming* and the *Streamlet*. He employed these to haul wheels to Philadelphia, New York, Baltimore, and to New England ports, delivering them directly to customers whenever possible, or turning them over to shipping lines for forwarding. Lobdell's ships brought coal, sand, axles, and scrap and pig iron back to Wilmington if a load was available.[35] Other producers shipped their products the same way. Often a ship would load locomotives from Baldwin or Norris in Philadelphia, drop down the Delaware to pick up cars at Harlan and Hollingsworth and wheels at Lobdell, then proceed south.

In the 1850s much of Lobdell's output went south, for many of the firm's best customers were southern railroads, car builders, and commission merchants. The firm had maintained and expanded its southern connections (originally made to sell machinery and castings), and thus was able to take advantage of the spurt in southern railroad construction in the 1850s. This business put an added strain on the firm's resources, however, for southern enterprises were generally less well financed than their northern counter-

[34] Erie Railroad to Bush & Lobdell, July 17, 1860; Bush & Lobdell to Erie Railroad, January 19, 1860; and correspondence between Bush & Lobdell and Trego, 1860, *passim*; Lobdell Car Wheel Papers.

[35] The wanderings of the *Maria Fleming* can be followed in the telegrams and letters of her captain, Richard Shaw. When no cargo for Wilmington was available, Shaw picked up any freight he could find headed in the right direction.

parts. They usually demanded long-term credit and the right to make partial payment in securities. Lobdell was reluctant to grant either; nevertheless, he did both. Faced with large debts, and burdened with fixed and operating costs, he could do little else, for the alternatives were capitulation or the loss of sorely needed business. He extended long-term credit to car builders, such as Wharton and Petsch of Charleston, and accepted the bonds of the Mobile and Ohio, Memphis and Charleston, Mississippi Central, San Antonio and Mission Gulf, Nashville and Northwestern, Fernandina and Gulf, and other roads.

Neither action was without precedent. On paper the firm had an ironclad policy of extending credit for a maximum of four months, the debt being secured by interest-bearing notes. This policy worked only with prosperous railroads, some of whom paid cash and received a discount. Others paid their bills monthly, and the firm had often extended credit for six, nine, twelve months or longer. Lobdell also accepted securities in payment, including the stock and bonds of the Western Maryland and Pennsylvania railroads.[36]

Other railroad equipment manufacturers also had accepted such payments. For example, Stone and Harris of Springfield, Massachusetts, built a bridge for the Richmond and Danville in 1849 and took stock in payment. In 1847–48 Abram Hewitt sold Trenton Iron rails to the Hudson River Railroad and took $20,000 in stock. Hewitt had to do this to meet the competition of British ironmasters who were willing to sell rails for American railroad bonds. In 1857 George Whitaker sold $91,000 worth of rails to the Hempfield Railroad for $38,000 cash and $53,000 in securities. Matthias Baldwin and Rogers Locomotive Works accepted stock and bonds from a number of railroads north and south, including the Virginia Central, Pittsburgh, Fort Wayne and Chicago, Florida, and others.[37]

Railroad capitalization expanded swiftly from $318 million in 1850 to $763 million in 1855 to $1,149 million in 1860.[38] The presence of such quantities of securities in the market often depressed their value greatly, and Lobdell tried to hold them as long as possible; nevertheless, the need for cash sometimes forced him to sell at a severe discount. He also used securities to pay for raw materials when he could find a supplier willing to take them. For example, after accepting a quantity of Florida Railroad bonds from Harlan and Hollingsworth and Rogers Locomotive, he tried to foist them off on Trego in exchange for axles. Trego would have none of it, so Lobdell

36 Memo to E. O. Gibson, May, 1860, Lobdell Car Wheel Papers.

37 Richmond & Danville Railroad to Stone & Harris, January 15, 1849, Stone & Harris Papers; Nevins, *Hewitt*, pp. 89–104; N. Wilkinson to G. Whitaker, July 4, 1857, and Hempfield Railroad Account, both in Whitaker Iron Papers; Baldwin Ledgers, Baldwin Papers; and many letters between Rogers Locomotive and Lobdell, 1855–60, Lobdell Car Wheel Papers.

38 Chandler, *Railroads*, p. 15.

shopped around and finally managed to unload them on N. D. Thompson, proprietor of the Union Steam Forge in Bordentown, New Jersey.[39]

The 1850s thus presented the bizarre spectacle of northern car builders, locomotive manufacturers, wheel founders, iron brokers, and commission merchants trying to convince one another to accept payment in southern railroad paper.[40] Competition and expansion combined to force manufacturers to accept securities, buy materials on credit, and secure loans and advances. This patchwork financing worked well enough as long as prosperity endured, but it was a source of great embarrassment when the market collapsed in the Panic of 1857.

THE IMPACT OF RECESSION AND SECESSION, 1857–1862

The Panic of 1857 and the long recession that followed hit railroad equipment manufacturers hard. Not only did orders fall off rapidly, but many creditors defaulted on their bills. Many firms that had entered the field during the prosperous years were quickly forced into bankruptcy. Among these were some twenty locomotive producers (half of the firms in the field), including William Swinburne of Paterson. Swinburne, who had resigned as superintendent of Rogers Locomotive in 1856 to set up his own business, was bankrupted by the failure of the Chicago and Alton Railroad in 1857. The road owed Swinburne $60,000 when it went into receivership; after a long delay he received fifty cents on the dollar, but it was too little and too late.[41]

Only the strongest firms were able to survive, and they were forced to the brink as the recession continued through 1858, 1859, and 1860. Survival depended on outside resources, for current business was inadequate to meet past obligations. Harlan and Hollingsworth had the revenues of its shipbuilding division ($456,000 in 1860).[42] Rogers Locomotive had Jesup's participation in the firm. Lobdell and Baldwin got the assistance of commission merchants. Lobdell borrowed heavily from Cabeen and from Jesup, who advanced him $32,000 in 1859, and he added Cooper and Hewitt of New York to his list of patient iron suppliers. Baldwin borrowed from Cabeen ($52,500 in 1859) and others. His short-term obligations totaled $87,000 in 1859 and $105,000 in 1860 and 1861. He also got help from Jesup and another New York commission merchant, Gilead Smith.[43]

---

[39] Lobdell to Trego, February 15, 1860; Trego to Lobdell, March 7, 1860; and Thompson to Lobdell, December 18, 1860; Lobdell Car Wheel Papers.

[40] Southern railroad securities in the hands of northern businessmen played an important role in determining the control of prostrated southern railroads after the Civil War.

[41] White, *American Locomotives*, p. 24.

[42] *Memoir of Harlan and Hollingsworth*, pp. 233–35.

[43] Correspondence, 1857–61; and Bush & Lobdell in Account with M. K. Jesup, 1859–60; Lobdell Car Wheel Papers. See also Letterbooks, 1857–61, Baldwin Papers.

The fall of 1860 found Lobdell with a deteriorated credit rating, large debts to brokers, and a safe full of southern railroad bonds and business paper. He still owed Bush's heirs $21,000.[44] After Lincoln's election he was faced with the prospect of losing his best customers, the southern railroads and car builders, and of having to compete against equally unfortunate rivals for the remaining northern business. Lobdell's unhappy position was in part the result of his failure to anticipate the effect that political events could have on business. Like his fellow ironmasters Abram Hewitt of Trenton Iron and Joseph Anderson of the Tredegar Works in Richmond, Virginia, Lobdell viewed politics as secondary to business; when the two conflicted, the desire for profit invariably won out.[45] Like Anderson, Lobdell talked out of both sides of his mouth when pressed by customers for opinions on sectional differences. After Lincoln was elected Lobdell wrote the Central Railroad in Savannah that he hoped "our southern friends will not forget us at this time, as we are to a considerable extent by northern men being considered too southern in our sentiments."[46] He also took pains to assure a Charleston commission merchant that he was not opposed to slavery. On the other hand, a major northern customer, machinist and locomotive builder L. B. Tyng of Boston, believed Lobdell to be a fellow abolitionist, and Lobdell said nothing to disabuse him.[47]

Lobdell, like Hewitt, ignored the probable economic consequences of southern secession until events brought a sharp awakening. Throughout 1860 he continued to sell to southern customers and to take bonds and notes in payment. On October 5 he sold 40 sets of wheels to the Memphis and Charleston and accepted a note in payment. On October 24 he sold 50 wheels to the Mobile and Ohio and took payment in bonds. In November his Charleston agent advised that he could not make collections from roads until political affairs quieted down. In December the San Antonio and Mission Gulf, and the Florida defaulted on their notes. These events temporarily dampened Lobdell's enthusiasm for southern business.[48] By January, 1861, however, his optimism had revived, and he sold wheels to Wharton and Petsch in Charleston, taking $3,000 worth of Mississippi Central notes

---

[44] Memo, July 1, 1861, Lobdell Papers. Dun & Bradstreet listed Bush & Lobdell's credit as "Good as Old Gold," until July 1, 1861, when Lobdell was adjudged "at present though probably solvent he would not be able to pay if pushed" (Delaware, 2: 15, Dun & Bradstreet Collection).

[45] On Hewitt see Nevins, *Hewitt*, pp. 152–53; for Anderson see Charles B. Dew, *Ironmaker to the Confederacy*, pp. 38–60.

[46] Lobdell to Central Railroad, November 14, 1860, Lobdell Car Wheel Papers. Baldwin lost some business in the South because he had participated in a movement to educate free blacks; see Allen Johnson *et al.*, eds., *Dictionary of American Biography*, 1: 541–42.

[47] Central Railroad to Lobdell, October 18, 1860; and L. B. Tyng to Lobdell, January 4, 1861, Lobdell Car Wheel Papers.

[48] Correspondence, October–December, 1860, *ibid.*

(for eighteen and twenty-four months respectively) in payment.[49] In February he accepted an order from Savannah for 100 wheels and hastened to ship it before a proposed tariff on northern goods was enacted. In March and April he sold wheels on credit to the Richmond and Danville and the Richmond, Fredericksburg, and Potomac.[50] Altogether Lobdell's conduct justified Allan Nevins' observation that "our competitive industrialists, hoping that war could be averted, pressed on with an optimism that no political apprehensions could chill."[51]

In April, of course, the chill came, and in May Lobdell wrote that "business is stopped."[52] Creditors were soon pressing for payments that he could not meet. Surveying the situation in May, 1861, he wrote a friend in Virginia, "There is not much doing here and throughout all the free states except preparing for war." He believed that the war was purely to sustain the Union, not to free the slaves or subjugate the South. He warned that he had just completed a futile sales trip throughout the North and had found the people united to preserve the Union regardless of cost. With gloomy prescience he added: "It [the war] will bankrupt half of the business community. War will result in the freeing of the slaves and what will become of the poor ignorant Negroes God only knows. There is no probability of business matters improving here for some time. I can pay none of the drafts due. These are times which you and I never expected to see and the banks should be lenient at such a time."[53]

[49] Wharton & Petsch to Lobdell, January 5, 1861, *ibid.* Wharton & Petsch regretted the delay in ordering more wheels, but they had been ordered to make gun carriages for the South Carolina Militia.

[50] Baldwin also made sales in the South until the war broke out. He accepted bonds issued by the Georgia Railroad, the state of Tennessee, and the city of Louisville. See Baldwin Ledgers, Baldwin Papers.

Many northerners collected at least part of their southern accounts after the war. Anderson of Tredegar paid his debts (Dew, *Ironmaker*, p. 301). Lobdell collected in full with back interest from many railroads (Mobile & Ohio to Lobdell, September 13, 1866, Lobdell Car Wheel Papers). John F. Stover, *Railroads of the South, 1865–1900*, is unclear on the subject, but he indicates that southern railroads generally acknowledged prewar debts and eventually paid them. Tennessee railroads had to pay back interest to bond holders as a condition to their purchase of U.S. Military Railroads rolling stock. See Thomas Weber, *The Northern Railroads in the Civil War, 1861–1865*, p. 218.

Northern manufacturers in other fields had similar success. For example, southern commission merchants owed Fall River Iron $28,000 when the war broke out. Most of it was eventually repaid with interest: Dade Hurocthal of Mobile paid $4,277 in September, 1865; O. Mozangi of Mobile sent $17,000 (including $2,477 in interest) in June, 1867. See Dade Hurocthal to Fall River Iron, September 15, 1865; O. Mozangi to Fall River Iron, June 29, 1867; and Balance of Accounts, Ledger, 1861; Fall River Iron Works Papers.

[51] Nevins, *Hewitt*, p. 152. In fairness to Lobdell it should be said that he may have felt that the state of his finances forced him to accept orders, however problematical the payment.

[52] Lobdell to Trego, May 24, 1861, Lobdell Car Wheel Papers.

[53] Lobdell to J. Marston, May 15, 1861, *ibid.*

Fortunately, the banks were reasonably patient, and commission merchants were more so. Pratt, Hewitt, Cabeen, Stickney, Jesup, and others carried Lobdell throughout the rest of the year, which was a dismal chronicle of futile sales trips and a gradual liquidation of such railroad bonds as had any value. Not only were the southern markets gone, but railroad construction had virtually stopped. The only business obtainable amounted to small sales to maintenance departments of northern railroads and some overseas contacts dredged up by commission merchants.[54] In such straitened circumstances, only firms that enjoyed patient support from mercantile creditors avoided bankruptcy. Among these were Lobdell, Harlan and Hollingsworth, Baldwin, Norris, and Rogers, all of which eventually emerged from their prolonged slump when the Civil War revived demand.

Before the war brought relief, however, the recession that had begun in 1857 turned the railroad supply industry into a highly concentrated field. Markets once open to a multitude of small producers were dominated by a handful of large firms by 1860. The nine largest wheel foundries produced 74 per cent of the total national output; the two largest, Whitney and Lobdell, made 51 per cent of the total. The eight largest locomotive manufacturers controlled 80 per cent of the market; the three largest, Baldwin, Rogers, and Norris, controlled 55 per cent. The seven largest rolling mills contributed 73 per cent of all domestic rails produced.[55]

Concentration appeared because a period of high demand and prosperity, which brought many producers into the field, was followed by a prolonged recession in which the industry's capacity greatly exceeded the diminished market. In the absence of controls on production, only the few strongest survived.[56] In subsequent years, repetitions of this pattern would bring con-

---

[54] The firm sold 1,000 shares of Western Maryland Railway stock in late November, 1861; see Jesup to Lobdell, December, 1861, *passim, ibid.* Rogers Locomotive sold two engines in Chile; see *American Railroad Journal* 32 (1859):72.

[55] Computed from data in Census Office, *Eighth Census: Manufactures*, pp. clxxv, clxxvii, clxxix; White, *American Locomotives*, p. 20; and Lesley, *Iron Manufacturer's Guide*, p. 57.

[56] Baldwin Locomotive Works continued to prosper after its founder's death in 1866. In the first third of the twentieth century, under the superintendency of Samuel Vauclain, Baldwin became the foremost steam locomotive designer and producer in the world. After World War II the firm attempted to stave off dieselization by merging with Lima-Hamilton, an Ohio producer. When this strategy failed, Baldwin turned to the manufacture of diesels. Despite the fact that it designed and produced the finest diesel locomotives ever to run on American railroads, the firm was unable to compete with General Motors, American Locomotive, and General Electric, and went out of the locomotive business in the 1950s.

. Harlan & Hollingsworth continued to produce ships and railroad cars throughout the nineteenth century. In the 1870s and 1880s it and another Wilmington firm, Jackson & Sharp (founded in 1863), produced more railroad passenger cars than all other American car builders combined. In 1900 Harlan & Hollingsworth was absorbed by the American Shipbuilding Corp., which almost immediately went bankrupt. Bethlehem Steel then bought the plant, and, although production continued sporadically for some years, it discontinued after World War I. The firm is now defunct; its buildings, still

centration to many American manufacturing industries, particularly those serving concentrated markets.

The changing distribution patterns of the railway supply industry were also harbingers of future developments. Although independent middlemen continued to play a major role in the industry until the 1870s, their significance had already begun to decline by 1861. Their ability to control production and distribution depended on the relevance of their financial and mercantile abilities, and the changing nature of the market eroded that relevance.

By 1861 many railroads had demonstrated their ability to dispense with the middleman's assistance in financing transactions. Manufacturers were still dependent on merchants for capital, but the prosperity and inflation of the Civil War era greatly reduced that dependence.

Three factors diminished the value of the commission merchants' mercantile services. They were: (1) the development of the first concentrated market for American manufactures, a market in which a small number of readily identifiable customers generated sufficient demand to support high-volume, specialized producers; (2) the emerging bureaucratic structure of railroad management, which minimized material costs by eliminating the middleman and rationalized the flow of goods by assigning purchasing to a specialist or specialized department; (3) the increasingly complex technology of railroad equipment, a technology which required the search for more durable wheels and rails, the design of more powerful engines, and the construction of cars of greater capacity, technical abilities that few middlemen possessed.

By 1861 the combination of all these factors, and above all the existence of a concentrated market for specific goods, had diminished the importance of middlemen to the railroad supply industry. This development was almost unique to that industry. In the rest of the manufacturing economy, independent wholesalers, using traditional mercantile techniques, still controlled the distribution of more than 95 per cent of all manufactured products sold in the United States. On the eve of the Civil War, diffuse markets for generic goods still prevailed, as they had throughout American history. In this relatively static environment the merchants' marketing and financial resources remained relevant; however, their virtual monopoly in the field of manufacturing finance was destined to decline.

---

standing, house a multitude of small firms.

The Lobdell Car Wheel Co. remained under family control until 1949, when United Engineers & Foundry Corp. bought it. From the 1890s on, railroads and wheel foundries debated the relative merits of chilled iron versus steel car wheels. Unfortunately for the Lobdell firm, it stuck with chilled iron, and in so doing strapped itself to a cadaver. As steel wheels captured the market, the firm turned to the making of paper-mill machinery and produced nothing else after World War II. The plant is now closed.

American Locomotive of Schenectady absorbed Rogers Locomotive Works in 1904. The Paterson plant closed immediately after the merger.

CHAPTER VII

The Decline
of the Merchant
as Financier

In the decade 1860–70, few changes appeared in the marketing channels through which manufactured goods passed. With rare exceptions, such as railway equipment, most manufactured products continued to be generic goods; they were sold to relatively diffuse markets, and they required no technological advances in either marketing methods or facilities. Traditional networks therefore remained adequate. Despite the enduring relevance of the merchants' more visible function, marketing, the decade was, nevertheless, an era in which significant alterations often took place in the relationships between manufacturers and their suppliers and distributors.

In this decade some manufacturers freed themselves from long-standing financial dependency upon wholesalers. In so doing, these manufacturers not only effected significant reductions in the cost of doing business; they also greatly increased the vulnerability of the independent merchant's position in the economy. At the beginning of the decade, the wholesaler's indispensability rested firmly on the twin pillars of his marketing and financial expertise. When the decade ended, there were many instances of the wholesaler's continued importance resting solely on his ability to sell. Events in subsequent years undermined his importance as a source of long-term and working capital, as well as his usefulness as a financial agent.

The wholesaler's importance as a source of manufacturing capital declined during the decade of the sixties and thereafter for two principal reasons. First, many manufacturers began to meet a large part of their capital needs with current income and retained earnings. Second, manufacturers in general began to tap national capital markets from which they had previously been excluded.

In the prewar period most American manufacturing firms secured their long-term capital in one of two principal ways. The first, common only in the textile industry, was a parlay of stockholders' investments, retained earnings, and loans from financial intermediaries such as banks and insurance companies. The second, and far more common, capital structure was a patchwork consisting of the proprietor's (or partners') personal investment, loans on his real property, retained earnings, and short-term loans or advances from suppliers and distributors. Such loans were converted into long-term capital through the process of frequent renewal. Many of the firms in the first category (although by no means all of them) were relatively solvent in 1860. For example, the Pepperell Manufacturing Company's balance sheet showed a surplus of nearly a million dollars on December 31, 1860, and the firm had paid out $548,000 in dividends in the preceding decade.[1]

Such solvency was, however, confined largely to the textile industry, and isolated examples give a false impression of the profitability of antebellum manufacturing generally. Most firms belonged to the second category, and very few of them could boast of Pepperell's steady prosperity. Credit reports in the Dun Manuscripts reveal the shaky financial condition of these firms.[2] Even a casual examination of the Dun ledgers for the prewar years shows that manufacturing was a risky business indeed. Failures and bankruptcies were commonplace, and many firms that survived for years were habitually regarded as dubious credit risks unless they had access to mercantile capital. The credit reports on Daniel Reese, operator of Locust Point Iron Furnace, exemplified the fortunes of many. In a twelve-year period Reese was successively described as: "often pressed for money as most men are who engaged in that kind of business which is a precarious one, but he seems to have been a success.... Supposed to be backed by Stickney and Co. who are agents for sale of iron manufactured by him and his credit is good"; "broke and out of business"; "pays better but not desirable for credit"; "has improved considerable, now owns the property"; "same, but [property] heavily mortgaged."[3]

Reese's predicaments were far more typical of antebellum manufacturing than was Pepperell's prosperity. Recurring capital shortages forced most manufacturing entrepreneurs to resort to repeated borrowings from suppliers and distributors by either renewing old obligations or incurring new ones.

[1] Evelyn H. Knowlton, *Pepperell's Progress*, app. 32.

[2] The Dun Manuscripts (hereafter cited as Dun MSS) are part of the Dun & Bradstreet Collection.

[3] Credit reports on Daniel M. Reese, Locust Point Furnace in Maryland, Dun MSS, vol. 8.

The high interest charges attached to this method of finance constituted, in effect, a fixed cost that siphoned off profits in good times and deepened indebtedness in slack periods. As a result, periodic panics and recessions scythed down marginal firms by the hundreds. Even successful firms labored under debts that often grew as fast as (or faster than) sales, for the increasing demand for capital to underwrite expansion often consumed all available profits and then some. Thus, by 1861 Jones and Laughlin had increased its fixed assets by reinvesting all profits ($85,000) and an additional $71,000 contributed by Laughlin. The firm was unusually fortunate in that Laughlin was content to secure his cash investment with an expanding share in the partnership rather than increase the firm's costs by demanding interest or dividend payments.

Few firms were so fortunate, with the result that manufacturing entrepreneurs in general were a debtor class in the antebellum period. For example, the financial history of the Lobdell Car Wheel Company offers a marked contrast to that of firms such as Pepperell or Jones and Laughlin. By 1861 George Lobdell had built his firm into the largest of its kind in the world. He had also piled up a steadily growing debt to his partner's heirs, iron suppliers such as Cabeen, and distributors such as Morris Jesup.[4] For Lobdell, as for many of his contemporaries, the Panic of 1857 and the business collapse that followed Lincoln's election in 1860 threw an almost unbearable burden on resources that had been extended to finance growth in the preceding era of boom and optimism. Many firms failed.[5]

Many of those which survived soon enjoyed the most prosperous times they had ever known. As surely as the prelude to the war had pushed them to the brink of despair and disaster, so the War itself brought sustained, high-volume demand, rising prices, and shorter terms of payment. These factors raised profit levels to the point that many producers were able to break the vicious circle of deficit finance by meeting capital requirements with current income. This meant reduced borrowing; reduced borrowing meant decreased interest costs; decreased interest costs brought higher profits, which not only could supply current capital needs but also could be used to pay off prewar debts.

The Civil War economy was, of course, a paradise for debtor-manufacturers like Lobdell. While prices for their products rose as a result of wartime inflation and the fact that it was a seller's market, the amount of their antebellum debts remained constant. In effect this meant that it cost manufacturers from a quarter to a third less to pay off prewar debts in 1863 than it would have cost in 1860.[6] Consequently, for the first time, many northern

[4] Lobdell Car Wheel Co. Papers, 1850–60. The Lobdell financial records are incomplete, so it is impossible to determine Lobdell's exact indebtedness; however, it undoubtedly exceeded $200,000.
[5] W. F. Dunaway, *A History of Pennsylvania*, pp. 434–35.
[6] Wesley C. Mitchell, *A History of the Greenbacks*, chap. 7.

manufacturers were able to eradicate their indebtedness to their suppliers and distributors.

How widespread this phenomenon was it is impossible to say with certainty. It is nevertheless a fact that at the end of the war there were firms (often the largest producers) in virtually every manufacturing field which no longer required capital contributions from suppliers and distributors and which had paid off prewar debts to merchant capitalists. These firms achieved not only significant reductions in costs but also a greater degree of autonomy. It was no longer necessary to consign their entire output or a major part of it to a single merchant in order to secure his financial support, nor was it necessary to accept a supplier's price for materials in order to secure lenient terms or loans. Manufacturers who had competed for the favor of wealthy distributors before the war, could pick and choose among dealers after it.

As a result, the balance of financial power often shifted from the merchant's counting house to the factory office. For example, in the late 1850s, when declining demand led to surpluses and falling prices, it was the merchants who organized strategies of price-fixing and pooling of orders to combat ruinous competition. In the next sustained period of falling prices, following the Panic of 1873, the manufacturers themselves devised and implemented pools and trade associations in a vain attempt to rationalize production. To be sure, there were other factors that contributed to the manufacturer's ability to wrest control of his policies from the hands of his mercantile intermediaries, but in a number of important cases it was the prosperity of the war years which began the transfer and thus played a crucial role in determining the subsequent institutional development of producing and marketing firms.

MANUFACTURING PROSPERITY AND LONG-TERM CAPITAL DURING THE CIVIL WAR

As the gloomy events of 1861 unfolded, most northern businessmen grew steadily more pessimistic. Their correspondence reflected the prevalence of George Lobdell's fear that the war "would bankrupt half the business community," and that there was "no probability of business matters . . . improving for some time."[7] Here and there, however, more prescient souls anticipated the glorious opportunities of a war economy and urged their friends to come early to the barbecue. Sam Dinsmore, a Boston commission merchant, went to Washington in the summer of 1861 to dig up government contracts that his clients might supply. Writing from Clay's Hotel in August, he urged Bangor, Maine, machinists Hinckley and Egery to present themselves to the chief clerk of the Bureau of Contracting, who was on his way to Maine. Prompt action was necessary, said Dinsmore, because the government

[7] George Lobdell to J. Marston, May 15, 1861, Lobdell Car Wheel Papers.

was about to contract for the construction of a number of steamers, and "a Maine shop may have [the contract for] the machinery of one of those steamers for the asking. Two hulls would go to Maine if there were anybody to bid for them. . . . I trust you will come to Washington," he added, for "a great amount of money could be made by strong and enterprising parties."[8]

And so it proved; for whatever else the Union may have lacked, there was no dearth of "strong and enterprising parties" among its businessmen. As the Civil War deepened, government contracts revived markets and pumped money into the economy. Entrepreneurs shed their melancholy for frenzied activity, and the results are reflected in their correspondence. Threnodies for days gone by changed to hymns of celebration. Typical of such transmogrified attitudes was that of W. W. Watts, a Pennsylvania forgeman who converted pig iron into blooms, which he sold to the "Coatesville Mills." Watts's pungent correspondence forms a graphic (if sometimes hyperbolic) record of an antebellum manufacturer's endless struggles against the vagaries of nature and the markets. Like most of his fellows, he plunged into despair and occasional fury as his works fell idle in 1861. By March of 1862, however, he had changed his tune. Writing Huston and Penrose that he had shipped one order and was working all out on another, Watts closed triumphantly, "I am in no hurry for peace."[9]

Such bald expressions of satisfaction were rare. Most businessmen discussed their wartime prosperity in the curious argot into which they were wont to translate discussion of any sort of upheaval. In April, 1863, Edward Peters, a Boston commission merchant, wrote Hinckley and Egery, urging them to take the $60,000 he had collected for them and invest it somewhere at interest. "In such times as these it don't make so much difference to owe so much in one spot, but we have seen the times when such sums to be called for unexpectedly would not be so pleasant as a dinner at Parkers, and what times have been may be again. We . . . like to prepare for a storm when the sun is shining."[10]

At that time, Grant was bogged down in the swamps of the Vicksburg campaign, Lee and Jackson were readying the undefeated Army of Northern Virginia for the spring offensive, the *Florida* and *Alabama* were merrily destroying American merchantmen, and a greenback dollar brought sixty-eight cents in gold; nevertheless, for Messers Hinckley, Egery, and Peters, the sun was shining. Hinckley and Egery had indeed proved "strong and enterprising parties." Before the war they had relied heavily on their distributors for loans and advances. By the spring of 1863, their dealer was calling on them to pick up the money.

8 Sam Dinsmore to Hinckley & Egery, August 28, 1861, Hinckley & Egery Papers.
9 W. W. Watts to Huston & Penrose, February 12, 1862, Lukens Steel Co. Papers.
10 Edward Peters to D. B. Hinckley, April 8, 1863, Hinckley & Egery Papers.

Similar prosperity buoyed other manufacturing fields. Pepperell's profits reached a new high in 1862 ($285,000), nearly tripled in 1863, and declined only slightly in 1864. Wool manufacture, which had consumed 86 million pounds in 1859, used 200 million pounds at its wartime peak as old firms enlarged capacity and cotton mills switched to wool production. The expansion of the industry's capacity was financed by the "high level of profits," which exceeded all previous experience and subsequently remained unmatched until World War I. Pacific Mills of Lawrence, Massachusetts, for example, expanded from 1,000 looms in 1853 to 3,500 in 1869; most of the new equipment was added during the war years and was paid for out of profits. In addition, Pacific's stockholders, who had invested two and a half million dollars to start the firm in 1853, recouped their entire investment in wartime dividends, and the firm retained " 'a very large mount' of undivided profits."[11]

Metal industries also enjoyed the boom. Refiners such as Cornwall Furnace and the Watts bloomery were often hard pressed to supply the needs of iron processors such as Gibbons and Huston, who were kept busy making boiler plate for steamships and locomotives. Backed up orders were common throughout metal-working and fabricating industries. By 1863, Fall River Iron was writing prospective customers that it had "all the orders for nails that we can fill for months to come." Stone and Harris, machinery fabricators of Springfield, Massachusetts, sold all the lathes they could manufacture, turned away customers who offered premium prices, and suffered throughout the war from late deliveries of material from iron furnaces and foundries. Hollingsworth and Harvey, machinery builders in Wilmington, Delaware, also ran at full capacity after the first year of the war. For example, in September, 1864, they wrote, "We will hurry on with the machinery as fast as we possibly can, as we are as much interested in getting it completed as we can be, having other work pushing us which we cannot do until we get yours out."[12]

Such high-volume business soon restored the fortunes of many impoverished machine shops. A. and W. Denmead, a Baltimore foundry and machine works, had teetered on the edge of bankruptcy in 1860–61, meeting only 10 per cent of its notes at maturity. By 1863 the firm's credit was restored via "considerable business for the government." John Haskell of Baltimore is another example of a machinery builder who rose from near prostration to prosperity during the war, and an almost endless list of similar cases could be cited.[13]

[11] Knowlton, *Pepperell's Progress*, p. 462; Arthur H. Cole, *The American Wool Manufacture*, 1: 380 and chap. 20 *passim*.

[12] Fall River Iron to Frost & Ainsbury, November 29, 1863, Fall River Iron Works Papers; Stone & Harris Papers; Hollingsworth & Harvey to W. Clark, September 15, 1864, Hollingsworth & Harvey Papers.

[13] Credit Reports on A. and W. Denmead, and on John Haskell in Baltimore, Dun MSS, vols. 7, 8, and 9. These volumes contain dozens of similar examples, such as Trego Thompson & Co. and the Baltimore Iron & Rail Works.

Manufacturers of transportation equipment also enjoyed a resurgence of demand. In 1861 Harlan and Hollingsworth built three steamers for inventory in order to keep its work force employed and intact. By March, 1863, there were no ships for sale on the Delaware River, and shipyards everywhere had a backlog of orders which continued throughout the war. Shipyards fell so far behind demand that private owners often sold or chartered their steamers to the government at prices that yielded impressive profits. In 1863, for example, Fall River Iron sold its steamer *Canonicus* to the federal government for $86,000. *Canonicus* had cost $40,000 when built in 1850; at the time of the sale, Fall River Iron valued it at $20,000 on the books.[14]

The scarcity of shipping also forced many manufacturers such as Cornwall Furnace to ship extensively by rail for the first time. This development contributed to the resurgence of the railway equipment industry, which enjoyed a spectacular revival despite the fact that southern customers evaporated and railroad construction came to a standstill. The war generated so much demand for motive power and rolling stock that producers who had survived the prewar recession did more business than ever. The Baldwin, Norris, Rogers, and Schenectady locomotive works combined built 750 units between 1855 and 1860. During the war they constructed 1,200.

Orders came from both the U.S. Military Railroads (313) and private firms; railroads in Pennsylvania alone purchased 163. Car builders also kept busy supplying the U.S. Military Railroads, which bought 5,166 cars; Pennsylvania roads, which took 9,750; the Erie, which bought 1,000; the Philadelphia, Wilmington, and Baltimore, which ordered 659; and many others. These and other orders exceeded the capacity of existing firms; consequently, new firms appeared virtually overnight. Most of them promptly disappeared after the war, but one, Jackson and Sharp of Wilmington, was an immediate success and continued to build cars for railroads all over the world until its merger into American Car and Foundry in 1903.

Lobdell, of course, profited from the revived demand for railroad equipment. As an established producer with close ties to manufacturers and railroads, both directly and through purchasing agents, he was able to secure a number of large orders. He supplied all the wheels for the new and old cars of the Erie, the Pennsylvania, and the Philadelphia, Wilmington, and Baltimore. In November, 1862, the Philadelphia and Reading ordered 4,000 wheels. The Lehigh Coal and Navigation Company bought 5,000 a year in 1863 and 1864.[15]

---

[14] *Semi-Centennial Memoir of the Harlan and Hollingsworth Company*, p. 269; Letterbook, 1863–65, Hollingsworth & Harvey Papers; Ledgers, 1863, Fall River Iron Papers.

[15] Locomotive manufacturers' production was calculated from data in John H. White, Jr., *American Locomotives*, p. 20. Other information on wartime production of railroad equipment came from: *War of the Rebellion*, 5: 999; Herman K. Murphy,

Lobdell also supplied many wheels for government-purchased cars. Contracts let for U.S. Military Railroads' rolling stock often specified "wheels of Whitney or Bush and Lobdell pattern." Some wheels were sold directly to the Quartermaster Corps through the efforts of F. B. Sturgis, a Wilmingtonian on the quartermaster's staff at Nashville. Altogether wartime orders kept the firm so busy that Lobdell arranged for an inside contractor to handle all the firm's business in non-railroad castings.[16]

The great volume of wartime business generated inflated profits that enabled railway equipment manufacturers (like many others) to eradicate past debts to suppliers and to cease relying on them for credit and capital. In doing so, some manufacturers simply made permanent an arrangement originally invoked by the merchants themselves. During the slump of 1860 and 1861, many suppliers had put manufacturers on a cash basis, and many distributors had refused to make further loans or advances. Consequently, when business began to revive, manufacturers had to look elsewhere for capital to recommence production. For example, in January, 1862, Lobdell had $14,000 worth of orders in hand, but he could not operate, for he had no cash with which to pay wages or buy raw materials. He obtained the necessary cash by mortgaging his last unencumbered real estate to the Farmers Bank for $6,000. Denmead of Baltimore did the same, mortgaging his property to the Eutaw Savings Bank.[17]

Once production resumed, propitious business conditions frequently obviated the need for outside capital. The break between merchant and manufacturer, often initiated by the former's refusal to supply additional short-

---

"The Northern Railroads During the Civil War," p. 328; Thomas Weber, *The Northern Railroads in the Civil War*, 1861–1865, pp. 194, 222; Eva Swatner, "Military Railroads During the Civil War," 310–16; Lobdell Correspondence, 1861–65, Lobdell Car Wheel Papers, Contract, October 9, 1862, between Captain H. Robertson AQM and Harlan & Hollingsworth to supply boxcars for U.S. Military Railroads and MS Memoranda of Cars purchased from various persons for the U.S. Government, both in records of the Office of the U.S. Quartermaster General, Consolidated Correspondence File, 1794–1915.

No figures exist that would permit comparison of the number of cars built between 1855 and 1860 with the number built from 1861 to 1865. Albert Fishlow has constructed estimates of construction by decades after 1838. He estimates that approximately 68,000 freight and passenger cars (measured in eight-wheel equivalents) were built between 1848 and 1858, while 110,000 were constructed in 1868–69. It is difficult, however, to know how much of this growth is attributable to the Civil War and how much to the boom in railway construction that followed it. See Albert Fishlow's *American Railroads and the Transformation of the Ante-Bellum Economy*, app. D, and "Productivity and Technological Change in the Railroad Sector, 1840–1910."

[16] F. B. Sturgis to Lobdell, April 18, 22, 29, and May 12, 1862, and Lease of Upper Foundry to W. C. Hudson, August 1, 1862, Lobdell Car Wheel Papers; "George D. Lobdell, Claim for Car Wheels," MS in Register of Claims, Supplies, and Occupation of Real Estate, 1874, K File #4823, U.S. Quartermaster General's Records.

[17] M. K. Jesup & Co. to Lobdell, December, 1861, *passim*; Lobdell to Cabeen & Co., October 30, 1861; and Lobdell to David Wilson, January 1, 1862; Lobdell Car Wheel Papers. See also Credit Report on A. and W. Denmead, Dun MSS.

term funds, widened as prosperity provided the manufacturer with adequate funds to meet all his capital needs and to pay off prewar debts as well. In October, 1862, Lobdell wrote a friend that he hoped to be out of debt in a year. By the end of the war he had paid off all his obligations, and his credit rating was restored.[18] Never again in the firm's history did it rely on suppliers or distributors for capital. The same was true for many other firms in the industry, including Harlan and Hollingsworth, Rogers, Norris, and Baldwin.

Firms in other industries achieved similar independence. Rescued from bankruptcy in 1857 by watch distributor Royal Robbins, the Waltham Watch Company expanded its sales of watch movements from 2,000 in 1860 to 52,000 in 1865 and 73,000 in 1866. Waltham, like Pacific Mills and the railroad equipment producers cited above, financed expansion of its production facilities with wartime profits. Jones and Laughlin not only ceased drawing on Laughlin for added capital but paid its first dividends to the partners while continuing to add to its capital assets, which grew from $176,000 in 1861 to $1.5 million in 1870.[19]

Aggregate statistics indicate that rapid growth in capital assets was characteristic of the U.S. manufacturing economy as a whole. Producers' capital goods accounted for 3.4 per cent ($137 million) of the Gross National Product in 1859, and 6.9 per cent ($441 million) of it in 1869.[20] The records of individual firms appear to confirm the statistical trend, and they also show that many large firms stepped up long-term investment while simultaneously detaching themselves from financial dependence on suppliers and distributors.

A similar metamorphosis took place in the area of working capital. Considering the relatively greater importance of short-term funding to most manufacturers, it seems likely that the move toward self-sufficiency in long-

[18] Lobdell to Sturgis, October 10, 1862, Lobdell Car Wheel Papers; Credit Report on Lobdell Car Wheel Co., Dun MSS. Lobdell disposed of bonds through McComb, who assumed the balance of Lobdell's debt to Bush's heirs and paid $10,000 in bank stock besides. The deal was mutually advantageous. Lobdell achieved full control over his business; McComb used the bonds as a springboard to a postwar career as carpetbag railroad king in Mississippi. He was also one of the original stockholders in the Credit Mobilier & Union Pacific Railroad. See Correspondence between McComb and Lobdell, 1862–66, Lobdell Car Wheel Papers; Robert W. Fogel, *The Union Pacific Railroad*, pp. 56, 57, 62, 65; and John F. Stover, "Colonel Henry S. McComb, Mississippi Railroad Adventurer."

[19] George R. Taylor, *The Transportation Revolution*, p. 238; Harry Scheiber, "Economic Change in the Civil War Era," p. 410. Jones & Laughlin figures were derived from data in various articles of partnership and from H. S. Geneen to W. R. Compton, December 2, 1932, Old History Papers, Jones & Laughlin Steel Corp. Papers.

[20] Robert E. Gallman, "Gross National Product in the United States, 1834–1909," pp. 26, 34; figures are in 1860 dollars.

term funding was related to, and made possible by, developments in the Civil War economy, which often terminated the wholesaler's long-standing role as the principal source of manufacturing working capital.

THE WAR ECONOMY AND ITS EFFECT ON WORKING CAPITAL

Many historians and economists have noted a basic change in the conduct of northern commerce during the Civil War: a general shift away from long-term credit toward doing business for cash, or on current account with monthly billing. The explanation commonly offered for this striking development follows the comments of one contemporary businessman: "The fluctuating value of the depreciated currency made long credits quite hazardous, and when this became apparent in the early years of the War, sales were brought as nearly as possible to a cash or short-credit basis."[21] Wesley Mitchell, historian of the greenbacks, elaborated on his theme:

Men realized their inability to foresee the future and, knowing that it might bring great price fluctuations in either direction, sought protection against these changes by limiting their future pecuniary obligations as much as possible. . . . When no one could foresee with confidence what would be the relative purchasing power of a dollar three months in advance, it was obviously risky for a merchant to accept a note due in ninety days for goods sold, or to give such a note for goods bought. Consequently, cash business increased in importance and credit operations diminished.[22]

The diminution of credit operations was well underway by August, 1862, and spread even to the West, which had "long been wont to strain its credit to the utmost."[23]

Manufacturers as well as merchants abandoned past practices. Virtually every commodity from boilers and teaspoons to nails and textiles brought cash, for manufacturers often refused to sell on credit at all, or offered only monthly terms. To one customer who asked for a steam engine on credit, Hollingsworth and Harvey wrote, "We have to pay cash for nearly everything, and must request our customers to do the same." By 1865 Reed and Barton, Taunton, Massachusetts, silversmiths, were collecting more than 90 per cent of their accounts within sixty days. Fall River Iron flatly refused to ship nails except on a cash basis, and Pepperell cut its usual credit terms from six months to one. The records of other firms, such as Gibbons and Huston and Cornwall Furnace, reveal the same pattern: the volume of notes received

[21] Knowlton, *Pepperell's Progress*, p. 90. See also Joseph J. Klein, "The Development of Mercantile Instruments of Credit in the United States"; and Joseph E. Hedges, *Commercial Banking and the Stock Market Before 1863*, pp. 86–87.

[22] Mitchell, *History of the Greenbacks*, pp. 374–75.

[23] *Ibid.*, p. 375.

in payment declined drastically during the war; and the term of those notes accepted decreased, usually to thirty or sixty days.[24]

This new method of doing business had immediate and significant effects on manufacturers' finances. First, since manufacturers realized the proceeds from sales quickly, the amount of working capital needed to sustain any given volume of production diminished considerably relative to prewar requirements. Second, because manufacturers both paid and received cash, their need to seek loans and advances diminished, with the happy consequence that interest payments no longer siphoned off a large share of profits. Since profits in wartime were higher, and the manufacturer was able to retain a greater portion of them than he had in the antebellum period, manufacturers could and did use new affluence to eliminate old debts to their suppliers and distributors and to finance new construction without the wholesaler's aid.

For many manufacturers this was the realization of a long-standing goal, for they, like most Americans, had always exhibited a strong streak of independence which manifested itself in the desire to be beholden to no man. They regarded their businesses as personal creations, and they often felt that continued indebtedness reflected unfavorably on their character and industry and that it literally and figuratively constituted a mortgage on their heirs.

Practical considerations reinforced this sentimental repugnance to protracted indebtedness. Manufacturers were well aware that continued financial reliance on distributors meant continued merchant influence over the kinds of goods produced and over the prices and terms at which products were sold and materials purchased. They also understood that the first step toward independence was to get business on a cash basis, and that, if this could be done, significant cost reductions would result.

The Civil War presented many manufacturers with a long-awaited opportunity to get off the credit treadmill. They seized it with celerity, and this, as much as the hazards of doing a credit business in a period of fluctuating money values, explains the shift from credit to cash during the war. Manufacturers, after all, had always done business in an atmosphere of monetary uncertainty, for the lack of a national currency after the demise of the Second National Bank had forced them to use as "money" notes issued by banks, customers, and merchants. The value of the first two was, with a few exceptions, always uncertain. Merchants' notes were safer, but could be obtained only at a price, and the price fluctuated unpredictably.

Thus, from the manufacturer's point of view, the "monetary uncertainty" of the war differed little from his previous experience. What was different was the fact that, while in the antebellum period the manufacturer had little

[24] Hollingsworth & Harvey to William Shakespear, October 7, 1864, Hollingsworth & Harvey Papers; George S. Gibb, *The Whitesmiths of Taunton*, p. 183; Correspondence, 1864–65, Fall River Iron Papers; Knowlton, *Pepperell's Progress*, p. 90.

choice but to do business on credit and accept a variety of paper in payment, the high level of wartime demand made it possible to insist on cash.

In this sellers' market, manufacturers who had usually had to do business on the merchants' terms soon adopted policies that minimized the effect of fluctuating currency values. They offset rising material and labor costs, the result of inflation, by adjusting prices. Often this was done after their original quotation had been accepted, a practice that would have been unthinkable in prewar years. In August, 1864, for example, Hollingsworth and Harvey wrote commission merchant David Haines, "Since writing you . . . there has been another advance of iron prices which would make two . . . boilers cost $250 more than the price we gave you."[25]

The ability to minimize losses in this way, together with rising profits and reduced interest costs was a major factor in the manufacturer's increased ability to supply his own capital from retained earnings. In addition, the development of new methods of mobilizing and transferring capital during the Civil War and afterward made it possible for manufacturers to supplement their own resources by drawing on the nation's stock of capital as a whole.

MANUFACTURERS AND THE NATIONAL CAPITAL MARKET

Tracing the changes that made it possible for manufacturers to draw on the national capital market without utilizing their dealers as intermediaries is a perplexing problem. In general terms it is clear that significant developments in this area occurred during the 1860s. Before the war formal financial agencies that pooled the savings of the public at large rarely supplied capital to manufacturers outside the textile industry. In the 1870s such financing was common. Carnegie Steel and Pabst Brewing are but two of a number of major producers who secured large bank loans to help finance growth. In succeeding decades of the nineteenth century, banks and insurance companies routinely played a role in the building of giant firms such as Pittsburgh Reduction (Alcoa), Swift, and Standard Oil.[26] It seems reasonably certain that the Civil War hastened the change. Indeed, after an elaborate study of the American capital market, 1846–1914, economist Richard Sylla concluded that there was "one great catalyst of capital market development: the Civil War."[27]

[25] Hollingsworth & Harvey to David Haines, August 29, 1864, Hollingsworth & Harvey Papers.

[26] Joseph F. Wall, *Andrew Carnegie*, p. 335; Thomas C. Cochran, *The Pabst Brewing Company*, pp. 85, 404; Paul B. Trescott, *Financing American Enterprise*, pp. 71–75, 84–85, 103; Allan Nevins, *John D. Rockefeller*, pp. 194, 248–49; Raymond W. Goldsmith, *Financial Intermediaries in the American Economy Since 1900*, p. 59.

[27] Richard E. Sylla, "The American Capital Market, 1846–1914," p. iii; see also his "Federal Policy, Banking Market Structure, and Capital Mobilization in the United States, 1863–1913."

Although Sylla's exposition offers few specific examples to support his conclusions, he does posit some explanations for the war's effect on capital markets, and much of the available evidence seems to support them. He suggests, for example, that the federal government's wartime budget formed a link from capital markets to the industrial sector. The bulk of government bonds was sold in capital markets to which manufacturers had no access, but the proceeds often went to them to pay for government purchases of manufactured goods. Since the producer's profits on government contracts contributed to his capital, it appears that the combination of Civil War finance and purchasing effected the first significant transfer of capital from the general public into the manufacturing sector. In the transfer the manufacturing distributor played no part, and this too was a precedent, for it marked the first important infusion of outside capital accomplished without his assistance. The government marketed its bonds through the Philadelphia banker Jay Cooke, and it paid manufacturers either in cash or with certificates of indebtedness (notes, in effect) with terms of from one to three years.

The use of certificates of indebtedness as a means of payment marked a turning point in the manufacturer's conduct of his financial affairs because they were a means by which he established an enduring business relationship with private and commercial bankers. While few banks would lend money to, or discount notes for, manufacturers before the war, most of them apparently discounted federal certificates of indebtedness willingly and at relatively low rates. In 1863, for example, when a greenback dollar was worth sixty-eight cents in gold, Fall River Iron Works sold its certificates to banks for ninety-eight and a half cents on the dollar.[28]

The certificates obviously attracted bankers into dealings with manufacturers, and relationships thus cultivated may have ripened in the warmth of wartime prosperity. Sylla argues that they did, and that the development and proliferation of financial intermediaries facilitated an efficient transfer of capital into the industrial sector and "was a reflection of the growing division of labor and specialization in finance."[29]

Such specialization clearly took place, for there was a steady growth of private banks from 398 in 1853 to 1,108 in 1860.[30] Most private bankers were merchants who had abandoned the marketing side of the merchant's dual role to concentrate on finance. Many of them had been, like Alexander McKim of Baltimore, dealers in manufactured products, and they therefore possessed an extensive knowledge of the intricacies of the trade and the reliability of various producers. Wartime prosperity must have acted as a strong inducement to put that knowledge to work by engaging in manufac-

28 Fall River Iron Papers.
29 Sylla, "American Capital Market," p. 208.
30 *Ibid.*, p. 209.

turing finance. Historians of commerce have traced such an evolution in the textile industry, and, while confirmation must await more extensive research, it seems reasonable to assume that the practice became general during the Civil War.[31]

The war, then, contributed to the manufacturing distributor's declining role as a source of capital. Through government finance and purchasing policies and the activities of private bankers, the manufacturing sector as a whole secured its first access to the pool of capital formed by public savings. With this supplement to wartime profits, many American manufacturers replaced their patchwork capital structure with a firm financial base that enabled them to deal with wholesalers from a new position of strength. This position was buttressed by the manufacturer's ability to dispense with the merchant's services as a financial expert.

THE DECLINE OF WHOLESALERS AS FINANCIAL AGENTS

The merchant's value as a financial expert declined during and after the Civil War for several reasons. First, the switch from credit to cash virtually eliminated the merchant's role as credit consultant and guarantor of payment. Second, the use of cash and the re-establishment of a national currency reduced the prewar blizzard of commercial paper to a manageable trickle. Third, manufacturers, pressed to the limit in supervising production, often emulated textile mills and railroads by hiring treasurers to handle their financial affairs. Fourth, as a logical consequence of his involvement in manufacturing finance, the private banker replaced the merchant as consultant.

The Civil War thus often deprived the distributors of manufactured products of their financial relevance to manufacturers by providing a combination of greater retained earnings, new sources of capital, and simplified monetary structures. Postwar events not only guaranteed that the role would never be resumed but also made the separation between marketing and financial agencies a general phenomenon throughout the manufacturing sector. Profits continued high in most industries until 1873, and by that time the trickle of outside capital had become a river which flows yet. Selling for cash or on current account continued as a common practice after the war. Internal financial management became a departmentalized function of management bureaucracy. The financing of transactions became the province of specialized agencies that evolved from private banks and brokerage houses. Although the process was a gradual one, by the end of the century it was virtually complete. In 1850 it would have been difficult to find a producer not dependent on his distributors for capital; sixty years later one declared,

---

[31] William H. Hillyer, "Four Centuries of Factoring."

"the manufacturer who needs the jobber as a commercial banker is a weak manufacturer."[32]

At the end of the Civil War the transition was well underway; the wholesaler, however, remained a dominant factor in manufacturing distribution. Diminished though his financial role was, he retained his importance as a sales agent. As long as goods remained undifferentiated and markets were diffuse, he remained the most efficient and effective means of reaching customers. His position was vulnerable, however, for specialization and loss of financial relevance had reduced his traditional cluster of competencies to a single function, his diverse stock in trade to a single commodity, and his broad horizons to a single market.

[32] Beech Nut Packing Co. File, #72222–75–1, pt. 1, U.S. Bureau of Corporations Records.

CHAPTER VIII

The Manufacturer Ascendant: Changing Markets in Producers' Goods

The nineteenth-century experience of firms in the ferrous metals industry was typical of the many industries that manufactured or processed producers' goods. These industries shared similar patterns in the distribution of their products in the first two-thirds of the century, and they also shared the experiences that led to the gradual replacement of the old marketing network of independent middlemen with manufacturer-owned distribution organizations. An examination and analysis of the history of the iron and steel industry will suggest why it and many other producers' goods industries underwent these transformations in distribution.

Broad changes in the distribution pattern of the American iron and steel industry occurred in the latter part of the nineteenth century.[1] In this industry, as in so many others, the years from the end of the Civil War through the turn of the century witnessed the passing of the distribution function from the hands of the specialized commission merchant and broker to the hands of the manufacturer. In the early decades of the nineteenth century, brokers and commission merchants were the agents through whom iron and steel manufacturers filled many of their requirements for raw materials and sold

[1] This chapter concerns the producers of finished products (the large firms that made end products and that had their own furnaces, foundries, and rolling mills) and the makers of semifinished items such as pigs, blooms, and bars. The semifinished manufacturers arose, of course, before the firms that made the end products in their own foundries and rolling mills. The production process for the semifinished group was much simpler and far less capital intensive than that involved in the production of finished goods in the complex, technologically sophisticated steel plants of the years after the Civil War.

much of their finished product. In addition to their services as distribution agents, middlemen often provided crucial working capital for iron manufacturers, as they did for producers in many other manufacturing industries. From 1870 to 1900, however, the importance of these middlemen declined. As the industry was transformed from a highly diffuse one with relatively small producing units to a highly concentrated one with relatively large producing units, manufacturers came increasingly to assume the functions of wholesalers. As retained earnings accumulated and as sources of available capital grew, the financial usefulness of brokers and commission merchants decreased. As the increasingly large manufacturing firms adopted strategies of vertical integration backward into raw materials, the importance of middlemen as suppliers of these materials underwent a corresponding decline. As the sales volume of the large iron and steel firms increased, and as sales became concentrated among a relatively few large customers, manufacturers moved to create their own distribution networks.

Some economists, such as George J. Stigler, have argued that vertical integration (that is, the performance by a single manufacturing concern of a wide range of functions, including the purchase of raw materials, the fabrication or processing of materials into semifinished goods, wholesaling, retailing, and the like) is typical only of very young industries and declining industries.[2] A new industry, the argument goes, is forced to assume a range of functions because of problems it faces in establishing itself in the market. As the industry grows, many of these functions are taken over by other firms, which can profitably specialize in them because of the increased market. As the industry declines, so do its ancillary, specialized industries, and the manufacturing firm is compelled to reappropriate functions no longer in enough demand to support independent firms. Stigler further argues (citing the textile industry as an illustration) that the pattern of integration, disintegration, and reintegration is typical of firms in the modern economy. The evidence of the present study suggests that, while large firms may pass through the three stages described by Stigler, they frequently engage in reintegration or extended integration as a result of rising, not declining, demand.

Further, the evidence strongly suggests that control of the product, needs for warehousing, and product differentiation by advertising in brand names were not important factors in the decision of steel firms to do their own marketing. Only a handful of steel companies built chains of warehouses. Although quality control was of some importance, most iron and steel goods remained fairly simple and relatively standardized. Unlike firms in some other industries, steel companies did not utilize advertising or the idea of differentiated products. Far more important was the role of concentrated demand

---

[2] George J. Stigler, "The Division of Labor is Limited by the Extent of the Market."

among large consumers. That demand and the consequent creation of sales offices developed even before the great merger movement of the late 1890s, although the latter did further concentrate the demand for iron and steel goods.

The change to direct marketing came gradually throughout most of the iron and steel industry. The determining factors in the survival or decline of brokers and commission merchants in the distribution of ferrous products were the nature of the market and the degree of the product's technological complexity.

REVOLUTION IN THE FERROUS METALS INDUSTRY

Although the Civil War was a time of greatly increased prices and moderately increased output for the ferrous metals industry (in short, a time of rising profits), the structure of production and distribution in the industry was little affected.[3] As Victor Clark later observed, "no significant change occurred in the organization of the iron and steel industry during the Civil War and the subsequent decade."[4] During the following three decades, however, very important changes did occur in the industry. Change came not only in organization but in technology, distribution, and the kinds of ferrous products sold in the United States. The result was a transformation of the industry from its early nineteenth-century form to one very similar to that of the steel industry of today.

As Peter Temin has shown, the composition of primary iron and steel products changed greatly between 1869 and 1909.[5] At the beginning of that period, rails, bars, and rods (except rods for wire) accounted for more than two-thirds of the total American production of iron and steel. Indeed, rails were so important a part of the industry that *Appleton's Annual Cyclopedia* observed in 1882 that "the iron business is particularly subject to fluctuations, owing to its dependence on railroad-building, and to the fitful way in which railroad extension takes place."[6] That year was, however, the high-water mark for rail production. At the same time (the early 1880s), Andrew Carnegie shifted the newly acquired Homestead works from the production of rails, ingots, and billets to the production of structural shapes and steel specialities. Homestead pointed the way to the industry's future.[7] By 1909 the share of total production accounted for by rails, bars, and rods had fallen to about

---

[3] For several production and price series in the iron and steel industry before, during, and after the Civil War, see American Iron & Steel Assoc., *Annual Statistical Report* (1886), pp. 45, 49, 55–57.

[4] Victor S. Clark, *History of Manufactures in the United States*, 2: 83.

[5] Peter Temin, "The Composition of Iron and Steel Products, 1869–1909."

[6] *Appleton's Annual Cyclopedia and Register of Important Events of the Year 1882*, p. 115.

[7] James H. Bridge, *The Inside History of the Carnegie Steel Company*, pp. 159–61.

one-third. Four products increased their share of production, and three of them—wire rods, skelp (strips used primarily in the making of pipe), and structural shapes—became, as Temin notes, "newly important products."[8] New markets were created by the growth of America's cities, which needed structural shapes for the construction of buildings, as well as wire rope and cables for suspension bridges, elevators, and many other purposes. The cities and the new petroleum industry provided wider markets for skelp.[9]

Change also came to the iron and steel industry in other ways. Perhaps the most important development in the industry was the coming of heavy capital investment, especially in the production of primary iron and steel. The use of first the Bessemer furnace and later the open-hearth process for the production of steel, coupled with the construction of much larger and more costly blast furnaces, made ferrous metals one of the most capital intensive industries in the manufacturing sector. The iron industry had always been relatively capital intensive; before the Civil War only textiles had exceeded the capital requirements of iron. In 1850, a time when most American manufacturing was labor intensive and heavily reliant upon working rather than fixed capital, the mean invested capital per establishment (factory) in the pig iron industry was $46,000. By 1860 this figure had risen to about $86,000 per pig iron establishment, and factories producing rolled iron had a mean capital investment of $78,000.[10] In the crucial years from 1870 through 1900, the capital invested per establishment in the iron and steel industry increased tremendously (see Table III). As the Bureau of the Census noted in regard to the data in Table III, "this shows strikingly the concentration that has marked the development of the industry during this period."[11] Highly capital intensive factories appeared in the newer sector of the industry, steel. In 1880 the mean capital investment in active establishments producing steel ingots or castings and rolled steel was approximately $330,000. By 1900 the figure had climbed to slightly more than one million dollars per establishment. The number of steel works and rolling mills (establishments) rose during those twenty years by less than 20 per cent, but the capital invested increased by nearly 300 per cent.[12] The crude iron and steel industry had come very far indeed since its antebellum days. As one manufacturer observed in 1895: "the increased production of pig iron [in the

[8] Temin, "Composition of Iron and Steel Products," p. 451. The other product that enjoyed increased production belonged to the traditional category, plates and sheets (other than nail plate).

[9] On the importance of expanding urban markets in the latter part of the nineteenth century, see Edward C. Kirkland, *Industry Comes of Age*, chap. 12.

[10] U.S. Census Office, *Ninth Census of the United States, 1870*, 3: 601–8. The average investment in establishments producing cast iron was about $12,500 in 1850 and $17,000 in 1860.

[11] Both the data and the comment are drawn from U.S. Bureau of the Census, *Census of Manufactures, 1905*, pt. 4, p. 4.

[12] Abraham Berglund, *The United States Steel Corporation*, p. 34.

United States] up to 1855 was due chiefly to an augmented number of blast furnaces and enlarged dimensions of shafts. But what was at that time considered as a large furnace would now rank as small, while the quantity of metal obtained in a year from the greatest producers of [1855] was equaled by the monthly output of a number of modern blast furnaces in 1895."[13]

TABLE III: CAPITAL INVESTED PER ESTABLISHMENT IN THE IRON AND STEEL INDUSTRY, 1870–1900

	1870	1880	1890	1900
Number of establishments in iron and steel industry	808	792	719	669
Capital invested (in millions of dollars)	121.7	209.9	414.0	590.5
Capital per establishment (in thousands of dollars)	150.0	260.0	580.0	880.0
Value of products (in millions of dollars)	207.2	296.6	478.7	804.0

The increased capital investment, coupled with numerous technological advances, greatly reduced the unit costs in the industry in the latter part of the nineteenth century. The Bessemer process, which made possible the volume production of steel, was the first of many technological breakthroughs made after the Civil War. Improvements in technology subjected the ferrous metals industry to "substantial economies of scale."[14] In the estimate of one scholar, the average furnace of 1900 could produce a ton of pig iron at a cost of from 40 to 50 per cent less than the typical furnace of the early 1880s.[15] The increase in product per furnace is indicated by the fact that during the years 1889–1909 the number of furnaces (in active establishments) declined from 473 to 388, while the product leapt 190 per cent.[16] The most striking illustration of the new economies of scale is the average capital invested per ton of product in the iron and steel industry from 1870

[13] John Birkenbine, "Forty Years of Progress in the Pig Iron Industry," *Iron Age*, January 2, 1896, p. 21.
[14] Lance E. Davis, "Capital Markets and Industrial Concentration," p. 264; see also David E. Novack and Richard Perlman, "The Structure of Wages in the American Iron and Steel Industry, 1860–1890," p. 338. The best sources on technological change and the resultant economies of scale are Clark, *History of Manufactures*, 2: chaps. 12 and 13, and Peter Temin, *Iron and Steel in Nineteenth Century America*, chaps. 6–8.
[15] Berglund, *United States Steel*, p. 37.
[16] U.S. Bureau of the Census, *Thirteenth Census of the United States*, 1910, 10: 220–21.

through 1900. The average investment per ton of product in 1870 was $37.31, and thereafter it steadily declined, falling to $32.36 in 1880, $25.46 in 1890, and $20.01 in 1900.[17] The large, expensive, and enormously productive factories in the primary iron and steel industry clearly did achieve considerable economies of scale.

Concomitant to shifts in the composition of products, increased capital investment, and the increase of production in large, efficient plants was the concentration of productive facilities among fewer firms. In the Pittsburgh area in 1869, for example, there were numerous manufacturers of primary and finished iron and steel products; by the early years of the twentieth century, most of these had become part of the large firms, such as United States Steel or Crucible Steel, which had come to dominate the industry.[18] Similar concentration occurred all over the country, and much of it came even before the great merger movement at the turn of the century.

Iron and steel firms merged for a variety of reasons. The retained earnings of some successful producers allowed them to acquire by purchase the facilities of competing firms. Sometimes the financial talents of a particular businessman—Andrew Carnegie, for instance—allowed a firm to assemble unusually large pools of capital. By these means and others, the iron and steel industry became increasingly oligopolistic between 1870 and 1900, and this allowed firms to accumulate the financial resources necessary to compete in the increasingly capital intensive industry.[19] The cumulative effects of the many great changes in the industry after the Civil War—the shifting composition of products, new technological advances, increased capital investment, the achievement of substantial economies of scale, and the coming of oligopoly—wrought a revolution in iron and steel. Only against the background of that revolution can the passage of the distribution function from commission merchants and brokers to large manufacturers be understood.

[17] Bureau of the Census, *Census of Manufactures, 1905*, pt. 4, p. 4.

[18] See, for example, Willis L. King (president of Jones & Laughlin), "Recollections and Conclusions from a Long Business Life," p. 225.

[19] The financial problem of the transition from the prewar industry of small firms to the era of scale economies is discussed in Davis, "Capital Markets and Industrial Concentration," pp. 258, 264. For the purposes of this inquiry it is not necessary to explain the coming of oligopoly to iron and steel; the problem is to relate the fact of increasing concentration to changes in the distribution network. Further, it is clear that the cooperation of manufacturers, whether through associations, pools, mergers, or whatever, had other ends as well as the simple accretion of large amounts of fixed capital. Because cooperation through associations, pools, or other "loose" arrangements does not appear to have had any significant impact on distribution, such cooperation is not considered here. The various pools, especially in the 1890s, were either price or production agreements, and none worked very well. Although the pools did not have much impact on marketing methods, they may have had some effect on the volume of sales by individual firms; see *Iron Age*, January 7 and February 11, 1897, and December 1, 1898, as well as the many parts of File #1940 of the records of the U.S. Bureau of Corporations, Record Group 122, National Archives, Washington, D.C.

MOTIVES FOR CHANGE IN DISTRIBUTION

The velocity and extent of the changes in distribution were not uniform throughout the iron and steel industry. Where manufacturers faced special marketing problems (as in the sale of technologically complex finished machines), they often had to dispense with the existing wholesaling structure very quickly. Where the product was simple and the market diffuse (as in the case of wire and nails), producers of some finished goods continued to find the old means of distribution adequate. In the primary iron and steel industry, manufacturers assumed the distribution function for their relatively simple, standard products whenever demand warranted such action.

In primary iron and steel, in the absence of special marketing problems such as the need for rapid distribution, consumer credit, demonstrations, highly skilled repair personnel, and the like, the passing of the wholesale function from the commission merchant to the manufacturer was largely the result of increased demand for a firm's goods in a particular sales area.[20] Theoretically, the manufacturer should move to create a sales office in a city when the cost of commissions paid on goods sold by commission merchants in that city exceeds the cost of establishing and operating a sales office there. However, while the producer could readily determine his costs under the existing commission merchant system, determining the cost of a sales office was much more difficult. It was necessary to compute the rental or purchase of office space, furniture, and equipment, plus remuneration for sales personnel. In addition, it was essential to consider the less tangible question of the availability of knowledgeable sales personnel and that of accounts lost while the new sales force familiarized itself with the local customers and their needs. For the late nineteenth-century manufacturer—even for a very large firm—these were not simple tasks. As a result, the decision to create a sales office was made in an imprecise and unsophisticated manner. It probably came long after the firm had passed the theoretical line between the relative costs of the alternative distribution systems.

The new distribution system resulted not only from increased demand but from more concentrated demand—that is, greater demand per region or customer. Rising aggregate demand undoubtedly played a role in bringing about more concentrated demand, but the latter proved the more important cause of change in distribution. As a result of the growth of larger firms in the finished ferrous goods industry, the primary producer counted among his potential customers more large firms, firms whose steady and substantial orders could mean a jump in the producer's sales in the market areas used by those larger customers. Perhaps more important was the fact that a rise in

---

[20] The importance of special marketing problems is discussed in Alfred D. Chandler, Jr., "The Beginnings of 'Big Business' in American Industry."

demand for a particular firm's goods in a particular market area could result
from a decrease in the number of competitors in that area. Indeed, this did
occur in the primary iron and steel industry as a result of the increased concentration brought about by mergers, purchases, or other means. As larger
and more efficient producers arose in the industry, they came increasingly to
dominate the large urban markets. Smaller, less efficient firms that could not
reap the sweet harvest of economies of scale were pushed steadily toward the
gray subservience of marginal production. Indeed, many furnaces that were
active in the 1870s had been abandoned by the 1890s because of their inability to compete with the large firms that employed the newer, more costly,
but more highly productive furnaces.[21] The increasing concentration, both in
larger factories and in larger firms, significantly raised the demand for a
firm's goods in a particular area; this in turn led to the assumption of the
sales function by many large producers.

The large firms assumed the sales function reluctantly and without great
dispatch. The step does not appear to have been taken because of any inability on the part of commission merchants to handle the increased flow of
primary iron and steel goods; the wholesaling firms could have expanded, or
more wholesaling firms could have entered the market in response to the
increased aggregate demand. Instead, the manufacturer moved to create his
own sales network only when demand in a given market area or areas had so
risen that it became obvious that the old network was more costly than a
new, producer-operated system would be.

The importance of an increased volume of sales in encouraging the primary manufacturers to assume the sales function is clear in the contrast between small and large producers. The small producer of pig iron, for example,
continued to market his goods in the manner in which he had made sales
before the rise of large, efficient firms. As was pointed out previously, many
small manufacturers had to assume the role of marginal producers or else
shut down production. Some continued to do business, of course, into the
first years of the twentieth century, but the number of these anachronistic
survivors was small. They continued to produce the same goods, but, because
they remained relatively small, the sales volume in their market cities never
grew large enough to encourage them to open sales offices. The Cornwall
Furnaces continued to rely on their agent Cabeen and Company of Philadelphia through the 1870s. In the eighties and early nineties, Cornwall's owners,
the Coleman family, made most of their pig iron sales through iron commission merchants such as Nimick and Company of Pittsburgh and J. Tatnall Lea
and Company or Pancoast and Rogers, both of Philadelphia. These iron commission merchants sold the Cornwall pig iron to a wide variety of customers,
including such growing firms as Bethlehem Iron, Alan Wood Steel, and

21 See U.S. Census Office, *Eleventh Census of the United States, 1890*, pt. 3, p. 400.

Lukens Steel.[22] The Pine Grove Furnaces, which were located very near the Cornwall Furnaces, also marketed their small pig iron output through commission merchants in the eighties and early nineties.[23] Western iron merchants, such as Rogers, Brown, and Company of Cincinnati, continued to market the output of the surviving small firms in the Hanging Rock iron district in the 1880s.[24] This pattern was the natural one for the small, traditional pig iron producer to follow. Because his sales volume never warranted it, he did not attempt to supplant the commission merchants.

The small producers of processed iron goods, like those making pig iron, continued to market their goods in the traditional manner. A good example is the Fall River Iron Works Company, which sold hoop iron, iron bars, and nails. In 1877 it was operating a rolling mill, a nail mill, and an iron foundry. Some local sales were made by the company, but commission merchants throughout New England and in New York and Philadelphia marketed most of the firm's products. Borden and Lovell, New York iron brokers, acted as Fall River Iron's agents in New York City. With the exception of a company-owned hardware store in Providence, however, Fall River Iron never attained a sufficient volume of sales to encourage the operation of sales offices.[25] A similar pattern existed among the makers of cast iron pipe and other small iron producers.[26]

By contrast, the new, large firms followed a general pattern of gradual progression toward a company-operated sales network. Many sales, especially in the 1870s and 1880s, continued to be made through the specialized commission merchants in the cities. As the sales volume in a particular city grew, however, the producing firm often made arrangements with one particular iron-marketing company in the area, authorizing that company to act as exclusive sales agent for the producer's goods in that geographic region. Oc-

---

[22] Incoming Correspondence; Pig Iron Order Book, Cornwall Anthracite & Donaghmore Furnaces, 1866–81; Pig Iron Sales Book, R. W. and W. Coleman, 1858–78; Cornwall Anthracite Furnaces Pig Iron Orders, 1881–92; Pig Iron Order Book, Bird Coleman, Donaghmore, and North Cornwall Furnaces, 1882–84; and Pig Iron Order Book, Bird Coleman, Donaghmore, North Cornwall, and Robesonia Furnaces, 1886–88; all in the Cornwall Furnace Papers. We are grateful to Professor Stanley Engerman for bringing this manuscript collection to our attention.
The Coleman furnaces, like so many small producers, found it more and more difficult to compete with the new, larger firms. Some of the Cornwall furnaces were abandoned in the 1880s, others were closed during the 1890s. See Frederic K. Miller, "The Rise of an Iron Community," 1740–1865, pp. 141–42 and ff.

[23] Letterbooks, 1888–94, Pine Grove Furnace Papers.

[24] Vernon D. Keeler, "An Economic History of the Jackson County Iron Industry," p. 213. Producers in all parts of the country shipped both on consignment to commission merchants and (via merchants) direct to consumers.

[25] The Borden family (Borden and Lovell) owned most of the Fall River Iron Works Co. By the end of the century they were shifting from iron to the production of textiles. See Fall River Iron Works Co. Papers.

[26] Henry J. Noble, *History of the Cast Iron Pressure Pipe Industry in the United States of America*, pp. 64–65.

casionally the wholesale firm acted as sales agent for just a single company, but the common arrangement was for the wholesaler to be the agent for several producers at the same time. The agents received a commission on sales and occasionally a small salary as well. Whenever the volume of company sales in an area made it clearly profitable to create a sales office there, either the exclusive area agent was asked to work solely for one producing firm, or the producer hired other sales personnel to operate his offices. The 1890s saw a network of producer-operated sales offices open in major cities across the nation. Possibly the depression of the nineties made manufacturers more acutely conscious of the need to be as efficient as possible in distribution as well as in production. By the early years of this century the present pattern of wholesaling by manufacturing companies was clearly visible.

The firm that became the largest American iron and steel manufacturer before the formation of United States Steel, Carnegie Steel Company, pioneered in the development of the new sales pattern. The Carnegie enterprises invested heavily in the new production methods and were always among the most efficient producers in the industry.[27] Sales rose rapidly for the various Carnegie steel companies, and so did profits.[28] In the early years of the Carnegie companies, many sales were made through iron commission

[27] There is little point in reviewing here the rise of the Carnegie Steel Co. and its role in the formation of the giant U.S. Steel Corp. No good business or economic history of Carnegie exists at present, nor is it likely that one will be written until such time as U.S. Steel opens its massive archives to scholars. Some details of the Carnegie saga may be found in such secondary sources as Burton J. Hendrick, *The Life of Andrew Carnegie*; Bridge, *Inside History of Carnegie Steel*; Berglund, *United States Steel*; Bernard Alderson, *Andrew Carnegie*; Andrew Carnegie, *Autobiography of Andrew Carnegie*; John K. Winkler, *Incredible Carnegie*; Arundel Cotter, "The History of the United States Steel Corporation"; John Moody, "The United States Steel Corporation"; and Charles M. Schwab, "The Huge Enterprises Built Up By Andrew Carnegie." By 1900 the consolidated Carnegie Steel enterprises produced about 20 per cent of the pig iron and about 80 per cent of all the Bessemer and open-hearth steel made in the United States; see John Moody, ed., *Moody's Manual of Industrial and Miscellaneous Securities*, 1900, p. 401. A recent study of the Carnegie experience is Louis M. Hacker's *The World of Andrew Carnegie, 1865-1901*. Joseph W. Wall's recent biography, *Andrew Carnegie*, contains some new information on Carnegie's early career.

[28] The net profits of the various Carnegie steel enterprises (Edgar Thompson Steel Co., 1876-81; Carnegie Bros. & Co., 1881-92; Carnegie, Phipps & Co., 1886-92; and Carnegie Steel, 1892-97) were reported in a letter from F. T. Lovejoy, secretary of Carnegie Steel, to Andrew Carnegie, January 26, 1898, Andrew Carnegie Papers, vol. 48. The profits (rounded to the nearest thousand) were:

1875	$19,000	1883	$1,019,000	1891	$4,300,000
1876	$172,000	1884	$1,301,000	1892	$4,000,000
1877	$190,000	1885	$1,192,000	1893	$3,000,000
1878	$300,000	1886	$2,925,000	1894	$4,000,000
1879	$512,000	1887	$3,442,000	1895	$5,000,000
1880	$1,558,000	1888	$1,942,000	1896	$6,000,000
1881	$2,000,000	1889	$3,540,000	1897	$7,000,000
1882	$2,128,000	1890	$5,350,000		

merchants. By the latter part of the 1880s, however, these enterprises had begun using authorized, exclusive area agents for the sale of Carnegie products in their areas. These manufacturers' representatives acted for other producers as well, but they enjoyed the exclusive right to sell Carnegie iron and steel in their areas. The subsequent transition of the wholesale firm from agent for several companies to agent for only one was gradual, and the exact point at which the transition was completed is often unclear. For example, Carnegie's Philadelphia agent was J. Ogden Hoffman of J. W. Hoffman and Company, iron merchants. The Hoffman company made sales for Carnegie in the Philadelphia area to such customers as the Lukens Steel Company.[29] At the same time, Carnegie sales in New York were made through A. R. Whitney and Company, iron and steel brokers. In the early nineties, Whitney and Company styled itself as an "Agency of Carnegie Steel," as well as an agency of the Glasgow Tube Works, the Brooklyn Wire Nail Company, and the Riverside Iron Works.[30] Both the Hoffman and Whitney agencies had become sales offices of Carnegie Steel by the late nineties; J. O. Hoffman and A. R. Whitney even attended several meetings of the Board of Managers of Carnegie Steel in those years.[31] John C. Fleming, Carnegie's Chicago sales agent from the late 1880s to the early years of this century, was a co-partner in two iron commission houses in that city prior to his employment with the Carnegie firm.[32] A Carnegie office was opened in Boston as early as 1888, serving New England customers such as the Washburn and Moen Company.[33] By the end of the nineteenth century, Carnegie Steel had company sales offices in New York, Philadelphia, Boston, Chicago, Montreal, Pittsburgh, Cincinnati, Cleveland, Saint Louis, New Orleans, Atlanta, Detroit, Denver, Buffalo, and other cities.[34] The growing Carnegie firm em-

[29] Correspondence between Hoffman and the Lukens Company, 1888–92, Lukens Steel Co. Papers; see also the telegrams from the Philadelphia agency to the Carnegie enterprises in 1890, Andrew Carnegie Papers, vol. 11.

[30] Correspondence of A. R. Whitney to Andrew Carnegie, 1893, Andrew Carnegie Papers, vol. 23; see also J. E. Moore to Andrew Carnegie, May 5, 1886, *ibid.*, vol. 9.

[31] It was the practice of the Carnegie Board of Managers to invite their sales agents from major cities to sit in on board meetings; see the Minutes of the Meetings of the Board of Managers, 1897–99, *ibid.*

[32] The two firms were Rogers & Co. and Whittemore & Co. See *Lakeside Directory of the City of Chicago* (Chicago: Chicago Directory Co.), 1881 ed., pp. 435, 1017; 1885 ed., p. 1451; and 1900 ed. pp. 379, 653.

[33] The *Boston Almanac and Business Directory* (Boston: Sampson, Davenport, 1888) first listed a Carnegie office in its 1889 edition. See the letters of Washburn & Moen to Wilbur S. Locke, Carnegie's sales agent, 1897–98, American Steel & Wire Co. Papers.

[34] New York, Philadelphia, Boston, Chicago, and Montreal are discussed elsewhere. For the remaining cities see: *Pittsburgh and Allegheny Directory, 1899* (Pittsburgh: R. L. Polk & Co. and R. L. Dudley, 1899), p. 274; *Williams' Cincinnati Directory, 1901* (Cincinnati: Williams Directory Co., 1901), pp. 322, 1730; *Cleveland Directory, 1901* (Cleveland: Cleveland Directory Co., 1899), p. 1356; *Gould's St. Louis Directory, 1900* (St. Louis: Gould's Directory Co., 1900), p. 344; *Soard's*

ployed a general sales agent who sent weekly letters to the various sales agents informing them of the over-all sales picture and urging them to push whatever items were overstocked or moving slowly. The general sales agent sat on the Board of Managers and reported regularly on the volume and composition of the firm's sales.[35]

Whenever Carnegie Steel could not secure the services of an iron merchant who had acted as the company's area agent, it tried to hire a local merchant already familiar with the customers in the region. In 1897, for example, Carnegie's Montreal sales agent died, and the company consulted some of the large customers of the Montreal office, seeking recommendations for a good local man. A suitable substitute was found, but he had no experience in selling structural steel. The company was then forced to send another man to Montreal to assist the first in sales of structural shapes.[36] The Carnegie sales offices throughout North America made direct contact with customers, supplying them with occasional needs or negotiating large contracts for annual supplies.[37]

When Carnegie Steel expanded beyond North America into overseas markets, the firm followed the same pattern in creating a sales network. Again, the demand for the company's goods in a particular market area was the determining factor in the decision whether to rely on manufacturers' agents or to create company sales offices. When Carnegie expanded from its British market base in an attempt to secure a share of the continental market, the Board of Managers decided to make "commission arrangements with leading brokers" in Europe, "giving each certain exclusive territory."[38] The

---

New Orleans Directory, 1903 (New Orleans: Soard's Directory Co., 1903), pp. 186, 816; Atlanta City Directory, 1901 (Atlanta: Maloney Co., 1901), pp. 634, 915; Detroit City Directory, 1900 (Detroit: R. L. Polk & Co., 1900), p. 395; Denver City Directory, 1900 (Denver: Ballenger & Richards Co., 1900), pp. 1163, 1462; Buffalo City Directory, 1900 (Buffalo: Courier & Co., 1900), pp. 311, 1205. Many of the offices had been created by the time of the consolidation of the Carnegie enterprises into the Carnegie Steel Co., Ltd., in 1892. "In addition to the general offices located at Pittsburgh," noted the industry's leading trade journal, "sales offices for the sale of the various products of the firm are located in the following cities: Boston, New York, Philadelphia, Buffalo, Cleveland, Detroit, Chicago, Minneapolis, Cincinnati, Atlanta, St. Louis, Denver, and San Francisco" (Iron Age, June 30, 1892).

[35] The letters to sales agents and the general sales agent's reports to the Board of Managers during the final years of the decade are scattered throughout the Andrew Carnegie Papers for those years.

[36] Minutes of the Board of Managers of Carnegie Steel, November 21, 1897, ibid., vol. 45. Sales agents were normally paid a commission of 1 per cent on area sales; the arrangement with the new Montreal agent stipulated that he should receive that commission and that he should conduct the office and pay all the expenses except the salary of the assistant sent to handle the structural work.

[37] See, for example, John Leishman to Andrew Carnegie, December 6, 1895, ibid., vol. 34; Minutes of the Meetings of the Board of Managers of Carnegie Steel, February 8, 1898, ibid., vol. 49; and Minutes of the Meetings of the Board of Managers of Carnegie Steel, January 3, 1899, ibid., vol. 60.

[38] Minutes of the Meetings of the Board of Managers of Carnegie Steel, August 8, 1897, ibid., vol. 43.

directors cautioned the Sales Department against going to "any expense to establish Agencies," because they felt that there was as yet insufficient demand for the company's products in European markets. Charles M. Schwab pointed out that entry into the Latin American market had been achieved in the same way; he noted that Carnegie Steel had a "very satisfactory arrangement with a firm of Commission Agents in Mexico City. We are at no expense." He suggested a similar tack in attempting to keep sales costs down until a sufficiently high volume of demand should emerge in China and Australia.[39] In later years, when that demand was achieved, United States Steel opened sales offices around the world.

Another important producer of primary ferrous goods, the Lukens Iron and Steel Company (post–Civil War successor to Gibbons and Huston), made its sales in much the same manner as did the giant Carnegie company. The Lukens firm was one of the largest producers of open-hearth steel and steel plates in the eastern United States and was a pioneer American manufacturer of plates.[40] In the eighties and nineties the firm made sales in several different ways. Traveling salesmen were in the company's employ, although they also acted for other producers. A. M. Castle, for example, was a Lukens traveling agent in the West. He received a salary from Lukens but also derived commissions on sales made for other firms. Castle handled accounts for midwestern customers such as Standard Oil of Ohio and Pabst Brewing. He placed orders, heard complaints, and collected on unpaid accounts.[41]

In addition to the sales made by traveling agents, Lukens sales were made all over the country through iron merchants who placed orders with the firm.[42] Many sales were placed through leading Philadelphia iron merchants, such as J. Tatnall Lea and Company, Lindsay, Parvin, and Company, C. W. and H. W. Middleton Company, and J. F. Bailey.[43] These commission merchants relayed their customers' orders and specifications and provided routing and shipping information; Lukens then shipped direct to the customer.

Sometimes the Lukens firm authorized a particular manufacturer's agent to market its products in a specified geographic area. F. X. Froment Company and Coolbaugh, Pomeroy, and Company of New York, Gilchrist and Taylor of Boston, and J. F. Corlett of Cincinnati were authorized agents who also

[39] Minutes of the Meetings of the Board of Managers of Carnegie Steel, August 18, 1897, *ibid.*

[40] John Moody, ed., *Moody's Manual of Railroads and Corporation Securities, 1908*, p. 2367. According to that *Manual*, the annual capacity of the Lukens plants was 380,000 net tons of steel plates.

[41] Correspondence of A. M. Castle, Lukens Steel Papers; see also the correspondence of another traveling agent, R. S. Groves, *ibid.* Castle was also the owner of a Chicago iron brokerage house; see *Chicago City Directory, 1900*, p. 2272. Plates were used most often for the construction or repair of industrial boilers and other machinery.

[42] General Orders, 1880–95, Lukens Steel Papers.

[43] See the correspondence from these firms to Lukens Iron & Steel, *ibid.* Needless to say, some local sales were made by direct contact between Lukens and Philadelphia area customers.

ran a general iron commission business.[44] A Lukens contract with one of the firm's authorized agents, Thomas J. Adams and Son of Cincinnati, authorized the Adams firm to "represent us as our Sales Agents in the following cities," listing the Ohio cities of Richmond, Hamilton, Dayton, Ironton, Marietta, and Cincinnati. Adams was to receive 2.5 per cent on all sales, with "all shipments to be made direct to the customer and invoices to be rendered direct, you to be furnished with copies of same." The contract further stipulated that "of course in all cases where business comes direct to us by mail, or otherwise from your customers we will allow you your commission on same."[45] Similar arrangements probably existed with other authorized Lukens agents.

By the end of the 1890s, however, Lukens (like Carnegie) was turning to the use of company sales offices run by sales agents who worked only for the company. An office was opened on Boston's Oliver Street in 1892. Charles Neblett, a Cincinnati iron broker in the early nineties, became that city's sales agent for Lukens by the turn of the century. In 1900, Lukens offices run by full-time managers were supplying customers in New York City and New Orleans. A Baltimore office appeared in 1904. Whenever the market was sufficiently large, Lukens departed from the old commission merchant or manufacturer's agent system and created its own sales offices.[46]

The iron enterprises of Peter Cooper and Abram S. Hewitt appear to have followed the same pattern of development. In the 1880s the Trenton Iron Company sold most of its goods (primarily wire) through Cooper-Hewitt in New York (which acted as agent and financier for the producing firm) and through many western houses such as Myers and Company of Cincinnati and Gates and Company of Saint Louis. The larger Hewitt enterprise, the New Jersey Steel and Iron Company (formed shortly after the Civil War), did less business through iron commission merchants as the volume of sales expanded. By the nineties, the firm was creating its own wholesale outlets (primarily for structural shapes) in such concentrated market areas as New York, Boston, and Chicago.[47]

---

[44] See the correspondence of F. X. Froment Co. and Gilchrist & Taylor to Lukens, *ibid.*; F. W. Coolbaugh to Andrew Carnegie, April 19, 1893, Andrew Carnegie Papers, vol. 20; and *Cleveland Directory, 1900*, p. 677. Sometimes there was frequent turnover in authorized agents for steel companies, especially in the New York area.

[45] Contract between Lukens Iron & Steel Co. and Thomas J. Adams & Son, October 5, 1893, General Orders, Lukens Steel Papers. It is impossible to say how widespread in the industry was the practice of allowing the agencies a commission on direct sales, or how faithfully the manufacturers adhered to the practice.

[46] *Boston Directory, 1892* (Boston: Sampson, Murdock, 1892), p. 842; *Williams' Cincinnati Directory, 1893*, p. 1140; *ibid.*, 1901, pp. 1083, 1264; *Boyd's Greater New York Co-Partnership and Residence-Business Directory, 1899* (New York: Boyd New York Directory Co., 1899), pp. 366, 709; *Soard's New Orleans Directory, 1894*, p. 550; *ibid.*, 1903, pp. 571, 726; *R. L. Polk's Baltimore City Directory, 1904* (Baltimore: R. L. Polk Co., 1904), pp. 409, 1065.

[47] Correspondence of Trenton Iron and the New Jersey Steel & Iron Co. with

Large producers of wire, such as the Washburn and Moen Company of Worcester, Massachusetts, also built their own nationwide sales networks in the 1890s. Because of the extremely diffuse nature of the midwestern and western market for bale ties, barbed wire, and other flat wire, manufacturers relied on many jobbers to make the individual contacts important in the sale of those small-lot items. When sales offices were opened they functioned more as suppliers and contractors for jobbers than as agencies for contact between the producer and the ultimate consumer. Some traveling salesmen (not jobbers) were employed by Washburn and Moen, especially in the Northeast, where the market was more concentrated.[48] By 1893 Washburn and Moen had established regional sales offices in Worcester, New York, Chicago, San Francisco, and Houston. After the firm became a part of American Steel and Wire (and then a division of U.S. Steel upon its formation in 1901), the program of expanding the company-operated sales system was stepped up; by the end of 1906 American Steel and Wire had twelve sales offices in the United States, one in Montreal, and one in London.[49] By 1913 there were fourteen American sales offices and a network of thirty warehouses serving customers and jobbers across the country.[50] Here, then, is another example of how the manufacturers moved to elaborate their own sales networks as the market for their goods increased.

Although by the beginning of the twentieth century the revolution in iron and steel had led large manufacturers to assume the wholesaling function, the iron commission merchant was by no means gone.[51] He served many small producers and even some large manufacturers in the less important market areas. The day of the independent middleman acting as primary

Cooper-Hewitt, Cooper-Hewitt Business Papers; Allan Nevins, *Abram S. Hewitt*, chaps. 5–8, 13, 14; *New England Business Directory and Gazetteer, 1898* (Boston: Sampson Murdock, 1899), p. 1112; *Phillips' Business Directory of New York City, 1899* (New York: Phillips Co., 1898), p. 638; *Chicago City Directory, 1900*, pp. 1311, 2272. Jones & Laughlin Steel also seems to have followed the general outlines of the Carnegie pattern. It had salaried agents in several cities, including Buffalo and New York, by the turn of the century, and by 1910 it had sales offices in a dozen cities. See the various catalogs, pamphlets, and several letters of W. L. King in the historical papers of the Jones & Laughlin Steel Corp.

[48] H. W. Wilson Letterbook, 1892–94; A. R. Webb Letterbook; F. H. Daniels Letterbook, 1898; and Incoming Correspondence, Washburn & Moen Co.; American Steel & Wire Papers.

[49] James A. Welch & Co. to Washburn & Moen, March 2, 1892, and March 7, 1893; and *Catalogue and Price List of Bale Ties, January 1, 1907*; ibid.

[50] American Steel & Wire Co., *American Wire Rope*.

[51] In 1899 a partial list of iron and steel companies with sales offices in New York City included producers such as Carnegie Steel, Federal Steel, American Steel & Wire, New Jersey Steel & Iron, Lukens Iron & Steel, Passaic Rolling Mills, Pencoyd Iron Works, Bartlett & Hayward, American Steel Foundry, Bethlehem Iron, Cambria Steel, Cleveland Rolling Mill, Lorain Steel, Park Steel, Maryland Steel, Pennsylvania Steel, Jones & Laughlin, Lackawanna Iron & Steel, and Latrobe Steel. See *Boyd's Greater New York Co-Partnership and Residence-Business Directory, 1899, passim.*

salesman for the iron and steel industry, however, had passed. As a large manufacturer's sales in a city rose, he turned from several local brokers to only one—the authorized agent or manufacturer's representative. The merchant probably accepted the lower commissions of an authorized agent because the higher volume of business made it profitable for him to do so. When area demand increased still more, the manufacturer turned to his own sales office, which was often managed by a man who had previously been a wholesaler in the area.

The manufacturer was not driven to create sales offices by any inadequacy in the existing distribution system. The iron merchants, who usually never even saw the goods they sold, could have adapted to the increased demand in the industry well beyond the point in time when the manufacturers began to supplant them. Manufacturers were encouraged to eliminate the middlemen only when it became apparent that they could sell their products at a lower cost per unit by doing so. Because they faced no special marketing problems in iron and steel, because they had always been oriented more toward production problems than toward sales problems, and because they lacked the ability to determine accurately when it was profitable to create sales offices, producers moved slowly to take command of the sales function. By the turn of the century, however, the new pattern in sales had clearly emerged. The manufacturer was ascendant, the independent merchant in decline.

As the commission merchant's role was eclipsed, some merchants shifted their functions to those of the jobber. Jobbers had played (and still play) a considerable role in the sale of finished hardware, but they had not been very important in the primary iron and steel industry. Iron merchants had been reluctant (especially in the latter part of the century) to tie up capital in inventories, and much iron and steel was shipped directly from producer to customer. Improved communications and transportation made direct shipping increasingly easy and inventories increasingly unnecessary. Only the simplest of iron goods, such as pigs, bars, and plates, were normally stockpiled. Those goods which were inventoried were sold on consignment in small lots by the commission merchant. By the end of the century, a few merchants, such as A. M. Castle and Company and Joseph T. Ryerson and Son, both of Chicago, had begun to buy large quantities of iron and steel from major producers and to sell the goods (especially structural shapes) to numerous relatively small construction firms in the large cities.[52] Such sales by jobbers constituted, however, a minority of the iron and steel sold.

So small was this market that, of the major manufacturers in the mid-

---

[52] The Castle firm is the same Chicago concern mentioned in connection with Lukens Steel. It grew into one of the nation's leading steel warehouse companies in the twentieth century. See Norris Willatt, "Agile Middlemen." For the Ryerson story see "Ryerson's Steel-Service Plants."

nineties, only Jones and Laughlin appears to have had any warehousing or jobbing outlets.[53] Carnegie Steel was considering a New York warehouse in 1896, but it did not have one at that time. Andrew Carnegie wrote John Leishman, suggesting the possible creation of a warehouse in New York to handle emergency beam orders from impatient contractors. "None of our competitors," Carnegie wrote, "do a business large enough to justify them in following us in this."[54] The Scotsman's opinion was apparently correct; even by the early 1930s only three major steel producers had bothered to obtain their own warehouse systems.[55] Clearly, the market for steel jobbers was not large enough to draw many commission merchants into the warehousing business.[56] Some commercial houses did go into jobbing, some metamorphosed into sales offices of the large firms, and others, such as Baltimore's Enoch Pratt Company, passed permanently from the scene when the firm's proprietor died.[57] The middleman was clearly on his way out as a sales agent for the industry. His prospects as supply agent for the large firms were even more grim.

THE SUPPLY PATTERN, 1870–1900: BACKWARD INTEGRATION AND INTRACOMPANY SALES

In the supply of raw materials, as in the sale of manufactured goods, the three decades from 1870 through 1900 saw the deterioration of the wholesaler's position as the manufacturer moved to assure his sources of supply. Small manufacturers continued to obtain most of their supplies in much the

[53] Jones & Laughlin's warehouse and jobbing outlet in Chicago dated from 1856; see Seelye A. Willson, "The Growth of Pittsburgh Iron and Steel," p. 569.

[54] Andrew Carnegie to John A. Leishman, April 6, 1896, Andrew Carnegie Papers, vol. 37.

[55] Inland Steel's 1935 acquisition of the Joseph T. Ryerson firm brought the total to four major producers with warehouses (*Iron Trade Review*, August 12, 1935, pp. 14–15, cited in Gertrude C. Schroeder, *The Growth of Major Steel Companies, 1900–1950*, p. 124). The earliest available and reliable estimates of the proportion of steel and iron sold by jobbers are for the 1920s. In the years 1926–32, when *Iron Age* compiled "data on shipments of semifinished steel to jobbers and warehouses, these middlemen took only 3.6% of total distributed shipments of these products." See Carroll R. Daugherty, Melvin G. de Chazeau, and Samuel S. Stratton, *The Economics of the Iron and Steel Industry*, 1: 46–47; chap. 3 of this excellent work is the best source on distribution in the modern iron and steel industry.

[56] Walter S. Doxsey, executive secretary of the American Steel Warehouse Assoc., declared in 1933 that "the number of steel warehouses that were organized for the single purpose of being steel warehouses may be numbered on the fingers of one hand. Almost all our steel warehouses, large and small, trace their inception back to wholesale hardware houses, ship chandleries, fabricating shops, smithies, brokerage houses, and what not" (Daugherty et al., *Economics of the Iron and Steel Industry*, p. 94). The importance of brokerage houses as forerunners of warehouses is perhaps reflected in their ordinal place in Doxsey's list (just before "what not").

[57] Enoch Pratt died in 1896 and within two years his firm disappeared from the pages of *R. L. Polk and Company's Baltimore City Directory*.

same way as they had before the revolution in iron and steel. The large companies that were the product of that revolution, however, moved steadily toward self-sufficiency in raw materials by integrating backward. At the same time, the new, large firms also integrated their production facilities, thereby causing a great increase in the proportion of intracompany sales of primary iron and steel. The result of these developments—backward integration into iron ore, coke, and other raw materials, and the consequent rise in intracompany sales—was a further diminishing of the role of the wholesaler as a supplier of coal, coke, ore, limestone, and pig iron. The primary manufacturers' increasing control of their sales systems meant, of course, a decline in the wholesaler's function as supplier of crude iron to manufacturers of finished ferrous products.

Carnegie Steel led the way in the development of integrated production facilities and intracompany sales, as it did in the manufacturers' assumption of the sales function. Carnegie's Edgar Thompson Steel Company began the production of Bessemer steel in Pittsburgh in 1875; its prime source of pig iron was Carnegie's own Lucy Furnaces, which boasted a monthly capacity of 5,000 tons. Andrew Carnegie noted, in a comment that must have chilled alert middlemen throughout the industry, that the Lucy Furnaces rendered Edgar Thompson Steel "entirely independent of the general market."[58] Just as his Bessemer converters were fed by his furnaces, so Carnegie's rolling mills were fed by his converters (and his other enterprises by his rolling mills). The Keystone Bridge Company, for example, drew upon Carnegie's Union Iron Mills for its materials.[59] Although few manufacturers could approach Carnegie in the degree of intracompany consumption, integrated production operations significantly reduced the manufacturers' dependence on outside sources. By 1905, for example, 59.7 per cent of all the pig iron produced by American blast furnaces "was for consumption in steel works and rolling mills under the control of the same company."[60] This growth of intracompany sales not only spelled less work for the middleman but it also signaled the large manufacturer's growing ability to regulate and assure the flow of raw materials through his production process.

Because the new, large manufacturers produced iron and steel on an unprecedented scale, they required enormous quantities of raw materials. A

[58] Clark, *History of Manufactures*, 2: 234. The Pennsylvania Steel Co. of Harrisburg built blast furnaces for its own pig iron in 1872; see the Pennsylvania Steel Co. Catalog dated 1879 in the miscellaneous collection of items in accession #884 at the Eleutherian Mills Library in Wilmington, Del. In the 1870s Jones & Laughlin acquired its own sources of coal; see B. F. Jones Notebook, Jones & Laughlin Papers.

[59] Instances of such consumption are legion. See, for example, the stories about the Keystone Bridge Co. in *Railway World*, March 29, 1884, and in *Iron Age*, May 15, 1884; see also Andrew Carnegie's undated letter to W. L. Abbott, president of Carnegie-Phipps, Andrew Carnegie Papers, vol. 240.

[60] Bureau of the Census, *Census of Manufactures*, 1905, pt. 4, p. 35.

steady, reliable flow of those raw materials at an acceptable and reasonably stable cost became highly desirable for these firms, but it was impossible for a single commission merchant or even several commission merchants to assure that steady flow. The large manufacturer, who was in a financial position to insulate his production process from the vagaries of the raw-materials market, moved to acquire the inputs necessary for the continuous, efficient operation of his blast furnaces, steel works, and rolling mills. As Andrew Carnegie later wrote of his decision to integrate backward after the formation of Edgar Thompson Steel, "the difficulties and uncertainties of obtaining pig iron soon compelled us to begin the erection of blast furnaces."[61] It was to overcome such "difficulties and uncertainties" that the Carnegie companies led the way in the steel industry toward backward integration.

From the mid-seventies through the mid-nineties, the Carnegie companies moved toward a completely integrated production process. The Carnegie interests acquired extensive ore lands, limestone sources, coal lands, and coke ovens. Carnegie's tie with Henry Clay Frick's huge coke company assured the Carnegie Steel enterprises a cheap, reliable flow of fuel from the rich Connellsville region of Pennsylvania. Carnegie Steel obtained its own fleet of lake steamers and even built its own railroad from Pittsburgh to the Great Lakes. As a later commentator said of Carnegie's raw materials, "from the moment these crude stuffs were dug out of the earth until they flowed in a stream of liquid steel in the ladles, there was never a price, profit, or royalty paid to an outsider."[62] Andrew Carnegie proudly noted in 1897 that "cost [of production] can be estimated, everything being within ourselves."[63]

Other major manufacturers soon followed suit. The giant Illinois Steel Company, formed in 1889, was a highly integrated firm which controlled its own coal lands, coke ovens, ore lands, and all the essential agencies of production.[64] Many other large firms pursued a similar policy, if only in self-

[61] Carnegie, *Autobiography*, p. 220. Peter Temin argued in *Iron and Steel* (p. 155) that producers integrated backward primarily to control the quality of the pig iron used in their Bessemer converters. By producing their own pig iron, they could avoid the irregular quality of pigs available on the open market. While this consideration undoubtedly played a role in the decision to build blast furnaces, the need to obtain a steady, reliable flow of inputs at an acceptable and reasonably stable cost was perhaps a more important factor. Joseph Wall (*Andrew Carnegie*, p. 323) argues that the integration by Carnegie in the early 1870s was motivated by a desire to reduce the costs of pig iron used by the firm.

[62] Bridge, *Inside History of Carnegie Steel*, p. 169. Carnegie explained his railroad to Frank Thompson (president of the Pennsylvania Railroad) as a necessity to meet the competition of steel producers located on the shores of the Great Lakes. "Pittsburgh," Carnegie declared, "had to become practically a Lake Port or be bottled up" (Carnegie to Thompson, 1896, Andrew Carnegie Papers, vol. 40).

[63] Andrew Carnegie to F. T. Lovejoy, October 8, 1897, Andrew Carnegie Papers, vol. 45.

[64] Clark, *History of Manufactures*, 2: 235–37.

defense.[65] The Bureau of the Census noted in 1890 that "a large number of iron and steel manufacturers not only operate blast furnaces, rolling mills, and steel plants, but also control the iron ore and coal mines, coke ovens, and timber lands which supply the works the larger part of the raw materials consumed."[66] By the turn of the century, most large American manufacturers of iron and steel had integrated back to the production of their own ore and fuel.[67]

The integration of major producers was, of course, an incomplete step toward total self-sufficiency. At times when they had planned the flow of materials poorly or when demand was especially heavy, the large companies would still buy raw materials, pig iron, or other crude ferrous items directly from each other or through large middlemen such as Preston and Company of Pittsburgh or J. Tatnall Lea of Philadelphia.[68] Sometimes the purchases from competitors were made through annual contracts. In 1899, for example, only about one-third of the output of the H. C. Frick Coke Company went to its parent company, Carnegie Steel; the rest was sold through contracts to competitors such as Federal Steel, Lackawanna Iron and Steel, American Steel Hoop, and Reading Iron.[69]

Nevertheless, by 1900 the large manufacturers had virtually eliminated the middleman in the acquisition of raw materials. The integration of productive facilities from blast furnaces through steel works and the resulting increase in intracompany sales greatly reduced the proportion of iron and steel handled by middlemen. The producer's strategy of backward integration into raw materials, undertaken to assure the flow of inputs, also served to reduce the need for middlemen. Large producers who had more raw materials than their plants required (such as Carnegie) sold the excess directly to other manufacturers. Backward integration meant that in the supply of raw materials, as in the sale of goods, the commission merchant faced a greatly re-

[65] Frank W. Taussig, "The Iron Industry in the United States," pp. 159–60; Andrew Carnegie to J. A. Leishman (then president of Carnegie Steel), November 11, 1895, Andrew Carnegie Papers, vol. 34.

[66] Census Office, *Eleventh Census*, pt. 3, p. 388.

[67] See the description of various iron and steel companies in *Moody's Manual, 1900*, *passim*, and also the *First Annual Report of the Federal Steel Company*, available in File #1938 of the records of the U.S. Bureau of Corporations, Record Group 122, National Archives, Washington, D.C.

[68] This pattern is clear throughout the various sections of the Andrew Carnegie Papers (such as H. C. Frick to Andrew Carnegie, January 17, 1898, vol. 48, and the Minutes of the Meetings of the Board of Managers of Carnegie Steel, February 8, 1898, vol. 49), and is evident in the Lukens Steel Papers and the American Steel & Wire Papers.

[69] Minutes of the Board of Directors of the H. C. Frick Coke Co., October 25, 1899, Andrew Carnegie Papers, vol. 70; see also H. C. Frick to Andrew Carnegie, January 18, 1896, *ibid.*, vol. 36. Some companies, such as Carnegie, were very nearly self-sufficient; others supplied internally only a part of their needs. John W. Gates, president of American Steel & Wire, estimated in 1899 that his firm supplied 55–60 per cent of its own raw materials and bought the rest on the open market. U.S. Industrial Commission, *Report of the Industrial Commission*, 1: 1005.

duced role. Salesmen in the minor markets and for the minor producers, suppliers only in emergencies or in remote markets, the mighty had fallen.

THE TRANSITION

It has been argued thus far that iron and steel manufacturers assumed the sales function primarily as a result of the increased demand in particular market areas, and that they did so slowly and hesitantly. It has perhaps not been emphasized enough that sales volume was the major determinant only when the product itself was relatively uncomplicated. Primary producers in the nineteenth-century iron and steel industry produced goods that were very heavy in relation to their value, and that usually required only reheating and reshaping by the consumer. The first characteristic tended to discourage jobbing; it facilitated direct shipping from producer to consumer and thus kept transport and storage costs at a minimum. The second characteristic meant that very little contact between producer and customer was required. That is to say, iron and steel goods carried with them no special marketing problems. Manufacturers seldom gave much thought to their sales methods, because sales presented relatively few difficulties. Producers of ferrous metals were almost entirely production oriented; the vast majority of their time and effort went into seeking ways to reduce the unit costs of production. The cost of sales was a very small part of the manufacturer's total costs, and he naturally was not inclined to give much attention to the sales mechanism. Even in times of depression in the industry, the producer's solution to falling sales was not innovation in sales methods; it was reduced prices. "The policy to-day is what it has always been in poor seasons," Andrew Carnegie declared in 1896: " 'scoop the market,' prices secondary; work to keep our mills running the essential thing."[70] The importance of the nature of the product in influencing the degree of attention given by the producer to the sales function can hardly be overestimated.

The years 1870–1900 marked the transition from the old iron and steel industry to the new. By the end of that period the manufacturing firm had assumed its place in the center of the economic stage. The changes in distribution which took place in the iron and steel industry from 1870 through 1900 pointed the way clearly to the marketing pattern of the twentieth century. Modern steel firms sell the vast majority of the nation's iron and steel directly to the customer, and middlemen play a very small role in the industry.[71]

[70] Andrew Carnegie to the Board of Managers of Carnegie Steel, July 13, 1896, Andrew Carnegie Papers, vol. 38.

[71] See Daugherty et al., Economics of the Iron and Steel Industry, vol. 1, chap. 3. In the years since World War II, steel warehouse firms have expanded their operations; they provide a wide range of services to customers and now warrant the name "steel service centers." Such firms (both independents and those which are subsidiaries of major producers) now handle about one-fifth of the steel shipped by the major producers. See Willatt, "Agile Middlemen."

Modern steel firms own the sources of supply for most of their raw-material needs.

FIRMS IN OTHER PRODUCERS' GOODS INDUSTRIES FOLLOW THE PATTERN OF THE IRON AND STEEL COMPANIES

Developments similar to those in the iron and steel industry also occurred in many other industries that supplied producers' goods. This was most apparent among the large firms that produced and marketed non-ferrous metals. Makers of copper, nickel, lead, silver, aluminum, and the like came to have a similarly dense, concentrated market involving a few consolidated firms. Other examples included firms manufacturing explosives and industrial chemicals. As manufacturers of producers' goods grew, they often found that their customers also were expanding their size and output. Because the phenomenon of increasing firm size was a fairly generalized one throughout much of the manufacturing sector, as a producer's size rose, so too did the size of many of the firms that consumed his goods.

In addition to integrating forward, many manufacturers, like those in the iron and steel industry, turned to backward integration. In non-ferrous metals, such firms as Phelps-Dodge, Anaconda, National Lead, American Smelting and Refining, Calumet and Hecla, U.S. Smelting and Refining, Alcoa, and International Nickel supplied substantial portions of their input requirements through company-owned sources. A large array of manufacturing corporations in many other industries (including such firms as International Paper, Union Bag and Paper, Virginia-Carolina Chemical, Pittsburgh Plate Glass, du Pont, American Agricultural Chemical Company, and International Salt) also engaged in backward integration during the early years of the twentieth century. The effect of this trend in many industries was to render the commission merchant and jobber increasingly irrelevant as a distributive agent.[72]

These changes usually came slowly. The inertia inherent in the old distribution system was very powerful. Manufacturers had found that system adequate for decades, and they were understandably slow to abandon it. Because of their accounting methods and the imponderables of sales lost while training personnel, manufacturing concerns were not able to determine when conditions had changed enough to encourage them to create their own wholesale outlets or warehouses. Usually the changeover was made only after it had become quite clear that the market was concentrated enough and the custom-

---

[72] Information on the firms mentioned is drawn from our extensive study of corporate annual reports in the Corporation Records Division of the Baker Library, Harvard University, from the early volumes of Moody's and Poor's industrial manuals, and from numerous secondary works, which include: Robert G. Cleland, *A History of Phelps Dodge, 1834–1950*; and Isaac Marcosson's *Anaconda* and *Metal Magic*. Materials from our study are summarized in Harold C. Livesay and Patrick G. Porter, "Vertical Integration in American Manufacturing, 1899–1948."

ers well enough known to make it profitable to dispense with commission agents and substitute full-time, company sales personnel. The new conditions prevailed most often, of course, for the large firms in the concentrated industries, and, as the combination movement spread, more and more of these firms arose. By the early years of this century they had moved to consolidate their functions and thus brought into being company distribution systems. In the producers' goods industries, however, the manufacturer's assumption of the wholesaling function came in the wake of the concentrated markets created by the rise of the large corporation in concentrated industries.

CHAPTER IX

The Manufacturer Ascendant: Concentration and Consumers' Goods

The pattern of change in distribution which resulted from concentrated urban demand was visible in some firms manufacturing consumers' goods as well as among those making producers' goods. The kind of concentrated market faced by the former was, however, quite different from that encountered by the latter. In the late nineteenth century, two types of concentrated markets appeared in the economy. One involved a relatively few consolidated firms. By and large, it was important to companies competing in the producers' goods sector, as the previous chapter suggested. The other was the dense market presented to makers of consumers' goods by the concentration of population (and hence of customers) in the large cities growing across the land. The new market was accessible via the nearly completed rail network, and thus manufacturers could compete more effectively than ever in a truly national market. Although goods were sold to their ultimate consumers through retail outlets, the concentrated demand represented by the cities led some large firms to create their own wholesaling organizations, which in turn supplied urban customers with a variety of goods. Depending on the industry, all or a part of the wholesaling function passed from the independent middleman to the manufacturer as what Adolf Berle and Gardiner C. Means termed the "modern corporation" rose to dominance in the American economy.[1]

[1] Adolf A. Berle, Jr., and Gardiner C. Means, *The Modern Corporation and Private Property*. Berle and Means were the first scholars to call attention to certain aspects of the changed nature of the business enterprise, although the process of change had been at work for many decades. As Berle noted in the Preface, "it is of the essence of revolutions of the more silent sort that they are unrecognized until they are far advanced" (*ibid.*, p. vii).

The pace of economic life quickened as the old order gave way to the new. In the last three decades of the nineteenth century, the Gross National Product (measured in constant dollars) increased approximately fourfold.[2] Much of the additional demand came from the new markets in America's burgeoning cities. The number of cities with a population in excess of 25,000 was 52 in 1870; by 1900 there were 160 such urban areas.[3] These cities needed improved streets, lighting facilities, water and sewage systems, and urban transportation networks, as well as many new buildings. The concentration of population created huge potential markets for many industries.[4] The rapid economic growth in this period substantially increased the aggregate demand for the products of manufacturing firms, but the increased aggregate sales volume enjoyed by many companies was not in itself a sufficient cause for the creation of wholesale networks by manufacturers; the increased sales had to be concentrated in large cities.

In most cases, the individual firm moved to eliminate the middleman only when the sales volume in a particular city grew large enough to indicate clearly that the firm's products could be marketed more efficiently by a full-time company sales force in that city. In industries that had no special marketing problems, this concentrated demand was usually the result of the rise of the modern corporation and the coming of oligopoly. The assumption of the wholesaling function by producers occurred largely, but not exclusively, among the large, modern corporations born during the period under consideration. It also came about largely, but not exclusively, in industries wherein production was concentrated in the hands of a relatively few firms.

THE RISE OF THE LARGE FIRM AND ITS CONSEQUENCES

From the time of the creation of John D. Rockefeller's Standard Oil trust in 1882 through the first years of this century, the large, modern manufacturing corporation developed in many industries, both in producers' and consumers' goods. As Populists and then Progressives writhed and moaned in confusion and protest, the "trusts" proliferated.[5] Mergers between industrial

---

[2] U.S. Bureau of the Census, *Historical Statistics of the United States*, p. 139.

[3] *Ibid.*, p. 14.

[4] A good discussion of the rise of cities and their economic impact appears in Edward C. Kirkland, *Industry Comes of Age*, chap. 12.

[5] Most of the large firms created in the 1890s and in the first few years of this century were not trusts. In the trust form of organization, first developed by Standard Oil in 1882, a group of trustees received the common stock of different corporations in exchange for trust certificates, which gave the trustees complete control over the various properties in the trust. This legal device avoided the common law prohibition against one corporation holding the shares of another, a prohibition which became much less important after 1889, when New Jersey enacted corporate laws allowing a corporation chartered in that state to hold the stock of other corporations. Because the trust form was under severe legal attack, and because the New Jersey law offered a seemingly safe harbor, virtually all large combinations put together after 1889 were

firms occurred on a scale unmatched before or since. In the ten year period
from 1895 through 1904, the average annual number of firms that disappeared via mergers was 301.[6] Many of the giant manufacturing companies of
the modern American economy were the products of mergers and combina-
tions that took place in the quarter-century after the formation of Standard
Oil.[7] By the end of Theodore Roosevelt's administration, such companies as
International Paper, National Enameling and Stamping, American Can, Allis-
Chalmers, American Car and Foundry, American Locomotive, Nabisco, U.S.
Steel, U.S. Gypsum, American Smelting and Refining, du Pont, International
Nickel, National Lead, Standard Oil, Texaco, U.S. Rubber, B. F. Goodrich,
Anaconda, and Phelps-Dodge had emerged as important factors in the na-
tional economy.[8] Although these large firms appeared occasionally in indus-
tries that remained relatively unconcentrated, they arose most often in industries dominated by a few large producers.[9] The effect of the merger or combination movement was to reshape the structure of American industry. As
Ralph Nelson has commented, the combination era "transformed many industries, formerly characterized by many small and medium-sized firms, into
those in which one or a few very large enterprises occupied leading positions.
It laid the foundation for the industrial structure that has characterized most
of American industry in the twentieth century."[10]

The emergence of the large firm and of oligopoly led many companies, in
both the producers' and consumers' goods sectors, to change their marketing
systems. Before the concentration movement, a number of small and medium-
sized firms competed in most industries. These enterprises usually continued
to rely on the old network of independent middlemen to handle the distribution of their commodities. Because they had always found the system of
brokers, commission merchants, and manufacturers' agents adequate to their

---

legally holding companies, not trusts. Background material on the question of legal
forms of combination and cooperation between corporations is available in William Z.
Ripley, ed., *Trust, Pools and Corporations*, pp. ix-xviii.

[6] Ralph Nelson, *Merger Movements in American Industry, 1815–1956*, p. 34. Nelson defines a merger as "the combination into a single economic enterprise of two or
more previously independent enterprises" (*ibid.*, p. 3).

[7] See, for example, *ibid.*, p. 4.

[8] These companies are listed in A. D. H. Kaplan's *Big Enterprise in a Competitive
System*, chap. 7, and in Nelson, *Merger Movements*, pp. 161–62. Other well-known
corporate giants (including American Tobacco, General Electric, Westinghouse, Swift
& Company, Armour, United Fruit, Pabst, Eastman Kodak, International Harvester,
and Singer) also had reached the status of major American firms, but they will be
treated in later chapters.

[9] In 1909, oligopoly was most prevalent in the tobacco, petroleum, rubber, primary
metal, and electrical machinery industries. It was least prevalent in the textile, apparel,
lumber and wood, furniture, paper, printing, and leather industries. See P. Glenn
Porter and Harold C. Livesay, "Oligopolists in American Manufacturing and Their
Products, 1909–1963," p. 283.

[10] Nelson, *Merger Movements*, p. 5.

needs, there was little incentive for innovation. The independent middlemen continued to market manufactured goods much as they had throughout the century, taking a commission on all transactions. After the wave of mergers, however, the large firms built through horizontal combination turned to consolidating their various enterprises and activities. This process of consolidation involved the imposition of centralized control over the component parts of the company, the concentration of production in the most efficient plants, the creation of purchasing departments, and the construction of a new distribution network. One effect of the combination movement was to reduce substantially the number of buyers and sellers in many industries, thereby reducing the need for an elaborate network of middlemen, whose job had formerly been to connect the mass of producers with customers. As in the case of iron and steel, concentrated sales volumes (either in a city or among a few large customers) made it clearly advantageous for manufacturers to create their own selling networks. As Alfred D. Chandler, Jr., has argued, after the rise of the large corporation, firms making both consumers' and producers' goods "set up nation-wide and often world-wide marketing and distributing organizations."[11]

These changes in distribution came largely in those industries in which the large firm and oligopoly were present. These included industries that will be discussed in subsequent chapters (such as tobacco, electrical machinery, and consumer perishables), as well as the iron and steel, petroleum, rubber, and non-ferrous metals industries.[12] The old marketing patterns tended to continue primarily in those industries which had few if any large firms and in which oligopoly did not appear. These industries included food products, hardware, lumber, leather, furniture and fixtures, and apparel and related products.[13]

Many large firms that supplied the wants of urban customers experienced changes in distribution. The following section focuses on industries in which manufacturers of consumers' goods moved to assume all or part of their own wholesaling, marketing their products to large numbers of jobbers and retailers in the large cities. The concentrated demand represented by the urban market encouraged large producers to create their own sales organizations in the cities. The firms described in the balance of this chapter all produced what we have termed generic goods, involving no particular marketing diffi-

---

[11] Alfred D. Chandler, Jr., "The Beginnings of 'Big Business' in American Industry," p. 16. Several firms making consumers' goods are discussed in Chapter X of this volume.

[12] Porter and Livesay, "Oligopolists in American Manufacturing," pp. 282–89. The interrelationships among the large firm, oligopoly, and vertical integration are analyzed in Alfred D. Chandler, Jr., "The Structure of American Industry in the Twentieth Century."

[13] Some of the industries in which the old marketing patterns continued will be discussed in Chapter XIII.

culties, and they all moved to take charge of a portion of their own whole-saling because it was cheaper to do so than to rely on independent whole-salers.

PETROLEUM AND OTHER CONSUMERS' GOODS INDUSTRIES

The pioneer industry in this story was, of course, petroleum. In the in-dustry's early years (after E. L. Drake's first successful oil well in 1859), refiners faced no special marketing difficulties for their products. Illuminat-ing oil found ready markets through the same channels that had served to distribute other illuminants (principally coal oil). Commission merchants soon specialized in petroleum products, doing most of their business on a commission basis, but sometimes taking title to these generic goods and sell-ing on consignment. These merchants sold to other wholesalers, including large wholesale grocery and drug merchants, who in turn distributed the items to a mass of local retailers. The marketing of American petroleum goods to foreign countries also was handled by a network of independent merchants. In the period before the dominance of the Rockefeller firm, then, the petroleum industry was a perfect example of the mid-nineteenth-century distribution network.

During the 1870s Standard Oil made a few hesitant moves toward build-ing a company distribution system. It acquired partial control of petroleum marketing firms such as Chess, Carly, and Company of Louisville and Waters-Pierce and Company of Saint Louis. Such marketing enterprises began to make innovations in the bulk transport of petroleum products in special tank cars and also built a storage and distribution network which extended throughout several states.

In the latter part of the seventies and throughout the eighties, Standard moved to take more control of the wholesaling of its products as the growth of cities increased its markets. "The rapid rise in population and incomes," noted Harold Williamson and Arnold Daum, "increased the market for artificial illumination in factories, hotels, office buildings, and homes."[14] Standard's policy of acquiring marketing affiliates continued as the urban markets grew. These specialized wholesaling affiliates assumed the function formerly performed by large grocery and drug wholesalers—they distributed petroleum goods to local grocery and drug jobbers in the nation's towns and cities.[15] Thus Standard replaced middlemen as it began to do a portion of its own wholesaling in urban centers across the country.[16]

[14] Harold F. Williamson and Arnold R. Daum, *The American Petroleum Industry*, 1: 680.

[15] Indeed, the growth of these firms was "a major factor in the decline in the rela-tive position of the large grocery and drug wholesaler in the domestic distribution of refinery output" (*ibid*., p. 536).

[16] In the 1890s Standard extended its distribution activities to include direct con-

The pattern of development in the rubber industry seems somewhat similar. In the rubber boot, shoe, and glove industry, for example, marketing was carried on through an elaborate system of independent jobbers in the decades before the combination of leading producers into the U.S. Rubber Company early in the 1890s. The new firm, however, turned to the consolidation of production, purchasing, and marketing. In the mid-nineties a centralized selling department was created to replace the jobber apparatus with a more efficient and less costly distribution system, a system which included branch offices in major cities across the United States and in Europe as well.[17] Firms that were to enjoy rapid growth and expansion through the production of rubber tires for carriages, bicycles, and (of course) automobiles also created company distribution organizations. The Goodyear Company, for example, utilized a number of independent wholesale outlets for its products at the turn of the century. Late in 1902, it "took over these offices, put the men on salary and started its first direct sales branches" in New York, Boston, Chicago, Detroit, Cincinnati, and Saint Louis. During the following decade the firm virtually eliminated independent middlemen and built a chain of wholesale agencies in twenty-three cities.[18]

In some small manufacturing industries, where mergers produced medium-sized firms and oligopoly, combinations often remade marketing channels. In the soda-water apparatus industry, for example, it was all but unheard of for any manufacturer to operate sales offices in more than one city before the nineties. The merger movement touched this industry as it did so many others, and in 1891 the four leading producers combined to form the American Soda-Fountain Company. After an interregnum of several years, during which the firm established centralized control over its constituent parts, a chain of sales branches was constructed in major market areas. By the end of the nineties the company had sales offices in eleven major cities across the country.[19]

When the Bureau of Corporations conducted an extensive inquiry into the structure of resale prices in the years just before the outbreak of World War I, replies from many medium-sized firms emphasized the role of concentrated sales volumes in making profitable company-owned marketing sys-

---

tact with retailers, but the primary motivation then was to discourage competition and control the market. Another important reason was the need to impose rational control over the complex flow of its goods. The company succeeded in gaining control over wholesaling partly because the newness of the product meant that there were only a relatively few specialized petroleum jobbers, almost all of whom were large and could be bought out.

[17] U.S. Rubber, *Annual Reports*, Corporation Records Division, Baker Library, Harvard University, Boston, Mass.; see also Chandler, "Beginnings of 'Big Business,'" pp. 13–14.

[18] Hugh Allen, *The House of Goodyear*, pp. 29, 337–45.

[19] John J. Riley, *A History of the American Soft Drink Industry*, esp. p. 68. American Soda-Fountain was initially capitalized at $3,750,000.

tems. The Eaton, Crane, and Pike Company (a major manufacturer of stationery), for example, pointed out that it had largely ceased selling through merchants and jobbers in concentrated market areas and had substituted its own branch offices and warehouses in large cities. From these branches the company dispatched salesmen to contact retailers directly. Eaton, Crane, and Pike continued to rely on jobbers to serve those markets "at long distance where the salesman of the manufacturer cannot reach and where orders are not large enough ... to make it profitable for the manufacturer to solicit business in such points." Jobbers remained "a factor in distributing goods in the small towns" where sales volume was too small to encourage the producing firm to assume the wholesaling function.[20]

The Sherwin-Williams Company of Cleveland provides another example. Throughout most of the nineteenth century the paint and varnish industry utilized the usual network of independent middlemen to handle the distribution of its goods to large numbers of small retail dealers, hardware wholesalers and retailers, and building firms. As the volume of sales for Sherwin-Williams products grew in the concentrated market areas, however, the company set up its own warehouses and "line sale branches" in those areas. By the time of Woodrow Wilson's election to the presidency, the Cleveland firm had about thirty such branches in principal cities, and its officials could declare flatly that "the wholesaler and jobber are not essential to the economical distribution of our product." This highly integrated company (which owned linseed oil mills, lead and zinc mines and smelters, white-lead plants, tin-can factories, etc.) enjoyed high-volume, concentrated demand in major cities, and thus it was led to integrate forward into wholesaling.[21]

Another example is the manufacture of collars and cuffs. Important producers such as Cluett, Peabody, and Company and United Shirt and Collar Company (both in Troy, New York) sold their goods in major cities by means of their own warehouses and wholesale branches. An official of the United company noted that "the wholesalers and jobbers in the collar trade are a very small factor. ... the most economical distribution is without ques-

---

[20] The U.S. Bureau of Corporations' files on the resale prices inquiry, as well as many other of their investigations, are a rich source of information about distribution in the early years of this century. The resale prices inquiry was conducted in two ways: by means of written questionnaires filled out by high company officials, and by interviews of officials by agents of the bureau, who turned in detailed written accounts of the interviews. The information on Eaton, Crane & Pike is in File #7222–73–1 of the records of the U.S. Bureau of Corporations. The value of the records as a whole is suggested in Patrick G. Porter, "Source Material for Economic History."

[21] The Sherwin-Williams information is in File #7222–59–1, *ibid.* The company also operated a few retail stores. Volume distribution meant many savings for Sherwin-Williams, including the cheaper transportation costs resulting from the firm's ability to "ship to these [major] distributing points in solid car-loads." Sherwin-Williams was, however, the only manufacturer of paints and varnishes to become so highly integrated before World War I.

tion direct to the retail dealer." Cluett and Peabody's *Arrow Collar & Shirt Style Book* (1914) revealed that wholesale branches and a chain of warehouses had been opened in more than a score of U.S. cities. These firms used independent middlemen only in diffuse and remote markets.[22]

The middleman was sometimes eliminated even in small manufacturing industries in which oligopoly prevailed. Although oligopoly is usually associated with the large firm, it has also existed (even in the present-day economy) in many small industries.[23] Most of these industries have been closely related to the older, agrarian-based economy of the mid-nineteenth century. A few firms assembled pools of capital, organizational talent, and productive skills to meet the needs of the agrarian-oriented economy. Markets remained large enough to sustain a core of producers, but they did not become large enough to tempt many new entrants. Often the technology of production was sophisticated enough, or the supply of skilled labor was scarce enough, to discourage would-be competitors. In some cases the necessity of importing scarce raw materials helped keep the industries oligopolistic. Firms in such industries were so few in number that they were highly visible and well known to their customers. Many such firms could ignore the wholesaler and make sales via catalogs, mail orders, and a few traveling salesmen.[24]

In many of the small, oligopolistic industries, manufacturers could supplant the web of commission merchants and jobbers, in part because very low freight rates made direct distribution to retailers profitable. The fountain pen industry exemplifies this pattern. That industry was oligopolistic in the last decades of the nineteenth century, and all makers of high-quality pens sold in the same manner. As George S. Parker (president of the Parker Pen Company) told an agent of the Bureau of Corporations, "We consider neither the jobber or wholesaler essential or desirable for the distribution of our goods."[25] The market served by the Parker firm was a very diffuse one; most of Parker's pens found their consumers in thousands of small retail stores scattered across the country. In most such industries (that is, those with diffuse markets), jobbers played a crucial role.[26] Pen manufacturers, however, made virtually no sales through jobbers. This was true not only because the industry was oligopolistic but because the product was sufficiently light in weight, small in bulk, and high in value to allow manufacturers to

---

[22] Information on the United Shirt & Collar Co. and on Cluett, Peabody & Co. are in Files #7222–60–1 and #7222–70–1, *ibid.*

[23] This phenomenon is discussed in Patrick G. Porter and Harold C. Livesay, "Oligopoly in Small Manufacturing Industries."

[24] See, for example, the materials on the Henderson-Ames Co. (maker of regalia, badges, lodge uniforms, etc.), the L. M. Taylor Barber Supply Co., and the Victor Safe & Lock Co. (all of which competed in oligopolistic industries) in Files #7222–20–1, #7222–15–1, and #7222–29–1, Bureau of Corporations Records.

[25] File #7222–80–1, *ibid.*

[26] See Chapters XII and XIII.

distribute the item directly from the factory to the retailer. "Owing to the lack of bulk of the article we manufacture," George Parker observed, "the whole world is our market. We have sold upwards of 15,000 dealers in the United States and Canada." Salaried company traveling salesmen reached the retailers, and then the producer used "the express and mails to good advantage."[27] The Parker company utilized the widely known brand name of its pens and their high value in relation to their bulk to ship directly to retailers.

The nation's few makers of spectacles and eyeglasses marketed in much the same way as did the Parker company. E. Kirstein, Sons, and Company of Rochester, for example, shipped directly to retailers orders placed by mail and by company traveling salesmen. "Transportation costs are a very small part of the original cost of articles," the company president pointed out. "One hundred dollars' worth of Shur-on mountings can be sent to Cleveland, O. [from Rochester], for instance, by Parcel Post, Insured, for twenty-five cents." The Kirstein enterprises used jobbers to distribute goods only in remote areas with low sales densities, "the very smallest centers which we could not possibly reach."[28]

CONCLUSION: THE ROLE OF MARKETS IN CONSUMERS' AND PRODUCERS' GOODS

Throughout most of the nineteenth century, the manufacturing sector was composed of many producers who sold to many consumers. In most cases the manufacturer and the consumer were unknown to each other. The large number of consumers tended to make many small purchases. Commercial middlemen brought the diffuse mass of buyers and sellers together. No single manufacturing company could profitably pay a full-time sales force to find the many buyers in the numerous and widely scattered markets of the antebellum American economy. Instead, the independent middlemen served as distributing agents for the producers. They coordinated the flow of goods by providing the nexus between the numerous producing and consuming units. Their store of capital allowed commission merchants and jobbers to buy in quantity the products of individual manufacturing firms and thereby enabled the manufacturer to dispose of his goods with a minimum of bother and expense. In turn, the goods were parceled out to many consumers, thus enabling the consuming units to obtain inputs quickly and easily without the

[27] The interview with George S. Parker is available in File #7222–80–1, Bureau of Corporations Records.

[28] The marketing system of E. Kirstein, Sons & Co. is explained in File #7222–62–1, *ibid*. See also the history of marketing by the Dennison Manufacturing Co. in N. S. B. Gras and Henrietta M. Larson, *Casebook in American Business History*, pp. 440–48.

time-consuming difficulties of contacting various producers to see if they could provide the needed materials.

The wholesaler provided many services to manufacturers, but the most important was his fund of knowledge about the makers and users of the line of goods in which he specialized. Wholesalers knew who produced what, how quickly, and at what price. They knew who needed which commodities, in what quantities, at what time and price. Equally important, they understood the transportation system and its relation (both in time and money) to their ability to bring buyer and seller together efficiently. They knew the current status of transportation rates and were able to bargain effectively to reduce them. They were aware of alternate transportation routes, and they knew of forwarding merchants and storage facilities. All the various kinds of expertise and services represented by the mercantile community made the independent middlemen a virtually indispensable element in the economy throughout most of the nineteenth century.

Even the steady improvement of the nation's transportation and communications systems did not destroy the usefulness of the commission merchants and jobbers. Poor transportation and uncertain communications had undoubtedly helped make the independent wholesaler necessary. Until the construction of the nationwide rail network, goods could not be shipped quickly (and sometimes not at all if water routes were frozen). Middlemen reduced the uncertainties and the lengthy wait for delivery of goods by assembling pools of commodities in the regional distribution centers, the cities. A manufacturer in urgent need of materials to keep his mill or factory in operation would often obtain them from the wholesaler's store or warehouse in a nearby city, rather than wait for the goods to be produced and shipped from a distant manufacturer. Furthermore, the individual transaction most often involved only a small lot, which meant paying higher shipping costs per sale than would be the case in the shipping of large lots. Middlemen bought and shipped in larger lots than did individual consuming units, and they therefore seem to have allocated the flow of resources more efficiently than could individual buyers and sellers. Similarly, poor communications also made the independent merchants relevant. Because communications were often slow and unreliable, consumers preferred to contact middlemen, who could be counted upon to act quickly and effectively to fill orders, whereas one might wait weeks to hear from an individual producer, only to discover that he could not supply the commodities requested. Although the construction of better transportation routes and the advance of communications greatly reduced the uncertainties and the slow pace of commerce, they did not eliminate the independent middleman. Improved shipping facilities, better mechanisms for the dissemination of information, the consolidation of railroad systems, and the stabilization of rates were necessary but not sufficient conditions for the assumption of the wholesaling function by producers. Still necessary were growing city markets, the rise of the large firm, and the concentration of productive capacity known as oligopoly.[29]

Once these conditions emerged, however, many firms discovered that new conditions had arisen which made independent middlemen far less relevant in the economy. Improved transportation and communications— exemplified by the efficient traffic departments of consolidated railroads and by the speed and reliability of the parcel post—diminished the importance of the commission merchants and forwarding agents. Most important, however, manufacturers in the consumers' and producers' goods areas faced a new, concentrated market. The old, diffuse, scattered market of the first part of the century had vanished, and with it had gone the imperative of having a large connecting web of independent middlemen to bring the many small and widely dispersed buyers and sellers together.

Firms in the consumers' goods sector were not confronted by large, consolidated firms which acted as highly visible consuming units. They did, however, enjoy a high degree of visibility in their own businesses because they were almost invariably competitors in oligopolistic industries. If they were large firms, the volume of sales in the cities was often enough to make it economically sensible for the manufacturer to open a sales office in those urban areas. Most small firms that competed in consumers' goods industries did not (as Chapter XIII will show) find it economically feasible to integrate forward into wholesaling. The ones that did were almost always companies in small but oligopolistic industries with special characteristics. The Parker Pen Company, for example, was one of only a handful of producers of quality fountain pens, and retailers in the large cities were well aware of the company and its products. Goods produced in small, oligopolistic industries (such as fountain pens and eyeglasses) were usually lightweight and very inexpensive to ship, even in considerable quantities. Companies making such items could make good use of the mails, the railroads, and the parcel post to distribute their goods without wholesalers.

[29] One indication of the growing size of producing units is the fact that from 1879 to 1899 the average estimated capital (fixed and working) per establishment rose from approximately $19,000 to more than $36,000. These figures are derived from tables in the Bureau of the Census' *Historical Statistics*, pp. 409–10. To the perpetual grief of many economic historians, the Bureau of the Census has always compiled its manufacturing data on the basis of establishments, not firms. As noted on page 401 of the source just cited, "an establishment is a geographically isolated manufacturing unit maintaining independent bookkeeping records, regardless of its managerial or financial affiliations. An establishment may be a single plant, a group of closely allied plants operated as a unit, or a group of closely located plants operated by a single company without separate records for each. The establishment is also the basic unit of industrial classification, being assigned to an industry on the basis of its reported product volume." In the years 1849–99 all establishments making goods listed at a minimum annual product value of $500 were included in census studies. This naturally resulted in the inclusion of many tiny establishments in "hand and neighborhood" industries. From 1899 to 1919 all establishments whose shipments were valued at $500 or more were considered. From 1921 to 1939, only establishments making shipments valued at $5,000 or more were included.

In the consumers' and producers' goods industries, then, the usual reason for the assumption of the wholesaling function by a manufacturing firm was the new, concentrated markets created by the growth of the nation's cities, on the one hand, and by the rise of the large corporation and the coming of oligopoly on the other. Many brokers, commission merchants, and jobbers disappeared as the old condition of a scattered, diffuse market passed from the scene. Independent middlemen survived in the industries discussed in this chapter and the previous one only in the low-density markets, where the nineteenth century lived on.

CHAPTER X

The Imperatives
of Technology:
Marketing Perishable
Goods

This chapter and the next consider manufacturers who created their own wholesaling organizations, but who did so for reasons that differed from those which motivated the firms discussed in the previous two chapters. The great difference was that the producers discussed in this and the following chapter faced complex problems in the marketing of their goods. They did not merely react to increasingly concentrated demand, but were forced to make innovations in marketing techniques because of shortcomings in the existing system of independent wholesalers. In these industries, manufacturers found the web of independent commercial agents inadequate or inappropriate, and they consequently took the initiative to handle their own wholesaling. Integration forward into wholesaling and backward into purchasing often took place before the rise of truly giant firms.

Like the firms considered in the preceding chapter, the manufacturing enterprises discussed here were producers of generic consumers' goods. They too found their markets primarily in growing cities. They were, however, virtually new industries, and had to overcome very serious marketing problems in order to establish their products in the urban markets. Entrepreneurs built increasingly large firms by making innovations in marketing. The companies analyzed below were not the products of the combination movement, but were built before that movement gained full force. They resulted from a strategy of growth wherein a single manufacturing firm expanded through integration. The integration forward into marketing resulted from serious shortcomings in the old system.

In the industries considered here, the importance of advanced technology is clear. Although the goods produced were for the most part generic items, their efficient distribution into national markets often required an extremely expensive, technically advanced delivery apparatus. The independent middleman failed to supply the apparatus in an integrated, coordinated system; the manufacturer then did so.

THE DISTRIBUTION OF ICE

Perhaps the earliest example of a manufacturer creating his own distribution system for the marketing of a perishable good is the ice industry. Ice was traded in a haphazard way almost from the first settlement of the colonies. Farmers in the northern part of the country harvested ice in the winter and sold it to city ice houses. Yankee skippers heading south often ballasted their ships with ice, thereby turning a profit on what otherwise would have been dead weight. Inventive Americans, such as Benjamin Franklin and Oliver Evans, tinkered with ice-making machines in a desultory way, but the man who first turned the production and sale of ice into a systematic business was a Boston spice merchant, Frederick Tudor.[1]

Tudor had the same sort of perceptions about the sale of perishables which later carried manufacturing entrepreneurs such as Gustavus Swift to prominence. He combined these with the traditional shrewdness of the Yankee trader and the combative competitiveness of a Commodore Vanderbilt. He first entered the ice trade in 1806, sending a cargo to Martinique, but the rapidity with which the ice melted convinced him that the business required special methods of distribution based on the control of proper storage facilities. Because no comprehensive chain of such necessary facilities existed at that time, and because no independent merchants in possible market cities moved to supply them, Tudor resolved to create his own wholesaling network.

Development of the trade was interrupted by the Embargo Act of 1807, Orders in Council, and finally the War of 1812, but after the war Tudor began building a network of ice warehouses by opening establishments in Charleston and New Orleans in 1818. His well-insulated buildings gave him a substantial edge over his competitors, who had either to sell at ruinous prices or watch their cargoes melt away. By the 1820s these methods had proved so successful that Tudor was exporting 2,000 tons of ice each year and was having difficulty in securing adequate supplies. To eliminate this problem, he integrated backward.

[1] For Tudor's story see Richard O. Cummings, *The American Ice Harvests*, pp. 1–64, and Oscar E. Anderson, Jr., *Refrigeration in America*, pp. 1–20.

In theory the supply of ice was impossible to control because it was cut from the surface of ponds and rivers that were public property. Ice harvesting, therefore, was a case of every man for himself; Tudor, however, entered into an agreement with a young inventor named Nathaniel Wyeth, who produced a series of innovations which turned ice harvesting into a systematic, mechanized production process. As a result, Tudor was provided with larger supplies that were secured at less cost than those obtained by any of his competitors. Wyeth patented a series of ice cutters which not only cut up large quantities of ice quickly but also harvested it in rectangular blocks that were easier to store and less susceptible to melting than irregular pieces hacked out by hand. Wyeth also developed a conveyor belt to lift the ice blocks from the water and carry them into the ice house, a mechanical device that stacked blocks in the warehouses, and insulated railroad cars to carry the ice from the pond or ice house to dockside. Tudor himself secured a patent on the use of sawdust as an insulating material and built special ships to carry cargoes of ice. As a result, Tudor had at his disposal a completely integrated firm in which production was mechanized and distribution facilities were specially designed for the perishable product. He then turned these advantages into a successful world-wide trade, with outlets in the Caribbean, South America, and India.

Tudor's experience demonstrated that the existing distribution system was unprepared to handle perishable goods. In order to gain access to the necessary facilities, he had to build them himself; in the process he integrated his enterprise forward into distribution, eliminated all middlemen, and achieved significant competitive advantages.

This pattern recurred in the post–Civil War period as other enterprising entrepreneurs began to develop long-distance trade in perishables. In these postwar examples, as in the antebellum ice industry, elimination of the middleman resulted from a strategy of growth wherein a single manufacturing firm expanded through integration.

The Meat-Packing Industry

The industry that best exemplifies the marketing problems faced by producers of perishable goods and the steps they took to overcome those difficulties is the meat-packing business. In the decades before 1870 the industry was a very diffuse and unconcentrated one. Although processors of cured pork built medium-sized firms that produced pork goods and shipped them great distances, they marketed their output through the old network of independent jobbers. Fresh beef was never transported over great distances in any form other than on the hoof because of its highly perishable nature. Live cattle were moved by rail from the great stockyards in the Midwest, then were butchered and sold in the nation's cities and towns. Processing was thus in the hands of small, local firms that supplied only limited market areas. The development of competition among beef firms in a national market awaited advances in the technology of refrigeration. By the mid-1870s, experimental shipments of dressed beef began arriving in eastern cities, but the refrigerated railroad car was still an imperfect and often unreliable device.[2] Pioneers such as George H. Hammond led the way in the exploration of the applicability of the new technology to the dressed-beef business.[3] The full exploitation of further advances in refrigeration, however, came with the innovations of the man who reshaped the entire structure of the American dressed-beef industry—Gustavus Franklin Swift.

As a young man, Swift had worked in a Massachusetts butcher shop, then had begun his own small wholesale meat business in New England. In 1872 he became a partner in a Boston meat concern operated by James A. Hathaway. Swift came increasingly to handle the buying in the midwestern stockyards, and by 1875 he had established an office in Chicago, the great center of the meat-packing industry. While working in Chicago, Swift, like George Hammond, conceived of a means by which the beef business might be changed. The enormous potential market for fresh western beef in large eastern cities might be connected with the supply of cattle in midwestern stockyards via the refrigerated railroad car. If cattle could be slaughtered and dressed in the Midwest, and the dressed beef then shipped to the East in refrigerated cars, costs could be substantially reduced. Freight charges would be levied only on the dressed meat rather than on the entire animal. In addition, if slaughtering and processing could be concentrated in large, efficient plants in the Midwest, considerable economies of scale could be realized. Swift presented his proposals to his partner Hathaway, but the older man regarded the scheme as unsound. They dissolved the partnership and Swift proceeded on his own. In 1878 he formed a new partnership with his brother Edwin Swift and began the fight to implement his ideas.[4]

The heart of Swift's plan was to build a nationwide network of branch houses which could store and merchandise the chilled beef. This was necessary because of the inability of established jobbers to handle the perishable meat and because local butchers and packers in the East opposed the sale of western chilled beef. Independent jobbers refused to pay what Swift regarded as fair prices for the beef because they feared it would spoil before they could dispose of it and because they were unable or unwilling to invest

[2] The best source on the technology of refrigeration and its impact on the nation's economy is Anderson, *Refrigeration in America*, esp. chaps. 3–11.

[3] See Rudolf A. Clemen, *George H. Hammond (1838–1886)*.

[4] For additional information on the beginnings of the dressed-beef industry see Louis F. Swift and Arthur Van Vlissingen, Jr., *The Yankee of the Yards*; U.S. Bureau of Corporations, *Report of the Commissioner of Corporations on the Beef Industry*; Louise A. Neyhart, *Giant of the Yards*; and Rudolf A. Clemen, *The American Livestock and Meat Industry*.

in large refrigerated warehouses in which to store the beef until they could sell it. Because the existing channels of distribution for meat proved unsuitable to his needs, Swift created in the 1880s his own system of company-owned jobbing houses (often forming partnerships with local jobbers) in order to achieve outlets to the consuming markets in the nation's urban areas.[5]

The branch houses of Swift and Company consisted of a refrigerated warehouse and a merchandising organization. Dressed beef arrived by refrigerated rail car from the Midwest and was immediately transferred to the chilled storage area. There the sides of beef were further butchered by Swift employees. Sales personnel (in some cases salaried, in some cases working on a commission) contacted local retailers, conferred with them regarding their needs, and closed the sales. Retailers would then call at the branch house (often called a "box" or "cooler") and pick up their goods.[6]

Swift's operations met with much success. Demand increased, and the company opened additional slaughtering and packing plants in cities across the center of the country; in Kansas City, East Saint Louis, Omaha, Saint Paul, Saint Joseph, and Fort Worth new Swift plants arose. In order to meet the needs of his packing plants for larger quantities of ice for refrigeration, Swift also established ice houses in the cities mentioned above.[7]

Swift's innovations proved so successful that other packers soon followed his lead. By the 1890s such firms as Armour, Morris, National Packing, Cudahy Packing, and Swartzchild and Sulzberger had built similar chains of distributing houses in most of the leading cities and in many towns of medium size. By the turn of the century, all the large packing firms merchandised in the way pioneered by Gustavus Swift.[8]

---

[5] E. L. Rhoades, *Merchandising Packinghouse Products*, pp. 263–64. In addition to the inadequacy of the jobbing network, Swift had to overcome the prejudice against chilled beef, which had been slaughtered many days earlier in distant cities. Scare campaigns and appeals to support local businesses were backed by local butchers and the National Butchers' Protective Assoc. Advertising was one of the several ways in which Swift managed to conquer such opposition. See Alfred D. Chandler, Jr., "The Beginnings of 'Big Business' in American Industry," p. 7.

[6] Bureau of Corporations, *Report on the Beef Industry*, pp. 21, 207–9, 253–55.

[7] Louis Unfer, "Swift and Company," pp. 43–44.

[8] The beef industry had always been characterized by many small, local units until Swift's innovations led to the creation of large, nationwide firms. By the early years of the twentieth century, the six firms of the so-called beef trust (Swift, Cudahy, Armour, Morris, Swartzchild & Sulzberger, and National Packing) had achieved national prominence. They exercised little real control over prices, however, and were estimated to sell only about 45 per cent of the nation's fresh beef. The absence of patents, of secret processes, of control over raw materials, and a relative ease of entry prevented the large firms from controlling prices and taking exorbitant profits. See Bureau of Corporations, *Report on the Beef Industry*, pp. xxi, xxiii, 57–65. Successful medium-sized packing firms became smaller versions of the model presented by the "Big Six." The T. M. Sinclair Co. of Cedar Rapids, for example, had built eight wholesale branches throughout the Midwest and in Oregon by 1904. See T. A. Carroll to the Commissioner of Corporations, July 9, 1904, in File #666 of the records of the Bureau of Corporations. Carroll was a field investigator for the Bureau of Corporations.

The systems of branch houses, originally built to distribute chilled beef, soon served also to handle the marketing of other products as well. Pork, lamb, and mutton were sold through the branches. When the packers turned to the production of various inedible by-products such as soap and glue, the chain of company-owned jobbing outlets served to market these items in addition to a full line of meat products.[9]

The establishment of networks of branch houses by the packers was, as indicated above, a response to the inadequacies in the existing jobber system. Jobbers were unwilling to bear the heavy costs of adjusting their activities to the problems presented by the handling of chilled beef. The great variety of grades of beef and the variability in quality from one batch to another called for an expertise which jobbers did not have; more important, this variation called for close contact between jobber and supplier in order to insure that supply was carefully adjusted to demand for a perishable product. Furthermore, the jobber—that is, the independent wholesale butcher—had no way of responding to the challenge of the packers unless he joined forces with them, for he did not have access to the supplies of chilled beef. Consequently, many butchers chose to form partnerships with Swift and thus to avoid restriction to the butchering and sale of local cattle and those still carried on the hoof by the railroads.

Swift's branch houses presented complex problems because of the distance of these units from the controlling company and the resulting necessity for intimate contact between the producing plant and the field sales organization in order to control intelligently the flow of goods. Records had to be kept of the exact nature of the supply on hand in the branches and of the supply available (and potentially available) in the plants. A constant flow of communications was required in the form of reports, letters, telegrams, and (later) long-distance telephone contacts between the field organization and the packing plants. Some jobbers chose not to handle fresh beef because of the high costs of maintaining this flow, as well as the variety and varying quality of fresh beef and the costs of constructing refrigerated storage facilities.[10] The result was, of course, that they were replaced by full-time personnel in the field sales organizations of the large packing firms.

---

[9] See the replies of Swift & Co. and of Cudahy Packing Co. to a questionnaire circulated by the Bureau of Corporations to manufacturers of soap in File #7054, *ibid.*

[10] An excellent description of the complex problem of flow maintenance is found in Rhoades, *Merchandising Packinghouse Products*, pp. 294–303. See also Bureau of Corporations, *Report on the Beef Industry*, p. 21. The system of branch houses carried with it the imperative always present in organizations with relatively high fixed costs—the system had to be kept in operation if at all possible. J. Ogden Armour noted that his company sometimes sold at a loss in some areas where the supply of local beef was particularly bounteous. The reason was that "we have our investment there and a staff of men, so that the expense goes on constantly, and because we have a certain line of trade we must keep on our books. We can not close up one month and open the following month with any success" (cited in *ibid.*, pp. 80–81).

Sometimes the problem of flow maintenance proved very difficult for small packers

Although the packers did largely eliminate the wholesaler from the sale of their processed goods, they made much less of an attempt to remove them as a source for their raw materials, cattle and hogs. The independent cattle commission houses performed their functions in much the same way as they had done before the coming of large firms in the meat-packing business. To be sure, the big packers did systematize their buying of animals and did hire some company-employed buyers to work in the great stockyard centers such as Chicago, Kansas City, Omaha, and others.[11] They continued, however, to buy considerable quantities of their animals from independent commission firms such as Clay, Robinson and Company, Rosenbaum Brothers, Wood Brothers, and the Bowles Livestock Commission Company, all of which had offices in the major stockyards.[12] In addition, the large packing companies never integrated backward to the actual raising of animals. Conditions in the area of raw-material supply afforded few reasons for any serious backward integration because the existing system provided the beef at acceptable prices. The old system of purchasing through independent commission houses continued alongside the operations of buyers employed by the large packers. Swift, Armour, and their fellows faced no problems in supply comparable to those they encountered in the distribution of their processed goods, and hence they made few innovations in that area.

The fresh-beef industry had undergone a transformation by the end of

---

attempting to expand. The Agar Packing Co. of Des Moines, for example, had four wholesale houses by 1904, in Chicago, Milwaukee, Saint Louis, and Memphis. Company officials encountered many problems in managing the flow of beef, however, and grew doubtful of the wisdom of having many branch houses. Beef had often been misallocated, and the overstocked branches had sold at whatever prices they could get. Fixed expenses at the branches had to be met "whether the receipts are on the right side or not," because "packers who have a large number of branch houses must keep them running and bear losses incident to changes in economic conditions" (T. A. Carroll to the Commissioner of Corporations, July 13, 1904, File #666, Bureau of Corporations Records.

[11] See, for example, Bureau of Corporations, *Report on the Beef Industry*, p. 16, and *National Provisioner*, April 2, 1904, in File #666, Bureau of Corporations Records. The big packers also bought shares of common stock in major stockyards in Omaha, Fort Worth, Saint Louis, Saint Paul, Kansas City, and Sioux City. This gave them some influence (in the form of places on the boards of directors) in the yards, but they never made any real attempts to gain control of stockyard operations. See *Report on the Beef Industry*, pp. 28–39.

[12] Bills from these and other livestock commission companies in 1903 and 1904 are in File #667, Bureau of Corporations Records. Files #666 and #705 contain additional data on such firms. The firms operated in much the same manner as early commission merchants had in the iron industry. The animals were sent on consignment and sold; the proceeds (less freight, yardage, hay, shipping charges, and commission) were then returned to the rancher. The commission houses allowed ranchers to draw on them as soon as the animals arrived in the stockyard city, and they also often acted as bankers for their customers. An excellent portrait of the cattle commission houses of the late nineteenth century is drawn in Gene M. Gressley, *Bankers and Cattlemen*, chap. 7.

the nineteenth century. In 1870 a mass of local wholesalers handled the output of many local suppliers. As the refrigerated rail car became a reality in the late seventies and early eighties, entrepreneurs moved to utilize this technological advance to break the old patterns by connecting the eastern markets with western sources of supply. The wholesalers did not adapt to the needs of these entrepreneurs, and thus forced them to innovate in marketing. By the nineties the major packing firms had all followed Swift's plan of a nationwide chain of company branch houses equipped and staffed to handle the marketing of chilled beef and other meat items and inedible by-products. Backward integration into purchasing by the large firms also diminished the role of middlemen, but to a lesser extent than did backward integration into the marketing of processed goods. At the turn of the century, independent jobbers sold fresh beef in the small cities and towns, but most of the great market areas—the large cities—had passed into the hands of the manufacturing firms.

FORWARD INTEGRATION IN OTHER PERISHABLE GOODS INDUSTRIES

Gustavus Swift's experience in the beef business was paralleled in other industries that sold perishable goods in urban areas. This section considers several firms that processed and merchandised agricultural products as well as one company that produced a non-agricultural item but also dealt with the problem of distributing perishable goods.

A business that encountered difficulties very much like those in beef and solved them in much the same way was the processing and marketing of bananas. Like chilled beef, the banana was an unknown product in American markets at the time of the Civil War. The first known importations of the tropical fruit from the Caribbean occurred near the end of the 1860s at the ports of New Orleans and New York.[13] The fruit often arrived in American ports already rotten or in a high state of readiness for sale after a slow journey in sailing ships, the only available means of transportation. Beginning in the 1870s, however, the technology of the steamboat was applied to the banana trade, thus allowing quicker movement of the highly perishable fruit from the tropics. By the early 1880s "steamships were deciding the present and indicating the future" of the trade.[14]

Even the improvements in seagoing transportation, however, did little to make the banana a genuine competitor in any areas of the United States other than the port cities on the Atlantic and the Gulf of Mexico. Bananas were bought in large lots at a seaport by a produce merchant who disposed of them as best he could in that city. After local demand was satisfied, the merchant then shipped the rest on consignment to other middlemen in the

[13] Philip K. Reynolds, *The Story of the Banana*, p. 11.
[14] Charles M. Wilson, *Empire in Green and Gold*, p. 35.

interior.[15] Because the produce jobbers lacked adequate refrigerated (in sum-mer) and heated (in winter) warehouses, the fruit sent to the interior often arrived in an inedible state. In addition, several large shipments often arrived at once, and most found no immediate buyers; the fruit often rotted before it could be disposed of through other jobbers. The poor distribution system in the interior meant that the markets for bananas were almost entirely in the port cities where the fruit was imported. As late as the latter part of the 1890s the inland market was neglected. Five port cities received at least 95 per cent of the total amount of bananas imported into the United States, and approximately 80 per cent of these were consumed in the same cities. The population of the five main ports represented only about one-sixth of the American consuming public; the vast potential market of other urban areas lay open to the man who could create an adequate distribution system.[16]

The man was Andrew Woodbury Preston of the Boston Fruit Company. Preston had been active in the banana trade for many years and had conceived of a system of distributing bananas in inland markets along the lines of Swift's innovations in the beef industry. Preston was the prime mover in the transformation of the Boston Fruit Company into the United Fruit Company in 1899, and he was the first president of that firm. He carried out his plan through a subsidiary of United Fruit called the Fruit Dispatch Company. That company's task was to build a nationwide network of company jobbing houses equipped with the necessary cooling and heating apparatus to insure that the bananas ripened at a time when there was a market for them. The crucial problem of flow maintenance obtained in bananas as it did in beef; supply had to match demand as closely as possible lest the perishable fruit be ruined. Close communications between coastal and interior offices had to be maintained at all times.

Preston's Fruit Dispatch Company solved the distribution difficulties, and soon company branches expanded to many other cities. The operation began with outlets in Boston and New York early in 1899. By the end of that year marketing organizations had been established in Pittsburgh, Buffalo, Cleve-land, Washington, Richmond, Chicago, Detroit, Columbus, Cincinnati, Indianapolis, Kansas City, Saint Louis, Minneapolis, New Orleans, and San Francisco.[17] Preston's chain of wholesale outlets resulted in increased con-sumption of the product and led to further expansion. By 1901 United Fruit's marketing subsidiary had twenty-one distributing divisions in major cities in the United States and Canada.[18] In the annual report for that year

[15] See Frederick U. Adams, *Conquest of the Tropics*, pp. 72–73.

[16] Wilson, *Empire in Green and Gold*, pp. 72, 99.

[17] *Ibid.*, pp. 170–71.

[18] These data were assembled by the Bureau of Corporations and are available in File #4560–19 of the Bureau of Corporations Records. The bureau conducted numer-ous preliminary investigations into industries that were thought to be in possible violation of the antitrust laws. Field investigators made studies of suspicious large firms in order to determine whether full-scale investigations should be launched.

Andrew Preston proudly reported to stockholders that, "through its distributing department, the Fruit Dispatch Company, your Company has organized a most thorough and systematic method of disposing of its products throughout the United States, agencies for marketing the fruit having been established in all of the principal cities of the country."[19] As new outlets were opened, the company also provided the necessary apparatus for handling the perishable merchandise. Preston noted in the 1904 annual report, for example, that two new branches had been established and that "a new 'warm house' has been built at Springfield, Missouri, capable of receiving and reheating forty cars of bananas at one time."[20]

In its relations with the many produce jobbers and retailers who bought bananas, United Fruit used its position as the only reliable supplier of the fruit to try to rationalize the flow of goods. The company would sell to any produce dealers, of course, but, if a dealer agreed to sign a contract committing him to the regular purchase of a previously agreed upon quantity of bananas, he would receive a discount from the distributing arm of United Fruit. By 1907 approximately 150 independent wholesalers and retailers located all over the country had agreed to this plan. The contracting dealers agreed to buy bananas from no other source for a period of two years, and to place a standing order for a fixed number of cars per week (except from December through February, when the order was for that number of cars every two weeks). For its part, Fruit Dispatch contracted to supply the bananas, "it being understood that orders of this character are to have preference over all others." The dealer got a discount ranging from 1 to 2.5 per cent, depending on the volume of his order. The discount was held by Fruit Dispatch for six months and was forfeited if the dealer failed to meet his end of the bargain. The supplying firm set the price per carload each week, and the dealer had to accept that price or opt out of the arrangement. These contracts allowed the management of United Fruit to gauge demand much more accurately than before, and to plan the storage and movement of its fruit much more intelligently.[21] They and their national distribution organization helped assure the steady flow of goods needed to make the costs of refrigerated transportation and storage reasonable enough to assure a low price.

United Fruit, unlike the meat-packing companies, was able to gauge ac-

[19] United Fruit Co., *Annual Report for 1901*. The annual reports of United Fruit for the years 1900–1912 are available in the Eleutherian Mills Historical Library, Wilmington, Del.

[20] United Fruit Co., *Annual Report for 1904*. Such large-scale facilities became necessary as United Fruit's pathbreaking innovations tapped the large markets across the interior of the continent.

[21] Information on the marketing arrangements between the Fruit Dispatch Co. and its preferred dealers was taken from File #4560–19 of the Bureau of Corporations Records. That file also contains a copy of the contract between Fruit Dispatch and the dealers who agreed to place standing orders.

curately the supply of its raw materials (subject always to the tropical weather) because, from its inception, it owned its own banana plantations. These spread throughout the Caribbean and Central America, along with a network of telegraph lines, railroads, and (later) radio stations to maintain good communications. The company also owned and operated its own fleet of refrigerated steamships for transporting its goods. Middlemen played almost no role in this end of United Fruit's operations, so thorough was the process of backward integration.[22]

The evidence in Thomas C. Cochran's excellent study of the Pabst Brewing Company suggests that the beer industry underwent a pattern of development somewhat similar to that of the beef and banana firms. The Pabst firm began brewing beer in Milwaukee in 1844, and in the early 1850s established a branch office in Chicago. Late in the seventies the company embarked on a general policy of expansion in order to compete in the urban markets across the country. In reaching out to distant markets, Pabst usually had to provide refrigeration facilities in which to store the beer until the company wholesale outlet could sell it. Frederick Pabst noted in a letter to a Memphis jobber whom he wanted as manager for a company wholesale branch: "one very important problem is that of an ice house. Can a suitable one be rented, or must one be built?"[23] Branch offices for the firm spread rapidly in the eighties and nineties, and by the turn of the century there were approximately fifty of them. The branches contacted wholesalers and retailers in the vicinity and dispatched traveling salesmen to outlying areas. The expansion by Pabst into the national market via company-owned wholesale outlets came as a result of the problem of perishability and the inability of jobbers to handle that difficulty as well as the manufacturing firm itself could.[24]

The problem of perishability was not restricted to processors and vendors

---

[22] Such complete backward integration was rare among firms that processed agricultural products (either plants or animals). The supply was usually so widely available that companies seldom saw any reason to go into the business of actually raising their own plants or animals. Notable exceptions were the sugar-growing and refining enterprises of Claus Spreckels in Hawaii and on the West Coast of the United States. See Jack S. Mullins, "The Sugar Trust," pp. 76–78; Jacob Adler, *Claus Spreckels*; and Alfred S. Eichner, *The Emergence of Oligopoly*, pp. 87–92. Whenever supplies came mostly or largely from abroad, however, manufacturers in such industries as sugar, chocolate, and chewing gum often purchased their own land for raw-materials production in foreign areas in order to assure a steady flow of supplies.

[23] Thomas C. Cochran, *The Pabst Brewing Company*, pp. 170–71.

[24] *Ibid.*, pp. 171–75, 237, and chap. 7. In addition to wholesale branches, brewers often had to buy saloons as well in order to insure the presence of sufficient retail outlets for the individual firm's beer. Between 1887 and 1893, for example, Pabst invested about $1,400,000 in saloon real estate. Additional information on the beer industry (though certainly not as thorough as Cochran's study) can be found in: Stanley Baron, *Brewed in America*; G. Thomann, *American Beer*; Roland Krebs and Percy J. Orthwein, *Making Friends Is Our Business*; and Alvin Griesedieck, *The Falstaff Story*. Pabst, like Swift and United Fruit, owned and scheduled its own railroad cars.

of agricultural products. The early history of Eastman Kodak bore some similarity to the experience of the firms already discussed. George Eastman divined a vast market for a simple, reliable, inexpensive means by which the public could provide itself with photographs. He, like Swift and Preston, envisioned a large, untapped domestic market; his market was that of amateur photography. His goal was to provide masses of consumers with cameras and film, to expand greatly the number of Americans actually taking photographs. Eastman found, however, that his goals and strategies were incompatible with those of existing wholesale houses dealing in photographic supplies, and the problem of perishability played a part in that incompatibility.[25]

George Eastman entered the business of cameras and photographic apparatus in 1880 and was moderately successful in that decade. In the eighties he marketed gelatin photographic plates, but he encountered serious difficulties with wholesalers because of the perishability of the plates; the sensitivity of the photographic emulsion declined with the passage of time. Wholesalers held the goods too long. Photographers complained bitterly about the worthless plates that had been sold too late.[26] As a result of such difficulties with the existing merchants in photographic supplies, Eastman began opening his own wholesale stores. When he moved into the production of sensitized photographic film in the latter part of the eighties, his business boomed "so that a change in the capital structure was necessary to finance new factory buildings and additional distribution agencies."[27] Eastman later recalled his early experiences with the independent distributors: "When I started in the photographic business, it was wholly in the hands of three houses, who were in turn manufacturers, importers, and jobbers. Practically all of the trade passed through their hands, and they . . . sold to about seventy-five dealers in photographic goods, no one of whom could have carried on his business except in connection with those houses. My attempts to do business through them were unsatisfactory and my concern started out to interest other people."[28]

As the business grew, distributing warehouses and company-owned wholesale and retail stores spread across the country. Three large storage and distributing centers were built in New York, Chicago, and San Francisco to

---

[25] The established houses, still attuned to the needs of the traditional market, did not promote Eastman's goods in a manner he found satisfactory. Only by building his own system of outlets could he control flows, avoid wastage of perishable film, and tap a national amateur market. Professor Reese V. Jenkins, who is currently working on a study of the American photographic industry, generously contributed his thoughts on this topic. Of course, he is not responsible for errors in the interpretation here presented, but his help is appreciated.

[26] Carl W. Ackerman, *George Eastman*, pp. 31, 42–43. In addition to Ackerman's biography, a good sketch of Eastman is Blake McKelvey's "George Eastman," in *Dictionary of American Biography*, ed. Harris E. Starr, pp. 274–77.

[27] Ackerman, *George Eastman*, p. 92.

[28] *Ibid.*, p. 265. Eastman's comments came in a letter to Thomas Wallace of the Expo Camera Co. of New York City, probably late in 1912.

serve their respective geographic areas. The firm trained its personnel in the wholesale and retail stores to control carefully the flow of sensitized film goods in order to prevent them from deteriorating before they could be sold. In a letter to the Bureau of Corporations in 1914, George Eastman explained that his firm had completely eliminated independent wholesalers, and he emphasized the importance of the perishability of the goods in that connection: "The wholesaler or jobber is a detriment to our business because a large proportion of it is in sensitized goods which are perishable. . . . We have organized our distribution facilities so as to get the goods into the hands of the consumer as quickly as possible. Our sensitized goods carry an expiration date. Our own retail houses . . . have been educated to control their stocks very accurately so that the goods are kept moving."[29]

Conclusion

Eastman Kodak, like firms selling perishable agricultural goods in a national market, found the old system of wholesalers inappropriate. The response of the Rochester firm, like the response of Swift and Company, United Fruit, Pabst Brewing, and others, was to create its own marketing organization. These organizations included the necessary mechanical apparatus and the needed trained personnel to coordinate the flow of perishable goods from source of supply to market. Because the nature of the products they sold created new, important problems for independent wholesalers, the middlemen could not handle them properly. In each case the producing firm was led to invest in a nationwide network of wholesale outlets which allowed it to tap the potential demand the company had discerned. Most of the firms considered in this chapter were processing and selling relatively new products for urban consumers. Because their goods were perishable in nature, they did not fit well into the old distribution systems, which were accustomed to being able simply to store unsold goods until the market improved. Attempts by entrepreneurs to merchandise their perishable products in widely separated markets through existing mercantile methods often ended disastrously. Jobbers and commission merchants did not have and were not quick to acquire

---

[29] Eastman's communication to the Bureau of Corporations came on October 24, 1914, and is located in File #7222–45–1 of the Bureau of Corporations Records. Of course, Eastman was not entirely candid; the elimination of middlemen brought other advantages as well. By retaining effective control of the means by which retailers could obtain its products, Eastman Kodak was better able to prevent price cutting for its goods and to discourage the widespread distribution of competing products.

Independent retailers selling photographic supplies sometimes complained vigorously about Eastman's distribution methods. Jackson & Semmelmeyer of Chicago, for example, denounced the large firm: "The Eastman company prohibits every retailer from handling any other competitive goods, except a few sundries, on penalty of having the entire Eastman line taken away. It also forces the distribution of its goods through exclusive agencies in exclusive territory" (File #7222–11–1, *ibid.*).

either the special physical plants or the new expertise called for by the new products. They were similarly incapable of creating the organizations vital to the intelligent management of the flow of goods.

Although some backward integration toward raw materials was undertaken (notably in the case of the United Fruit Company), such integration was less widespread in these perishable goods industries than in the various industries described in Chapters VIII and IX of this study. Purchasing organizations did eliminate many middlemen, but the replacement of independent commercial agents with company personnel was much more apparent in marketing organizations.

Because the old marketing order proved inflexible and inappropriate, producers in the perishable goods industries considered in this chapter seized the initiative and largely eliminated wholesaling middlemen from the distribution process. By the early years of the twentieth century, the firms discussed above had built nationwide marketing organizations designed to do well what the independent merchants could do only poorly, if at all. These marketing organizations seem to have resulted in substantial economies of scale in distribution; the large, steady flow of goods made the costs of special transport, storage, and handling facilities reasonable enough to assure a low selling price. Such economies of scale contributed to the success of these firms.

None of the products considered in this chapter was complex; all were generic. They did not, however, fit into the old marketing system for generic products, because of their peculiar requirements for elaborate, technically complex, expensive, nationwide merchandising and delivery systems. Because the traditional mercantile network did not meet the needs of the expansionary and innovative businessmen considered in this chapter, these producers created their own advanced marketing apparatus, utilizing new techniques in refrigeration, transport, and the rational control of flows within their path-breaking enterprises.

CHAPTER XI

Other Products
with Marketing
Complexities

The preceding chapter considered the experience of firms that elaborated their own marketing organizations as a result of the failure of independent middlemen to meet the special problems involved in the distribution of perishable goods. This chapter describes other companies that integrated forward into wholesaling as a result of merchandising difficulties other than perishability. For the most part these enterprises were making and selling producers' goods, although some consumers' goods industries encountered problems and created solutions very similar to those experienced by the producers' goods firms.

The business enterprises discussed below all found the usual structure of brokers, commission merchants, jobbers, and other merchants unsuitable for the peculiar marketing methods required by their products. In the years before the Civil War, perhaps the most outstanding example of this situation was the industrial machinery industry. The specific requirements of individual customers, the technological complexity of the products, their high unit cost, the need for special instruction in their operation, and the difficulty of repairs meant that the manufacturer had to establish close contacts with his customers. Such contacts could not be achieved through independent commercial agents, and manufacturers therefore had to build their own marketing systems to meet their particular needs. These producers met new and difficult problems in marketing because their goods were very specific ones, unlike the generic goods that characterized most of the early nineteenth-century economy.

The same pattern obtained in the post–Civil War period and was very important in determining the marketing structure of new producers' goods industries such as the early electrical industry. Makers of new consumers' goods sometimes found like problems in the distribution of their products, including such difficulties as the need for a demonstration, the necessity of providing repair service, and the need to provide consumer credit to allow widespread sales of relatively expensive items to the consuming public. Like all the firms discussed thus far, the companies considered here moved to effect changes in their distribution systems. They did not do so in response to concentrated demand, however, as did some businesses. Instead, they faced special marketing problems that led them to take charge of their own merchandising operations. Because their highly specific, complex goods would not flow smoothly through the older marketing channels, these manufacturers were compelled to bypass the traditional channels.

The Marketing of Industrial Machinery

From the earliest days of mills and factories in the United States, firms that manufactured machinery for such establishments found that the usual marketing channels in the economy would not serve for the special requirements of their products. The machinery was often technologically complex, very expensive, and difficult to repair. The customer almost always had special needs for the particular machinery he wanted for his factory, which meant that only rarely were any two machines exactly alike. As noted in Chapter V, the producer often had to send a skilled mechanic great distances to demonstrate the proper operation of the machines and to see that they functioned as intended. As a result of these requirements, manufacturers seldom could rely on commission merchants or brokers to act as distributors. The producing firm itself had to assume the marketing function. Sales usually came in the wake of personal visits by producer to customer (or vice versa), personal contacts by full-time traveling salesmen, or elaborate and extensive correspondence (which often included blueprints).

The first large-scale industrial enterprises to require complex machinery in this country were the textile mills. Firms such as the Whitin Machine Works and the Saco-Lowell Shops arose in New England to specialize in the manufacture of industrial machinery, primarily for textile mills. From their earliest days, such firms found independent commercial agents of little use, except occasionally as forwarding agents. They contacted mill owners directly in New England and in the South, and they built their products to meet the unique needs of factory owners. Leading makers of textile machinery spurned the middleman as a marketing agent throughout the nineteenth century because they "continued to believe that the only satisfactory way to conduct a machinery business was by direct contact between the manufacturer and his customers."[1]

A similar pattern of direct contact between producers and consumers obtained before the Civil War in the sale of other forms of industrial machinery. Makers of sugar mill machinery, industrial boilers, and large, stationary steam engines also communicated closely and extensively with their customers, and often they sent mechanics to superintend the installation and initial operations of the machines.[2]

In the years after the Civil War, the same marketing methods prevailed. Large iron and steel producers bought their machinery in much the same manner as did the textile mills; a close, intimate contact prevailed between the maker and the user of the goods.[3] Large companies producing industrial machinery in the latter part of the century often had several regional offices to afford better close contact with customers. The largest machinery firms, such as New Jersey's Babcock and Wilcox, often enjoyed the same kind of concentrated market which marked the steel industry, and they also responded with company sales offices. These offices allowed the machinery makers to use more efficiently the distribution methods that had always existed in their industry.

A good portrait of the distribution pattern of machinery makers late in the nineteenth century is provided by the records of the Shawmut Fibre Company, a New England paper concern. Shawmut utilized a range of special machinery in its mill and therefore had contacts with many leading machinery manufacturing firms. These firms, like the makers of textile machinery, spurned the network of commercial intermediaries. Exact specifications for goods continued to be required. Charles W. Pusey of Wilmington's Pusey

---

[1] Thomas R. Navin, *The Whitin Machine Works since 1831*, p. 96. Navin's excellent study is paralleled by George S. Gibb, *The Saco-Lowell Shops*. These two books give a thorough and detailed picture of marketing methods in the textile machinery industry. For an example of such techniques applied in the South, see Richard W. Griffin and Diffee W. Standard, "The Cotton Industry in Ante Bellum North Carolina," pt. 2, pp. 139–40.

[2] For examples of such sales see Correspondence, 1840–87, J. C. Hobbs & Sons (makers of steam engines and other machines) Papers, and the letters from Corliss Steam Engine Co. to Fall River Iron Works, Fall River Iron Works Papers. See also the William D. Wiegand Papers, 1852–61. Wiegand was a partner in the Baltimore engineering firm of Hazlehurst & Wiegand, which operated the Vulcan Iron Works in that city. Additional examples of the marketing methods of machinery manufacturers are given in such secondary sources as Kathleen Bruce, *Virginia Iron Manufacture in the Slave Era*, pp. 209–11; and Vernon D. Keeler, "An Economic History of the Jackson County Iron Industry," p. 144.

[3] See, for example, Minutes of the Operating Department of Carnegie Steel, December 18, 1897, Andrew Carnegie Papers, vol. 47, and Minutes of a Meeting to Discuss the Manufacture of Steel Cars, January 13, 1899, *ibid.*, vol. 60. See also F. H. Daniels (of American Steel & Wire) to Edwin Reynolds, general superintendent of the E. P. Allis Co., March 18, 1899; Daniels to W. P. Palmer, general manager of the American Steel & Wire plant in Cleveland, April 21, 1899; and Daniels to F. L. Brown of San Francisco, April 12, 1899; American Steel & Wire Co. Papers.

and Jones cautioned the Shawmut firm, "In ordering please give all the information asked for by the enclosed blueprint, since we are not sure of completing a [pulp] Screen satisfactorily without it."[4] J. H. Horne and Company of Lawrence, Massachusetts, noted that "we have made specifications as we understand what you want but should you wish to make any changes or have a different size engine if you will let us know exactly what you want we shall be pleased to submit price and specifications for same."[5]

Trained personnel employed by machinery makers often visited customers to make certain that they fully understood the wants of the buyer. "Our engineer will be at your works sometime this week," wrote the Providence Steam and Gas Pump Company, "to take the measurements for the plans, and make arrangements."[6] The time-honored practice of installation of the costly machinery by skilled company employees continued in the Gilded Age. When the Union Machine Company of Fitchburg, Massachusetts, sent Shawmut its plans for a piece of mill machinery priced at more than $8,000, it assured Shawmut that "further, we propose to furnish a competent man to superintend the setting-up of the machine, free of expense to you."[7] Other machinery manufacturers, including the Bigelow Company of New Haven, Wilmington's J. Morton Poole Company, the Link-Belt Engineering Company of Philadelphia, and Babcock and Wilcox, a New Jersey corporation, dealt with Shawmut Fibre Company in the same way.

Early in the twentieth century other such producers followed the supply pattern exemplified by the firms that dealt with Shawmut Fibre. The Union Steam Pump Company of Battle Creek, Michigan, for example, almost never made standardized machines that could properly be sold through jobbers. "Almost every article is specifically made, with special features adapted to some special use. The designs and finished products are largely based upon individual specifications. Only one man in the United States buys from us and pays cash and takes his chances on a resale."[8] Other large industrial equipment (for example, printing presses) was built to the specifications of the customer, and direct contact between consumers and the marketing force of manufacturers was essential.[9] Because their products were often unique, technologically complex, and quite expensive, and because the installation and

---

[4] Charles W. Pusey to Shawmut Fibre Co., December 7, 1888. All information on the paper firm is from the Shawmut Fibre Co. Papers, 1885–89.

[5] J. H. Horne & Co. to Shawmut, December 8, 1888, *ibid*.

[6] Providence Steam & Gas Pump to Shawmut, May 16, 1889, *ibid*.

[7] Union Machine to Shawmut, December 13, 1888, *ibid*.

[8] The quotation is from the company's response to a questionnaire distributed by the Bureau of Corporations and is in File #7222–17–1 of the records of the U.S. Bureau of Corporations.

[9] Newspapers wanted specific features in their printing presses and made their wishes known to the sales personnel of such firms as the Duplex Printing Press Co. of Michigan. The Duplex company's sales methods are described in File #7222–22–1, *ibid*. Also of interest are the similar operations of S. F. Bowser & Co. of Fort Wayne, Ind., makers of oil pumps and oil tanks; see File #7222–3–1, *ibid*.

repair of their goods required trained personnel, most makers of heavy industrial machinery utilized their own marketing systems from the 1830s throughout the nineteenth century.

Only small, standardized machinery was sold through commission merchants and jobbers. Some stationary steam engines were marketed in that manner beginning in the 1850s, when standardization was first used for those machines; they could be sold via the usual marketing network because they were simple and uncomplicated.[10] In general, they were smaller, less complex, and much less expensive than the special-order devices built for large mills and factories. A similar pattern prevailed in the manufacture of small, standard boilers, lathes, and other machines.[11] Some middlemen even specialized in the sale of such machinery.[12] Because items did not carry with them the special marketing requirements that attended large-scale, special-order goods, the usual marketing channels served.

THE EARLY ELECTRICAL INDUSTRY

Similar problems and responses occurred in the formative years of the electrical industry in the United States. The industry did not begin in any real sense until the 1880s, but it quickly encountered marketing difficulties similar to those involved in the sale of heavy industrial machinery. Thomas Edison began his business enterprises in 1879 and expanded them in subsequent years. The Edison Lamp Works at Harrison, New Jersey, produced the incandescent lights used in Edison's system of lighting, and the manufacture of heavy equipment such as dynamos was concentrated in the Edison Machine Works at Schenectady, New York. In 1889 the various enterprises were consolidated to form the Edison General Electric Company. That firm was one of two components in the formation of the General Electric Company in 1892. The other part was the Thomson-Houston Electric Company, which first appeared in 1882 as a reorganized form of the American Electric Company, a Connecticut corporation begun in 1880. The union of Thomson-Houston and Edison General Electric laid the foundations for one of the nation's largest firms, General Electric. GE's largest competitor, Westinghouse, was started in 1884 by George Westinghouse. Although other, smaller

[10] The coming of standardization to small, stationary steam engines is discussed in Victor S. Clark, *History of Manufacturers in the United States*, 1: 505, 509.

[11] The machinery sold through commission merchants seldom cost more than $1,000, whereas the special-order products for mill machinery, engines, boilers, and other industrial machinery usually were far more costly.

[12] The D. L. Harris Co. of Springfield, Mass., for example, marketed its lathes through commission houses such as Wells Chase & Gehrmann of Baltimore and Hawkins & James of Chicago; see Correspondence, 1864–66, Stone & Harris Papers. The Erie City Iron Works also sold standard boilers and engines through machinery commission merchants; see Incoming Correspondence, 1879, Erie City Iron Works Papers.

firms existed in the early electrical industry, these were the largest, and this section will concentrate on the activities of the three that dominated the industry, Thomson-Houston, Edison General Electric, and the Westinghouse Company.[13]

The primary line of business for all these companies was the production of apparatus to generate electricity and to convert that energy into usable light. The transformation of electricity to light was accomplished by means of two kinds of lamps, the incandescent and the arc. The first, in which Edison made various technical improvements, involved running a current through a filament in a vacuum until the filament was heated and glowing. The second, which was most widely used by the Thomson-Houston Company, utilized an intensely hot, glowing path of electricity, a path formed when two touching electrodes were slightly separated and the current continued to flow between them. Both of these lighting systems were sold to two kinds of consuming units in the late nineteenth century. One was the growing network of central power stations in the cities, and the other was individual units (usually factories or stores) that purchased isolated lighting systems in order to generate their own power rather than draw it from a central station. In marketing their apparatus to central stations and to isolated consumers, the early electrical manufacturers faced serious problems.

The first difficulty was that of allaying the public's fear of a new and mysterious source of power and light. The careless installation and incompetent operation of lighting systems in the eighties and early nineties led to several disastrous accidents and fires, and these served to frighten the populace and to impede its acceptance of electricity. Electrical manufacturers were acutely conscious of the problem of the public's fear of electricity. Elihu Thomson wrote an executive of the Thomson-Houston Company in 1887, warning him to take precautions in the installation of a new lighting system: "A disastrous fire originating from any such apparatus would of course be a serious drawback to its introduction, just as the burning of the Temple Theatre in Philadelphia as a consequence of bad wiring on the part of the

---

[13] Information about the early electrical industry's operations is drawn from a variety of sources. The Westinghouse Co. has very few surviving records, although a small collection of historical materials is available at its plant in East Pittsburgh, Pa. General Electric, on the other hand, has voluminous records, which are open to scholars at the company's main library in Schenectady, N.Y. GE's records include many original company documents as well as thousands of items compiled by John W. Hammond in the preparation of his book, *Men and Volts.* Hammond was a GE employee who had access to company files and who compiled a massive collection of information drawn from those files and from extensive personal interviews with company personnel. His notes and the transcripts of his interviews are available in the company's library. The General Electric Co. was extremely cooperative and helpful, and we are grateful both to that firm and to Westinghouse for the privilege of consulting their historical files. An outstanding secondary study of the industry, Harold C. Passer's *The Electrical Manufacturers, 1875–1900,* is based primarily on the company collections described above.

Edison Co. will undoubtedly hurt the introduction of incandescent light-ing."[14] A speaker at a meeting of the newly formed American Institute of Electrical Engineers commented on the problem that same year: "There is an air of gloom and anxiety on every face; the unseen tremendous power not always under control . . . may be made to react at any moment with destruc-tive energy." Most of the fear was unfounded, the speaker continued. "I think I could count on my ten fingers the number of accidents that have occurred so far. And yet, like sweet morsels between their teeth the repor-torial tongues roll these things about until every newspaper in the land speaks of death and desolation from electrical currents."[15] The leading trade journal in the industry, *Electrical World*, voiced a similar complaint: "It seems to be the rule now that if the cause of a fire is unknown it is immediately attrib-uted to electricity."[16]

To avoid the disastrous accidents that retarded the industry's growth, a force of technically trained company employees was needed to insure the proper installation and operation of lighting systems and other electrical ap-paratus. The long-term success of the entire industry depended in large part on public acceptance of the safety of electrical devices. It also depended on the efficient functioning of the lighting systems themselves, and that too in-volved careful installation and thorough instructions on the operation of the systems. Elihu Thomson repeatedly emphasized the importance of careful installation and instructions to users. Thomson-Houston's arc and incandes-cent systems, he believed, should be sold and delivered only by skilled com-pany personnel and only under strict rules enforced by the manufacturer. Lighting apparatus, Thomson asserted, "must, from the very delicate nature of the conditions involved, be handled by men who are measurably within our control . . . [and we must not supply any] apparatus without supplying that other necessary concomitant; men who have seen the making and work-

[14] Elihu Thomson to Charles A. Coffin, February 7, 1887, Elihu Thomson Papers. The Thomson papers reflect Elihu Thomson's specialized areas of interest (the scien-tific, technical side of the enterprise), but some useful information on the operation of the business as a whole is also obtainable.

[15] Statement on Incandescent Lighting from Central Stations by Dr. Otto A. Moses, *Transactions of the American Institute of Electrical Engineers, 1887*, pp. 2–3.

[16] *Electrical World*, January 7, 1893. Apprehensions about electricity may have increased rather than decreased in the wake of manufacturers' attempts to instruct the users of their equipment. For example, in 1890 Edison distributed a lengthy circular for adventurous do-it-yourselfers. The document was called (in the marvelously direct prose of nineteenth-century American business) *Directions for Setting Up and Running Edison Electric Motors.* "In preparing these instructions," the company declared, "it has been assumed that the electrical and mechanical features of the machine are under-stood." Those willing to venture beyond that caveat then encountered a welter of un-settling phrases including "under no circumstances," "exercise great care," "do not touch it," "never, under any circumstances or in any manner," "will cause the part to be burned out," and "invites disaster." This document is part of the Trade Catalogue Collection at the Eleutherian Mills Historical Library, Wilmington, Del.

ing of the plant sufficiently to know, when they are using it aright, or when it is not being used aright by others."[17] In another letter Thomson declared: "Our agents should not take contracts to furnish apparatus without specifying that the conditions of the sale are that our rules shall be observed. . . . our Company ought not to supply . . . anybody unless [the systems] are put up by our own experts and under our own rules."[18] A trained sales and installation force meant not only greater safety but also more efficient installation; Thomson was aware of the necessity of "educating agents so as to be able to estimate and figure on the wiring for . . . plants. . . . the matter of wiring economically is one of great intricacy and should not be trusted in the hands of a man who has not had a practical training in electrical matters."[19]

In addition to the problem of the danger of fire and destruction from the equipment, electrical manufacturers faced the range of marketing difficulties which had long been present in the production and sale of heavy industrial machinery. Customers had special needs and requirements that made standardization extremely difficult in the industry's early years. Electrical machinery was even more technologically complex than lighting apparatus, and it required installation and initial operation by expert mechanics. Close contact between the manufacturer and the consumer was as essential to the electrical machinery business as it was to the industrial. So the producers of both types of products naturally found the web of independent commercial agents who distributed so much of the nation's goods to be less useful in the merchandising of these new, complex electrical devices. Accordingly they moved very early to handle their own marketing by creating company sales organizations of the type urged by Elihu Thomson.

The necessity of having a trained company marketing force applied to electrical machinery and both principal lighting markets, the isolated systems and the central stations. In the early years of the 1880s the demand for isolated lighting systems was quite brisk. The customers were almost invariably businesses. In 1881 and 1882, for example, the Edison Company for Isolated Lighting installed incandescent systems for such firms as the McCormick Harvesting Machine Company, Marshall Field and Company, Baldwin Locomotive Works, Trenton Iron, and National Tube, as well as in the private residence of J. P. Morgan.[20] As the number of central stations expanded, however, demand for the isolated systems fell rapidly. In 1891, for example, the Thomson-Houston Company estimated that only slightly more than 10 per cent of its total business to date had been in isolated systems, the rest

[17] Thomson to S. A. Barton, January 22, 1886, Elihu Thomson Papers.
[18] Thomson to S. A. Barton, June 5, 1885, and Elihu Thomson to Frederick Thomson, June 1, 1886, *ibid.*
[19] Thomson to S. A. Barton, September 3, 1885, *ibid.*
[20] Edison Co. for Isolated Lighting, *Prices of Edison Incandescent Light Apparatus for Lighting Factories and Other Buildings, 1882,* p. 6. This pamphlet is part of the Trade Catalogue Collection at the Eleutherian Mills Historical Library.

having gone to central stations.[21] Both the isolated and central systems required close contact between the manufacturer and the consuming unit. Because electricity was so new, neither individual businesses nor central stations had the skilled personnel and technical knowledge required to operate their systems in the infancy of electric lighting. Their personnel had to be trained by employees of the electrical manufacturers.[22]

They moved quickly, however, to meet the special merchandising needs of their customers. As early as 1882, Edison established the procedure of installation and instruction by a trained company employee: "On completion of a plant we allow one of our men to remain for a reasonable period of time, at our expense, to instruct the purchaser in its use. It may be run by any workman of ordinary intelligence, and requires no more attention than would be given by any engineer without interfering with his regular duties."[23] An engineering department employing a corps of inspectors was created to make certain that Edison materials sold to central stations were installed and operating properly.[24] Competing firms built comparable organizations.

From its earliest days Westinghouse, for example, included a specialized engineering subsidiary firm, Westinghouse, Church, Kerr, and Company. The company was keenly aware of the key role of its subsidiary in its over-all operations. "In a business such as ours," Westinghouse declared in a company publication in 1898, "it is fully as important that the product shall be intelligently sold, as that it shall be honestly and skillfully made. In pursuance of this principle, the engineering establishment of Westinghouse, Church, Kerr, and Company was incorporated in 1884, to market the product of the Westinghouse Machine Company, and to conduct a general engineering and

[21] Thomson-Houston Electric Co., *Annual Report, 1891*, General Electric Co. Papers. "While some electrical manufacturing companies," Thomson-Houston noted, "have confined their operations principally to the supply of mills, factories, hotels, etc., ... which is known as 'isolated' business and which is of inferior value and importance, nearly ninety per cent. of the business of your company has been in the sale of its apparatus to corporations organized to furnish light and power from central lighting and power stations."

The central stations were local corporations that operated under licenses granted by the manufacturing concerns holding patents on lighting systems. Often the manufacturing company received a minority percentage of the common stock of the stations. The central stations bought their equipment from the licensing firm and sold electricity to local users. Sample contracts and licenses between Thomson-Houston and General Electric and their local central stations are available in the General Electric Papers. An interesting and detailed account of how the local Edison Illuminating companies were organized is given in Sidney A. Mitchell, *S. Z. Mitchell and the Electrical Industry.*

[22] The central stations were well aware of this problem, and one of the prime goals of the Assoc. of Edison Illuminating Cos. was to improve and increase the flow of technical information from Edison to the central stations. Several resolutions by the association reflected that desire, including one in 1886 calling on Edison to "write up some general instructions in regard to the handling and placing of lamps ... so that new Illuminating Companies may be instructed in the fullest manner." Assoc. of Edison Illuminating Cos., *Minutes, 1886*, p. 37.

[23] Edison, *Prices of Edison Incandescent Light Apparatus*, p. 3.

[24] Assoc. of Edison Illuminating Cos., *Minutes, 1887*, p. 56.

contracting business." The subsidiary firm designed and installed complete electric power and lighting plants and could provide for the unique needs of its customers. "A wide experience in all parts of the country has given them [the firm's engineers] unusual opportunities for determining how far the suitability of any piece of apparatus, however excellent in itself, may be limited by local conditions or character of service required," the company proclaimed. "Their engineering force is large and comprises men especially skilled in each line."[25]

The Thomson-Houston Company operated in much the same way as the Edison and Westinghouse enterprises. The New England firm's marketing organization furnished specifications for individual customers, spelling out the exact size and nature of the dynamo and wiring system to be built. These written proposals also committed the company to "furnish the services of an electrician for the period of construction, to start plant and give instructions in operating the same, purchaser agreeing that a competent man shall be detailed to receive such instructions during the time needed."[26] In addition to installation and instruction services. Thomson-Houston employees also often made frequent visits to customers to insure satisfaction. Early in 1885 the firm sold a lighting system to the Alan Wood Steel Company in Conshohocken, Pennsylvania, for example, and subsequently contacted that firm several times to make repairs and to give additional training to Alan Wood personnel.[27] Such expert training and close contact could be provided most reliably by Thomson-Houston's own marketing organization.

Company marketing organizations spread rapidly, and soon the major electrical manufacturers had nationwide marketing systems with offices in cities across the country. Thomson-Houston expanded from its Boston headquarters in the eighties, and by 1890 had established offices in Chicago, New York, Atlanta, Washington, Kansas City, Saint Paul, Cincinnati, Philadelphia, and San Francisco.[28] Westinghouse, Church, Kerr, and Company also stead-

[25] Westinghouse Machine Co., *A Description of the Westinghouse Single Acting Compound Engine, 1898,* p. 5, Trade Catalogue Collection, Eleutherian Mills Historical Library. Additional information on Westinghouse, Church, Kerr & Co. may be found in the Westinghouse historical collection at the firm's East Pittsburgh plant. See especially the advertisements in the Westinghouse Scrapbook for the 1890s and a pamphlet entitled *Programme for Westinghouse Day, September 7, 1898,* p. 17.

[26] See, for example, the proposal of the Thomson-Houston Electric Co.'s isolated lighting department to provide a lighting system for the Grafton & Knight Manufacturing Co. in Worcester, Mass., dated June 21, 1889, in the General Electric Papers.

[27] Thomson-Houston to Alan Wood Steel, January 13, September 17, November 2, 24, and 27, 1885, Alan Wood Steel Co. Papers. For further illustration of the continuing efforts by Thomson-Houston to provide technical advice and help to customers after the initial installation, see Outgoing Correspondence, 1885 and 1886, Elihu Thomson Papers.

[28] Thomson-Houston Electric Co., *General Catalogue, 1890,* p. 7, Trade Catalogue Collection, Eleutherian Mills Historical Library; see also Recollections of T. A. McLoughlin, General Electric Papers.

ily increased its sales offices until it had a company marketing force in many major cities.[29]

Edison General Electric built a widespread marketing structure following the company's reorganization in the wake of the consolidation of the Edison enterprises in 1889. The new company created a system of salaried company employees in order to give the New York headquarters more control over sales and to reduce marketing costs. Edison General Electric divided the country into seven sales districts, sending each a district manager and a force of skilled men. This organization proved very successful, and, when the General Electric Company was created in 1892, it simply adopted the sales system used by Edison General Electric. In the nineties the control imposed from the central office resulted in standardized procedures that made the sales organization even more efficient.[30] By 1900 the firm had offices in twenty-three American cities.[31]

Although the vast majority of sales made by the electrical manufacturers were the result of the efforts of the company-owned marketing organizations, some sales were made to electrical jobbers and supply houses. The independent wholesalers dealt in small, simple, standardized goods—the items usually referred to as "electrical accessories." These accessories (such as porcelain insulators, lamp cords, and some lamps) usually were not patented, and they carried with them none of the marketing problems that marked the more complex electrical products. "Approach all supply houses of good standing," General Electric's General Manager of the Sales Department charged his district organizations in 1894, urging them to make greater efforts to increase sales of accessories to jobbers.[32] To supply the demand of independent jobbers and other local customers, General Electric and Westinghouse established a network of warehouses which stocked standard accessory items and lamps.[33]

The electrical manufacturers also broke with the past in purchasing. Although they engaged in some backward integration into raw materials in the

---

[29] See Westinghouse, *Description of the Single Acting Compound Engine*, p. 5, and *Westinghouse Diary for 1909*, Westinghouse Co. Historical Papers.

[30] See Minutes of the Sales Committee, August 21, 1891, and the very useful extracts from circular letters issued by the first vice-president (who was in charge of sales), December 15, 1894–July 12, 1900, General Electric Papers. Harold C. Passer gives an excellent analysis of the operations of the General Electric sales force in the 1890s in his "Electrical Manufacturing Around 1900," pp. 383–89.

[31] Information on the back cover of the General Electric Co.'s *Edison Incandescent Lamps, 1900*, Trade Catalogue Collection, Eleutherian Mills Historical Library.

[32] J. R. Lovejoy, Circular Letter #61 to Sales Managers, June 20, 1894, General Electric Papers.

[33] General Electric, *Edison Incandescent Lamps*, p. 1; Westinghouse, *Westinghouse Diary for 1909*, p. 1; and *Electrical World*, January 7, 1893.

initial years of operation, they did not choose to do so very extensively.[34] They did, however, create their own purchasing departments, which secured the various materials required for production. Silas A. Barton of Thomson-Houston, for example, organized a central purchasing department for that company in Boston in 1891. The fundamental features of organization and routine originally devised by Thomson-Houston were retained in the purchasing department of GE after the union of Thomson-Houston and Edison General Electric.[35] Most of the purchasing was done via direct contact with producers, not through middlemen.

The special marketing needs of electrical products gave rise to the distribution methods adopted by electrical manufacturers. The industry's new goods did not flow smoothly through the old channels. To merchandise electrical equipment, the sales apparatus had to have a new and quite specialized expertise in engineering. Very few merchants and jobbers possessed such skill, and few showed the inclination to flee established, going concerns and lines of trade in order to involve themselves in a novel and somewhat risky industry. In addition, manufacturers required a force of genuinely skilled and informed personnel to handle the installation of the equipment and the task of educating customers in its proper operation; to gamble on the work of men not measurably within their control (as Elihu Thomson phrased it) was to risk fire and destruction, which would seriously cripple the industry's efforts to expand. As in the case of the heavy industrial machinery business, the specific needs of individual customers called for close and continuing contact between manufacturer and consumer. All these marketing requirements had to be met quickly if the industry was to succeed; the electrical producers could not afford to wait for possible changes in the web of independent marketing agents. Therefore, such firms as Thomson-Houston, Edison General Electric, and Westinghouse built widespread marketing organizations and purchasing departments even before the appearance of the firm that was to dominate the industry thereafter, the General Electric Company.

---

[34] L. G. Banker, the chief purchasing agent for GE, recalled the difficulties the firm encountered in the early days when trying to obtain some raw materials needed for the manufacture of electrical apparatus. Thomson-Houston could not secure sufficient mica (used in insulation), so the firm purchased mica mines in northern Canada. It also acquired a casting company and a wire concern. See Reflections of L. G. Banker, General Electric Papers. Such integration was not widespread in the industry.

[35] L. G. Banker, "How the General Electric Company Buys," *The Purchasing Agent: The Magazine of Centralized Buying* 14 (1925): 1351–53, on file with the General Electric Papers. Thomson-Houston (and then General Electric) did most of its buying directly from producers, not through middlemen. See, for example, Elihu Thomson to S. A. Barton, January 22, 1886; Thomson to Pittsburgh Steel Castings Co., September 14, 1886; Aylworth & Jackson Co. to Elihu Thomson, May 9, 1896; and Aultman & Taylor Machinery Co. to General Electric, March 10, 1897; Elihu Thomson Papers.

OTHER PRODUCERS' GOODS INDUSTRIES

Firms in other industries making producers' goods also encountered marketing difficulties that led them to build nationwide marketing organizations by the early years of the twentieth century.

A system of commissioned, exclusive local agents marketing finished producers' goods was developed at mid-century by the McCormick Harvesting Machine Company. During the 1850s McCormick created a network of agencies in the United States and Canada to sell and service farm machines. Its agents pushed the sale of the machines, saw to delivery, collected payment, and agreed to "devote themselves actively to putting up, starting and setting to work the said Reapers."[36] After the Civil War, when the firm produced and sold increasingly complex machines such as binders, the salesman's role as instructor and repairman grew even more important. "The company," wrote the leading historian of the McCormick business, "hesitated to put such a complicated mechanism as a binder in a farmer's hands until it had taught its field force how to operate and repair it."[37] By the early eighties the firm had a large field force of about 150 traveling experts who assisted local agents in instructing farmers in the use of the firm's goods.[38] From 1884 to around 1900, major harvesting machinery producers expanded their distribution systems still further by establishing branch houses and eliminating the old sales system. Much of the impetus for that expansion, however, apparently resulted not from genuine distribution problems but from increased competition, which led to intensive efforts to increase sales.[39] Other firms competing in the industry early in the twentieth century followed the lead of McCormick and its largest competitors.[40]

Makers of various types of office machines provide another example. This

---

[36] William T. Hutchinson, *Cyrus Hall McCormick*, 1: 356. The early McCormick agents often engaged in other lines of work in addition to selling harvesting machinery. McCormick's early sales system is described in *ibid.*, chap. 15.

[37] *Ibid.*, 2: 711.

[38] *Ibid.*

[39] Indeed, after about 1884 the changes in distribution "involved a relatively inefficient use of capital and labor"; see Helen M. Kramer, "Harvesters and High Finance," p. 284. The Kramer article provides a fine treatment of the harvesting machinery industry at the end of the nineteenth century. See also File #5888–1 of the Bureau of Corporations Records; Cyrus McCormick, *The Century of the Reaper*; and Herbert N. Casson, *Cyrus Hall McCormick*.

[40] The Nichols & Shepard Co. of Battle Creek, Mich., for example, had thirteen branch houses distributing threshing machinery and tractors to about 1,500 retailers; these retailers were commissioned agents who also engaged in other work. "Jobbers and wholesale men," the company said in 1914, "are not used in this business to any extent. We only make contracts with them to handle our products in a few localities where we have no selling organization of our own and do not want to start one, because if we did we would have to build a warehouse. There are localities where trade does not warrant a warehouse, although some sales are affected" (File #7222–16–1, Bureau of Corporations Papers).

industry, like the electrical business, was a new one. For centuries office workers had conducted business without the benefit of anything more complicated than pen, ink, and paper; companies selling such devices as adding machines, cash registers, and typewriters had to overcome the inertia of businessmen. Producers had not only to make a good machine but, equally important, to convince businessmen of the usefulness and reliability of the machine. Advertising helped solve the problem of introducing the goods to potential customers, and the producing firms built marketing organizations designed to merchandise their products efficiently. The Burroughs Adding Machine Company, for example, was founded in 1905 and very quickly created a chain of agencies that specialized in the sale and service of the Burroughs machines. The dealers got the exclusive right to market Burroughs products in a certain geographic area, and they were paid a commission on their sales. The dealers agreed to do nothing else but sell the Burroughs machines, to provide an office and a sales force of appropriate size, and to sell the machines only at the company's price. Burroughs required that the workers at the local dealerships teach all customers how to use the machines and how to care for them properly so as to keep them in good working order. If the machines could not be repaired by the local sales outlet, the dealers were responsible for seeing that they were taken to one of Burroughs' regional repair shops ("Service Stations").[41]

The National Cash Register Company, begun in 1899, marketed in much the same manner as the Burroughs company. National Cash Register utilized local agencies that specialized in its goods and worked on commission. The company's dealers also provided the service of installment purchasing if the customer desired it. John H. Patterson, president of NCR, recognized that the real problem in the growth of his concern was mass distribution, not mass production. "The important things to do are to improve our advertising and improve our sales force. If we get the orders we can easily manufacture the product and make the proper records, but first we must get the orders."[42]

Typewriter makers, like the producers of adding machines and cash registers, often built large marketing systems that provided sales and service to businessmen who desired to make use of the new writing machines. The Remington typewriter firm, for example, had offices in sixteen American cities as early as 1892.[43]

[41] Information on the Burroughs Adding Machine Co. is from File #7222–74–1, *ibid.* That file also contains copies of the agency agreement signed by Burroughs and its various local dealers.

[42] Ray W. Johnson and Russell W. Lynch, *The Sales Strategy of John H. Patterson, Founder of the National Cash Register Company,* p. 50. On the cash register industry see also Isaac F. Marcosson, *Wherever Men Trade,* and Samuel Crowther, *John H. Patterson.*

[43] See Wyckoff, Seamans & Benedict to Andrew Carnegie, Andrew Carnegie Papers, vol. 16.

The use of franchised agencies in the harvester, adding machine, and cash register industries made it possible for the producing firm to insure that the needed services of instruction and repair would be performed. The products considered above were widely known, often mechanically superior items, and manufacturers could exercise significant control over their sales outlets because dealers were eager to retain their lucrative franchises. At the same time, however, manufacturers avoided the large investments that would have been required if they, not the dealers, had had to pay the expenses of the office and of sales and repair personnel, as well as take the risks of selling the goods on credit to consumers. The franchised dealership was less costly than company-owned outlets, and it provided many of their advantages.

Marketing Innovations in Consumer Durables

The distribution problems described above were not restricted to the makers of finished producers' goods; they also occurred in some industries manufacturing consumer durables. A brief examination of the experience of firms making two such durables, sewing machines and automobiles, will illustrate the range of marketing requirements imposed by some finished consumers' goods.

The sewing machine industry began around 1850, and manufacturers immediately encountered serious problems in distributing the new devices. Edward Clark of the I. M. Singer Company then introduced marketing innovations that cleared the way for his firm's growth and prosperity. Initially, the Singer machines were sold through commissioned agents who worked only in the Singer line. As the 1850s progressed, however, Clark built a network of company-owned sales outlets.

To market the sewing machines adequately, the company had to provide demonstrations and service to customers. Because the sewing machine was a new item, the operation of which was hardly self-evident, sales personnel had to instruct the public in the proper methods of using it. Because it was a moderately complicated piece of machinery, few customers could effect repairs when the machine broke down. Thus a trained company sales force was needed to distribute and repair sewing machines, and to do so more efficiently than the commission agents. As the leading historian of the young Singer firm wrote, "The company learned early in its New York sales offices that adequate selling demanded demonstration and servicing by men who were completely conversant with the mechanical features of the sewing-machine and could adjust or repair them on short notice."[44] By 1856 Edward Clark had concluded that "the only way" to sell the machines was through a nationwide network of company outlets.[45]

[44] Andrew B. Jack, "The Channels of Distribution for an Innovation," p. 122.
[45] *Ibid.*, p. 121.

The Singer stores had spread into fourteen American cities by 1859, and they provided a wide range of services which furthered the marketing of the firm's products. They engaged in promotional, educational, and service activities, including demonstration, repairs, and the storage of parts, and they furnished information on the credit reliability of local customers, which allowed the company to sell more and more machines by installment plans. The merchandising efforts of the company's own outlets proved so successful that by the mid-1860s Singer had stopped using franchised commission agents.[46]

When the early automobile industry began to expand a half-century after the introduction of sewing machines, its marketing needs proved somewhat similar to those of the Singer company. Unlike the sewing machine firm, auto makers did not turn to company-owned outlets manned by salaried personnel, but they did require that their franchised dealers perform many of the same services provided by the Singer stores and harvester agencies. Auto dealers had to engage solely in the sale of the cars of a single firm, and they enjoyed the exclusive right to market those cars in their particular geographic area. The Ford Motor Company required in its contracts with dealers that they supply full demonstrations and instructions for customers unschooled in the operation of the new vehicles. Furthermore, the dealers agreed to instruct consumers in the proper methods of caring for the cars and to keep on hand a supply of parts and a force of mechanics capable of repairing the autos.[47] Other young automobile firms, such as Packard, Studebaker, Chalmers, and the Waverly Company, marketed their vehicles in much the same way as Ford.[48]

CONCLUSION

We have recounted the experience of firms in many industries that turned to their own distributing organizations as a result of other marketing difficulties. The nature of their products and markets shaped the business strategies of these manufacturers. Most of the nation's manufactured goods could be sold easily through the old system of commission merchants and jobbers, but the articles considered above could not. As the antebellum history of the

[46] *Ibid.*, pp. 124, 132–33. On Singer's distribution methods abroad see Robert B. Davies, "The International Operations of the Singer Manufacturing Company, 1854–1895." Some of Davies' findings were later published in his article, " 'Peacefully Working to Conquer the World.' "

[47] Information on the Ford Motor Co., including contracts between Ford and its dealers for the years 1904–14, is available in Files #7222–68–1 and #7222–68–2 of the Bureau of Corporations Records.

[48] See Files #7222–44–1, #7222–49–1, #7222–76–1, and #7222–109–1, *ibid.* The Waverly Co. made electric vehicles. Occasionally an early auto firm operated one or two retail outlets, but even then most of its sales came through the franchised, exclusive dealerships.

heavy industrial machinery industry demonstrates, the merchandising of some goods called for skills and services that conventional middlemen simply could not provide as efficiently as the manufacturers themselves. Non-standardized, expensive, technically complicated products necessitated a close and continuing contact between producer and consumer. In its first couple of decades the electrical industry met these difficulties, which were complicated by the technological sophistication of electrical apparatus and the element of danger to the careless or ignorant consumer. Company personnel had to be trained to assess the needs of the individual customer and to see that the company met those needs. Somewhat similar problems beset firms marketing such producers' goods as harvesting machinery, adding machines, cash registers, and typewriters, as well as new consumer durables such as sewing machines and, later, automobiles.

The marketing of goods such as those described here was a very involved proposition. The new, technologically advanced products that entered American markets in the last half of the nineteenth century found little of relevance in the old distribution system, wherein producers sold relatively simple, often standard items to anonymous (to the producers) customers through commercial middlemen. Manufacturers had to figure out new ways to introduce the goods, to instruct customers in the proper use of costly machinery, to effect quick and reliable repairs, to supply needed parts, and to arrange installment purchasing. It no longer sufficed for a manufacturer simply to sell an article to a handy middleman and be done with it. These items carried with them a wide range of requirements which ran from the initial sale through repeated repair jobs. Technical expertise was a necessary element in the composition of the sales and service organizations that evolved to do the job that commission merchants and jobbers could not do. The difficulties of efficiently distributing such goods presented strong challenges to manufacturers, and the pressure of the marketing needs of their products soon led to innovations in merchandising. By the early years of the twentieth century, many firms had responded to the marketing challenge by building extensive company distributing organizations.

CHAPTER XII

The Continued Relevance
of the Jobber:
The Tobacco Industry

Earlier chapters in this study centered on manufacturers' assumption of the functions of the wholesaler and sometimes even those of the retailer. We have argued that the old system of commercial middlemen declined and often disappeared in many American industries in which the large firm integrated forward in response to the new, concentrated markets represented either by the cities or by a few consolidated firms. We have also chronicled the merchandising initiatives taken by manufacturers who faced particular marketing problems with their products, problems related to the perishability of their goods or to the need for a close and continuing contact between producer and consumer. Many firms, especially those manufacturing semi-finished producers' goods, also engaged in backward integration into purchasing and/or the ownership and production of raw materials. The moves by manufacturers forward into marketing and backward toward raw materials resulted in a revolution in distribution.

The changes in distribution described herein did not, however, result in the complete elimination of the middleman from the American manufacturing scene. In several broad areas of manufactured goods, producers' expansion into distribution was very limited in scope. In those areas the jobber proved very durable because of the survival of many of the conditions which had long made him relevant. In the distribution of the complex of items sold in the grocery, drug, and hardware trades, wholesale marketing continued to be the province of the independent middleman, even in the twentieth century. This chapter and the next will explain the reasons for the survival of middlemen in these sectors of the economy and will point out that, although jobbers endured here, their role changed significantly.

The distribution of manufactured goods through such outlets as hardware, grocery, drug, furniture, dry goods, and jewelry stores represented the only major portion of the economy in which manufacturers continued to face the extremely diffuse and scattered markets that could be served most efficiently by a network of jobbers. The many thousands of retailers who sold goods in these areas dealt in hundreds of different items, most of which were made by many different producers. Oligopoly and concentration of production remained relatively infrequent phenomena in these trades. Manufacturers did not enjoy the concentrated market of a few consolidated firms, and even in major cities, they rarely experienced the high sales volume that would justify their assumption of the jobbing function. Because the goods were standard, uncomplicated, low-cost items (what we have called generic goods), manufacturers encountered none of the distribution problems which marked the merchandising of the products discussed in Chapters X and XI. A multitude of small manufacturing units sold a mass of simple, standard goods to a mass of small retailers, and that equation perpetuated the need for an interconnecting body of independent middlemen. These themes will be developed more thoroughly in the following chapter, but here we will examine the experience of the tobacco industry. That industry sold to the same diffuse and scattered markets as did producers in the grocery, hardware, and drug businesses, but it was an industry in which the large firm and concentration of production did arise.

The purpose of this chapter is to illustrate that the existence of a diffuse market of many thousands of retailers made the jobber an economically useful agent even· in industries dominated by a single large firm. American Tobacco, like other large companies, made some attempts to take over the wholesaling of its goods, but, even when the firm handled a part of the wholesaling operation in major market areas, it continued to find jobbers useful in distributing its goods to the thousands of grocers, druggists, and tobacconists who retailed its products. And, like other large firms processing agricultural goods, American Tobacco made some changes in its purchasing methods for raw materials, though it never felt the need to expand into the full-scale growing of its own tobacco. The middleman was, therefore, never eliminated entirely from the tobacco industry, even though, from the late 1890s to 1911, it was one of the few virtually monopolistic American industries.

BEGINNINGS OF THE CIGARETTE INDUSTRY

The dual symbols of American tobacco consumption in 1850 were the cigar and the spittoon. In succeeding decades, however, chewing tobacco and cigars were increasingly supplanted as the dominant forms of tobacco use by the little white slaver, the cigarette. For a variety of reasons—its low price, its popularity with women, its vast advertising, and its role as what one perhaps overwrought observer has termed a "natural accompaniment of the creeping neurasthenia of urban existence"—the cigarette grew enormously in popularity after the Civil War.[1]

Cigarette production began in this country in New York around the end of the Civil War. There were two reasons why New York was the birthplace of the American cigarette industry. First, the Civil War ended Richmond's dominance as the distribution point for leaf tobacco and as the major manufacturing center for tobacco products. After that war began, most leaf tobacco grown outside the Confederacy flowed through New York markets, and that city began its rise as the major production center of the tobacco industry.[2] Second, New York was the mecca for immigrants, and immigrants founded the tobacco industry in the United States. Those who began the production of cigarettes came mostly from Eastern Europe and the Middle East, where the modern cigarette originated.[3] The early cigarettes were somewhat exotic, expensive products made from Turkish tobacco, and they had a very narrow market.[4] Use of the cigarette was confined to the large urban centers, especially New York, where it was consumed by immigrants, "the few natives who had acquired the habit during a residence abroad, and ... foreigners."[5] As the cigarette became more popular, however, domestic manufacturers turned to its production.

In most cases the firms that later came to dominate the industry expanded an already existing tobacco business into cigarette production. Francis S. Kinney, founder of the Kinney Tobacco Company of New York, moved into cigarettes in 1869 as an addition to his smoking tobacco business.[6] William S. Kimball, president of W. S. Kimball and Company of Rochester, had begun

---

[1] The quotation is from Jerome E. Brooks, *The Mighty Leaf*, p. 252. The product was apparently introduced into the United States in the 1850s, although this is not entirely clear. Robert K. Heimann (*Tobacco and Americans*, p. 204) makes a persuasive case for the appearance of the cigarette in the fifties. Charles D. Barney & Company (*The Tobacco Industry*, p. 19) places the date at about 1860; William W. Young (*The Story of the Cigarette*, p. 8) says "about 1866"; and Charles E. Landon ("Tobacco Manufacturing in the South," p. 44) asserts that the cigarette was introduced from England in 1867.

[2] Victor S. Clark, *History of Manufactures in the United States*, 2: 34; *Commercial and Financial Chronicle*, August 17, 1867. Richmond never regained its antebellum dominance. In the decades after the Civil War the growing popularity of bright-leaf tobacco caused the focus of southern tobacco manufacturing to shift farther south into the bright-leaf belts of North Carolina and southern Virginia.

[3] Heimann, *Tobacco and Americans*, pp. 203–6.

[4] Brooks, *The Mighty Leaf*, p. 241.

[5] *U.S. Tobacco Journal*, May 1, 1877.

[6] Testimony of Francis S. Kinney, U.S. Department of Justice manuscripts relating to the case of *United States* v. *American Tobacco Company*, U.S. Circuit Court, Southern District of New York, Equity Case Files E1–216, 1908, Record Group 60, National Archives, Washington, D.C. (hereafter cited as Circuit Court MSS).

tobacco manufacture during the Civil War and became a cigarette producer in 1876.[7] The firm that later became the largest manufacturer in the industry, W. Duke, Sons, and Company of Durham, North Carolina, had produced smoking tobacco since 1866, but it did not make the move into cigarettes until 1881.[8] An interesting exception to this pattern was a former furniture dealer and unsuccessful New York stock broker, Lewis Ginter. He formed a tobacco partnership with John F. Allen in Richmond in 1872, and Allen and Ginter began producing cigarettes three years later.

All the domestic companies that turned to cigarettes faced a common production problem, and all met it in the same way. The problem was that cigarettes were handmade by skilled rollers, who were scarce in the United States. The cigarette companies found that the solution was either to import skilled immigrants or to hire away the immigrant laborers already working for New York firms making the expensive Turkish or Egyptian brands.[9] The Kinney Tobacco Company induced East European cigarette rollers to immigrate, and W. Duke brought 125 immigrant rollers from New York to Durham.[10] Often these skilled laborers worked at several successive American firms.[11] They usually supervised cigarette production and trained large numbers of young girls in the art of rolling cigarettes by hand. These factory girls provided a cheap source of labor and were the industry's main line of defense against labor unions after they had replaced their instructors in the factories.[12]

Once the domestic firms had solved the labor problem, they began to expand their markets, driving sales of imports and of the expensive Turkish and Egyptian brands downward by means of a lower-priced product. By the latter part of the 1870s it was clear that the domestic, bright-leaf tobacco cigarettes were becoming the dominant type. Domestic producers were acquiring an ever-increasing superiority in American markets.[13]

The cigarette remained a kind of orphan, however, in the family of American tobacco manufacturing. As a trade journal later pointed out:

For about fifteen years . . . the cigarette business did not attract much attention in the trade, nor develop as rapidly [as it did during the decade of

[7] Blake McKelvey, *Rochester*, pp. 236–38; *Tobacco*, February 25, 1887.

[8] Testimony of James B. Duke, Circuit Court MSS.

[9] This was a common practice for other domestic industries in need of skills; see Edward C. Kirkland, *Industry Comes of Age*, chap. 16.

[10] Heimann, *Tobacco and Americans*, pp. 206, 212.

[11] For example, J. M. and David Siegel, immigrant brothers from Kovno, Russia, worked for Goodwin and Co. in New York, were hired by the Dukes to supervise the Duke cigarette department in Durham for a time, and later set up their own company; see Hiram V. Paul, *History of the Town of Durham, N.C.*, pp. 111–12.

[12] Women proved far less troublesome than did men, and were far less prone to strike; see *U.S. Tobacco Journal*, November 2, 1878.

[13] *Tobacco*, June 19, 1877.

the 1880s]. This was due not so much to . . . small profits, as to the fact that established tobacco manufacturers took up the cigarette as a side issue, but, having organized departments for making and selling them, found little difficulty in putting them on the market along with a line of smoking tobaccos, and under these conditions the growth and development of the cigarette in its early stages was slow.[14]

The industry in its early years was thus relatively small-scale and unimportant, but with the eighties came a new competitor who was to revolutionize the entire industry in a decade—James Buchanan Duke.

THE EARLY INNOVATIONS OF JAMES B. DUKE

"Buck" Duke was a shrewd and tough businessman, ambitious and fiercely competitive. He drove W. Duke, Sons, and Company to the top of the cigarette trade in less than a decade. More than any other individual, he was responsible for the formation of the American Tobacco Company, and he ran that vast combination for a score of years after its founding. When the courts dissolved the company, the only man who understood the complex interrelationships of the combination well enough to dismantle it rationally was James Duke. His Horatio Alger story is genuine, and his biographers have done him more than justice.[15]

James Duke's father, Washington Duke, founded the business after the Civil War. The Dukes ran their business from the family farm outside Durham until 1875, when they built a factory in the town. In 1878 a five-man partnership was created. Washington Duke, James Duke, James's brother Benjamin N. Duke, Richard H. Wright, a local tobacco manufacturer, and George W. Watts, a Baltimore businessman, each contributed $14,000. The partnership ended in 1885 and the firm then incorporated under its previous name, W. Duke, Sons, and Company.[16]

The Duke firm achieved moderate success, mostly in granulated smoking tobacco, but this was not enough to satisfy the ambitious James Duke. He believed that as long as the company stayed in the production of smoking tobacco it had no real future. The predominance of the "Bull Durham" brand, manufactured by W. T. Blackwell and Company, also of Durham, was apparently unshakeable. As Duke allegedly remarked: "my company is up against a stone wall. It can't compete with Bull Durham. Something has to be done and that quick. I am going into the cigarette business." The other partners were less certain of the wisdom of the decision, but Duke ultimately persuaded them. In 1881 the company began producing cigarettes.[17]

[14] *Ibid.*, January 31, 1890.
[15] See John W. Jenkins, *James B. Duke*; John K. Winkler, *Tobacco Tycoon*; and Watson S. Rankin, *James Buchanan Duke (1865–1925)*.
[16] Testimony of James B. Duke, Circuit Court MSS.
[17] Jenkins, *James B. Duke*, p. 65.

For the first two years after the shift into cigarettes, the older partners had good reason to regret their decision, for the move had all the earmarks of a rousing disaster. The Duke firm made little headway because the government at that time was considering a reduction of the cigarette tax from $1.75 to $.50 per thousand. The Duke brands were not established in the market, and many dealers refused to buy them and take the chance of losing the difference in tax, should the tax be lowered. The Dukes accumulated a large quantity of cigarettes and were forced to close their factory. James Duke thus found himself in an unenviable position: his warehouses bulged with unsold cigarettes, his brands were making little progress in the market, and his factory had shut down.[18]

When the government, its coffers overflowing, finally reduced the tax in March, 1883, Duke made the first in a long chain of bold decisions. He immediately reduced the price of his cigarettes from ten to five cents per pack of ten cigarettes. He declared that jobbers' orders would be filled at the lower price, provided that at least three-quarters of the goods were delivered after the tax reduction in May.

The Duke products instantly became the lowest-priced ones on the market, and, in the two months before the tax reduction went into effect, Duke sold his backlog of cigarettes, though at a loss. His factory reopened. He then firmly established his brands in the trade through a combination of low prices and a massive advertising campaign.[19] Duke had caught his competitors napping. A journalist later overstated the case, but he was not far from the truth when he wrote, "the coup gave him a start over his rivals from which they never recovered."[20]

Duke's heavy advertising at the time of the tax reduction taught him a lesson he did not forget. His share of the market expanded rapidly. Advertising was an important factor in making low production costs possible through the stimulation of his sales. Duke followed up on the lesson in 1884, when he established offices and a factory in New York in order to be nearer his markets and to secure better advertising facilities.[21] He was described as "an aggressive advertiser, devising new and startling methods which dismayed his competitors; and [he was] always willing to spend a proportion of his profits which seemed appalling to more conservative manufacturers."[22]

James Duke was the leading innovator in the cigarette business during the 1880s. Although he came to the industry almost as a novice, he made entrepreneurial contributions in marketing, purchasing, and protection, and those

18 Testimony of James B. Duke, Circuit Court MSS.
19 *Ibid.*; Neil H. Borden, *The Economic Effects of Advertising*, p. 221; and Jenkins, *James B. Duke*, pp. 70–72.
20 "The Beginnings of a Trust," *Collier's*, August 10, 1907, p. 15.
21 Borden, *Economic Effects of Advertising*, p. 221; Alfred D. Chandler, Jr., *Strategy and Structure*, p. 32; and American Tobacco Co., *"Sold American!"* p. 20.
22 "The Beginnings of a Trust," p. 15.

contributions were the driving forces for change and for eventual combination.

Duke's vigorous, imaginative merchandising placed his company among
the five dominant cigarette producers of the eighties. The others were Allen
and Ginter of Richmond, W. S. Kimball and Company of Rochester, the
Kinney Tobacco Company of New York, and Goodwin and Company, also
of New York. These five companies followed the same basic pattern in production, in distribution, and in the means of acquiring their leaf tobacco. In
each area, however, the Duke company went further in terms of efficiency
and innovation.

Changes in Purchasing and Distribution
before the Combination

In the decade before the formation of the American Tobacco Company,
manufacturers made tentative attempts to remove the middleman from both
the supply of raw materials and the merchandising of cigarettes. In each
case, however, the role of jobbers and tobacco brokers remained very important in the industry.

The major producers obtained most of their leaf tobacco (their prime
raw material) through tobacco brokerage houses in the bright-leaf belts of
the South. These brokers purchased the leaf at warehouse auctions, stored
and dried it in their own warehouses, then resold it to the cigarette manufacturers.[23] Especially in years when there was a serious shortage of crops,
this arrangement made it possible for speculators and rehandlers to make
handsome profits.[24] One such broker purchased cutters (the particular kind of
leaf tobacco used in the production of cigarettes) on the Durham market at
thirteen cents per pound, then resold it a few months later to W. S. Kimball
and Company at slightly more than twice that price.[25] Such occurrences were
common. Because competition in the cigarette industry became less and less a
competition in price of product and increasingly a competition of advertising
and gimmickry, producers apparently paid relatively little attention to the
cost of raw materials. "The whole attention of these manufacturers," recalled
a tobacco broker, "seems to have been taken up with the sale of goods, and
it left a good opening for . . . speculators and dealers to get a profit out of
them."[26]

Manufacturers began in the eighties to create their own purchasing departments in a half-hearted attempt to reduce these raw-material costs. They

---

[23] For an excellent description of the entire warehouse and auction system see
Nannie M. Tilley, *The Bright-Tobacco Industry, 1860–1929*, pp. 191–308.
[24] File #4766, sec. 1 and 2, records of the U.S. Bureau of Corporations.
[25] Testimony of John B. Cobb, Circuit Court MSS.
[26] *Ibid.*

made some purchases directly at warehouse auctions in order to eliminate middlemen. Probably in an attempt to avoid bidding against each other and thereby increasing the price, the buyers for each company bought almost exclusively in different auction areas. Allen and Ginter bought most of their leaf in the market at Henderson, North Carolina. W. S. Kimball and Company confined its purchasing to Oxford, North Carolina. The Duke firm bought almost entirely in Durham, but occasionally in Danville, Virginia, which was the market used by the Kinney Tobacco Company. Of the five major producers, only Goodwin and Company apparently had no buyers in the bright-leaf belt.[27]

The big cigarette companies, however, continued to buy most of their leaf through brokers and commission merchants. Purchases through company agents in the latter part of the eighties in most cases amounted to no more than one-fourth of the companies' requirements, the rest coming from commercial middlemen.[28] Only the Duke company made real efforts to eliminate the middleman. Duke, as he later testified, appreciated the value of reducing the role of "the speculator who had been . . . buying and selling to the manufacturers, with the exception of Duke's Sons & Co. We had been buying a good part of our tobacco in the loose warehouses direct from the farmer."[29] The independent middleman remained clearly evident at the end of the 1880s.

The major producers also established warehouse storage facilities in the bright-leaf belts during the eighties. The Duke Company, of course, had such warehousing almost from the beginning of its business, for the firm arose in the North Carolina bright-leaf belt. Manufacturers farther removed from the markets found the facilities more difficult to obtain, but most did acquire warehousing. The Kinney company did so very early, opening a rehandling and storage plant in Danville, Virginia, in 1877.[30] There the cutters were re-dried, stemmed, and prized for shipment to their factories in New York and Baltimore.[31] Allen and Ginter established stemmeries and re-drying and storage houses in North Carolina in 1887. W. S. Kimball and Company obtained similar facilities a year later.[32] The warehousing system and the use of company leaf buyers marked significant vertical integration in purchasing well in advance of the combination of the leading producers.

---

[27] *Ibid.*; see also testimony of Francis S. Kinney and William H. Butler, *ibid.*

[28] Testimony of John B. Cobb, *ibid.*

[29] Testimony of James B. Duke, *ibid.*

[30] Nannie M. Tilley, "Agitation Against the American Tobacco Company in North Carolina, 1890–1911," p. 213. See also the testimony of Francis S. Kinney and William H. Butler, Circuit Court MSS; and *Tobacco News and Prices Current*, February 15, 1879.

[31] The re-drying process reduced the weight of the tobacco by about one-tenth, thereby reducing shipment costs to the factories; see testimony of T. B. Yville, Circuit Court MSS.

[32] Tilley, "Agitation Against American Tobacco," p. 213.

In the distribution of finished goods, as in the supply of raw materials, the cigarette makers made some effort to reduce the importance of middlemen. From its earliest years, the industry sold its products by means of traveling salesmen. The drummer was one means through which the producing companies made potential jobbers and retailers aware of the product. Drummers traveled all over the country, attempting to stimulate demand for cigarettes. They took orders from grocery and drug jobbers, who in turn distributed the goods to the many retailers who sold the cigarettes to their ultimate consumers. From the very earliest days of the industry, then, the manufacturers handled a part of their own wholesaling. The vast majority of the goods, however, were marketed by independent wholesalers.

During the eighties some significant organizational changes occurred in the distribution system. Each of the five leading producers continued to sell to jobbers via traveling salesmen.[33] But the manufacturers organized and maintained a system of company-owned distributing centers in the largest market cities. Connected with these wholesale outlets were generally a manager, a city salesman, and one or two traveling agents. These distributing centers sold cigarettes to the jobbers, who in turn distributed them to the retailers.[34]

The effect of the manufacturers' creation of wholesale outlets in the eighties was primarily to eliminate the commission merchants and perhaps some of the largest urban jobbers from the distribution system for cigarettes. From the very first, cigarette producers had tended to go directly to local jobbers by using traveling salesmen; when several company wholesale offices opened in the eighties, the local independent jobbers could be reached more efficiently. Although the company-owned wholesale outlets sold some cigarettes directly to large urban retailers, the vast majority of their sales went to the jobbers. Although the creation of company branches represented a substantial inroad by manufacturers into the distribution process, the network of local independent jobbers continued to carry the burden of marketing the cigarettes to the thousands of small retailers who ultimately disposed of the goods.

The Formation of the American Tobacco Company and Its Effect on the Distribution System

The late 1880s were marked by increasingly fierce competition, spurred by the coming of machine production and its consequence, overproductive capacity. In the replacement of hand labor with machines, James Duke led the way. He boldly backed the use of the best of the several cigarette rolling

---

[33] Defense stipulation marked Government Exhibit A, Circuit Court MSS.

[34] This information is derived from an extensive report in the *Western Tobacco Journal*, July 15, 1889. See File #4766, sec. 1 and 2, Bureau of Corporations Records.

devices that appeared in the eighties and he encountered great success in reducing production costs. Other manufacturers followed his lead, and the industry soon faced the specter that troubled so many others—vast productive capacity, much in excess of the level of demand. The ensuing competition led to heavier expenditures for advertising and merchandising gimmickry. By the end of 1889 the five major producers had come to the conclusion that cooperation would prove more salutary than competition. As a result, they agreed early in 1890 to the combination of their firms in order to form the American Tobacco Company.[35]

In the score of years after its formation, American Tobacco used the base of its virtual monopoly of the cigarette business to expand into other parts of the tobacco industry, employing competitive policies that ultimately led to the court-ordered dissolution of the firm in 1911. Producers of plug and smoking tobacco were acquired (usually through exchanges of stock and occasionally through cash purchases), and the company started the so-called Plug Wars of the 1890s.[36] American Tobacco used its economic size to full advantage by selling various "fighting brands" of plug below cost, sacrificing "several millions" of the profits from cigarettes in order to force the plug manufacturers to combine with the company.[37] In December, 1898, an agreement was reached with the major independent plug producers, and their firms were joined with the plug business of American Tobacco to form the Continental Tobacco Company.

The purchase of independent concerns (often in secrecy) and the competitive practice of selling below cost brought more and more companies into the tobacco combination. The same competitive methods that were used successfully in acquiring a majority of the plug and smoking tobacco output worked equally well in the case of snuff, which culminated in the creation of the American Snuff Company in 1900. The cigar industry proved much more difficult to dominate, but an effort was made through the formation of the American Cigar Company in 1901.[38]

The growth and the competitive tactics of the American Tobacco Com-

[35] The events summarized here are described in unnecessary detail in Patrick G. Porter, "Origins of the American Tobacco Company," pp. 67–74.

[36] On Christmas Eve, 1892, James Duke informed his brother that he had no time to take part in holiday festivities because of important business meetings related to the Plug Wars. He exuberantly analyzed the present condition of the wars and forecast their outcome: "We are making Rome howl on plug and are making preparations to do great work the 1st of the year. We will make the plug manufacturers hustle like we once did Cigarette Manufacturers" (James B. Duke to Benjamin N. Duke, December 24, 1892, Benjamin N. Duke Papers).

[37] U.S. Bureau of Corporations, *Report of the Commissioner of Corporations on the Tobacco Industry*, 1: 2.

[38] Cigars were produced by very simple machines in small lots or were hand rolled; they could not be mass produced by machine as could cigarettes. The cigar industry was characterized by many relatively small competitors, a fact which made the task of acquiring control of the market very difficult.

pany brought it increasingly under the scrutiny of the newly formed Bureau of Corporations and the Department of Justice. The company was acutely aware of this problem and paid close attention to the workings of the anti-trust division. After the *Northern Securities* case of 1904, all the various enterprises of the tobacco combination were merged under the name American Tobacco Company. This failed, however, to bring the desired immunity from prosecution, and the Department of Justice brought suit against the firm in 1907 under the Sherman Act. After lengthy trials and appeals, the Supreme Court, shortly after its ruling against Standard Oil, ordered the dissolution of American Tobacco in an effort to restore competition in the tobacco industry.[39]

From 1890 through 1911, American Tobacco enjoyed its greatest degree of control in the tobacco industry, and it made important changes both in the area of raw-material supply and in the distribution of its finished goods. In the supply of raw materials, the firm engaged in considerable backward integration. American Tobacco acquired a number of subsidiaries which produced a variety of non-tobacco items needed by the company. Such subsidiaries made licorice (used in tobacco manufacture), boxes, cotton bags, tin foil, machinery for American Tobacco's factories, pipes, and other accouterments of the tobacco trade.[40] Despite its acquisition of these subsidiary concerns, however, the company never chose to integrate back to the production of its major input, tobacco itself. Although a couple of small Cuban tobacco-growing firms were bought, all but a tiny fraction of the company's tobacco needs were purchased on the open market. The company always felt assured of a supply of tobacco; because it never was threatened there, it never felt the need to involve itself in agricultural operations.[41]

As indicated previously, however, manufacturers had begun to create their own tobacco purchasing departments even before 1890, and this process was accelerated by American Tobacco. The leaf-buying activities of the various parts of the company were consolidated into the Leaf Department. That department assessed the needs of the company each year, assigned salaried company buyers to leaf markets across the country, and supplied the required tobacco.[42] The company did not do all its own buying, but it did most of it. Sometimes, independent tobacco brokers acted as suppliers in markets where American Tobacco had no salaried buyers. N. R. Bowman and Company of

---

[39] See *United States* v. *American Tobacco Company*, 164 F. 700 (1908), 221 U.S. 106 (1911), and 191 F. 371 (1911).

[40] Bureau of Corporations, *Report on the Tobacco Industry*, 1: 16–17.

[41] *Ibid.*, pp. 16–17, 251–52.

[42] The Benjamin Duke Papers are the best source for activities of the Leaf Department. Duke was a member of the Leaf Committee, which oversaw the operations of the department, and his correspondence for the 1890s contains many examples of the department's workings; see, for example, the letters of John Cobb, John Pope, and W. R. Harris to Benjamin Duke throughout the 1890s.

Lynchburg, Virginia, for example, served as the supplier of certain grades of tobacco from the Lynchburg market.[43] The growth of American Tobacco and its policy of conducting most of its own buying operations did, however, substantially reduce the importance of independent tobacco merchants and brokers. The number and economic significance of independent leaf middlemen declined from 1890 until the outbreak of World War I. Some left the business, others became salaried employees of American Tobacco, and still others continued in business, supplying small manufacturers and even selling to American Tobacco when the giant firm incorrectly gauged the flow of leaf and was forced to buy from middlemen.[44]

The forward integration of American Tobacco into marketing finished goods was not so extensive as its backward integration into purchasing. In the first decade of its existence, the company made few efforts to change its distribution methods. During the early 1890s American Tobacco experienced a kind of interregnum which was marked by the continued independent operation of the several firms that had been formally united. During this period "there was very little change in the methods of manufacturing and distributing cigarettes."[45] American Tobacco's constituent companies maintained the salesmen and sales agencies they had developed during the late eighties, and each advertised its own brands. After several years, however, the sales responsibility was transferred to the central office in New York as Duke consolidated the functions of American Tobacco and centralized its operations. By the end of 1895 the sales of all branches of the company were being processed through the New York office.

The company adopted a slightly modified version of the marketing apparatus utilized by the various cigarette makers in the late eighties. The traveling salesman remained the primary means by which the manufacturer contacted wholesalers. The company's several wholesale offices in major cities continued to dispatch salesmen to the jobbers, who in turn distributed the goods to retailers. All orders placed through the salesmen were reported to the New York office, which arranged for the shipment of goods from the nearest factory.[46] American Tobacco's sales organization was quite extensive,

---

[43] See J. B. Cobb, manager of American Tobacco's Leaf Department, to N. R. Bowman & Co., October 31, 1893, *ibid.* American Tobacco required weekly statements showing total purchases and average prices paid for each grade, as well as weekly samples of the grades bought.

[44] Tilley, *Bright-Tobacco Industry*, pp. 268–86, 307. In 1903 American Tobacco created a purchasing subsidiary called the Amsterdam Supply Co. That company, like the Leaf Department of American Tobacco, acted as a purchasing department, ordering such goods as sugar, rum, extracts, machinery, tools, furniture, stationery, and other items needed by American Tobacco. Amsterdam Supply brought to American Tobacco the advantages of high-volume purchasing. See Bureau of Corporations, *Report on the Tobacco Industry*, 1: 265–66.

[45] File #4766, Bureau of Corporations Records.

[46] Bureau of Corporations, *Report on the Tobacco Industry*, 1: 256–57.

and it provided prompt shipments to wholesalers in an attempt to maintain the complex flow of goods from the factories through the distribution system. As Richard Tennant has pointed out, "The selling force could check inventory, prevent stale goods from reaching the public, and, in general, impose some rational central control upon a highly complex flow of supplies."[47]

Although American Tobacco made no attempt to eliminate the network of jobbers which handled the marketing of its goods to retailers, it did try to exercise controls over the jobbers during the 1890s. The firm used rebates in an effort to encourage jobbers to deal only in the products of American Tobacco. Initially, jobbers received extra rebates if they agreed to sell only American Tobacco's goods, but this raised a storm of protest and a cloud of legal challenges which led the company to abandon the system temporarily (early in 1892).[48] Very soon after that legal action, however, the rebates were resumed under the guise of a so-called consignment plan. The same jobbers dealt in the same goods in the same way as before, except that American Tobacco retained legal title to the goods until they were sold. The agreement the jobbers signed with American Tobacco contained a clause which stated that the jobber would receive his rebates as long as the company determined that he had cooperated with the company, had promoted American Tobacco's interests, and had sold goods entirely to the company's satisfaction.[49] In practice, the revised rebate system functioned as the old one had, with American Tobacco withholding rebates from jobbers whom they knew were dealing in other goods.

The rebates were designed to reduce competition from other companies by discouraging jobbers from handling their goods and to prevent price cutting on American Tobacco's products. Although it is very difficult to judge the success of this policy in reducing competition, it is clear that rebates failed to stop price cutting by jobbers. The company was interested in maintaining its prices not as an end in itself but rather as a means of keeping its goods out of the hands of jobbers who sold competitors' goods. The independent wholesalers, however, often made secret deals with one another, agreeing to fix prices at whatever level they chose. Frequently a jobber who appeared to be maintaining prices, selling only to retailers, and abstaining

---

[47] Richard Tennant, *The American Cigarette Industry*, p. 250.

[48] George W. Watts, one of James Duke's original business partners, wrote Benjamin Duke that "the American Tobacco Company on Saturday decided to abolish all rebates. Buck fought against it ever since you left [to become manager of the Durham plant] as he agrees with me that it is the worst thing we have ever done and we will soon see it" (Watts to Benjamin Duke, February 8, 1892, Benjamin Duke Papers). The rebates were soon resumed.

[49] On the rebate system see the *New York Times* for November 17 and 21, 1893, and April 7, 1896; see also Files #4754 and #4760 of the Bureau of Corporations Records. The clause was intended, of course, to give American Tobacco the power to retain rebates if the jobber sold the goods of other manufacturers, but it avoided the legal difficulties of prohibiting him in writing.

from trade in the goods of other companies was in fact splitting his rebates with others (in effect) by selling American Tobacco goods to other whole-salers below the agreed-upon prices. It proved impossible for the company to prevent price reductions and the consequent flow of its products to jobbers who dealt in others' goods.[50] Because of the failure of the system to achieve its ends, and because of an ever-growing welter of legal difficulties resulting from its attempts to manipulate the jobber trade, American Tobacco in 1897 finally abandoned its efforts to prevent its jobbers from dealing in any other company's goods.[51]

The only attempt by American Tobacco to eliminate many independent middlemen came in the wake of its efforts to gain control of the cigar trade. As mentioned earlier, the company had much success in the nineties in ex-tending its dominance from the cigarette business into other lines of the tobacco industry, including smoking tobacco, plug tobacco, and snuff. The cigar trade, however, proved much more difficult to conquer, primarily be-cause it was composed of many small producers (and hence could not be overcome by successful battles with a few large companies) and was not sub-ject to economies of scale in production. American Tobacco signaled its in-tent to move into cigars in 1901 when it created the American Cigar Com-pany. Its labors in cigars did not yield much success, however, and the company then attempted to increase its influence over the cigar wholesaler apparatus. The rebate system designed to force jobbers to sell only American Tobacco's goods was temporarily revived and brought to bear on cigar out-lets. American Tobacco extended extra credit to jobbing houses in an at-tempt to encourage them to push its cigars rather than others. To aid in its struggle to gain control of the cigar business, the company even bought a controlling interest in several wholesale firms. In addition, in 1901 the firm established a subsidiary called the United Cigar Stores Company, which opened a chain of retail cigar outlets. These efforts to move into the whole-sale and even the retail end of the industry proved very expensive, and American Tobacco endured substantial losses in its war on the cigar trade.

The company was unsuccessful in its attempt to do with cigars what it had been able to do in the other branches of tobacco manufacture; even at the height of its efforts it never produced more than about 20–25 per cent of

[50] The company even resorted to numbering lots of its goods and attempting to trace them through the distribution network in order to find out which jobbers were responsible for the leaks. All such espionage efforts failed to provide effective control.

[51] See *New York Times*, March 31, 1897; and Bureau of Corporations, *Report on the Tobacco Industry*, 1: 309. American Tobacco was the object of many legal actions during the 1890s and this proved very bothersome, especially when the company's offi-cials began to be convicted frequently. In January, 1897 (just before the company abandoned its attempts to make jobbers deal only in its goods), James B. Duke and nine other officials of American Tobacco were convicted in New York for price fixing and for attempting to restrain trade. See *People* v. *Duke et al.*, 44 N.Y. Supp. 336–37 (1897).

the nation's cigars.[52] Even the forward integration that the company tried in its efforts to acquire dominance in cigars resulted in the distribution of only a very small portion of the firm's output. The overwhelming majority of American Tobacco's goods continued to be marketed through independent wholesalers to independent retailers.

CONCLUSION

During the years when American Tobacco enjoyed a near monopoly of the tobacco industry, it chose to leave the marketing of its products almost completely in the hands of independent middlemen. As the commissioner of corporations reported in 1909, "The Tobacco Combination [that is, American Tobacco] has followed in general the method of other tobacco manufacturers by disposing of its products through the regular wholesale and retail channels."[53] The rise of the modern corporation and of concentrated production did not lead the tobacco manufacturers to supplant the independent wholesalers and retailers in the tobacco industry. Because the market that the industry served did not change in structure, the old system of distribution continued to be the most economical and efficient. Leaf middlemen were seriously affected by American Tobacco's backward integration in purchasing, but with the rise of the giant combine their counterparts who marketed American Tobacco's goods were left largely intact.

No particular marketing problems arose in the tobacco industry, and the market remained scattered and diffuse.[54] Although the industry sold in the urban markets, the number of retailers remained so large and the volume and value of the individual orders from retailers remained so small that American Tobacco found it logical and efficient to use jobbers. As the New York Times observed of the tobacco trade in 1893, it was "done through jobbers, as the smallness of the orders put in by retailers makes a direct dealing on the part of the manufacturers impossible, because it leaves no profit."[55] For

[52] Files #4707-29 and #4758, Bureau of Corporations Records; Bureau of Corporations, Report on the Tobacco Industry, 1: 25, 312-14. This is an example of a manufacturing company's attempt to force competitors out of business by involving itself in distribution even though it was much more costly to do so. Independent middlemen could distribute the goods more cheaply. The American Sugar Refining Co. engaged in a similar effort to drive its competitor John Arbuckle out of business by buying into wholesale and retail grocery houses to discourage the sale of Arbuckle's sugar. The attempt failed miserably and proved very costly. See Jack S. Mullins, "The Sugar Trust," pp. 119-30.

[53] Bureau of Corporations, Report on the Tobacco Industry, 1: 309.

[54] There was some problem with the perishability of cigarettes in pre-cellophane days, and that may have been one factor which led cigarette manufacturers to establish their several wholesaling centers. This problem was not nearly so serious in the tobacco industry as it was in the industries considered in Chapter X; cigarette makers were never led to build widespread, elaborate distribution networks.

[55] New York Times, November 17, 1893.

American Tobacco to have supplied all its retailers, the company would have had to pay a very sizable force of its own wholesalers. The firm recognized that it would be less costly simply to put its goods through the old channels of grocery and drug jobbers. Because the turnover of items handled by the jobbers for the grocery and drug trades was fairly rapid, the jobbers could also handle tobacco products (which went to the same retailers who took the rest of their line of goods) at a very low cost to manufacturers. American Tobacco produced only a single line of goods, and that line was too narrow to justify the company's doing its own jobbing; a company jobbing force would have spent too much time making sales that were too small to justify the time spent by the jobbers. Therefore, the whole line of goods needed by grocers and drug retailers was most efficiently distributed by middlemen whose full line brought enough small sales in a single visit to a retailer to repay the time spent in the visit.

The economic force of that set of relationships among manufacturers, retailers, and wholesalers in the grocery and drug trades was so strong that virtually all manufacturing concerns whose products are retailed by drug and grocery stores have continued to rely on jobbers for the distribution of their goods, even in the twentieth century. Although the modern tobacco industry has been concentrated and oligopolistic, the distribution methods of manufacturers have remained much the same as they were before the founding of American Tobacco. A 1939 study of the industry revealed that manufacturers still sold to independent jobbers, most of whom sold a wide range of goods, including tobacco products, groceries, drugs, and alcoholic beverages.[56] The nature of the market that tobacco products found determined the distribution channels through which they would flow, and that has meant the continuing relevance of the jobber.

In one important respect, however, the American Tobacco Company did exert a powerful influence for change in distribution. Although the company chose to leave the jobber network largely intact, the heavy advertising in which the firm engaged significantly altered the role of the jobber. Even before American Tobacco, cigarette manufacturers found heavy advertising to be their most potent weapon for increasing sales, and American did not cease to use massive advertising during its first two decades. In the eighties and even in the nineties tobacco jobbers played an important part in introducing new items and encouraging their sale by engaging in considerable advertising themselves. The role of the jobber in that period was, in short, to act not only as distributor but also as salesman for his goods.[57]

The national advertising of American Tobacco after 1890, however, steadily eclipsed this part of the jobber's activities. The manufacturing firm

[56] U.S. Bureau of the Census, *Census of Business, 1939,* pp. 142–81; see also Tennant, *American Cigarette Industry,* p. 246.
[57] See Bureau of Corporations, *Report on the Tobacco Industry,* 3: 71, 171.

began to go directly to the consumer via advertising, and the jobber increasingly became only a delivery vehicle, not a salesman. "The function of the cigarette retailer," a scholar of the modern cigarette industry has noted, "is primarily to make change, and the function of the wholesaler is to provide the retailer with what the customers want."[58] The jobber endured in tobacco, but his functions were permanently altered by the advertising of manufacturers. As Nannie M. Tilley said of the tobacco industry in this period, "While existing channels of distribution, wholesale and retail, were not destroyed, they were greatly changed by advertising which drew manufacturer and consumer closer."[59] The significance of the middleman in the tobacco industry declined, but he remained the prime agent of distribution.

[58] Tennant, *American Cigarette Industry*, p. 248.
[59] Tilley, *Bright-Tobacco Industry*, p. 528.

CHAPTER XIII

Survival of the Old Order: Continuity in Consumers' Goods

This chapter considers the broad sectors of the manufacturing economy in which independent wholesalers continued to serve as distributors of goods to independent retailers. The experience of American Tobacco pointed up the particular market and product conditions which gave jobbers a role in distribution even when the manufacturer was a highly integrated firm that enjoyed a position of great power and influence in an industry. The same set of relationships among producers, jobbers, and retailers also marked the complex of goods sold through retail outlets such as grocery, drug, hardware, jewelry, liquor, and dry goods stores. A study of the distribution methods of manufacturers who sold through such outlets clearly demonstrates that the old, nineteenth-century marketing channels continued to be dominant. The incidence of oligopoly and the large firm was much less frequent among those industries than in other parts of the manufacturing sector. Insofar as the changes in production, organization, and distribution described in this study may be said to have foreshadowed the rise of the modern corporate order, the industries considered in this chapter may be said to have lagged behind. Even in the early decades of the twentieth century, these industries continued to resemble their nineteenth-century counterparts far more than they resembled contemporary corporations.

The old pattern of diffuse markets served by many producers who sold through jobbers to many small retailers prevailed. Manufacturers found little in the way of concentrated markets to encourage them to do their own wholesaling. Nor did they encounter merchandising difficulties that might have led them to integrate into marketing. The products made by these manufacturers were, by and large, simple, standard, relatively inexpensive goods that neither required nor repaid attempts by producers to assume the wholesaling or the retailing function. The retailers to whom these producers sold generally dealt in a wide range of goods produced by a large variety of manufacturers, and they placed relatively small orders. Jobbers who carried a large stock of disparate items proved to be the most efficient, for theirs was the least costly way in which the goods could be filtered down to the mass of small retailers. Manufacturers found, as American Tobacco did, that the expense of trying to handle the jobbing of their own products to retailers was prohibitive. Substantial economies of scale were virtually unrealizable in the distribution of these manufacturers' goods, and so they, like their predecessors, continued to rely on the web of independent middlemen for the marketing of their goods.[1]

Although the old order endured, some changes came even to the industries with which this chapter is concerned. Some manufacturers who had sufficient sales volumes in the large urban centers built chains of warehouses and small sales offices in those cities in order to take advantage of the slight economies of scale which were available in that way. These manufacturers, however, continued to sell their goods to jobbers; the construction or rental of warehouses and the use of small sales forces represented little in the way of forward integration. And, as had been the case in the tobacco industry, producers in these industries turned increasingly to the use of national advertising of brand names in order to create consumer demand by direct contact with the public. The jobber's old role as salesman atrophied as manufacturers relied more on advertising and less on their distributors in their efforts to build consumer demand for their goods.

THE GROCERY TRADE

The grocery business involved a wide range of products comprising not only foodstuffs but other items as well, and virtually all manufacturers who supplied items to grocers relied on jobbers and wholesalers throughout the nineteenth and early twentieth centuries. The reason they did so was tersely summarized by the sales manager of the Kellogg Toasted Corn Flake Company: "We distribute 100 per cent of our stuff—our entire product—through the jobber and wholesaler; we do this because they work cheap."[2]

---

[1] See, for example, the recent study by William Becker, "The Wholesalers of Hardware and Drugs, 1870–1900."

[2] Statement of Andrew Ross, sales manager for the Kellogg Toasted Corn Flake Co., File #7222–36–1, records of the U.S. Bureau of Corporations. This chapter relies heavily on the large collection of materials accumulated by the Bureau of Corporations in its "Resale Prices Inquiry" conducted in the years just prior to the outbreak of World War I. In interviews and questionnaires from sources of manufacturers, wholesalers, and retailers the bureau assembled a wealth of information about the distribution of goods in the industries with which this chapter deals. The bureau's files constitute an excellent source of primary information on this topic, perhaps the best such source available.

The jobber, W. K. Kellogg declared, was absolutely essential to the grocery business; if manufacturers were to take over the jobber's function, "our cost of distribution would be prohibitive and if we passed it on to the consumer the price of our goods would be mulitplied several times."[3]

The sentiments of the Kellogg officials were echoed by their fellow cereal makers. The Postum Cereal Company of Battle Creek, the Cream of Wheat Company of Minneapolis, and the Grain Products Company of Detroit all marketed their products through the wholesaler network. The merchandising channels of the Postum firm illustrated the extremely diffuse and scattered market faced by makers of foodstuffs. Postum sold its cereals through about fifty food brokers who in turn directed the goods to approximately 3,000 jobbers across the country; the jobbers then sold the cereals to the 250,000 retailers who carried Postum products.[4] Because the individual retailer's orders for cereal were small in volume and in value, manufacturers found it much cheaper to distribute through grocery wholesalers.

Manufacturers of other goods sold through grocery stores faced a marketing situation comparable to that of the cereal companies, and they also relied principally on the jobber. Cocoa and chocolate firms, such as Walter Baker and Company and the Walter M. Lowney Company, both of Boston, recognized the importance of middlemen in the distribution process. "The cost of distributing our grocery articles direct to the retail dealer," noted the latter firm, "would be very considerable—the individual shipments would be small."[5] Such food processors as the Van Camp Products Company, McCormick and Company, the Calumet Baking Powder Company, Horlicks Malted Milk, and the Beech-Nut Packing Company all sold, in the words of a Van Camp official, "almost exclusively to the jobber."[6]

Grocery retailers sold many goods which were not foodstuffs, and the makers of these items, like the food processors, utilized the independent wholesalers. For example, the Pacific Coast Borax Company (maker of the Twenty Mule Team brands) sold to grocery and drug wholesalers; the firm reported that it dealt "exclusively with jobbers." "We rely upon the jobber

[3] Statement of W. K. Kellogg, president of the Kellogg Toasted Corn Flake Co., *ibid.*

[4] Information on Cream of Wheat, Grain Products, and Postum is from Files #7222–82–1, #7222–5–1, and #7222–40–1, *ibid.* These manufacturers sold a very small portion of their output directly to retailers. Grain Products also made cereals for other firms (such as Sears, Roebuck), which then sold them under company brand names. Of course, such cereals were sold directly from Grain Products to the customer firm without the use of a middleman.

[5] On the Baker and Lowney companies see Files #7222–41–1 and #7222–55–1, *ibid.*

[6] Data on the distribution methods of these firms supplied by company officials in 1913 and 1914 are in Files #7222–61–1, #7222–20–1, #7222–90–1, #7222–83–1, and #7222–75–1, *ibid.* In addition to spices, Baltimore's McCormick Co. also made a number of drug products. As they reported, "We sell to wholesale grocers and the wholesale drug trade."

as our exclusive distributor," said a Borax executive, "because of the convenience and economy of such an arrangement over direct dealing with the retailer or consumer."[7] Other firms making non-foodstuffs for the grocery trade shared the opinions of the Borax company.[8]

The usual means by which manufacturers contacted wholesalers was traveling salesmen. These salesmen operated from the various firm's headquarters, taking orders from jobbers or conferring with food brokers. In the case of the larger companies, offices were sometimes opened around the country to afford easier access to wholesalers.

If the producing company's sales volume was large enough, the firm often established warehouses at strategic distribution points to facilitate the flow of goods into the wholesalers network and to reduce shipping costs. The large meat-packing companies, which handled their own wholesaling of meat, found their warehousing useful also in the marketing of the inedible items they produced. In the distribution of these nonperishable goods, the meat packers relied on the jobber system, although they made good use of their own storage facilities and personnel in the companies' distribution networks for beef. The existence of the marketing apparatus for beef made transportation and storage for their other goods available at a very small additional cost. The Cudahy Packing Company, for example, sold its nationally known Old Dutch Cleanser through the usual channels of grocery jobbers, but the firm made use of its beef facilities to distribute more cheaply the cleanser and other similar items to the trade. "We have warehouses of our own in a great many central points throughout the country," the Cudahy company reported, "enabling us to facilitate distribution and secure a saving which enters into the aggregate economy in distribution to the benefit of the ultimate consumer."[9] Swift and Company made similar use of its marketing organization to distribute its soap products.[10]

Other producers who enjoyed a large volume of sales also found company warehouses to be an effective means of reducing distribution costs. The Kellogg Toasted Corn Flake Company pointed out, "We maintain warehouse stock at . . . different points throughout the country, to facilitate deliveries and reduce shipping costs."[11] The Walter Baker Company, a major maker of cocoa and chocolate, acquired warehouses in strategic cities (New York, Philadelphia, Chicago, and two cities on the West Coast) in order to secure

[7] See File #7222–57–1, *ibid.*, for the operations of Pacific Coast Borax, a Chicago-based concern.

[8] See, for example, the data on the J. B. Ford Co., makers of washing soda, scouring soap, and related items in File #7222–105–1, *ibid.*

[9] File #7222–85–1, *ibid.*

[10] Replies from Swift and Cudahy on the marketing of their soap items are in File #7054, *ibid.* On the use of company goods as soap, glue, and cleansers see E. L. Rhoades, *Merchandising Packinghouse Products*, chaps. 16 and 17.

[11] File #7222–36–1, Bureau of Corporations Records.

reduced costs. "At first we thought we could cover our territory from New York," an official of the firm recalled, "but it became evident that we could not. Our warehouses are the result of our idea of developing business."[12] By shipping in large lots to their warehouses and then disposing of the goods as the regional markets required, firms with a large enough sales volume could handle that part of the distribution process more cheaply than could the wholesalers.

For others, however, acquiring and staffing a chain of warehouses was not profitable. The prime determinant, of course, was the volume of shipments made, although other considerations also played a part. The Walter Lowney Company (one of Baker's smaller competitors) gave as one of its reasons for relying entirely on jobbers the fact that, if they were to handle a part of their own marketing, "we should have to have a succession of warehouses for such distribution."[13] Lowney preferred simply to sell to the jobber and let the middleman take care of the costs of warehousing and shipping. Some producers also relied on the wholesaler to bear the risk of spoilage of food-stuffs. The Beech-Nut Packing Company, which marketed a wide range of goods, including olive oil, vinegar, chewing gum, bacon, peanut butter, beans, and jellies, experimented with a warehouse system but soon concluded that "the maintenance of our own warehouses over the country don't pay—it always ends up in a loss."[14] Beech-Nut's goods were semiperishable,[15] and the firm found that it was more costly to attempt to manage its own flows; by selling directly to jobbers, it disposed of its goods and any worries about their spoilage, transferring those troubles to the wholesalers.

Even for the firms that could reduce a portion of their distribution costs by using company warehouses, however, the economies of scale in marketing were quite limited. A manufacturer could not extend himself very far into the marketing process without adding substantially to his costs. Goods sold through grocery stores were, in general, rather bulky and quite low in unit value. The result was that the costs of shipping, storing, handling, and delivering the products to retailers constituted a considerable portion of the ultimate retail price of the article. An item such as canned beans or soap powder, for example, was relatively cheap to produce but relatively expensive to distribute, especially when it was wanted in small quantities by the retailer, as was almost invariably the case. All items subject to high freight and handling costs per unit sold were likely candidates for the jobber network. As a Beech-Nut official pointed out, "We feel that the jobber is essential in

[12] File #7222-41-1, *ibid.*
[13] File #7222-55-1, *ibid.*
[14] All information about the Beech-Nut Packing Co. is from File #7222-75-1, *ibid.*
[15] As a company official wryly noted, "While vacuum packed articles in glass keep pretty well, we do not feel that they improve with age." (*ibid.*).

our business, more so than he would be for the manufacturer who . . . might sell to any store such a quantity . . . as would enable the manufacturer to prepay the freight at the minimum cost on such shipments."[16] If the jobber was to be eliminated, each sale had to be either large in volume or high in value in order to make freight and handling costs lower than those the middleman could set. Because of the nature of the products and of the diffuse market, the distribution of goods in the grocery trade continued to make the wholesaler the most attractive marketing channel for manufacturers.[17]

DRUGS AND HARDWARE

The marketing conditions that governed the mode of distribution throughout most of the grocery business also prevailed in the drug and hardware trades. Both of these trades were supplied by many producers, and both involved the marketing of a great many simple, standard items. The usual retail drugstore, for example, stocked several thousand different items, while the wholesale druggist stocked an even greater variety. As a Columbia University scholar later noted: "These facts in themselves are sufficient to explain the existence of the drug wholesaler as an important factor in the distribution of drug products. It is manifestly impractical for a retail druggist to attempt to buy every item in his stock directly from the manufacturers. The cost of such a practice would be prohibitive both for retailers and for many manufacturers."[18]

Makers of pharmaceuticals and of the many patent medicines sold through drugstores were very conscious of the importance of the drug wholesaler. Parke, Davis, and Company and Frederick Stearns and Company, both of Detroit, agreed that the jobber served them far better as a distributor than they could serve themselves. "We believe the Jobber is essential to the economical distribution of our products," declared the president of the Stearns firm, "since he is in a position to supply the limited buyer in small quantities on short notice at convenient distances."[19] Patent-medicine producers, such as the Dr. Miles Medical Company and the Pinex Company, found the jobber indispensable for the same reasons. An official of the former company explained the role of the middleman: "In our judgment the wholesaler or

[16] *Ibid.*

[17] An excellent analysis of the distribution process in the grocery trade is given in Nathaneal H. Engle, "Competitive Forces in the Wholesale Marketing of Prepared Food Products." Engle's findings were summarized in a series of four articles in the magazine of the National Wholesale Grocers' Assoc., *The Bulletin*, in November and December, 1929, and January and March, 1930. Data on retail grocery stores are available in the many sections of File #7224, Bureau of Corporations Records.

[18] Paul C. Olsen, *The Merchandising of Drug Products*, p. 102.

[19] File #7222-52-1, Bureau of Corporations Records. Information on Parke, Davis & Co. is in File #7222-51-1, *ibid.*

jobber is vitally essential to the economical distribution of our product." The reason for this was that, "if the jobber were eliminated and if the [retail] dealer were to buy direct, ... the expense of carrying a very large number of accounts and probably of paying freight on small quantities [would be prohibitive]."[20]

Companies producing some of the many non-medical goods sold at least in part through drugstores expressed sentiments very much like those of the pharmaceutical and patent-medicine firms. I. W. Lyon and Son of New York, makers of tooth powder, sold exclusively through jobbers; the Western Clock Company, producers of the Baby Ben clocks, marketed much of its output through drug wholesalers.[21] Another company whose goods found their retail market in drugstores was the United States Playing Card Company. That firm's products were retailed through many thousands of outlets—drug, stationery, tobacco, hardware, department, and general stores—and distribution direct to those retailers would have been very costly. As a company official expressed it: "The average dealer carries a very small stock of cards. To ship small quantities direct to dealers would be entirely too expensive." He illustrated the importance of shipping costs in discouraging direct contact with retailers: "For example, it costs 40 cents to send three gross (432 decks) of cards to Chicago [from the firm's headquarters in Cincinnati] by freight, and 30 cents to send five decks by the cheapest method afforded us."[22]

Thus, manufacturers who supplied the nation's drugstores tended by and large to use the old distribution channels, though in some cases producers dealt directly with retailers. When the retailer was in very close proximity to the manufacturer, or when the retailer placed large orders, direct contact occurred. Also, a few producers had marketing problems with their goods which led them, like the producers of perishables described in Chapter X, to assume the wholesaling function.

The marketing methods of Whitman's, the candy concern, were instructive of the latter case. Whitman's made two kinds of candies, and each was merchandised differently. The high-grade, packaged candies were sold directly to retailers so that the company could regulate the flow of the perishable goods and avoid alienating customers through the sale of a single spoiled package. The small, inexpensive, bar and packaged candies had a quick turnover rate and usually went to children; this kind traveled through the usual drug-jobber network (and the wholesale grocery houses) because it presented none of the thorny marketing difficulties associated with the high-grade

<hr>

[20] For the Dr. Miles Medical Co. see File #7222–48–1, *ibid.* The Pinex Co. (a purveyor of cough medicine) statement is from File #7222–4–1, *ibid.*

[21] Files #7222–6–1 and #7222–64–1, *ibid.*

[22] Information on the U.S. Playing Card Co. is obtainable from File #7222–34–1, *ibid.*

items.[23] Only in such special circumstances did manufacturers deviate from the broad pattern of sales through independent wholesalers.[24]

The prevailing distribution pattern in groceries and drugs was also typical of the marketing of manufactured goods in the hardware trade. Hardware retailers, like their counterparts in drugs and groceries, dealt in a wide range of different items which they generally ordered in small lots from wholesalers. The papers of John Wilson, a Pennsylvania hardware retailer from the 1870s through the 1890s, demonstrate distribution methods that were common throughout the trade. Wilson bought often from wholesalers such as the Smith-Seltzer Hardware Company, a Philadelphia jobbing house that carried a full line of hardware items. Goods generally referred to as "heavy hardware"—metal bars, plates, shapes, and other semifinished metal items—were supplied by specialized metals commission merchants such as C. W. and H. W. Middleton of Philadelphia and Phelps, Dodge of New York, although the sales in heavy goods through retail stores tended to decline at the end of the nineteenth century. The Wilson Papers indicate the breadth and variety of the goods handled by hardware retailers.[25]

The information provided to the Bureau of Corporations by another hardware retailer, Abbott and Son, outlined the reasons for the continuing relevance of the jobber in hardware. "The jobber is today," declared the Iowa retailers, "very essential to the retail trade. 75% of the retailers buy from the jobbers almost exclusively." Because of the frequent, small orders placed by retailers, direct dealing was not economical. Furthermore, the retailer's "requirements do not justify factory buying and his finances do not permit it. . . . Turn stock quickly is his salvation," Abbott explained. "By doing so he can make a profit if he follows a few well worn statements made at every State Hardware Convention for the past ten years."[26]

Manufacturers dealt directly with large or nearby retailers, but most firms that marketed through hardware stores did so through the independent middleman. Jobbers sold the mass of standard, simple items that were the staples of retailers across the country, and they also handled the sale of many nationally known brand name products to retailers. For example, jobbers distributed to hardware stores Bissell carpet sweepers, Community (Oneida) flatware, Disston saws, Ingersoll watches, Baby Ben clocks, and Gillette razors.[27] Makers of many items in the range of goods sold by hardware deal-

[23] See Olsen, *Merchandising of Drug Products*, pp. 21–22.

[24] The operations of retail druggists may be discerned through the many interviews and questionnaires with such businessmen in the various parts of File #7224 of the Bureau of Corporations Records; see, for example, the information about the Campbell Drug Store of Lowell, Mass., in File #7224–19–1.

[25] John Wilson Papers, 1872–1903.

[26] Information on Abbott & Son of Marshalltown, Iowa, is in File #7224–18–1, Bureau of Corporations Records.

[27] See the data in File #7224–9–1, *ibid.* A separate source on the Bissell Carpet Sweeper Co. is File #7222–39–1, *ibid.*

ers—including plumbers' supplies, fly paper, wall tints and coatings, nails, and small tools—relied primarily on jobbers to handle the marketing of their products.[28]

The economic conditions that governed the distribution of drugs, groceries, and hardware also obtained in some related consumers' goods industries. Much of the dry goods trade, a traditional haunt of the middleman, remained in the hands of the jobber. Manufacturers of underwear, hosiery, and garters—including the B. V. D. Company, Chalmers Knitting, Burson Knitting, and the George Frost Company—all testified to their heavy reliance upon jobbers, which resulted from the diffuse market and the high costs they would face in attempting to run their own distribution systems.[29] Makers of other goods marketed in dry goods and general department stores, including such items as cloth, shirts, men's straw hats, and gloves, also sold almost entirely through jobbers.[30]

Although the evidence is less clear, the same marketing channels appear to have been used in merchandising many of the products sold through retail jewelry stores. The distribution methods of the Elgin Watch Company, makers of watch movements and parts, are illustrative. Elgin's products found their ultimate markets in many thousands of retail jewelry outlets, and the firm utilized the web of jewelry jobbers to disperse its items. Charles W. Hulburd, Elgin's president, noted some minor reasons for the firm's use of the jobbing network, then observed that "back of all this is the fact that we, selling one article, cannot economically distribute the goods throughout the country as cheaply as the jobber, who carries a very large line of goods, jewelry, diamonds as well as watches, and the selling force would be distributed over all these articles instead of being confined to one product."[31]

Hulburd also pointed out another very important (and historic) reason why manufacturers in such trades as groceries, drugs, hardware, dry goods, and jewelry continued to use the jobber—the middleman bore credit risks that manufacturers did not care to assume. Direct dealing between producers and retailers would necessitate costly additions such as greatly expanded bookkeeping and communications departments to service thousands of scat-

---

[28] See, for example, Files #7222–1–1, #7222–21–1, #7222–23–1, #7222–25–1, ibid. The position of the independent wholesaler in drugs and hardware was so strong that newly expanding institutions such as catalog houses and department stores "were at worst annoying, not threatening"; see Becker, "Wholesalers of Hardware and Drugs," p. 267.

[29] For the firms mentioned see Files #7222–103–1, #7222–47–1, #7222–94–1, and #7222–78–1, Bureau of Corporations Records.

[30] See, for example, information on M. S. Levy & Son (straw hats) and Oppenheim, Oberndorff & Co. (cloth and shirts), both of Baltimore, in Files #7222–98–1 and #7222–101–1, ibid. File #7222–52–1, ibid., outlines the operations of the Eisendrath Glove Co. of Chicago.

[31] File #7222–50–1, ibid.

tered retailers about whose credit standing the producer knew nothing. As Charles Hulburd phrased it, "One reason why we sell to the jobber is because it is much easier for us to sell to one hundred responsible jobbing houses, who pay us promptly, than to sell to twenty-five thousand jewelers and carry credits and have a very extensive credit department."[32] Jobbing houses were generally familiar to manufacturers and were very reliable customers. For a producer to have ventured into extensive direct dealing with retailers would have meant giving credit to a large number of unknown, small retailers, thereby involving the manufacturer in attempts to collect on bad or slowly repaid debts. The jobber usually knew many of his customers and was far more informed about their credit reliability than a distant manufacturer could be.[33] The jobber's traditional function as a supplier of credit to retailers, then, was another significant reason for his survival in the areas of the economy considered in this chapter.

In the grocery, drug, and hardware trades, however, as in the tobacco industry, the last years of the nineteenth century and the first years of the twentieth witnessed the erosion of a portion of the jobber's importance as a result of the impact of national advertising. Advertising was not, of course, a new phenomenon in American life, but the two decades around 1900 marked the first widespread attempts by manufacturers to reach a mass audience through national media. The success in the nineties of such low-priced, mass-circulation magazines as *McClure's*, *Saturday Evening Post*, *Cosmopolitan*, *Ladies' Home Journal*, and *Munsey's* created a medium through which producers could reach the American middle class. In that same decade, advertising enjoyed its first genuine impact on the nation.[34] Makers of the kinds of goods considered in this chapter took up advertising as the way to answer the challenge implied in the famous remark by Thomas J. Barratt of Pears' Soap: "Any fool can make soap. It takes a clever man to sell it."[35] Many of the products of the firms discussed here, as well as those of numerous others, were heavily advertised; even a partial listing includes Gillette razors, the cereals of the Kellogg and Postum companies, Baker's chocolate, Old Dutch Cleanser, Ingersoll watches, Bissell carpet sweepers, Calumet bak-

[32] *Ibid.*

[33] Manufacturers, wholesalers, and retailers of the early twentieth century were very conscious of the importance of the jobber's function as bearer of questionable credit risks. Many of the files in the records of the Bureau of Corporations dealing with its "Resale Prices Inquiry" contain remarks by businessmen on this topic.

[34] The rise of national advertising is covered in such secondary sources as Frank Presbrey, *History and Development of Advertising*; George B. Hotchkiss, *Milestones in Marketing*; Ralph M. Hower's study of the N. W. Ayer agency, *History of an Advertising Agency*; and James P. Wood, *The Story of Advertising*.

[35] Barratt's comment is cited in Frank Rowsome, Jr., *They Laughed When I Sat Down*, pp. 2–3.

ing powder, and Van Camp's pork and beans.[36] Indeed, the early use of national advertising seemed to be concentrated in the trades considered in this chapter, especially the grocery business. As one student of early advertising has commented: "In time it grew clear that iteration coupled with a memorable slogan or image was vastly more effective than just announcement alone. But difficulties were still encountered. The approach seemed to be suited only for widely distributed and broadly consumed commodities such as soap, tobacco, and the new packaged foodstuffs."[37]

It is impossible to measure the effect of advertising and brand names on the jobbers of groceries, drugs, hardware, dry goods, and jewelry, but it appears to have been considerable. The atrophy of much of the selling function of wholesalers served to make them less important and less powerful actors on the economic stage. Prior to the rise of national brand advertising, the wholesaler exercised some autonomy in the sense that he could choose to push whatever goods he wanted and to sell other products in a somewhat desultory fashion. That role as salesman gave him some leverage against producers and probably made it possible for him to exercise influence over the terms and service he received from manufacturers. Once the manufacturer went over the wholesaler's and retailer's heads direct to the consumer via advertising, however, jobbing became more and more a distributive mechanism which routinely supplied the goods demanded by the public as the result of that advertising. Jobbers who grew disenchanted with a particular producer in the wake of some real or imagined grievance had little choice but to continue carrying his goods if they were nationally known, widely demanded items. The remark of a scholar of the drug business is pertinent to all the trades discussed here: "A manufacturer of a product that is widely accepted by consumers is not going to be hurt much by [the actions of individual jobbers]. In most sections of the country competition between wholesale druggists is keen."[38]

An excellent analysis of the changes brought by nationally known brands was made by a manufacturer who had engaged in national advertising for his product. Recalling the situation on the eve of the advertising revolution of the nineties, the president of a major maker of soap and washing powders declared:

[36] Advertising played an important part in the success of some of the firms mentioned in Chapter IX, firms that could distribute directly to retailers as a result of their advertising and the fact that their goods were extremely inexpensive to ship, relative to their value. Examples include Arrow's collars and cuffs and George Parker's pens.

[37] Rowsome, *They Laughed When I Sat Down*, pp. 26–27.

[38] Olsen, *Merchandising Drug Products*, pp. 119–20. Some large hardware jobbers tried to solve the problem of advertising and brand names by creating their own brand names and contracting with manufacturers to produce them. See Becker, "Wholesalers of Hardware and Drugs," pp. 80–81, 122, 143.

Twenty-five years ago the manufacturer went to the jobber, related the merits of his goods, and arranged the terms. The jobber said: "Send me two cars at the agreed terms." The jobber then went to the retailer and told him that he had goods of exceptional quality, stated the terms, and the retailer ordered several cases. When the consumer came to the retailer, she asked for an article but did not specify the brand. She relied upon the retailer, who supplied her from his stock on hand. The method of twenty-five years ago is reversed today. The manufacturer goes first to the consumer. By advertising he burns it into the consumer's mind that he wants a certain brand. Through premiums, gifts or bribes if you please, he induces her to try his brand. At tremendous expense the manufacturer educates her to ask for Fels Naphtha, Ivory, Rub-No-More, Arrow collars, etc., as the case may be. The demand created, the retailer goes to the jobber asking him to furnish the articles called for. Then the jobber goes to the manufacturer.

Our company sells through the jobber, and we do the rest. We create the desire for our product through advertising.[39]

CONCLUSION

This chapter has briefly surveyed the distribution methods of manufacturers who produced goods for the grocery, drug, hardware, dry goods, and jewelry trades. These lines of business represented the only major sector of the manufacturing economy in which the independent middleman maintained his primary role, wholesaling goods to retailers as he had done since the nation's earliest days. Although national advertising seriously reduced his role as salesman, he remained the primary agent in the distribution process. This and the preceding chapter have shown that the wholesaler (primarily the jobber) endured here while his fellows in most other manufacturing industries were largely or entirely replaced by the marketing organizations of producing firms. The reason for the survival of much of the old order in the distribution of the goods considered here was, of course, the survival of the generic nature of goods and of the diffuse market in which these commodities were sold. The latter involved several sets of characteristics, each of which tended to discourage moves by manufacturers to assume the distribution function.

The first characteristic of the diffuse market was that it was the stage for the interaction of many buyers and sellers. The industries considered in this chapter were seldom concentrated, oligopolistic ones; the giant corporation that arose in so many other areas of the economy at the turn of the century appeared much less frequently in these trades. The absence of patents, secret processes, and complex technology, coupled with the ready accessibility of raw materials, labor, and other factors of production, meant that there was

---

[39] Statement by Gustav A. Berghoff, president of the Rub-No-More Co. in File #7222–30–1, Bureau of Corporations Records.

considerable ease of entry. The prevalence of medium-sized and small firms tended to make less likely the manufacturers' achievement of sales volumes large enough to encourage forward integration. The presence of so many small buyers meant that the makers of the commodities discussed here were denied the kind of concentrated markets enjoyed by the manufacturers of many producers' goods. Firms competing in the kinds of consumers' goods sold through numerous independent retail outlets could not be encouraged to take over their own wholesaling, for their market was not composed of a few consolidated companies.

The second characteristic of the diffuse market was the fact that a retailer's orders for a single item remained small, both in volume and in value. These goods went to consumers through thousands of retail dealers, each of whom carried hundreds or even thousands of different commodities produced by many different manufacturers. Each order for a particular product was so small that it did not pay manufacturers to employ a sales force of the magnitude required by the task of dealing directly with so many small retailers. The commodities sold through the independent retail stores were usually low in price and often were bulky; this meant that the costs of shipping and handling each unit were quite high, especially when the orders were for only a small amount. The result was that such products could be marketed most cheaply by middlemen who assembled a full line of goods from a great many producers and supplied the varied wants of retailers. Although the grocery, drug, hardware, and dry goods items sold in such establishments were consumers' goods that sold in urban markets like many of the products of firms discussed in Chapter IX, their markets remained diffuse rather than concentrated because of the economic conditions just described.

Another characteristic of the diffuse market was that most of the products sold there shared an immunity to merchandising problems. Unlike the goods described in Chapter X, they were not subject to the difficulties resulting from perishability. And, unlike the products considered in Chapter XI, they did not require close and continuing contact between producer and consumer. The commodities in the retail trades were simple, standard items that exhibited almost no technological complexity. Customers did not require any instructions in the use of such products, and the goods called for no specialized repair services. Because of this immunity to merchandising difficulties, manufacturers were not pressured to integrate forward into wholesaling.

In short, the economic conditions that had always governed these trades were not disturbed by new technologies or new or changed markets, and so the old distribution channels continued to handle the task of wholesaling and to do the job more efficiently than could the manufacturers themselves. The absence of many economies of scale in distribution meant that the producer was content to let the jobber provide the service he had traditionally performed. The jobber invested his funds in large inventories, thus relieving the manufacturer of that task. He accumulated a wide variety of products from many producers, saw to their transportation, to their storage in his warehouse, and to their delivery to retailers. He contacted retailers and carried hundreds of their accounts, often extending credit to his customers. All these tasks would have fallen to the manufacturer had the jobber been eliminated, and manufacturers understood very clearly that they could not do the jobs so cheaply. Although the rise of national brand advertising diminished the wholesaler's autonomy, he remained in the early years of the twentieth century what for sound economic reasons he had been throughout the nation's past—the agent who brought together manufacturers and retailers in the grocery, drug, hardware, dry goods, jewelry, and similar trades.

CHAPTER XIV
The Contours of Change

By the early years of the twentieth century, the new order in American marketing had emerged in many industries. Although it is impossible to say precisely when most manufactured goods in the U.S. economy came to be distributed by the producers themselves, it seems clear that the marketing revolution occurred between the mid-1890s and World War I.

When the Bureau of the Census conducted the first systematic investigation of the distribution of manufactured products in 1929, the results clearly revealed the dimensions of the change that had taken place in marketing since the early nineteenth century.[1] Independent wholesalers, for so much of our economic past the dominant marketers of manufactured goods, handled less than one-third of the flow of such goods from American factories in 1930.[2] Most manufactured products were marketed in various ways by the producing firms themselves. Almost one-third of the goods were sold directly to industrial consumers, and the rest went to the manufacturers' own wholesale and retail branches, to independent retailers directly (without the use of wholesalers), or directly to home consumers.[3]

The shift toward this new marketing system was quite clearly under way by the turn of the century. In industry after industry, firms developed their own marketing divisions. Just a partial listing of the large companies that by

---

[1] U.S. Bureau of the Census, *Fifteenth Census of the United States, 1930*.

[2] The actual figure was 29.6 per cent of the selling value FOB factory (that is, excluding transport and handling costs from factory to customer) of manufactured goods (*ibid.*, 2: 5–7). The sampling period (the early part of the Great Depression) obviously was not a "typical" one, but the over-all pattern of manufacturing dominance is clear.

[3] The breakdown was: 31.6 per cent to industrial consumers; 18.6 per cent directly to retailers; 16.1 per cent to the manufacturers' wholesaling branches; 2.5 per cent to home consumers; 1.9 per cent to the manufacturers' retailing branches; and 29.6 per cent to wholesalers (*ibid.*).

1910 had built their own systems to distribute their goods in the national market includes: food processing enterprises such as Armour, Swift, Morris, Wilson, Cudahy, Nabisco, United Fruit, Corn Products, American Ice, and National Distillers; metals firms such as U.S. Steel, Bethlehem Steel, Crucible Steel, and National Enameling and Stamping; petroleum products companies such as Standard Oil, Pure Oil, Union Oil of California, Sun Oil, General Asphalt, Texaco, and Gulf; makers of crude chemicals such as du Pont and International Salt; automobile firms such as General Motors, Ford, and Packard; as well as producers of a variety of technologically complex goods— firms such as General Electric, Westinghouse, Pittsburgh Plate Glass, International Harvester, Singer, Eastman Kodak, Worthington Pump and Machine, U.S. Rubber, and Allis-Chalmers.[4]

During the first half of this century, the process of integration forward into marketing continued to spread. By mid-century the vast majority of large corporations were handling some of their own marketing. Of a sample of 153 large manufacturing firms operating in 1948, 79 per cent engaged in wholesaling operations, and 87 per cent were involved in wholesaling and/or retailing activities.[5] Sometimes this occurred in the form of a sales department with offices across the nation, sometimes through company wholesaling and/or retailing branches that kept inventories, sometimes via the creation of a subsidiary marketing corporation, or through some combination of these methods. Whatever the particular form they assumed, the merchandising activities of manufacturing concerns represented the overturning of an economic order whose lineage in the Western world was centuries old.

In the colonial and early national period, the pattern had been an extension of the European configuration. Virtually all manufactured goods that entered markets other than strictly local ones passed through the hands of sedentary merchants. With the exception of a few industries, this pattern continued without visible prospects of change until the 1870s. The mercantile community experienced internal alterations as a result of expanding trade and specialization after 1815, but these changes did not affect the fundamental dominance of the mercantile community as the agent of distribution or as coordinator of national and regional flows. Merchants acted as merchandisers and as financiers of economic growth. Their financial role began to atrophy after 1860, and they were forced to rely on their specialized marketing activities.

[4] This incomplete list is drawn from evidence presented earlier in this volume, as well as from our study of large twentieth-century American firms based on company annual reports, Moody's and Poor's manuals, and a variety of secondary sources. Some of the results of that study appeared in Harold C. Livesay and Patrick G. Porter, "Vertical Integration in American Manufacturing, 1899–1948."

[5] Based on data collected for the Livesay and Porter article, "Vertical Integration in American Manufacturing." An outstanding statistical analysis of the distributive sector's place in the over-all twentieth-century economy is provided in Harold Barger's *Distribution Place in the American Economy since 1869*.

These activities had always rested on the twin pillars of the generic nature of manufactured goods and the diffuse markets in which they were sold. Only when those conditions changed could a new marketing order emerge. The fundamental changes came in the wake of improvements in transportation and communications. These developments made possible the expansion of manufacturing firms into large regional, national, and even international markets. In adapting to these changes, merchants sacrificed versatility for specialization. Once the expansion had occurred, independent wholesalers became vulnerable to changes in the nature of products and of markets.

As the last decades of the nineteenth century unfolded, products and markets changed. Advancing technology brought to many industries new merchandising requirements for their goods. The old economy of simple, uncomplicated products was joined by the many new scientifically and technologically oriented industries that were to become the backbone of the modern American economic system. These new industries found that the traditional marketing arrangements did not function very well for them; consequently they built a new network of manufacturer-dominated merchandising channels. Similarly, the increasing concentration of markets in the wake of the rise of the modern corporation, the emergence of oligopoly, and the concentration of population in urban areas altered the traditional nature of the market for many industries. Many manufacturing firms then found it more efficient to deal directly with their customers and to dispense with much of the old web of commercial intermediaries. These two basic developments, coupled in some industries with backward integration and intracompany sales, spelled the decline of the independent wholesaler in the twentieth-century economy.

Although the independent wholesaler obviously did not disappear from the national scene, he became largely restricted to those broad sectors considered in Chapter XIII. Only where goods remained generic and markets diffuse—in those sectors wherein numerous retailers sold a wide variety of relatively simple goods produced by many manufacturers—did the wholesaler retain his primary distributive role.

The independent wholesalers were unable to adjust to the different economic order of the late nineteenth century primarily because their traditional function was no longer relevant in many industries. They were specialized men of business whose time had simply passed; they cannot fairly be faulted for inadequate will or poor entrepreneurship. Their methods, their organization, their whole orientation toward the economy made them ill equipped to function in the emerging environment of advanced technology and giant corporations. They had served long and well, but their expertise, resources, and training were not adaptable to large portions of the corporate world of the twentieth century.

We have explored in this volume the structure of the marketing of manufactured goods in the nineteenth century, tracing the process of change and suggesting reasons for that change. The evolution of marketing techniques is a part of the over-all story of the fundamental alterations in American society brought about by the metamorphosis from the older, agrarian-oriented, merchant-dominated economy to the modern, industrialized, concentrated economy. Observers have long noted that ours is above all a business civilization; towering office buildings dominate our cities and reflect the values of our civilization as surely as the magnificent cathedrals of the twelfth and thirteenth centuries reflected those of medieval Europe. For more than two centuries after the initial English settlements in what was to become the United States, our business civilization lay in the hands of independent merchants. Their power derived from their strategic position at all the crossroads of commerce, at the nexus between producer and consumer. When they surrendered their place of leadership, first to the men who built the great manufacturing firms and then to their corporate heirs, they did so in large part as a result of having lost that strategic position. The modern manufacturing corporation assumed the marketing role, not because of a failure of will or vision on the part of the merchants, but because of the alterations in the nature of products and of markets. Once these fundamental dimensions of the economy had changed, there followed a lasting revolution in the relationships between merchants and manufacturers.

Bibliography

Manuscript Sources

Alan Wood Steel Co. Papers. Eleutherian Mills Historical Library. Wilmington, Del.

American Steel & Wire Co. Papers. Baker Library. Harvard University. Boston, Mass.

Baldwin Locomotive Works Papers. Historical Society of Pennsylvania. Philadelphia.

Betts, Pusey & Harlan Papers. Eleutherian Mills Historical Library. Wilmington, Del.

Bonney & Bush Receipt Book. Historical Society of Delaware. Wilmington.

Builder's Iron Foundry Papers. Baker Library. Harvard University. Boston, Mass.

Carnegie, Andrew. Papers. Division of Manuscripts. Library of Congress. Washington, D.C.

Carter & Scattergood Papers. Eleutherian Mills Historical Library. Wilmington, Del.

Chicago, Burlington & Quincy Railroad Papers. Newberry Library. Chicago, Ill.

Colt, Samuel. Papers. Connecticut Historical Society and Connecticut State Library. Hartford.

Cooper-Hewitt Business Papers. Division of Manuscripts. Library of Congress. Washington, D.C.

Cornwall Furnace Papers. Pennsylvania State Historical and Museum Commission. Bureau of Archives and History. Harrisburg.

Drug Trade Collection. Eleutherian Mills Historical Library. Wilmington, Del.

Duke, Benjamin N. Papers. Duke University Library. Durham, N.C.

Dun & Bradstreet Collection. Baker Library. Harvard University. Boston, Mass.

Erie City Iron Works Papers. Eleutherian Mills Historical Library. Wilmington, Del.

Fall River Iron Works Papers. Baker Library. Harvard University. Boston, Mass.

General Electric Co. Papers. General Electric Co. Schenectady, N.Y.

Haldeman, Jacob. Papers. Eleutherian Mills Historical Library. Wilmington, Del.

Hazlehurst & Wiegand Collection. Maryland Historical Society. Baltimore.

Hinckley & Egery Papers. Baker Library. Harvard University. Boston, Mass.

Hollingsworth & Harvey Papers. Eleutherian Mills Historical Library. Wilmington, Del.

Illinois Central Railroad Papers. Newberry Library. Chicago, Ill.

J. C. Hobbs & Sons Papers. Baker Library. Harvard University. Boston, Mass.

Jones & Laughlin Steel Corp. Papers. General Documents File. Jones & Laughlin Steel Corp. Pittsburgh, Pa.

Lewis, William D. Manuscript Diary. Historical Society of Delaware. Wilmington.

Lobdell Car Wheel Co. Papers. Historical Society of Pennsylvania. Philadelphia.

Lobdell Papers. Eleutherian Mills Historical Library. Wilmington, Del.

Lukens Steel Co. Papers. Eleutherian Mills Historical Library. Wilmington, Del.

Mount Hope Iron Co. Papers. Baker Library. Harvard University. Boston, Mass.

Philadelphia Merchants. Miscellaneous Papers of, 1774–1890. Eleutherian Mills Historical Library. Wilmington, Del.

Phoenix Iron Co. Papers. Eleutherian Mills Historical Library. Wilmington, Del.

Pine Grove Furnace Papers. Pennsylvania State Historical and Museum Commission. Bureau of Archives and History. Harrisburg.

Plimpton Papers. Baker Library. Harvard University. Boston, Mass.

Principio Furnace Papers. Maryland Historical Society. Baltimore.

Pusey & Jones Papers. Eleutherian Mills Historical Library. Wilmington, Del.

Reese, James & Co. Papers. Inland Rivers Collection. Cincinnati Public Library. Ohio.

Richwine Carriage Co. Papers. Cincinnati Public Library. Ohio.

Shawmut Fibre Co. Papers. Baker Library. Harvard University. Boston, Mass.

Singer Sewing Machine Co. Papers. Wisconsin Historical Society. Madison.

Stone & Harris Papers. Baker Library. Harvard University. Boston, Mass.

Thomson, Elihu. Papers. American Philosophical Society. Philadelphia, Pa.

Troth, Henry and Samuel. Papers. Eleutherian Mills Historical Library. Wilmington, Del.

U.S. Bureau of Corporations. Records. Record Group 122. National Archives. Washington, D.C.

U.S. Department of Justice. Manuscripts relating to *United States* v. *American Tobacco Company,* U.S. Circuit Court, Southern District of New York. Equity Case Files El–216, 1908. Record Group 60. National Archives. Washington, D.C.

U.S. Quartermaster General. Office Records. Consolidated Correspondence File, 1794–1915. National Archives. Washington, D.C.

Westinghouse Co. Historical Papers. Westinghouse Co. East Pittsburgh, Pa.

Whitaker Iron Papers. Maryland Historical Society. Baltimore.

Wiegand, William D. Papers. Maryland Historical Society. Baltimore.

Wilson, John. Papers. Eleutherian Mills Historical Library. Wilmington, Del.

Wright, Richard. Papers. Duke University. Durham, N.C.

Dissertations and Theses

Becker, William. "The Wholesalers of Hardware and Drugs, 1870–1900." Ph.D. dissertation, The Johns Hopkins University, 1969.

Clayton, John M. "Railroad Building in Delaware." Master's thesis, University of Delaware, 1948.

Davies, Robert B. "The International Operations of the Singer Manufacturing Company, 1854–1895." Ph.D. dissertation, University of Wisconsin, 1967.

Engle, Nathaneal H. "Competitive Forces in the Wholesale Marketing of Prepared Food Products." Ph.D. dissertation, University of Michigan, 1929.

Holmes, William F. "The New Castle and Frenchtown Turnpike and Railroad Company." Master's thesis, University of Delaware, 1961.

Miller, Frederic K. "The Rise of an Iron Community: An Economic History of Lebanon County, Pennsylvania from 1740–1865." Ph.D. dissertation, University of Pennsylvania, 1948.

Moore, Terris. "Unsecured Bank Loans as Permanent Working Capital for Industry." Ph.D. dissertation, Harvard University, 1936.

Mullins, Jack S. "The Sugar Trust: Henry O. Havemeyer and the American Sugar Refining Company." Ph.D. dissertation, University of South Carolina, 1964.

Potter, Jack C. "The Philadelphia, Wilmington, and Baltimore Railroad, 1831–1840." Master's thesis, University of Delaware, 1960.

Rhame, William T. "Competitive Advantages and Disadvantages of Agencies Making Short and Medium Term Loans to Industry." Ph.D. dissertation, Harvard University, 1940.

Sylla, Richard E. "The American Capital Market, 1846–1914." Ph.D. dissertation, Harvard University, 1968.

Unfer, Louis. "Swift and Company: The Development of the Packing Industry, 1875–1912." Ph.D. dissertation, University of Illinois, 1951.

Whitman, William B. "Business and Government in Nineteenth Century Delaware." Master's thesis, University of Delaware, 1964.

Other Unpublished Sources

Annual Reports of American Corporations. Corporation Records Division. Baker Library. Harvard University. Boston, Mass.

Trade Catalogue Collection. Eleutherian Mills Historical Library. Wilmington, Del.

Books and Articles

Ackerman, Carl W. *George Eastman*. Boston: Houghton Mifflin, 1930.

Acworth, W. M. "Railroad Accounting in America vs. England." *North American Review* 191 (1910):330–39.

Adams, Frederick U. *Conquest of the Tropics: The Story of the Creative Enter-*

prises Conducted by the United Fruit Company. Garden City, N.Y.: Double-day, Page & Co., 1914.

Adler, Jacob. *Claus Spreckels: The Sugar King in Hawaii.* Honolulu: University of Hawaii Press, 1965.

Albion, Robert G. *The Rise of New York Port.* New York: C. Scribner's Sons, 1939.

Aldcroft, Derek. "The Efficiency and Enterprise of British Railways, 1870–1914." *Explorations in Entrepreneurial History.* 5 (1968):158–74.

Alderson, Bernard. *Andrew Carnegie: The Man and His Work.* New York: Doubleday, Page & Co., 1908.

Allen, Hugh. *The House of Goodyear: A Story of Rubber and Modern Business.* Cleveland, Ohio: Corday & Gross, 1943.

American Pharmaceutical Assoc. *Report of the Committee on the Drug Market.* Philadelphia: American Pharmaceutical Assoc., 1868.

American Steel & Wire Co., *American Wire Rope: Catalogue and Handbook.* N.p.: American Steel & Wire Co., 1913.

American Tobacco Co. *"Sold American!"* New York: American Tobacco Co., 1954.

Anderson, Oscar E., Jr. *Refrigeration in America: A History of a New Technology and Its Impact.* Princeton: Princeton University Press, 1953.

Appleton's Annual Cyclopedia and Register of Important Events of the Year 1882. New York: D. Appleton, 1883.

Armes, Ethel. *The Story of Coal and Iron in Alabama.* Birmingham: Published under the auspices of the Chamber of Commerce, 1940.

Assoc. of Manufacturers of Chilled Car Wheels. *Historical Sketch of the Lobdell Car Wheel Company.* N.p.: n.p., 1936.

Atherton, Louis E. "The Pioneer Merchant in Mid-America." *University of Missouri Studies* 14, no. 2 (1939).

————. *The Southern Country Store, 1800–1860.* Baton Rouge: Louisiana State University Press, 1949.

Bailyn, Bernard, ed. *The Apologia of Robert Keayne: The Self Portrait of a Puritan Merchant.* New York: Harper & Row, 1965.

————. *The New England Merchants in the Seventeenth Century.* Cambridge, Mass.: Harvard University Press, 1955.

Barger, Harold. *Distribution's Place in the American Economy since 1869.* Princeton: Princeton University Press, 1955.

Baron, Stanley. *Brewed in America: A History of Beer and Ale in the United States.* Boston: Little, Brown & Co., 1962.

Baughman, James P. *Charles Morgan.* Nashville, Tenn.: Vanderbilt University Press, 1968.

Baxter, William T. *The House of Hancock: Business in Boston, 1724–1775.* Cambridge, Mass.: Harvard University Press, 1945.

"The Beginnings of a Trust." *Collier's,* August 10, 1907, pp. 15–16.

Berglund, Abraham. *The United States Steel Corporation: A Study of the Growth and Influence of Combination in the Iron and Steel Industry.* New York: Columbia University Press, 1907.

Berle, Adolf A., and Means, Gardiner C. *The Modern Corporation and Private Property*. 2nd ed. New York: Macmillan, 1937.

Billinger, R. D. "Beginnings of Bethlehem Iron and Steel." *Bulletin of the Pennsylvania Department of Urban Affairs* 20 (1952): no. 1, pp. 3–7; no 4, pp. 7–10; no. 5, pp. 13–18.

Bining, Arthur C. *Pennsylvania Iron Manufacture in the Eighteenth Century*. Harrisburg: Pennsylvania Historical Commission, 1938.

Biographical and Genealogical History of Delaware. Chambersburg, Pa.: Runk, 1899.

Black, Robert C. *Railroads of the Confederacy*. Chapel Hill: University of North Carolina Press, 1952.

Borden, Neil H. *The Economic Effects of Advertising*. Chicago: R. D. Irwin, 1942.

Bridge, James H. *The Inside History of the Carnegie Steel Company*. New York: Aldine Book Co., 1903.

Brooks, Jerome E. *The Mighty Leaf*. Boston: Little, Brown & Co., 1952.

Brown, William A. *Morris Ketchum Jesup: A Character Sketch*. New York: C. Scribner's Sons, 1910.

Bruce, Kathleen. *Virginia Iron Manufacture in the Slave Era*. New York: Century, 1930.

Bruchey, Stuart. *Robert Oliver, Merchant of Baltimore, 1783–1819*. Baltimore, Md.: The Johns Hopkins Press, 1956.

———. *The Roots of American Economic Growth, 1607–1861*. New York: Harper & Row, 1968.

———. "Success and Failure Factors: American Merchants in Foreign Trade in the Eighteenth and Nineteenth Centuries." *Business History Review* 32 (1958): 272–92.

Bryan, James. *Bryan's Druggists' Manual*. Rochester, N.Y.: By the author, 1860.

Buck, Norman S. *The Development of the Organization of the Anglo-American Trade*. New Haven, Conn.: Yale University Press, 1925.

Bullis, Harry A. *Buffalo: Its Flour Milling Heritage*. New York: Newcomen Society, 1948.

Bush & Lobdell. *Catalog, 1851*. Wilmington, Del.: Bush & Lobdell, 1851.

Canby, Henry S. *The Brandywine*. New York: Farrar & Rinehart, 1941.

Cappon, Lester J. "Trend of the Southern Iron Industry Under the Plantation System." *Journal of Economic and Business History* 2 (1930): 353–81.

Carnegie, Andrew. *Autobiography of Andrew Carnegie*. Boston: Houghton Mifflin, 1920.

Casson, Herbert N. *Cyrus Hall McCormick: His Life and Work*. Chicago: A. C. McClurg, 1909.

Chandler, Alfred D., Jr. "The Beginnings of 'Big Business' in American Industry." *Business History Review* 33 (1959): 1–31.

———. *Giant Enterprise: Ford, General Motors, and the Automobile Industry*. New York: Harcourt, Brace & World, 1964.

———. *Henry Varnum Poor: Business Editor, Analyst, and Reformer*. Cambridge, Mass.: Harvard University Press, 1956.

————. "The Role of Business in the United States: A Historical Survey." *Daedalus* 98 (1969):23–40.

————. *Strategy and Structure: Chapters in the History of the American Industrial Enterprise.* Paperback ed. New York: Doubleday, 1966.

————. "The Structure of American Industry in the Twentieth Century: A Historical Overview," *Business History Review* 43 (1969):255–81.

————. ed. *The Railroads: The Nation's First Big Business.* New York: Harcourt, Brace & World, 1965.

Charles D. Barney & Co. *The Tobacco Industry.* New York: Charles D. Barney, 1924.

Clark, Malcolm C. "The Birth of an Enterprise: Baldwin Locomotive, 1831–1842," *Pennsylvania Magazine of History and Biography* 90 (1966):423–44.

Clark, Victor S. *History of Manufactures in the United States.* 3 vols. New York: McGraw-Hill, 1929.

Cleland, Robert G. *A History of Phelps-Dodge, 1834–1950.* New York: Alfred Knopf, 1952.

Clemen, Rudolf A. *The American Livestock and Meat Industry.* New York: Ronald Press, 1923.

————. *George H. Hammond (1838–1886): Pioneer in Refrigeration Transportation.* New York: Newcomen Society, 1946.

Cochran, Thomas C. *The Pabst Brewing Company: The History of an American Business.* New York: New York University Press, 1948.

————. *Railroad Leaders, 1845–1890: The Business Mind in Action.* Cambridge, Mass.: Harvard University Press, 1953.

Cole, Arthur H. *The American Wool Manufacture.* 2 vols. Cambridge, Mass.: Harvard University Press, 1926.

————. "Marketing Nonconsumer Goods Before 1917." *Business History Review* 33 (1959):420–28.

Cole, Arthur H., and Williamson, Harold F. *The American Carpet Manufacture.* Cambridge, Mass.: Harvard University Press, 1941.

Conrad, Henry C. *History of the State of Delaware.* 3 vols. Wilmington: By the author, 1908.

Corning, Howard, ed. "A Letter from John Griffin, Ironmaster, 1878." *Journal of Economic and Business History* 4 (1932):687–703.

Cotter, Arundel. "The History of the United States Steel Corporation." *Moody's Magazine* 18 (1915) and 19 (1916).

Crowther, Samuel. *John H. Patterson: Pioneer in Industrial Welfare.* New York: Doubleday, Page & Co., 1923.

Cummings, Richard O. *The American Ice Harvests.* Berkeley and Los Angeles: University of California Press, 1949.

Dailey, Don M. "The Early Development of the Note Brokerage Business in Chicago." *Journal of Political Economy* 46 (1938):202–17.

Daugherty, Carroll R.; de Chazeau, Melvin G.; and Stratton, Samuel S. *The Economics of the Iron and Steel Industry.* 2 vols. New York: McGraw-Hill, 1937.

Davies, Robert B. "Peacefully Working to Conquer the World: The Singer

Manufacturing Company in Foreign Markets, 1854–1889." *Business History Review* 43 (1969):299–325.

Davis, Lance E. "Capital Markets and Industrial Concentration: The U.S. and the U.K., a Comparative Study." *Economic History Review* 19 (1966): 255–72.

———. "The New England Textile Mills and the Capital Markets: A Study of Industrial Borrowing, 1840–1860." *Economic History Review* 20 (1967): 1–30.

Degler, Carl N. *Out of Our Past.* New York: Harper & Row, 1970.

Dew, Charles B. *Ironmaker to the Confederacy.* New Haven, Conn.: Yale University Press, 1966.

Diamond, Sigmund. "Values as an Obstacle to Economic Growth." *Journal of Economic History* 27 (1967):561–75.

Dunaway, W. F. *A History of Pennsylvania.* New York: Harper & Bros., 1948.

Edwards, Richard, ed. *Industries of Delaware.* Wilmington: By the author, 1880.

Eichner, Alfred S. *The Emergence of Oligopoly: Sugar Refining as a Case Study.* Baltimore, Md.: The Johns Hopkins Press, 1969.

Ellis, C. Hamilton. *British Railway History.* 2 vols. London: George Allen & Unwin, 1954.

Ewing, John S., and Norton, Nancy P. *Broadlooms and Businessmen.* Cambridge: Mass.: Harvard University Press, 1941.

Fairchild, Byron. *Messrs. William Pepperell.* Ithaca, N.Y.: Cornell University Press, 1954.

Ferguson, Eugene. ed. *Early Engineering Reminiscences [1815–1840] of George Escol Sellers.* Washington, D.C.: Smithsonian Institution, 1965.

Fishlow, Albert. *American Railroads and the Transformation of the Ante-Bellum Economy.* Cambridge, Mass.: Harvard University Press, 1965.

———. "Productivity and Technological Change in the Railroad Sector, 1840–1910." In *Output, Employment, and Productivity in the United States After 1800.* National Bureau of Economic Research, Studies in Income and Wealth, no. 30. New York: Columbia University Press for NBER, 1966.

Fitzgerald, F. Scott. *The Great Gatsby.* New York: C. Scribner's Sons, 1953.

Fogel, Robert W. *Railroads and American Economic Growth: Essays in Econometric History.* Baltimore, Md.: The Johns Hopkins Press, 1964.

———. *The Union Pacific Railroad: A Case in Premature Enterprise.* Baltimore, Md.: The Johns Hopkins Press, 1960.

Freiday, Dean. "Tinton Manor: The Iron Works." *Proceedings of the New Jersey Historical Society* 70 (1952):250–61.

Fritz, John. *Autobiography.* New York: John Wiley, 1912.

Gallman, Robert E. "Commodity Output, 1839–1899." In *Trends in the American Economy in the Nineteenth Century.* National Bureau of Economic Research, Studies in Income and Wealth, no. 24. Princeton: Princeton University Press for NBER, 1960.

———. "Gross National Product in the United States, 1834–1909." In *Output, Employment, and Productivity in the United States After 1800.* National Bureau of Economic Research, Studies in Income and Wealth, no. 30. New York: Columbia University Press for NBER, 1965.

Gibb, George S. *The Saco-Lowell Shops: Textile Machinery Building in New England, 1813–1949.* Cambridge, Mass.: Harvard University Press, 1950.
————. *The Whitesmiths of Taunton: A History of Reed and Barton, 1824–1943.* Cambridge, Mass.: Harvard University Press, 1943.
Goldsmith, Raymond W. *Financial Intermediaries in the American Economy Since 1900.* Princeton: Princeton University Press, 1958.
Gras, N. S. B. *Business and Capitalism: An Introduction to Business History.* New York: F. S. Crofts, 1939.
Gras, N. S. B., and Larson, Henrietta M. *Casebook in American Business History.* New York: F. S. Crofts, 1939.
Gray, James. *Business Without Boundary: The Story of General Mills.* Minneapolis: University of Minnesota Press, 1954.
Gray, Ralph D. "The Early History of the Chesapeake and Delaware Canal." *Delaware History* 8 (1959):207–64, 354–99; 9 (1960):66–98.
————. "Transportation and Brandywine Industries." *Delaware History* 9 (1961):303–25.
Gressley, Gene M. *Bankers and Cattlemen.* New York: Alfred Knopf, 1966.
Griesedieck, Alvin. *The Falstaff Story.* N.p.: Simmons-Sisler, 1951.
Griffenhagen, George B., and Romaine, Lawrence B. "Early U.S. Pharmaceutical Catalogues." *American Journal of Pharmacy* 131 (1959):14–33.
Griffin, Richard W., and Standard, Diffee W. "The Cotton Textile Industry in Ante-Bellum North Carolina." *North Carolina Historical Review* 34 (1957):15–35, 131–64.
Hacker, Louis M. *The World of Andrew Carnegie, 1865–1901.* Philadelphia: J. B. Lippincott, 1968.
Hammond, John W. *Men and Volts: The Story of General Electric.* Philadelphia: J. B. Lippincott, 1941.
Hart, Richard H. *Enoch Pratt,* Baltimore, Md.: Enoch Pratt Free Library, 1935.
Hartley, Edward N. *Ironworks on the Saugus.* Norman: University of Oklahoma Press, 1957.
Hartz, Louis. *The Liberal Tradition in America.* New York: Harcourt, Brace & World, 1965.
Hedges, James B. *The Browns of Providence Plantations: The Colonial Years.* Cambridge, Mass.: Harvard University Press, 1952.
Hedges, Joseph E. *Commercial Banking and the Stock Market Before 1863.* Baltimore, Md.: The Johns Hopkins Press, 1938.
Heimann, Robert K. *Tobacco and Americans.* New York: McGraw-Hill, 1960.
Hellet, John R. *The Impact of Railways on Victorian Cities.* London: Routledge & Kegan Paul, 1969.
Hendrick, Burton J. *The Life of Andrew Carnegie.* 2 vols. New York: Doubleday, Doran & Co., 1932.
Hidy, Ralph W. "The Organization and Functions of Anglo-American Merchant Bankers, 1815–1860." *Journal of Economic History,* suppl. (December, 1941), pp. 53–66.
Hidy, Ralph W., and Hidy, Muriel E. *Pioneering in Big Business, 1882–1911.* New York: Harper & Bros., 1955.

Hillyer, William. "Four Centuries of Factoring." *Quarterly Journal of Economics* 53 (1939): 305–11.

Historical and Biographical Encyclopedia of Delaware. Wilmington: Aldine, 1882.

Hotchkiss, George B. *Milestone in Marketing*. New York: Macmillan, 1938.

Hower, Ralph M. *History of an Advertising Agency*. Cambridge, Mass.: Harvard University Press, 1949.

Hughes, George W. "The Pioneer Iron Industry in Western Pennsylvania." *Western Pennsylvania Historical Magazine* 14 (1931):207–24.

Hungerford, Edward. *The Story of the Baltimore and Ohio Railroad*. 2 vols. New York: G. P. Putnam, 1928.

Hunter, Louis C. "Financial Problems of the Early Pittsburgh Iron Manufacturers." *Journal of Economic and Business History* 2 (1930):520–44.

Hussey, Miriam. *From Merchants to "Colour Men."* Philadelphia: University of Pennsylvania Press, 1956.

Hutchinson, William T. *Cyrus Hall McCormick*. 2 vols. New York: Century, 1930.

Jack, Andrew B. "The Channels of Distribution for an Innovation: The Sewing-Machine Industry in America, 1860–1865." *Explorations in Entrepreneurial History* 9 (1957):113–41.

Jackman, W. T. *The Development of Transportation in Modern Britain*. London: Frank Cass, 1966.

Jenkins, James W. *James B. Duke: Master Builder*. New York: George H. Doran, 1927.

Johnson, Allen, *et al.*, eds. *Dictionary of American Biography*. New York: C. Scribner's Sons, 1957.

Johnson, Keach. "The Baltimore Company Seeks English Markets: A Study of the Anglo-American Iron Trade, 1731–1755." *William and Mary Quarterly* 16 (1959):37–60.

Johnson, Ray W., and Lynch, Russell W. *The Sales Strategy of John H. Patterson, Founder of the National Cash Register Company*. New York: Dartnell Corp., 1932.

Jones, Fred M. "Middlemen in the Domestic Trade of the United States, 1800–1860." *University of Illinois Studies in the Social Sciences* 21, no. 3 (1937).

Kaplan, A. D. H. *Big Enterprise in a Competitive System*. Washington, D.C.: The Brookings Institution, 1964.

Keeler, Vernon D. "An Economic History of the Jackson County Iron Industry." *Ohio Archaeological and Historical Quarterly* 42 (1933):133–238.

King, Willis L. "Recollections and Conclusions from a Long Business Life." *Western Pennsylvania Historical Magazine* 23 (1940):223–42.

Kirkland, Edward C. *Industry Comes of Age: Business, Labor and Public Policy, 1860–1897*. New York: Holt, Rinehart & Winston, 1961.

Klein, Joseph J. "The Development of Mercantile Instruments of Credit in the United States." *Journal of Accountancy* 12 (1911):321–45, 422–49, 526–37, 594–607.

Knowlton, Evelyn. *Pepperell's Progress*. Cambridge, Mass.: Harvard University Press, 1948.

Kramer, Helen M. "Harvesters and High Finance: Formation of the International Harvester Company." *Business History Review* 38 (1964):283–301.

Krebs, Roland, and Orthwein, Percy J. *Making Friends Is Our Business: 100 Years of Anheuser-Busch.* N.p.: Anheuser-Busch, 1953.

Lander, Ernest M., Jr. "The Iron Industry in Ante-Bellum South Carolina." *Journal of Southern History* 20 (1954):337–55.

Landes, David S. *The Unbound Prometheus.* New York: Cambridge University Press, 1969.

Landon, Charles E. "Tobacco Manufacturing in the South." In *The Coming of Industry to the South.* Edited by William J. Carson. Philadelphia: American Academy of Political and Social Science, 1931.

Larson, Henrietta M. *Guide to Business History.* Cambridge, Mass.: Harvard University Press, 1948.

Lesley, J. P. *The Iron Manufacturer's Guide.* New York: John Wiley, 1859.

Livesay, Harold C. "The Lobdell Car Wheel Co., 1830–1867." *Business History Review* 42 (1968):171–94.

Livesay, Harold C., and Porter, Patrick G. "Iron on the Susquehanna: New Cumberland Forge." *Pennsylvania History* 37 (1970):261–68.

———. "Vertical Integration in American Manufacturing, 1899–1948." *Journal of Economic History* 29 (1969):494–500.

Livingood, James W. *The Philadelphia-Baltimore Trade Rivalry, 1780–1860.* Harrisburg: The Pennsylvania Historical and Museum Commission, 1947.

Lunt, Dudley C. "The Farmers Bank—An Assurance Company." *Delaware History* 8 (1958):54–79.

McCormick, Cyrus. *The Century of the Reaper.* Boston: Houghton Mifflin, 1931.

McKelvey, Blake. *Rochester: The Flower City 1855–1890.* Cambridge, Mass.: Harvard University Press, 1949.

McKesson & Robbins. *The Road to Market: 125 Years of Distribution Service.* New York: n.p., 1958.

McMaster, John B. *The Life and Times of Stephen Girard.* Philadelphia: J. B. Lippincott, 1918.

McNair, James B. *Simon Cameron's Adventure in Iron, 1837–1846.* Los Angeles: By the author, 1949.

Marcosson, Isaac. *Anaconda.* New York: Dodd, Mead & Co., 1957.

———. *Metal Magic: The Story of American Smelting and Refining Company.* New York: Farrar, Straus, 1949.

———. *Wherever Men Trade: The Romance of the Cash Register.* New York: Dodd, Mead & Co., 1945.

May, Earl C. *From Principio to Wheeling.* New York: Harper & Bros., 1945.

Mencken, August. *The Railroad Passenger Car.* Baltimore, Md.: The Johns Hopkins Press, 1957.

Mitchell, B. R. "Coming of the Railways and British Economic Growth." *Journal of Economic History* 24 (1964):315–36.

Mitchell, Sidney A. *S. Z. Mitchell and the Electrical Industry.* New York: Farrar, Straus & Cudahy, 1960.

Mitchell, Wesley C. *A History of the Greenbacks.* Chicago: University of Chicago Press, 1903.

Moody, John. "The United States Steel Corporation." *Moody's Magazine* 7 (1909):7–24.

Morison, Samuel E. *The Oxford History of the American People*. New York: Oxford University Press, 1965.

Murphy, Herman K. "The Northern Railroads During the Civil War." *Mississippi Valley Historical Review* 5 (1918):324–38.

Navin, Thomas R. *The Whitin Machine Works since 1831: A Textile Machinery Company in an Industrial Village*. Cambridge, Mass.: Harvard University Press, 1950.

Navin, Thomas R., and Sears, Marian V. "The Rise of a Market for Industrial Securities, 1887–1902." *Business History Review* 29 (1955):105–38.

Nef, John U. "Dominance of the Trader in the English Coal Industry in the Seventeenth Century." *Journal of Economic and Business History* 1 (1929): 422–33.

Nelson, Ralph L. *Merger Movements in American Industry, 1895–1956*. Princeton: Princeton University Press, 1959.

Neu, Irene D. *Erastus Corning, Merchant and Financier, 1794–1872*. Ithaca, N.Y.: Cornell University Press, 1960.

Nevins, Allan. *Abram S. Hewitt: With Some Account of Peter Cooper*. New York: Octagon Books, 1967.

————. *John D. Rockefeller*. New York: C. Scribner's Sons, 1941.

Neyhart, Louise A. *Giant of the Yards*. Boston: Houghton Mifflin, 1952.

Noble, Henry J. *History of the Cast Iron Pressure Pipe Industry in the United States of America*. Birmingham, England: Newcomen Society, 1940.

North, Douglass C. *The Economic Growth of the United States, 1790–1860*. Englewood Cliffs, N.J.: Prentice-Hall, 1961.

Novack, David E., and Perlman, Richard. "The Structure of Wages in the American Iron and Steel Industry, 1860–1890." *Journal of Economic History* 22 (1962):334–47.

Olsen, Paul C. *The Merchandising of Drug Products*. New York: D. Appleton, 1931.

Ottley, George. *Bibliography of British Railway History*. London: George Allen & Unwin, 1965.

Passer, Harold C. *The Electrical Manufacturers, 1875–1900*. Cambridge, Mass.: MIT Press, 1953.

————. "Electrical Manufacturing Around 1900." *Journal of Economic History* 12 (1952):378–95.

Paul, Hiram V. *History of the Town of Durham, N.C.* Raleigh, N.C.: Edwards, Broughton & Co., 1884.

Payne, Peter L., and Davis, Lance E. *The Savings Bank of Baltimore*. Baltimore, Md.: The Johns Hopkins Press, 1956.

Pierce, Arthur D. *Iron in the Pines: The Story of New Jersey's Ghost Towns and Bog Iron*. New Brunswick, N.J.: Rutgers University Press, 1957.

Pillsbury, Philip W. *The Pioneering Pillsburys*. New York: Newcomen Society, 1950.

Pollard, Sidney. "Fixed Capital in the Industrial Revolution in Britain." *Journal of Economic History* 24 (1964):299–314.

Porter, Kenneth W. *The Jacksons and the Lees.* 2 vols. Cambridge, Mass.: Harvard University Press, 1937.

Porter, Patrick G. "Origins of the American Tobacco Company." *Business History Review* 43 (1969):59–76.

———. "Source Material for Economic History: Records of the Bureau of Corporations." *Prologue: The Journal of the National Archives* 2 (1970): 31–33.

Porter, Patrick G., and Livesay, Harold C. "The Ante-Bellum Drug Trade: Troth & Company of Philadelphia." *Pennsylvania Magazine of History and Biography* 94 (1970):347–57.

———. "Oligopolists in American Manufacturing and Their Products, 1909–1963." *Business History Review* 43 (1969):282–98.

———. "Oligopoly in Small Manufacturing Industries." *Explorations in Economic History* 7 (1970):371–79.

Presbrey, Frank. *History and Development of Advertising.* New York: Macmillan, 1938.

Rankin, Watson S. *James Buchanan Duke (1865–1925): A Great Pattern of Hard Work, Wisdom, and Benevolence.* New York: Newcomen Society, 1952.

Ransom, James M. *Vanishing Ironworks of the Ramapos.* New Brunswick, N.J.: Rutgers University Press, 1966.

Reynolds, Philip K. *The Story of the Banana.* Boston: United Fruit Co., 1921.

Rezneck, Samuel. "The Rise and Early Development of Industrial Consciousness in the United States, 1760–1830." *Journal of Economic and Business History* 4 (1932):784–811.

Rhoades, E. L. *Merchandising Packinghouse Products.* Chicago: University of Chicago Press, 1929.

Richardson, George A. "History and Development of Railway Passenger Car Building." *Railway Record* 74 (1924):1133–41.

Riley, John J. *A History of the American Soft Drink Industry: Bottled Beverages, 1807–1957.* Washington, D.C.: American Bottlers of Carbonated Beverages, 1958.

Ripley, William Z. *Trusts, Pools and Corporations.* Boston: Ginn, 1905.

Robbins, Michael. *The Railway Age.* London: Routledge & Kegan Paul, 1962.

Roe, Joseph W. *English and American Tool Builders.* New York: McGraw-Hill, 1926.

Rolt, L. T. C. *A Short History of Machine Tools.* Cambridge, Mass.: MIT Press, 1965.

Rowsome, Frank, Jr. *They Laughed When I Sat Down: An Informal History of Advertising in Words and Pictures.* New York: Bonanza Books, 1959.

Ryder, David W. *The First Hundred Years: Being the Highlighted History of the First and Oldest Wholesale Drug House in the West.* San Francisco: Coffin-Reddington Co., 1949.

"Ryerson's Steel-Service Plants." *Far Eastern Review* 19 (1923):143.

Scharf, J. Thomas. *History of Delaware.* 2 vols. Philadelphia: L. J. Richards, 1888.

Scheiber, Harry. "Economic Change in the Civil War Era." *Civil War History* 11 (1965):396–411.

Schroeder, Gertrude C. *The Growth of Major Steel Companies, 1900–1950.* Baltimore, Md.: The Johns Hopkins Press, 1953.

Schwab, Charles M. "The Huge Enterprises Built Up by Andrew Carnegie." *Engineering Magazine* 20 (1901):505–17.

Semi-Centennial Memoir of the Harlan and Hollingsworth Company. Wilmington, Del.: Harlan & Hollingsworth, 1886.

Shapiro, Stanley J., and Doody, A. F. *Readings in the History of American Marketing: Settlements to Civil War.* Homewood, Ill.: Irwin, 1968.

Siegenthaler, Hansjörg. "What Price Style? The Fabric Advisory Function of the Dry Goods Commission Merchant." *Business History Review* 41 (1967):36–61.

Spear, Dorothea. *Bibliography of American Directories Through 1860.* Worcester, Mass.: American Antiquarian Society, 1961.

Starr, Harris E., ed. *Dictionary of American Biography.* Vol. 11, pt. 1, suppl. 1. New York. C. Scribner's Sons, 1944.

Stecher, Paul, ed. *The Merck Index: An Encyclopedia of Chemicals and Drugs.* Rahway, N.J.: Merck & Co., 1968.

Steinman, D. B. *The Builders of the Bridge: The Story of John Roebling and His Son.* New York: Harcourt, Brace & Co., 1945.

Stigler, George J. "The Division of Labor Is Limited by the Extent of the Market." *Journal of Political Economy* 59 (1951):185–93.

Stout, Wilbur. "The Charcoal Iron Industry of the Hanging Rock Iron District— Its Influence on the Early Development of the Ohio Valley." *Ohio Archaeological and Historical Quarterly* 42 (1933): 72–104.

Stover, John F ."Colonel Henry S. McComb, Mississippi Railroad Adventurer." *Journal of Mississippi History* 17 (1955):177–90.

———. *Railroads of the South, 1865–1900.* Chapel Hill: University of North Carolina Press, 1955.

Swatner, Eva. "Military Railroads During the Civil War." *Military Engineer* 21 (1929):310–16, 434–39, 518–26.

Swift, Louis F., and Van Vlissingen, Arthur, Jr. *The Yankee of the Yards: The Biography of Gustavus Franklin Swift.* New York: A. W. Shaw, 1927.

Sylla, Richard E. "Federal Policy, Banking Market Structure, and Capital Mobilization in the United States, 1863–1913." *Journal of Economic History* 29 (1969):657–86.

Taussig, Frank W. "The Iron Industry in the United States." *Quarterly Journal of Economics* 14 (1900):143–70.

Taylor, George R. *The Transportation Revolution, 1815–1860.* New York: Harper & Row, 1968.

Temin, Peter. "The Composition of Iron and Steel Products, 1869–1909." *Journal of Economic History* 23 (1963):447–71.

———. *Iron and Steel in Nineteenth Century America: An Economic Inquiry.* Cambridge, Mass.: MIT Press, 1964.

Tennant, Richard. *The American Cigarette Industry.* New Haven, Conn.: Yale, University Press, 1950.

Thomann, G. *American Beer: Glimpses of Its History and Description of Its Manufacture.* New York: United States Brewers' Assoc., 1909.

Throckmorton, Arthur L. "The Role of the Merchant on the Oregon Frontier: The Early Business History of Henry W. Corbett, 1851–1869." *Journal of Economic History* 16 (1956): 539–50.

Tilley, Nannie M. "Agitation Against the American Tobacco Company in North Carolina, 1890–1911." *North Carolina Historical Review* 24 (1947): 207–23.

———. *The Bright-Tobacco Industry, 1860–1929.* Chapel Hill: University of North Carolina Press, 1948.

Tocqueville, Alexis de. *Democracy in America.* 2 vols. New York: Schocken, 1961.

Tooker, Elva. "A Merchant Turns to Money-Lending in Philadelphia." *Business History Society Bulletin* 20 (1946):71–85.

———. *Nathan Trotter.* Cambridge, Mass.: Harvard University Press, 1955.

Trescott, Paul B. *Financing American Enterprise: The Story of Commercial Banking.* New York: Harper & Row, 1963.

Tyler, David B. *The American Clyde.* Newark: University of Delaware Press, 1958.

Walker, Joseph E. *Hopewell Village: A Social and Economic History of an Iron-Making Community.* Philadelphia: University of Pennsylvania Press, 1966.

Wall, Joseph F. *Andrew Carnegie.* New York: Oxford University Press, 1970.

Ware, Caroline F. *The Early New England Cotton Manufacture.* New York: Russell & Russell, 1966.

Warner, Arthur E. *A Historic Sketch of Economic Developments in Wilmington, Delaware, and Environs.* Newark: University of Delaware Press, 1962.

Weber, Thomas. *The Northern Railroads in the Civil War, 1861–1865.* New York: King's Crown Press, 1952.

White, Gerald T. *A History of the Massachusetts Hospital Life Insurance Company.* Cambridge, Mass.: Harvard University Press, 1955.

White, John H., Jr. *American Locomotives: An Engineering History.* Baltimore, Md.: The Johns Hopkins Press, 1968.

W. H. Schieffelin & Co. *100 Years of Business Life, 1794–1894.* New York: W. H. Schieffelin & Co., 1894.

Wilkinson, Norman B. "The Brandywine Home Front During the Civil War." *Delaware History* 9 (1961):265–81; 11 (1964):111–48.

Willatt, Norris. "Agile Middlemen." *Barron's,* May 1, 1961, pp. 5–6.

Williamson, Harold F., and Daum, Arnold R. *The American Petroleum Industry: The Age of Illumination, 1859–1899.* Evanston, Ill.: Northwestern University Press, 1959.

Willson, Seelye A. "The Growth of Pittsburgh Iron and Steel." *Magazine of Western History* 2 (1885):540–71.

Wilson, Charles M. *Empire in Green and Gold: The Story of the American Banana Trade.* N.p.: Henry Holt, 1947.

Winkler, John K. *Incredible Carnegie.* New York: Vanguard Press, 1931.

————. *Tobacco Tycoon: The Story of James Buchanan Duke*. New York: Random House, 1942.

Wood, James P. *The Story of Advertising*. New York: Ronald Press, 1958.

Woodman, Harold D. *King Cotton and His Retainers: Financing and Marketing the Cotton Crop of the South, 1800–1925*. Lexington: University of Kentucky Press, 1968.

Young, William W. *The Story of the Cigarette*. New York: D. Appleton, 1916.

GOVERNMENT PUBLICATIONS

Coxe, Tench. *A Statement of the Arts and Manufactures of the United States of America for the Year 1810*. Philadelphia: U.S. Treasury Department, 1814.

U.S. Bureau of Corporations. *Report of the Commissioner of Corporations on the Beef Industry*. Washington, D.C.: Government Printing Office, 1905.

————. *Report of the Commissioner of Corporations on the Tobacco Industry*. 3 vols. Washington, D.C.: Government Printing Office, 1909–15.

U.S. Bureau of the Census. *Census of Business, 1939*, vol. 2: *Wholesale Trade*. Washington, D.C.: Government Printing Office, 1942.

————. *Census of Manufactures, 1905*, pt. 4: *Special Reports on Selected Industries*. Washington, D.C.: Government Printing Office, 1908.

————. *Fifteenth Census of the United States, 1930: Distribution*. 4 vols. Washington, D.C.: Government Printing Office, 1933–34.

————. *Historical Statistics of the United States: From Colonial Times to 1957*. Washington, D.C.: Government Printing Office, 1960.

————. *Thirteenth Census of the United States, 1910: Bulletin. Manufactures 1909*. Washington, D.C.: Government Printing Office, 1913.

U.S. Census Office. *Eighth Census of the United States, 1860: Manufactures of the United States in 1860*. Washington, D.C.: Government Printing Office, 1865.

————. *Eleventh Census of the United States, 1890: Report on Manufacturing Industries*, pt. 3: *Selected Industries*. Washington, D.C.: Government Printing Office, 1895.

————. *Fifth Census of the United States, 1840*. Washington, D.C.: D. Green, 1842.

————. *Fourth Census of the United States, 1820: Digest of Accounts of Manufacturing Establishments in the United States and Their Manufactures*. Washington, D.C.: Gales & Seaton, 1823.

————. *Ninth Census of the United States, 1870: Statistics of the Wealth and Industry of the United States*. Washington, D.C.: Government Printing Office, 1872.

U.S. Industrial Commission. *Report of the Industrial Commission*. 19 vols. Washington, D.C.: 1900–1902.

U.S. Secretary of the Treasury. *Documents Relative to the Manufactures in the United States*. Washington, D.C.: Duff Green, 1833. Also known as *The McLane Report*.

War of the Rebellion: Official Records of the Union and Confederate Armies. Ser. 3, vol. 5. Washington, D.C.: Government Printing Office, 1900.

CITY DIRECTORIES

The number of city directories used in this study is so large as to warrant omission of individual listings. All directories cited are located in one of two sources. The pre-1860 directories are in the microfiche publication, *City and Business Directories of the United States Through 1860* (New Haven, Conn.: Research Publications, 1967). They are listed in Dorothea Spear, *Bibliography of American Directories Through 1860* (Worcester, Mass.: American Antiquarian Society, 1961). The post-1860 directories are on file at the Library of Congress, Washington, D.C.

NEWSPAPERS AND TRADE PERIODICALS

American Railroad Journal, 1830–67.
Annual Report of the Philadelphia, Wilmington, and Baltimore Railroad. 1840–66.
Commercial and Financial Chronicle. 1860–95.
Delaware Gazette (Wilmington). 1830–45.
Electrical World. 1890–1900.
Iron Age. 1890–1900.
Moody's Magazine. 1909–16.
New York Times. 1890–1900.
Tobacco. 1886–90.
Tobacco News and Prices Current. 1878–79.
U.S. Tobacco Journal. 1876–82.

OTHER PUBLISHED SOURCES

American Iron & Steel Assoc. *Annual Statistical Report.* Philadelphia, Pa.: American Iron & Steel Assoc., 1886.
Assoc. of Edison Illuminating Cos. *Minutes, 1886.* New York: Assoc. of Edison Illuminating Cos., 1886.
———. *Minutes, 1887. New York: Assoc. of Edison Illuminating Cos., 1887.*
Moody, John, ed. *Moody's Manual of Industrial and Miscellaneous Securities, 1900.* New York: O. C. Lewis, 1900.
———. *Moody's Manual of Railroads and Corporation Securities, 1908.* New York: Moody Manual Company, 1908.
People v. *Duke et al.,* 44 N.Y. Supp. 336 (1897).
Transactions of the American Institute of Electrical Engineers, 1887. New York: American Institute of Electrical Engineers, 1887.
United States v. *American Tobacco Company,* 164 F. 700 (1908), 221 U.S. 106(1911), and 191 F. (1911).

Index

Glenn Porter is director of the Hagley Museum and Library in Wilmington, Delaware. He has been the editor of the *Business History Review* and is also the author of *The Rise of Big Business, 1860–1910*, and editor of the *Encyclopedia of American Economic History*.

Harold C. Livesay is Clifford A. Taylor Professor of Liberal Arts in the Department of History at Texas A & M University. He has written numerous articles and books, including *Andrew Carnegie and the Rise of Big Business* and *American Made*.